Newsies vs. *The World*

How a War, a Newspaper
Rivalry, and a Trolley Strike
Sparked the Child Labor Riot
That Ended Up on Broadway

Ashley Varela

Theme Park Press
The Happiest Books on Earth
www.ThemeParkPress.com

Although every precaution has been taken to verify the accuracy of the information contained herein, no responsibility is assumed for any errors or omissions, and no liability is assumed for damages that may result from the use of this information.

Theme Park Press is not associated with the Walt Disney Company.

The views expressed in this book are those of the author and do not necessarily reflect the views of Theme Park Press.

Theme Park Press publishes its books in a variety of print and electronic formats. Some content that appears in one format may not appear in another.

Editor: Bob McLain
Layout: Artisanal Text

ISBN 978-1-68390-197-6
Printed in the United States of America

Theme Park Press | www.ThemeParkPress.com
Address queries to bob@themeparkpress.com

To Louis "Kid Blink" Ballatt, Racetrack Higgins, Spot Conlon, Jack Sullivan, "Crutchy" Morris, Dave Simons, Young "Mush" Myers, Jennie the newsgirl, Annie Kelly, Hannah Kleff, Winnie and Sadie Horn, Mary Welter, and every newsboy and newsgirl of New York City.

You deserved better.

"*The only people who lose their humanity are those who believe they have the right to render another human being powerless. They are the weak. To yield and not break, that is incredible strength.*"

—Hannah Gadsby, *Nanette*

"*What kind of citizens these Newsboys will make—what kind of creatures will spring from these mixed elements of turmoil, street-running, precocious activity of body and mind, and precocious profusion of cash, no one can guess; for the system—started some ten years since—has not been long enough in operation to bring any of them of age. ... Our best wishes are with the Boys.*"

—George G. Foster, *New York Tribune*, 1849

Contents

Introduction

Stories find us in unusual ways.

Before this one found me, it was buried in the pages of an old journalism survey, where historian David Nasaw first unearthed it in the 1980s. His 1985 child labor retrospective, *Children of the City: At Work and at Play*, illuminated his findings: among them, a two-week strike mounted in the summer of 1899, when a gaggle of school-age newspaper sellers fought back against the most influential publishers 19th century New York City had ever seen.

It was a compelling tale of David-and-Goliath proportions, albeit one that had been largely lost to history over the years. The book itself was well-received by critics, and on a spring day in '85, a favorable review in the *New York Times* introduced Nasaw's work to its most important reader: amateur actor and screenwriter Bob Tzudiker.

"In 1899 an event took place that would have been perfect for film use by the Dead End Kids," the *Times*' Avery Corman had written, "but as Mr. Nasaw points out, it has been a neglected episode."[1] His brief summary of the strike's events struck a chord with Tzudiker, who filed the story away in his notes for future use. He'd revisit it four years later with his wife and fellow screenwriter, Noni White. Together, the two fashioned Nasaw's account into a script and sold it to Disney. In 1992, *Newsies* was born.

My own run-in with the story felt no less serendipitous. It happened on a bright, sunny day in January, the kind that makes you feel doubly awful for staying home sick. I had curled up on the couch with a bottle of cold medicine and a box of tissues and started cycling through Hulu's limited menu of

Disney films. There, sandwiched between *Hercules* and *Mulan*, was *Newsies*, a campy '90s flick I vaguely remembered for a childhood friend's adolescent crush on a slingshot-swinging Gabriel Damon. Misty visions of choreographed dances, newspaper-waving, and Christian Bale swinging off the frame of a fire escape flitted through my mind, but beyond that, nothing but the faint glimmer of nostalgia forced me to press "play."

I watched it once, then twice, then a third time.

Crap. These were the warning signs of an oncoming obsession, and whether it was a side effect of the cold medicine or due to a sudden onset of sentimental feeling, I didn't care. There was something inexplicably wonderful about the tale of the newsbnoy-capped underdog taking on a cartoonish newspaper editor. I couldn't get enough of it.

A month later, I drove to the local theater. Among a smattering of the usual rom-coms and dirty comedies, the marquee advertised a one-night showing of *Disney's Newsies: Broadway's Smash Hit Musical*. I was enthralled. The clunky charm of the 1992 film had been buffed and polished to a professional shine. The colors were more vibrant, the lyrics sharper, the choreography sparkling with graceful pirouettes and big tap dance numbers, and at the heart of it, the newsies' story was endearingly unchanged. It still carried the same self-sure message of relentless hope, the kind that empowers the marginalized and downtrodden to rise up and fight for justice against insurmountable odds.

In other words, it was the stuff of your standard Disney tale. I found myself clasping hand to heart as *New York Sun* reporter Katherine Plumber stepped onstage, punching the keys of her typewriter as she attempted to put the newsies' story to page. Like David Nasaw and Bob Tzudiker and Noni White and Harvey Fierstein before her, she was captivated by the newsies' plight, irresistibly bound to a cause in need of a champion:

> There's a story behind the story
> Thousands of children exploited, invisible
> So speak up, take a stand
> And there's someone to write about it
> That's how things get better...

I left the theater in a daze, unable to shake the lyrics from my head. Disney had cast a pretty sheen over the newsies' story, one in which they triumphed over their one-dimensional villain with relative ease, but I wanted to peel back the curtain and take a look at the wizened face of the Wizard himself. Who were the real newsboys and girls of New York City? I wondered. What connection did they have with Joseph Pulitzer and William Randolph Hearst, and what inspired their protest against such powerful figures? Did they prevail easily and honestly, or had their real story been tossed aside to fit some tidy Hollywood narrative?

As Katherine put it, it was time to find the story behind the story.

A strike to end all strikes

New Irving Hall was no stranger to commotion. Among the chicer of the Lower East Side's two dozen-plus halls—venues for velvet-canopied weddings, lewd ballum-rancums* [*Footnote: A "ballum-rancum," as defined by historian Neil Hanson, was the colloquial term for a ball in which the majority of participants were considered criminals or sex workers.], charity events, mob-enforced fundraisers, and a smorgasbord of union gatherings—it attracted a cast of characters that touched every demographic in New York City. Within the wood-finished 1,200-person staging area, anarchists commissioned piano concerts, cloakmakers convened to abolish the piecework system, the Pants Makers' Union celebrated their annual strike, Jewish members of the Tenth Ward demonstrated against anti-Semitic hiring practices, and newspaper publishers traded entire rooms of Christmas decorations for a glowing write-up in their own publications. It was a rallying point and a safe house, amorphous in purpose and open to all who could command an audience and foot the $30 rental fee.

So, to the half-dozen policemen dawdling around No. 214 Broome Street on a school night in July 1899, it was no great surprise to see another swarm of protestors descend on the hall. Over five thousand child newspaper hawkers, or 'newsies,' burst from the underbelly of Manhattan, the

Bronx, and the Battery, dragging colleague and kin from as far as Brooklyn and Jersey City. They invaded the streets like a summer tempest, all noise and passion, and rushed upon the roundsman and his men with such force that the officers were quickly inspired to summon reinforcements. Twenty such men couldn't stymie the tide of aggrieved souls. The newsies had been wronged, and their appetite ran toward revenge.

Every man, woman, and child who did not wish to be swept up in the protest scurried indoors as the children's shrieks escalated to a unified roar. Two thousand bodies pressed upon the door of the hall until it cracked open, leaving some three thousand scattered along the pavement and under the windowsills.

Inside, a boy of about 14 years slicked back his bright red hair, buttoned his shirt and took the stage. An eyepatch dangled over one blind eye; his signature look.

"Yer know me, boys!" he began. "Well, I'm here to say if we are goin' to win this strike we must stick like glue and never give in. Am I right?"

Two thousand boys and girls cheered their approval.

"Ain't that 10 cents worth as much to us as it is to Hearst and Pulitzer, who are millionaires? Well, I guess it is. If they can't spare it, how can we?"[2]

He had a point.

For two weeks in the summer of 1899, Louis "Kid Blink" Ballatt helped orchestrate a city-wide strike against New York City newspaper superpowers Joseph Pulitzer and William Randolph Hearst. In the heat of the Spanish-American War of 1898, publishers had jacked up the wholesale price of their stock from 50 to 60 cents per hundred newspapers. The newsies didn't fight the price hike for long. Bad news was good for business, and they had already cornered the market with 60 percent of the city's papers in-hand.[*] On a good day, each kid could hawk a single paper for anywhere between one and five

---

[*]   During the strike of 1899, Don Carlos Seitz speculated in a memo to Joseph Pulitzer that "of this 60% [of newspapers handled by the newsboys], 50% of them quit selling." It is possible, though unlikely, that these percentages were inflated to make the strike seem direr than it actually was

cents, depending on how generous their customers were feeling or how long they could pretend to fumble for correct change. War inspired the worst kind of public hysteria, and the headlines were coming in fast, hot, and bloody from the battlefield.

Nearly a full year later, most publishers had returned to prewar prices, their front pages once again occupied with pedestrian scandals and local politics. Pulitzer and Hearst alone held out. The conflict in Cuba had long been resolved, but the two were embroiled in another fight on the home front: an old-fashioned circulation war. No expense proved bigger than their own inflated egos. They traded scathing editorials, took out targeted ad campaigns, and poached each other's most talented writers and editors. When the costs eventually caught up to them, the natural remedy—raising the sale price of their own newspapers—was a concession neither man was willing to make.

The casualties of this rivalry became the thousands of child workers employed by the city's newspapers. The average 19th century newspaper hawker couldn't count on an explosive headline or scintillating story to sell papers every day; they had to prove themselves reliable, courteous, knowledgeable creatures who always had an ear to the ground and a sob story to tell. Some newsies played on the late-night sympathies of wealthy theatre patrons and upper-class society figures, while others made their daily wage selling to harried businessmen and trolley riders. Still others resorted to outright schemes, peddling false stories in an attempt to stir up outrage for a bit of fun...and pocket change.

After spending an entire year trying to recoup lost profits, even the newsies' vast stores of creativity had run dry. The wartime scandals that once rocked American society had long been put to bed, and lingering debates over the morality of yellow journalism made the average consumer ever more wary of those who regularly cried fire, murder, and mayhem from the street corner. Without a nationwide crisis to boost their sales, it was getting harder and harder for the children to recoup lost profits. They needed change—both the literal and figurative kind—and they needed it fast. When it became all-too-obvious that Pulitzer and Hearst had no intention of reducing their wholesale prices, there appeared to be only one weapon left in the newsies' arsenal: a full-fledged, no-holds-barred strike.

They were hardly the first to do so. In turn-of-the-century America, boycotts and protests were as plentiful as, well, the dishonest employers who inspired the protestors. Trolley workers struck for ten-hour workdays and higher wages, bootblacks struck to keep their own tips, and messenger boys struck for regulated work hours. Of course, it was one thing to rally a few dozen kids for an afternoon demonstration and quite another to paint a target on the backs of two of the most prominent figures in New York City. The newsies of New York never did anything by half-measures, and this time, they had picked their Goliaths carefully.

In a city that boasted 17 daily newspapers, Pulitzer's *New York World* and Hearst's *New York Journal* topped the charts in both circulation and influence. Both papers shared a disconcerting appetite for sensationalism, it was true, but they strove to cater to both top-tier society members and the common people. Pulitzer's fiery editorials could gild the reputation of a presidential candidate and tarnish his rival's character with a single stroke, while Hearst's over-dramatized accounts of the war in Cuba almost single-handedly fanned the flames of public frenzy. The rival editors didn't just shape public opinion; they created it.

By the time Kid Blink took the stage in New Irving Hall, the strike was already on its last leg. The newsies left the two-hour rally feeling rejuvenated by promises of unions and parades, all but certain that a concession was right around the corner. What more could they ask for? how else could they prove, if not by the sentiment they stirred in the breast of every honest citizen of Lower Manhattan, that they were a force to be reckoned with?

Pulitzer and Hearst may have had time, money, and the brute strength of the city's police force on their side, but the newsies had a cause worth fighting for. And, not two weeks later, they managed their first real victory. After toiling in the streets every morning and afternoon, tearing papers from the hands of customers and scabs and delivery wagon drivers, petitioning the public to fund their boycott, and demonstrating in every square and plaza that would accommodate the swell of their ever-growing ranks, the newsies' combined efforts had diminished the *New York World*'s subscriber base from a stout 360,000 to just 125,000.[†]

It was an unprecedented triumph, and one that filled the publishers with a sense of dread. What had started as a minor nuisance was suddenly gnawing at their profit margins and scaring off their advertisers and, worst of all, turning the hearts and purses of loyal customers to other newspapers. If there was anything Pulitzer and Hearst could agree on, anything they truly cared about, it was the art of good business. With their backs to the wall, they sent proxies to meet with the strikers and offered only the smallest of olive branches: If the newsies would agree to distribute the *World* and *Journal* again, the publishers would absorb the expense of any unsold papers in the form of credits. It was a pittance compared to the 10-cent increase the newsies had originally sought from their employers, but the children, for all their bluster and swagger, didn't fully grasp the leverage they possessed. On August 2, 1899, the 15-day strike was officially dead in the water.

Goliath, it seemed, would have the last laugh after all.

Bringing *Newsies* from the streets to the silver screen

Today, the newsies' strike has become more fiction than fact.

In 1988, Walt Disney Feature Animation[‡] was crawling out of the "Dark Age," a period that spanned the two decades following Walt Disney's untimely death in 1966. Grief-stricken and uninspired, the studio's animators churned out small-budget features that fizzled at the box office and were routinely panned by critics.

Audiences who had connected so strongly with classics like *Snow White and the Seven Dwarfs*, *Peter Pan*, *Cinderella*, and *Lady and the Tramp* were now subject to recycled animation

---

† Exact data on the effect the newsies' strike had on the *New York Journal*'s subscriber total went unreported, though the losses were thought to be significant.

‡ Today, the studio is known simply as Walt Disney Animation Studios.

and peculiar, off-brand experiments like *The Black Cauldron* and *Oliver and Company*. A few stood on their own—like *The Aristocats*, the last film Walt worked on before his death, and *The Great Mouse Detective*, which effectively rescued the studio from bankruptcy—but it soon became clear that animated featurs films were dying a slow and painful death in popular culture.

Then, in 1989, a red-haired mermaid changed everything.

The Little Mermaid ushered in a new Golden Age of animation, not only proving that hand-drawn animation could still draw record crowds to the theaters, but revitalizing the entire concept of the classic movie musical. During its opening weekend, the film raked in $211 million worldwide and subsequently netted two Oscars for Best Original Score and Best Original Song. Disney's Renaissance Period had finally arrived.

Several years later, the studio rolled the dice with another Broadway-style musical, this one about a French peasant girl and a hideous monster sequestered in a remote castle. *Beauty and the Beast* was received even better than its predecessor. It was hailed as an unequivocal triumph by critics and audiences alike, matching *The Little Mermaid* in Oscar wins and becoming the first animated film to receive an Academy Award nomination for Best Picture.

With two smash hits on their hands, Disney had an intriguing thought: If they could mesmerize audiences with animated movie musicals, who was to say a live-action version wouldn't be as well-received? They had just received a compelling pitch about a bunch of ragtag newspaper hawkers who organized a strike against two of the fiercest editors in New York City. All it needed was a dash of Alan Menken's musical genius, some Kenny Ortega choreography and *presto!* Another instant classic for their pocketbooks.

On April 10, 1992, *Newsies* debuted in theaters across the United States. *Empire of the Sun* wunderkind Christian Bale headed the cast as charismatic (and fictional) strike leader Jack Kelly, flanked by Robert Duvall as the villainous Joseph Pulitzer, Bill Pullman as strike sympathizer and *New York Sun* reporter Bryan Denton, and a troupe of relatively unknown child actors as Jack Kelly's fellow newsies of Manhattan.

The story that unfolded on the silver screen was hardly a historical replica, however, even disregarding the melodramatic tap dance numbers and Menkensian ballads. Kelly, an enterprising salesman with dreams of heading out West, achieved much more than the real newsies of 1899 ever did. He sang and fight-danced his way into Pulitzer's office; he converted a showdown with scabs and newspaper distributors into a front-page story in the *New York Sun*; he convinced the same *Sun* reporter to break into Pulitzer's own printing press to dash off a few thousand strike pamphlets; he enlisted the help of then-New York governor Theodore Roosevelt to strong-arm Pulitzer into a concession; and he engineered a 10-cent raise for the newsies while simultaneously and inexplicably guaranteeing better working conditions for the city's bootblacks, messenger boys, and factory workers. It was a Herculean undertaking, even by Hollywood standards.

Disney had finally given the newsies their heartfelt happy ending, but audiences were slow to warm to the historical flick. *Newsies* didn't just fizzle at the box office; it imploded, recouping a paltry $2.8 million of its initial $15 million budget and becoming one of the lowest-grossing films in studio history.[3] Critics feasted on the cinematic carnage, decrying it as "campily perverse"[4] and "warmed-over Horatio Alger,"[5] a "misguided musical"[6] that looked like its own rehearsal ("an early one at that," the *Washington Post* griped[7]) and was a metaphorical "bullet in the head"[8] to the entire movie-musical genre.

Not all moviegoers were so disenchanted by the musical.

The resurrection of *Newsies*

"Adults don't have the same opinions as kids do," 12-year-old Cari Gelber wrote in a letter to the editor of the *New York Times*, "and when they say that a movie isn't good, I always end up loving it. For instance, this weekend I saw 'Newsies' and thought it was excellent though the reviewers didn't."[9]

Cari had tapped into something that the pundits and box office receipts missed: Kids loved *Newsies*. In the decade following the film's theatrical release, children sprawled out in front of their television sets and VHS tape decks, mouthing the words

to "Carrying the Banner" and "Seize the Day" and ogling Spot
Conlon and Racetrack Higgins and Jack Kelly as their parents
burned through an estimated $18 million in home video sales.
The Disney Channel used the film as filler for empty programming slots, further inflating its popularity on VHS and helping
develop the corny commercial flop into a virtual cult classic.
Newsies had an audience again, and a devoted one at that.

The children who loved *Newsies* became teenagers who loved
Newsies, and it didn't take long for Disney to notice. Numerous
amateur stage productions sprouted across the country as
devoted fans meticulously transcribed the film's dialogue and
soundtrack, bringing the newsies' timeless struggle to their
own auditoriums, community theatres, and summer camps.
That still wasn't enough to satiate the diehards. As word of the
film's growing popularity began to trickle back to its creators,
so too did the call for Disney Theatrical Productions to license
an official adaptation of the show.

In 2007, Disney decided to take action. According to Alan
Menken, the studio informed their composer that a stage
version of *Newsies* was in the works.[10] The musical wasn't
intended for the bright lights and star-studded casts of
Broadway, but it would provide a generation of self-dubbed
"fansies" with the rights to develop their own productions
on a smaller scale. For convenience's sake, Disney informed
Menken, they would let their internal team tackle all minor
script and song changes. Menken wasn't having it.

"There was no way I would let my baby be reworked by anyone
else but [lyricist] Jack Feldman and me," he recounted later.[11]

Even in Menken's hands, *Newsies* didn't strike the right
chord. Disney's creative team hemmed and hawed over the
finer points of the story, but the lack of a cohesive vision
became quickly and alarmingly apparent as they workshopped
a rudimentary stage adaptation. Despite the overwhelming
public demand—and, in theory, the fat profits to be made on
licensing rights—it looked like *Newsies* just didn't have the
chutzpah or the charm to make compelling theatre.

Then, in a fortuitous moment, Harvey Fierstein came along.

"We were sitting around Alan Menken's studio wondering
what project we could write together when I spotted the poster

for *Newsies* on the wall. 'How about a stage version of that?'"
he asked Alan.

"'Forget *Newsies*,' Menken said. 'We slaved over an adaptation. We even gave it two table readings. Disaster. It's never
going to work. Forget it.'"[12]

Egged on by a sense of nostalgia and the phantom clamoring of thousands of *Newsies* fans, Fierstein rose to the
occasion. He felt there was something worth salvaging in the
show and—unlike both Menken and Disney—had already
started to set his sights on Broadway. It might have seemed
like nothing more than wishful thinking at the time, but hind-
sight would prove it a rather lucky hunch.

By 2011, not only did Disney have a script for *Newsies*—it
had a thriving, electric adaptation playing at the Paper Mill
Playhouse in Millburn, New Jersey.

While the basic framework of the 1992 film was in place,
it had been thoughtfully reworked with new choreography,
lyrics, and characters. The plot hewed no closer to historical
events than it had before, but it made for damn good theatre
just the same. Strike leader Jack Kelly moonlighted as an
amateur Bob Ross, spending his spare moments painting
ethereal backdrops for a local vaudeville theatre. Katherine
Plumber supplanted *New York Sun* reporter Bryan Denton as a
charming Nellie Bly-lookalike who doubled as Jack Kelly's love
interest. The ensemble tap-danced and pirouetted across the
stage at every turn, scaling 24-foot metal towers with remarkable dexterity as they belted showstopper after showstopper.

And, out in the seats, the best change of all: passionate
crowds that sold out performance after performance, pro-
pelling *Newsies* to such success that Broadway was no longer
a question mark, but an inevitability.

Newsies the Musical made its first leap to Broadway in
March 2012, but Disney still had some reservations. Where
the success of *The Little Mermaid* and *Beauty and the Beast* had
buoyed hopes for a *Newsies* movie musical in 1992, the company's recent history of Broadway misfires paved the way for
more modest expectations with its newest show. Following
immensely successful productions like *The Lion King* and *Mary
Poppins*, Disney watched a $14 million staging of *Tarzan* tank

after a 15-month run in 2007. A surefire adaptation of *The Little Mermaid* lacked anything close to staying power: Armed with a budget of $15 million, it shuttered in 2009 after just 22 months in the Big Apple.[13] Disney wasn't going to take the same risk with *Newsies*, and even the enthusiastic patrons of the Paper Mill Playhouse couldn't erase the memory of the film's poor reception 20 years prior. After an acclaimed four-week run in New Jersey, the musical was handcuffed to a $5 million budget and a limited 101-performance run at the Nederlander Theatre in New York City. If things went well, the show would be cleared to book an open-ended run; if not, Disney Theatrical president Thomas Schumacher told reporters, the company could use the added publicity to drive licensing deals.[14]

He needn't have worried. The show grossed an unprecedented $735,991 in six preview performances, eclipsing the record established by *Rent* back in 2008 and recouping its initial investment faster than any other Disney stage production to date.[15] In mid-June, following considerable buzz at the Tony Awards, it continued to rake in estimated profits of $1 million per week and eventually became the highest-grossing show of Broadway's 2011-2012 season. Theatregoers, it seemed, couldn't get enough of the ragtag newsies and their fight against the penny-pinching Pulitzer and his cronies.

Two years, 999 performances, and eight Tony nominations later, *Newsies* seized its last day at the Nederlander. Some blamed a natural decline in ticket sales for the closure, precipitated by the turnover of its principal cast and the end of awards season, but Disney was already preparing to advance to the next stage: a 25-city national tour. The show had cleared every hurdle in its path with room to spare, becoming one of Disney's most profitable productions, meriting an open-ended run on Broadway, garnering substantial critical acclaim, and earning two Tony Awards for its exceptional score and choreography. It had taken two long decades to get to this point, but *Newsies* had finally gained the recognition and accolades it deserved.

Whether it had done justice to the real-life newsboys and newsgirls of New York City was another question altogether.

Reconciling the newsies of 1899 with the newsies of the 21st century

"If I've done my job right, [*Newsies the Musical*] makes a statement that's bigger than the newsies," Harvey Fierstein told the *New York Times*' Tammy La Gorce. "It's about a bunch of kids changing the world, about handing over the world to a new generation."[16]

He was right. Telling a story—any story—requires a certain degree of responsibility. It's not enough to tell something *accurately* or *well* or even *beautifully*. You have to get your hands dirty, digging your fingernail under layer after layer until you arrive at the core of your story, the thing that makes it real and alive and *true*.

If nothing else, that's what this book endeavors to do. We'll take a magnifying glass to the events leading up to the strike, from the way Hearst's particular brand of yellow journalism exacerbated a war to the way his employees got tangled in the crosshairs of a bloodthirsty newspaper rivalry. And we'll examine the breadcrumb trail that led from the war to the newsies' strike in 1899, culminating in a spectacular standoff between the publishers and their adolescent workforce.

Then, we'll turn our attention to Disney's *Newsies*, including the misguided movie musical that caused Christian Bale embarrassment and its über-successful Broadway adaptation. We'll ask ourselves the tough questions: Did Disney do a disservice to the real child newspaper hawkers of 1899? What happens when we sacrifice accuracy for great storytelling? How do we rewrite history in a way that amplifies the voices of the oppressed? Did Broadway successfully immortalize the newsies' story once and for all, or is it doomed to be forgotten yet again?

A Note on Sources

History isn't perfect. More often than not, it's told by people in power who are guilty of ignoring or misrepresenting those who lack the same privileges. Or, to put it in terms the newsies would understand: "If it's not in the papers, then it never happened."

Much of what we know about the child newspaper sellers of 19th and 20th century New York City has been gleaned from the publishers who employed them. Formal studies regarding the newsies' ages, ethnicities, annual earnings, and working and living conditions were not publicized until the early 1900s, when researchers used the data to both criminalize the juvenile working class and lend support to a nationwide child labor reform movement.[1] As a result, the information we are left with is incomplete at best and flawed at worst.

Sources for the 1899 strike

All reports of the 1899 strike have been traced back to original columns found in the *New York Times*, *New York Herald*, *New York Sun*, *New York Tribune*, *Evening Telegram*, *Brooklyn Eagle*, *New York Journal*, and *New York World*, as well as select correspondence between Don Carlos Seitz and Joseph Pulitzer. It's important to note that while this is as close as we can get to a first-hand accounts of the strike, there are strong biases present in each source.

In 1899, New York City publishers stood to profit during the strike, as the dwindling circulations of the rival *New York World* and *New York Journal* incentivized them to paint the newsies' efforts in a flattering, pitiable light. Rather than looking at the strike objectively, the city's journalists sought to engender sympathy for the newsboys and newsgirls, and by doing so, further cripple the *World* and *Journal*'s readership.

One of their most common tactics was the usage of "eye dialect," or the purposeful misspelling of words to produce a comic effect or denote the speaker's lack of education. This was most plainly seen in quotes given by the adolescent strikers. Several days into the boycott, the *New York Herald* reported a meeting between General Master Workboy "Blind" Diamond and District Master Workboy of the Brooklyn Union, Spot Conlon:

> "We bring youse greetings an' promises of support," Conlon was quoted. "We have tied up de scab sheets so tight dat y' can't buy one fer a dollar in de street. Hold out, me gallant, kids, an' to-morrer I meself, at de head of t'ree t'ousand noble hearts from Brooklyn, will be over here t' help youse win yer noble scrap for freedom an' fair play."[2]

On at least one occasion, journalists were asked to refrain from using eye dialect to describe the newsies' speech. The children wanted their cause to be taken seriously, not just by Pulitzer and Hearst, but by the public. The papers briefly honored the request before lapsing into eye dialect for the remaining eight days of the strike, perhaps unintentionally asserting their ability to control public perception of the child workers.

It's also worth noting that the reporters and publishers of the time were trained to keep an eye out for salacious and captivating stories. Beatings, arrests, bribes, extortion, homelessness, extreme poverty, and starvation were all fodder for eye-catching headlines and columns, while more mundane events were often left off the page. As a result, the papers did a poor job of providing readers with a well-rounded portrait of the average newsboy or newsgirl.

For obvious reasons, Pulitzer's *New York World* and Hearst's *New York Journal* declined to provide their readers with any substantial strike coverage. In modern terms, we might say they circumvented the "Streisand effect"; that is, they chose not to address the scandal in the hope that it would blow over with minimal attention. Following the resolution of the boycott on August 3, 1899, the *World* published an op-ed in order to provide their side of the story. It read in part:

"Because of the malicious reports circulated by those who hoped to profit thereby *The Evening World* deems it necessary to lay before the public a plain statement of facts concerning itself. There is no 'strike' of newsboys at present. The unorganized movement led by those who hoped to gain public confidence by lying about their successful rivals long ago collapsed. [...] Not knowing the facts, it was only natural that the public should sympathize with the boys. So does *The World*—so long as the boys are reasonable. But sympathy must be based on common sense and justice." [3]

This account, like others before it, remains relevant to the newsies' story even as it cannot be considered objective or free from bias. While the *World*'s self-serving slant is easy to spot, it was among many publications that twisted the truth for their own purposes.

A final word of caution

The historical events in this book have been drawn from biographies, newspaper articles, labor reform studies, interviews, photographs, and a variety of contemporary sources. Every attempt has been made to represent people, places, and events to the greatest degree of accuracy possible. Given the biased reporting, inconclusive data, and lack of available information, readers are encouraged to view the following history through a critical lens. A complete bibliography has been provided in the back of this book for further reading.

CHAPTER ONE

Carrying the Banner
A Portrait of New York City's Child Newspaper Salesmen

*When that bell rings, we goes where we wishes. We's
as free as fishes—sure beats washin' dishes! What
a fine life, carrying the banner home free all!*

"Got the declaration of war by Mexico!" the newsboys cried,
flapping pale copies of the *New-York Tribune* at the passersby
hustling home for the evening.[1] It was February, cold and dark,
and the seeds of the Mexican-American War of 1846 had yet
to bear fruit. Two months later, when spring blossomed in the
Southwest, Mariano Arista would direct 5,000 Mexican soldiers to reclaim their turf on Texas soil, and in doing so, spark
a fierce two-year conflict with the land-hungry United States.

The newsboys of New York City didn't know any of that.
They didn't need to. Even the whisper of war was good for business, and dealing in salacious stories, battlefront skirmishes,
and political scandals was the newsies' specialty. They were
experts at rifling through the day's news to find the most
sordid and woebegone copy, and whatever they couldn't find,
they happily invented.

Every morning and evening, the residents of the city flocked
to the newsboy and his companions, shelling out spare coins in
their haste to peruse the latest editions. Newspapers were the
be-all and end-all of breaking news and public opinion, and
though they would eventually be eclipsed by the popularity
of personal radios, Technicolor television sets, and the light-
ning-fast information dispensaries of the Internet, their daily

spread of local happenings and worldwide phenomena had no established rival.

If there was something worth knowing, you could bet it was tucked under the arm of a newsboy.

In the winter of 1846, however, the newsboys' con was short-lived. It only took one eagled-eyed customer to begin flipping through the pages of the *Evening Tribune* to discover the scam. There had been no declaration of war, not by Mexico or any other country, nor would there be for another three months.

Whether they were cognizant of it or not, the city's patrons had fallen for a common ruse, one of several the newsboys used to get rid of their surplus stock at the end of a slow news day. The publishers' distribution offices were not in the habit of buying back unsold newspapers, so the cost of any leftover merchandise was taken directly out of the newsies' pockets. When they couldn't persuade the overworked businessman or kind-hearted bum to pick up an extra paper, the young newspaper hawkers resorted to more desperate measures.

Such measures were routinely discouraged by irate customers, to say nothing of the local police force, but on a night like this one, no one seemed to care. The crowd dispersed, effectively separated from their pocket change and the promise of a compelling story, and the newsboys headed home with visions of tomorrow's big headlines swimming in their heads.

A new kind of newspaper seller

The modern American newsboy was invented on September 5, 1833, when 10-year-old Bernard Flaherty responded to a classified advertisement in the *New York Sun*.[2] The penny paper was brand-new; its first edition hit the streets only two days earlier as 23-year-old publisher Benjamin Day and his associates wandered the domain of lower New York to cry the papers themselves.[3]

Day was young, but he had the temperament, vision, and work ethic suited to a career in the publishing industry. Each of New York City's eleven newspapers represented an enormous undertaking. Its editors were cutthroat and talented, tasked with the responsibility of managing a small cadre of reporters, setting the tone for the publication, and overseeing the painstaking publishing process. Within the columns of their four-page, six-cent newspapers, they balanced explosive headlines against sharp-tongued editorials, international news, colorful police reports, myriad advertisements, and candid, if limited local coverage.

More than anything else, an editor's larger-than-life personality was counted on to drive the paper's sales, and in 1833, every customer counted. Over 250,000 people filled the boroughs of mid-19th century New York City, but just 26,000 of them regularly subscribed to the city's overpriced papers.[4] Day quickly spotted an opportunity. When his papers hit the streets, the first thing he wanted them to notice were the long black letters scrawled across the top of the first page: "PRICE ONE PENNY."[5]

He wasn't the first to experiment with a cheaper, more accessible newspaper geared toward the working class—Horace Greeley and Horatio Sheppard had already tried (and failed) to restructure their *Morning Post* as a penny paper—but he was the first to make it work. The only problem? Day lacked a suitable workforce to carry the paper to its patrons, and unlike the top publishers of the day, he was forced to resort to solicitation in order to recruit a broad readership.

When the second edition of the *Sun* hit the streets on September 4, it featured a prominent advertisement by its own editor. "To the UNEMPLOYED.—A number of steady men can find employment by vending this paper," the ad read. "A liberal discount is allowed to those who buy to sell again."[6]

A 10-year-old boy turned up at the *Sun's* office the next day. Bernard Flaherty was an Irish immigrant newly-transplanted in New York City and as hardworking as any unemployed day laborer. For the sum of two dollars a week, Flaherty traversed the city with a hundred papers tucked under his arm, shouting the headlines and growing the *Sun's* circulation by the hundreds.

He wasn't long for the job. By the time Flaherty was 13 years old, he had landed a minor speaking role in a production of *The Ice Witch*, marking his first significant foray into the world of theatre. Four years later, he shed his Irish moniker for the stage name "Barney Williams" and honed his craft on the stages of San Francisco, Philadelphia, London, Dublin, and Edinburgh, eventually returning home to New York as a thespian of moderate fame and great wealth.

Not all newsboys escaped the profession so easily, but Williams' great success helped shape the narrative of the hardworking immigrant and their pull-yourself-up-by-the-bootstraps American Dream. In the *Sun*'s first year, the paper reaped the benefit of that hard work and ambition: a circulation in the thousands and a regular troupe of young newspaper hawkers who shrieked the day's news with more fervor and less dignity than their adult counterparts ever could.

Rival publishers were quick to catch on. Their papers stretched four to six feet at full width and were stuffed full of foreign affairs and political intrigue, stories that resonated most strongly with the upper crust of New York society. Rather than depend on newsboys to push the paper's sales, they collected annual subscriptions upfront, some costing nearly a full week's wages. By the 1840s, their old business model no longer stood a chance against the penny paper. The *Sun* had sparked a revolutionary way of thinking, one that permeated every publishing office until the boys swarmed the streets by the hundreds, calling the news to every wealthy businessman and factory worker within earshot. Every literate person in New York City instantly became a potential customer.

The newsboys were instrumental to each newspaper's success, and unlike Bernard Flaherty, many didn't view the gig as a stepping stone to a more illustrious career path. In an age where the concept of childhood had yet to be marketed to American families, the boys and girls of 19th-century America were viewed as little more than a miniaturized work force. Every person in every family pulled their own weight as best they could, toiling long hours in the blackened bellies of coal breakers, meticulously separating shards of slate from coal, shucking seafood in canning sheds, tending the spindles of textile mills, and stoking the furnaces of glass factories. Each job had its own perils and pitfalls, even the more innocuous tasks of peddling papers for pennies on a street corner.

The average American newsboy entered the trade between the ages of eight and 15 years old, though the littlest newspaper hawker might have been as young as five or six. No matter their rank or experience, poverty kept the adolescent newsies on the streets far beyond their 18th birthdays. "Younger sells more papes," Disney's fictional newsboy, Jack Kelly, would later inform audiences. It was true in the 1800s, too. Though the children working the streets needed every penny they earned, they were adept at manipulating the sympathies of prospective customers in order to maximize their profits. Older boys often helped the young hawkers look as pitiable and isolated as possible as they dawdled along the sidewalks and wharves of the city. Patrons who believed the children were motherless and alone were far more prone to leave a generous tip.

Sometimes, the newsboys' ploys reflected an uncomfortable slice of real life. While some newsies had homes and families to return to at the end of their shifts, the juvenile homeless population was far greater. They were the barefoot and tattered lot, the ones who hoarded their spare change for cheap theatre tickets and hot buttered cakes and chilled oysters at the end of a long day and dozed in the cold nooks and crannies of City Hall Park until the circulation offices opened at dawn. By day, they ran rampant through the streets, waving papers, shooting craps, and weaving through busy thoroughfares for a hair-raising game of kick the can. Life could be bitter and miserable, but even the hardest times had their bright moments.

Census figures never quite got a handle on just how many newsies populated the stairwells and sidewalks of 19th century America, and historian David Nasaw notes that 20th century surveys collected limited data on the newsboys as they tried to prove the correlation between street trading and juvenile delinquency.[8] In 1872, author James McCabe estimated there were "ten thousand children living on the streets of New York, gaining their bread by blacking boots, by selling newspapers, watches, pins, etc., and by stealing." A fair number of the 10,000 homeless children were the newsies who frequented Printing House Square, spending bitter winter nights warming their bare feet over the street gratings that blew hot steam from the vaults of the printing presses below. The picture McCabe painted was a dreary one:

"[Newsboys] rend the air and deafen you with their shrill cries. They surround you on the sidewalks, and almost force you to buy their papers. They climb up the steps of the stage, thrust their grim little faces into the windows, and bring nervous passengers to their feet with their shrill yells; or, scrambling into a street car, at the risk of being kicked into the street by a brutal conductor, they will offer you their papers in such an earnest, appealing way, that, nine times out of ten, you buy from sheer pity for the child. [...] They are ragged and dirty. Some have no coats, no shoes, and no hat. Some are simply stupid, others are bright, intelligent little fellows, who would make good and useful men if they could have a chance."[9]

Ragged countenances and pitiable conditions notwithstanding, the newsboys of New York City possessed an entrepreneurial spirit and incredible work ethic that made them virtually indispensable to the newspaper industry. And they weren't the only ones the city depended on.

"The newsgirl is here to stay"

In 1868, 33 years after Bernard Flaherty applied for his post with the *New York Sun*, the *Brooklyn Daily Eagle* estimated a total 2,000 newsboys and 300 newsgirls were living within the city's borders.[10] By 1886, that number had grown exponentially:

"How many newsboys and newsgirls are there in New York? A Park row policeman, in answer to that question, replied with hasty emphasis, 'About a million, I believe.' [...] There are so many of the little creatures and they are so irrepressibly active, so shrill-voiced, tumultuous, and seemingly omnipresent, at all hours and in all public places, that one is apt to overestimate their real numbers."[11]

It may have felt as though the newsgirls were everywhere, overshadowing and outselling their male competitors, but they existed in much smaller numbers than the newsboys. Girls of varying ages, backgrounds, education, and classes could be spotted on the steps of Park Row's infamous publishing houses, lingering in railway stations and hotel lobbies, poaching newsboys' customers at the ferry landing, and rotating shifts at any number of established newsstands, never standing still long enough to be properly counted.

Most newsgirls fell within the range of eight to 20 years old, though, like the newsboys, they entertained a few as young as four or five. They, too, were beset with the financial burden of caring for large families, and in some cases their meager pay was all the income their families depended on for food and shelter. Such was the case with Mary Welter, a 16-year-old girl who made a name for herself hawking papers at the Twenty-Third Street Ferry.

A timid, if resilient teenager, Welter collected a dollar in daily paper sales and another three dollars a week from "trusties," the nickname given to the customers who couldn't afford their daily papers until the end of the week and often felt inclined to throw in a little extra cash as a kind of tip or convenience fee. She was under strict orders to attend to her business and ignore the two newsboys who ran a competing stand, and when the boys inevitably goofed off during the long afternoons, she gladly accepted their customers. At the end of each week, her $10 sum went straight to her parents, neither of whom had been able to secure a job in their mid-60s. Her father, she told the *Sun*, was 65 years old and had been blind for 11 years.

"I went to school until I was 13, and am crazy to go now, but of course I can't," she said. "I don't like to be a newsgirl at all, and if I could get some other work that would pay me $9 or $10 a week I'd quit to-night."

It didn't matter that Welter envisioned a different life for herself, one guided by a well-rounded education and her choice of career. Unrelenting hardship had already chiseled the shape of her future, one where work was scarce and unfulfilling and any gap in her wages would have dealt a serious blow to the well-being of her father and mother, not to mention herself.[12]

Other girls Welter's age had even more pressing concerns. An unnamed newsgirl, described only by her age (16) and the color of her eyes (green-black), was a fixed ornament on the steps of Park Street all throughout the winter of 1896. She entreated passersby with folded sheets of newspaper in one arm and a three-week-old infant in the other, taking turns "making change and kissing the sleepy little bundle in her lap."[13]

That's not to suggest that each newsgirl was shackled to infirm parents or fatherless infants. Some made a name for themselves alongside the newsboys as expert sellers, staking out their own

territories and adopting a variety of creative tactics to rid themselves of the day's stock. It wasn't unusual for both newsboys and
newsgirls to attract a devoted customer base, so loyal to their
preferred newsie that they were content to purchase whatever
the children were selling—even in times of scarcity or protest.

Despite the obvious draw of the self-made newspaper seller's profession, hawking sheets on the streets was far from the
only occupation available to young girls. Most adolescent and
teenage girls were put to work in domestic jobs; if they weren't
scrubbing fireplaces, polishing stovetops, ironing laundry,
darning socks and tailoring dresses, finessing choice cuts of
meat from the butcher, and clothing, and feeding, and tending
the younger children in their own homes, they were doing it
for someone else. Still others were occupied in factories and
shops, both of which were considered much more respectable
than any variety of work conducted on the streets outside, as
girls were thought to be less prone to adopt loose morals when
working in a controlled indoor environment.

Two of the most famous newsgirls of the late 1800s were
Winnie and Sadie Horn, affectionately known around town as
the "Soubrette Newsgirls." Clad in a ruffled dress, her curly gold-
en-brown hair obscured by the brim of a veiled Gainsborough
hat, Winnie co-opted the entrance to the Sixth Avenue train
station and left the opposite corner of Twenty-Third Street and
Sixth to her sister, where the two dispensed newspapers from
3 p.m. until 3 a.m. every day. On any given afternoon, commut-
ers and businessmen looking to pick up their daily paper on the
way to the station would have to wade through the girls' posse
of newsboys, who diligently monitored every transaction and
wagged their fingers at the backs of retreating customers.

The more well-known of the two, Winnie was born to an
English mother and Russian father. She was the eldest of
eight siblings and most distinctive in look. Those who caught
a close-up of the newsgirl might have noticed the way one curl
always fell strategically over her eye, disguising the thin film
that rendered her nearly half-blind.* Her effusive style and
charm worked its magic on the city, from the way she imitated

---

* In an 1896 interview with the *New York Sun*, Winnie claimed that she

Shakespearean English to her curt dismissal of would-be critics with a cool, "Immaterial" (or, to those who insulted her dress, "Are you jealous?"). She almost exclusively dealt in evening papers, making rare allowances for morning editions that advertised popular fights or eye-catching accidents, and often scribbled Bible verses and lines from popular literature in the margins of her copies—2 Corinthians 9:7 and quotations from Shakespeare's *Othello* were listed among her favorites, per a report from the *New York Journal* in 1896.

Her customers were hardly limited to the stream of passersby who tunneled in and out of the train station. They spanned a wide range of classes and stations, from New York City mayor William Strong to future state governor and U.S. President Theodore Roosevelt, as well as Chief of Police Peter Conlin and politicians John Goff and Richard Croker. Those who didn't have the good fortune to patronize her services directly could visit her likeness in wax at the Eden Musée or pay a visit to local theatres and casinos, where both Winnie and Sadie were frequently parodied and venerated by turns.

Occasionally, one of the younger Horn girls joined her sisters on the streets. Though Emma Horn claimed to be 16 years old, she had the frame and delicacy of an eight-year old and the cheer and resourcefulness characteristic of a young child. During her first day on the job, she found it difficult to offload her stack of newspapers in the same lickety-split manner as Winnie and Sadie often did. Eager to turn a profit, she set her newspapers down and began pirouetting and high-kicking on the street, drawing a crowd so vast and enthralled that the police were soon required to scatter it.

"She's made out of the right stuff," Winnie told the *Sun* after Emma had emptied her reserves for the sparkling sum of

---

had been taken away by the Gerry Society as a six-year-old and returned for the worse. "They said I must have my eye treated," she said. "They treated it, didn't they, now? I went there with two beautiful big brown eyes, and I came away with one." It wasn't the last unpleasant run-in she would have with the Society. Around 1894, the Gerry Society revoked Mrs. Horn's custody of her enterprising daughters for violating regulations on street-selling. Public outcry soon returned the children to their mother—and it wasn't long before Winnie and Sadie resumed control of their corners, newspapers in hand.

a dollar. "Bet cher life," Sadie echoed. "We are born news-girls." Hawking papers was clearly a talent reserved for the Horn family, and they wouldn't entertain the thought of switching careers before marriage.

"As we make from $1 to $2.50 every day, we propose to be newsgirls until some Princes, handsome ones, come along and want us for their brides," Winnie said. "It would kill us to be shut up in a shop. Why, [...] we would wither up an' go to nothin'."[14]†

Not everyone welcomed the newsgirls' enterprising efforts with open arms, however. The very same newspapers the girls hawked throughout the city also decried their hard work and ingenuity, claiming that the very idea of a girl working on the streets was both morally repugnant and intrinsically evil. Some were sure that the newsboys would be put out of business by the newsgirls as they were forced to take fewer customers out of sheer chivalry.

"Gallantry is so imbedded in the masculine breast that wherever a boy and girl are business competitors in selling papers it is the girl who first disposes of her stock," one *New York Sun* journalist opined, later complaining that the newsgirls did not return the favor by leaving the female patrons to the boys.[15]

Others believed that street trading would inevitably corrupt the girls' innate innocence and purity—a concern that did not appear to extend to the newsboys of the city. The youngest girls were often lost to the "abyss" and "hideous darkness" of the street, while the older ones were maligned for exhibiting the base behavior of the newsboys themselves: running wild through the city, shouting, swearing, boldly pushing their way into crowded saloons and upscale hotel lobbies, and bragging about the profits they made off of

---

† Winnie's words would become a self-fulfilling prophecy. After years of rebuffing interested suitors, she was whisked away by a bold young sailor in the spring of 1899 after he purchased her entire stock of newspapers and impulsively proposed marriage. The marriage was just as quickly annulled, but Winnie settled down with a Mr. Martinez not long afterward. Many of the Horn girls met tragic ends in the years that followed: both her father and Emma succumbed to a fatal bout of tuberculosis; her mother, Elizabeth, died of unreported causes; and the girls' heartbroken sister Jennie committed suicide by gunshot. She died in Winnie's arms on a June day in 1910. Months later, Winnie was found dead in her sleep, likely from an acute asthma attack.

businessmen and soft-hearted drunks. Worst of all, said one Mrs. E.S. Hurley of the Elizabeth Home lodging house, the girls refused to abandon their trade to take up dressmaking, typewriting, or laundry work, as they "scoffed at the idea of giving up their liberty."[16]

The very things the public loved about the newsboys—their scrappy behavior, their camaraderie, the way they epitomized the hardworking American man—they hated to see in the newsgirls.

"It is a hard life which the newsgirl leads," the *Buffalo Enquirer* told its readers. "Many boys who sell papers grow up to be useful, enterprising, respected citizens, but the after life of the newsgirl is seldom useful and happy."[17]

"Little girls are made hard and coarse and sent on the way of becoming bad women," the *Elmira Star-Gazette* added. "For the sake of a few cents they lose what is worth more than money and what they can never regain. They should not be allowed the run of saloons, stores, offices, hotels or other business or public places. It is bad for them and bad for the community."[18]

By the late 1880s, the community of New York had formally mobilized against the girls. It wasn't enough to complain about the newsgirls or debate about the dangers of unconventional gender roles; they felt compelled to end the conversation by getting the girls off the streets for good. Around 1886, the newly formed New York Society for the Prevention of Cruelty to Children, commonly termed the "Gerry Society," placed an age restriction on the city's juvenile work force. Girls under the age of 16 years old were no longer allowed to peddle flowers and papers, though any girl 16 years and older was welcome to try her luck among the boys.

The ban was characterized as a "kindness to the girl[s]," a way of preserving their moral dignity as they moved toward more traditional roles as housewives, mothers, and domestic help. It succeeded as a scare tactic for a while, but the girls soon realized that the Gerry Society was not planning on enforcing the rule. All manner of 16-year-old girls swarmed the streets once more, thick as mosquitos on a damp July afternoon. Some looked as young as eight; others appeared to be 12 or 14 years old. None of them looked the requisite 16, and it wasn't long before their outward defiance drew unwanted attention.

Not five years after the ban first swept through the streets of the city, the newsgirls of New York found themselves under attack once more. Citing continuous complaints from publishers, newsboys, and patrons due to the girls' unruly behavior, officers of the Gerry Society took up arms against the children, pulling underage girls from the streets to issue severe warnings. If the same girl returned to hawk her wares again, she was arrested with her parents and hauled off to court for a formal warning from the magistrate. A third offense was the most egregious, whereupon the girl's parents were arrested and punished and the newsgirl herself was turned over to the society.[19]

Winnie and Sadie Horn survived the purge, as did Mary Welter, though the Horn sisters were later denied permits for erecting their own newsstands. It might have been a slight consolation that they were counted among the few who could still call themselves newsgirls; by the end of the 19th century, Gerry Society superintendent E. Fellow Jenkins estimated that only 12-15 adolescent newsgirls were left in the entire city.[20] Three years later, in 1899, the ban reached the hordes of New York newsboys. Measures were put in place that forbade children under 14 years old to sell on the streets, and those who hawked papers in cities with populations exceeding 10,000 persons were required to carry a special license.

The newsboys suffered few ill effects from the new restrictions. This ban didn't appear to be as fiercely enforced as the regulations against the newsgirls had been; no one cared much if a boy of 10 or 12 was peddling newspapers alongside his elders, so long as he minded his business and respected the older boys' turf.[‡] (Certainly, no one was looking out for the

---

‡ By 1905, it appeared the city was taking the ban more seriously. Plain-clothes police officers were sent out in pairs to survey and apprehend boys who were openly flaunting the law, but they quickly realized how exhausting a task it was to round up the city's children every day (especially without the assistance of parents, caretakers, teachers, and other authority figures). Newsboys across the city devised a system to warn each other of the approaching officers—that is, when the cops weren't making themselves obvious by traversing the city blocks side-by-side—and falsified their identifying information when registering for their badges. Younger newsboys sewed their badges into their clothes so that the older boys couldn't steal them

state of his soul.) Further, there were thousands more boys on the streets of New York City than there were girls. They stood a good chance of lasting well into the 20th century by sheer volume alone.

The newsgirls, it seemed, had officially become a dying breed.

A day in the life of a newsie

The newsie's day began well before the first wash of morning light bathed the copper dome of the *New York World* Building. Although Manhattan was home to dozens upon dozens of newspapers, only the most prominent dailies were perched along Park Row, clustered so close together that it was eventually termed "Newspaper Row." Park Row branched off from Broadway and curved up to the foot of the Brooklyn Bridge, flanked by the stately offices of the *New York Herald*, *New York Times*, *New York Tribune*, *New York Sun*, and *New York World* on one side and the sprawl of City Hall Park on the other, its green lawns dotted with the bright white façades of City Hall and Tweed Courthouse. It was the very definition of imposing.

These were the stomping grounds of the newsies, the place where they took refuge at night and lined up before dawn to receive the day's supply of crisp new headlines. They crawled out from under stairwells and alleyways, burned-out safes and boxes of sand and ash, wiping in vain at the layer of grime that perpetually clung to their cheeks and clothes. On a good night, a few of the children might slink into the warm lobby of a publishing house, but the printers kept a watchful eye out and more than one newsie ended their night with a splash of cold water at their backs.

Most mornings, it was still dark outside when they gathered in front of the circulation offices. Each newsboy and newsgirl kept to their own habits. A few had the luxury of cashing in on the afternoon editions after school let out, running the family newspaper stands, or tag-teaming with a sibling to support

---

(and, consequently, run them off the street corners and ferry landings) while others concealed the badges under heavy coats for the sole pleasure of whipping open their coats to reveal them, as James K. Paulding wrote, "in the approved style of the stage detective."[21]

parents who toiled long hours in the city's factories and sweat-shops. Those with no families and no homes were among the hardest-worked of the lot, with shifts that began well before sunrise and extended past midnight. Many kept to a fairly consistent routine: they showed up when the offices opened and finished their business around 9 p.m., leaving a few hours to indulge in a cheap cigar and a lottery ticket—or, if they were lucky, a seat in one of the Bowery's finest theatres.

Before they earned the luxury of relaxation and play, the newsies had to tackle the first obstacle of the day: procuring a paper. Unlike their brothers and sisters in the coal mines and glass factories, newsies were required to do more than just show up to work. They had to make an initial investment in order to sell papers. The practice was thought to have been introduced back in the 1830s, when *New York Sun* editor Benjamin Day caught his newsies lending papers to customers and returning them, slightly worse for wear, to collect a refund from the office at the end of the day. From then on, he charged them 67 cents per 100 newspapers. If they sold all 100, they could pocket the 33-cent profit. If not, Day refused to buy back the leftover papers and the children were forced to find another 67 cents to purchase the next day's stock.[22]

Those who didn't get their papers directly from the approved distribution offices often bought them off of an independent wholesale dealer instead. The middlemen were a vital resource for the newsies, as they made a point of stocking multiple newspapers and, in doing so, spared the children the added trouble of sprinting from office to office each morning. Many of them had grown up on the streets as newsboys themselves, and were intimately acquainted with the ins and outs of the industry—which worked both to their own advantage and, in lesser ways, to that of the children who patronized them.

Knowing exactly how many papers to purchase presented another issue. Newsies didn't want to be saddled with unsold papers at the end of the night, even less so if the editions contained dull stories and lackluster headlines. No customer wanted yesterday's news, and if a newsboy or newsgirl couldn't recoup their costs by the end of the day, they might be forced to borrow from an older newsie or beg passersby for enough change to buy back in. They had to be shrewd to survive; more than that, they had to have their finger on the pulse of the city at all times.

Newsies had to remember yesterday's sales figures and customer demographics. They had to know how to pitch an international news item to a white collar suit and a political scandal to a passing housewife. They had to consider the time of day, the number of subscribers each paper drew, the flow of foot traffic, and whether or not it was going to rain. By the late 1800s, morning publications were being rapidly eclipsed by the more popular evening editions as technology fed a newer, faster brand of journalism and the citizens of New York enjoyed longer evenings thanks to the advent of streetlamps. Instead of purchasing their stock once in the mornings, the newsies were forced to return to the distribution offices a second time in order to satiate their customers' demand for brand-new evening editions. They had to balance risk against potential profits and hope that the headlines were strong and the gamble paid off.

It wasn't as simple as shoving a few quarters into the palms of the circulation managers, truckers, or route-men, however. There was a stringent protocol among the ranks of the newsies, one that had to be followed if each child wanted to be successful at their trade. The oldest newsies were given seniority. They got the papers first and hit the streets first. If they were feeling generous, some might even act as a proxy between the younger newsies and the publishers: distributing papers, taking a cut of the profits, and bailing out the few who had miscalculated the supply and demand of the day. The bigger and older a newsie was, the more power they wielded. They could stake their claim on a street corner without fear of intrusion from other children, and the more black-hearted of the bunch often took to plundering the pockets of smaller newsies in order to line their own.

Once they considered their investments and doled out their fees, the newsies erupted from Park Row like a tidal wave, their piercing cries crashing upon every street corner, sidewalk, and trolley[§] in the city. Those who stopped to listen were hit with

---

§   Newsboys and newsgirls were frequently spotted hawking their wares

bore after bore of bad news: fires and earthquakes, vicious battles in foreign lands, usurped kings and dirty politicians seemed to wash up on the front pages one day after the next. Only upon purchasing a paper could readers divine the truth, and even in the age of yellow journalism, it was guaranteed to be far milder than the newsies suggested.

Even so, fake news didn't always guarantee a sale. Newsies had to get creative if they wanted to sell out for the day, either by means of establishing a strong customer base, tricking their patrons, or tugging on their heartstrings.¶ One of the most common tactics was dawdling with a customer's change. Papers often cost one or two cents, but the unfortunate customer who didn't carry exact change walked straight into the newsie's trap. A newsboy might fumble in his pockets to make change for a nickel until the customer became exasperated and left, or he might run off to the nearest corner store to get the necessary four-cent return. The astute newsie deliberately took their time on such errands; sometimes, they didn't bother returning at all.

Other newspaper sellers preyed on the guilt of wealthier patrons. They loitered in Longacre Square** or in the entryways of upscale hotels and theatres, hoping to catch the upper-class couple on their way home and embarrass them into coughing up a couple of coins. More popular was the "last paper" sleight of hand, where the younger newsies would strike a mournful expression and beg a customer to buy their last paper so they could go home for the night...only to repeat the trick for the next sucker. Few customers escaped that encounter without shedding a few pennies; if the trickster was particularly

---

aboard the city's streetcars until the spring of 1894, when the First Avenue, Second Avenue, Third Avenue, Fourth Avenue, and Metropolitan Street Railway companies implemented a city-wide ban on newspaper sales. They offered two reasons for the ban: first, the disturbing number of injuries and fatalities that befell the young newsies who ran around the cars and leapt on and off the vehicles; and second, the frequent complaints from customers, who claimed they had been trampled and manhandled by the rowdy children.

¶   Most newsies collected around 25 to 60 cents per day, more if the selling conditions were ripe, the headlines juicy, and the customers hungry.

**   In 1904, Longacre Square was renamed when the *New York Times* building was repositioned at the intersection of 42nd Street and Broadway. Today, it's known simply as Times Square.

convincing, even a few tears. Luckier were the newsies who managed to worm their way into a saloon in the wee hours of the morning, where bleary-eyed drunks were likely to clean out their supply of papers before the next morning edition debuted at dawn.

A home for the newsies

The newsie made a pitiful picture against the backdrop of 19th century New York City. George G. Foster of the *New York Tribune* suggested that the children's common uniform was a "slouched cloth cap, dilapidated roundabout and breeches, no shoes or stockings, and a dirty face with hands to match." No one, Foster added, seemed to know where the newsies got their clothes: the tailors denied outfitting the children, as did the slop-shops and secondhand clothing stores. Some even speculated that the clothes were not purchased or picked from the garbage bins, but "[grew] upon the Newsboys by degrees, like moss about tree-trunks; that one day a pair of trousers comes, the next week what they call a coat, and then, as the season advances, an old cloth cap."[23]

Whatever the method of acquiring their coats and caps, the newsies bestowed a certain ragged charm upon the city. In their pockets, they hoarded marbles, pennies, dice, and cards to while away the hours between the morning and evening rush. Some spent the afternoon shooting craps in the alleys, while others dared to make the busy streets their playground. Late at night, when their shifts finished and the publishers were busy cranking out the next day's wares, the newsies could be found in saloons and cellars, picking apart hot biscuits and slurping down crimson-white concoctions that looked something like ice cream. When the air turned frigid, they traded in the sweets for penny cups of coffee.

For evening entertainment, there was nothing more enthralling than the theatre. In the decades before movie theaters and nickelodeons captured the imaginations and pennies of working class children, the newsies flocked to the playhouses of the Bowery. For no more than a dime or so, they were granted access to the pits of the Olympic and Chatham

Theatres, where they could cheer, hiss, and lob peanut shells to their hearts' content.[††] Some boys—for the pit strictly prohibited girls and women—carved their names into the hard benches to mark their territory; as the *Tribune* once remarked, they treated the whole affair with as much dignity as that of the well-to-do churchgoers who dropped $500 for polished nameplates on the pews of the city's distinguished congregations.[25]

When the theatres went dark and the sidewalks shed their last pedestrians, the newsies returned home to catch a few hours' sleep before the next morning rush. For the homeless newsie who had tired of coal boxes and doorsteps, the Newsboys Lodging House was the only respectable establishment in town.

Lodging houses hadn't always been available to the homeless children of New York City. They were the brainchild of philanthropist Charles Loring Brace, who founded the Children's Aid Society in 1853 and was eager to bring religious and social reform to the city. Brace had seen young newsboys curled up in alleyways at night and watched older boys getting drunk in the morning in the back rooms of gin shops. Appalled by their lack of education and propriety, he offered the orphaned and homeless practical resources as they transitioned from lives of abject poverty to ones as upstanding members of society.

In 1854, Brace opened his first lodging house to the boys. The building itself was mounted in the dilapidated loft of the "Sun Building," divided into neat sections that designated a school room, an office, a bathroom, and a sleeping area for up to 75 lodgers. The whole enterprise cost around $1,000.[26]

March 18, 1854 marked the grand opening. It cost six cents for a good night's sleep and a cold bath.[‡‡] The newsboys were thrilled. Not only were they assured a safe place to rest, but they had the benefit of evening school, church services ("It's a *Sunday-school trap!*" cried one boy), and a rudimentary bank

---

[††]   Theatre owners weren't always appreciative of the children's presence, despite the fact that they were frequent and paying customers. After one rowdy evening, one theatre manager threatened a few newsies and butcher boys with the only thing he knew would scare them straight: a price hike large enough to keep them out of the pit for good.[24]

[‡‡]   By 1865, the lodgers were required to shell out five cents for a bed, three for a meal, and one for a locker.[27]

that returned interest on their savings. Most, Brace noted, entered the building without much in the way of money, clothes, business savvy—or even a name:

> "They are generally known to one another by slang names, such as the following: 'Mickety,' 'Round-hearts,' 'Horace Greeley,' 'Wandering Jew,' 'Fat Jack,' 'Pickle Nose,' 'Cranky Jim,' 'Dodge-me-John,' 'Tickle-me-foot,' 'Know-Nothing-Mike,' 'O'Neill the Great,' 'Professor,' and innumerable others."[28]

Although the boys made their living preying on the pity of New Yorkers, Brace refused to treat them as objects of charity. He expected the newsboys and bootblacks and canal workers to pay their dues on time, keep order amongst themselves, eat healthy food, and invest their money wisely. There was no punishment, either, save for the grown-up consequence of paying fines when they broke a rule. The superintendent of the house organized a banking system to help the children save their pennies and resist the temptations of constant gambling, and the boys voted not to withdraw their savings for two months. "Some repented and wanted their money," Brace noted, "but the rule was rigid."[29] In the evenings, those who were interested were invited to participate in an evening school, where they could practice literacy and prepare to trade in their street professions for more honest careers and bigger paychecks.§§

The change did not go unnoticed by the publishers who employed the newsboys. *Sun* proprietor Moses Sperry Beach lavished praise upon Brace's methods of reform and education.

> "The contrast at the present time is remarkable," he wrote. "[...] A fight or a row among the news boys is seldom seen. The smaller ones pursue their traffic unmolested, and all things relating to the news boys give token of better times among them.
>
> If these changes are not all due to the Lodging House, I believe that by far the greater part of them can be traced directly to that as the cause."[31]

Even without the creature comforts the Lodging House provided the children of New York, there was no denying its

---

§§ "One of the boys is hired as *barber,*" Brace added, "and shaves some of the heads closely!"[30]

impact on the population. In its first 12 years of operation, Brace and his employees brought an estimated 273,969 kids off the streets and sent another 10,000 out West to find new homes and employers.[32]

The Newsboys Lodging House welcomed boys of all ages and ethnicities. Those who weren't native to New York were often orphaned immigrants from Ireland, England, Germany, and Scotland; others called Canada, France, Italy, and Switzerland home. Most fell between the ages of 13-15 years old, but a few arrived as young as five years old and as old as nineteen.

By 1907, the newsboys had another place to call their own: The Newsboys' Home Club. As the name suggested, the club wasn't a proper lodging house, but it afforded the children some basic amenities: an employment bureau, dental clinic, gymnasium, workshop spaces, commercial department, small dormitory, and best of all, a summer camp nestled in Woodland Beach on Staten Island, at which the boys could camp under the stars and plant and harvest their own crops of vegetables on a generous three-acre spread of land. The club was not organized by the newsies themselves, much as they delighted in making use of the facilities and running their private beachside colony. It was the brainchild of an esteemed group of influencers, including William Randolph Hearst and the son of Joseph Pulitzer (and successor to the *World*'s editorship), Ralph.[33]

The only group consistently excluded from the activities, naturally, were the newsgirls. In the 1860s, the city's homeless girls were given a refuge of their own in the Girls' Lodging House on New Canal Street in Lower Manhattan. Lodging cost five cents and three meals could be obtained for 15 cents more.[34] The food was plain and the beds iron-cast, but it was enough to beckon the children off the streets. Afraid that the steep price of $1.40 per week would drive some girls back to the alleys and stoops of New York, the Children's Aid Society offered them a discounted daily sum of just eight cents in exchange for their assistance with cooking, laundry, and needlework.[35]

Both the newsboys and newsgirls were affected by gendered biases perpetuated by the press and charity organizations.

Boys were characterized as "careless, jolly, mischievous" and were generally thought to be more inclined to idleness and violence if left to fend for themselves, though they were also trusted to be self-sufficient and capable of handling the rigors of street trades in a way that girls were not.¶¶

Girls, on the other hand, were often described as "bright, merry, [and] romping" and expected to be of a more refined and inherently well-behaved class.[37] Engaging in street trades were largely frowned upon, as the work shifted girls' attention away from stereotypical woman-led industries like household management and childcare and, some thought, even made them prone to promiscuous behavior and sex work. When homeless girls arrived at New York City lodging houses, they were not only fed and sheltered, but trained in typewriting, dress-making, and housewifery and expected to find their place within these narrow career choices. As a result, many ended up swapping their street work for employment as servants and caretakers in the homes of middle and upper-class families.

There were worse places for the children to end up than the streets. Every boy and girl knew of the House of Refuge, the state's first official juvenile delinquency center. Established in the heart of the Bowery on January 1, 1825, the reformatory sought to rehabilitate its adolescent inmates through one of three methods: education, evangelization, and employment. Corporal punishment comprised the fourth, unofficial measure by which Refuge leaders sought to keep their charges in line.

The House of Refuge opened its doors to boys and girls alike, albeit in separate quarters, and confined them to dormitories

---

¶¶   It's worth noting that gender bias wasn't the only thing working against the homeless children of the city. Children of poverty, immigrants, and non-white boys and girls were also stereotyped unfairly in the press and assumed to be more uncouth, less educated, and less capable of "rising above their station" or making their way in the world. In a 1915 advertisement for the Newsboys' Home Club, the *New-York Tribune* went so far as to suggest that the average newsboy was not forced into the street trade by circumstance and station, but elected to do so of his own free will. "Don't ever believe that a newsboy is just an urchin with papers," the ad read. "Some impulse, some urge inside of him has put him to selling papers. [...] he is meeting problems of life and mastering them."[36] In a contradictory manner, the children were, by turns, romanticized, pitied, and despised by the public at large.

and common areas where they were schooled in reading, writing, and arithmetic and trained in manual labor before being apprenticed out to nearby farms and houses. Boys were trained in making brushes, cane chairs, brass nails, and shoes, while girls were instructed to do laundry, make uniforms, and complete other varieties of domestic chores.

What began as a program of noble intentions quickly and viciously deteriorated. By 1911, newsies comprised approximately 32% of the asylum's inmates.[38] Most of the children had been scooped off the streets of New York City due to petty crimes or vagrancy, and there was no escaping the asylum until they reached adulthood. There was no stipulation that explicitly ordered the release of a child after they completed a certain period of servitude; rather, it was left up to the Refuge to decide when a delinquent boy or girl had been sufficiently reformed.

Those who refused to follow the rules or did not perform their work adequately were subject to swift and cruel punishments. A first offense might result in a child losing their recreational privileges, while a second sent them to bed without supper or limited them to a diet of bread and water for each meal. Additional provocation inspired harsher measures. Children were left in solitary confinement, handcuffed, and dunked in ice-cold water by a "ducking stool."***

Several decades later, investigations into the House of Refuge returned more appalling results. Inmates, many of them Irish Catholic, were denied visitations from priests and forced to practice Christian rites.††† Instead of using a system of gradual escalation to punish troublemakers, superintendents and overseers used the slightest excuse to torture their charges, often for nothing more egregious than failing to complete a task in a timely manner, daring to talk back, or getting distracted during church services. Even minor infractions were met with

---

*** A "ducking stool" was a contraption that allowed a girl to be strapped into a wooden chair and repeatedly dunked in a body of water.

††† Some estimate that as many as 63% of all Refuge occupants between 1825 and 1855 were Irish immigrants, and a large number were Catholic as well.[39]

physical abuses, where the supervisors punched and slapped the kids in the face, whipped them with straps and canes and hickory switches, strung them up by their thumbs until they bled, left them to fester in dark, dirty cells for as many as 36 consecutive days, maimed a one-legged inmate with his own crutch, and worse. Many such victims were lashed in excess of 20 or 30 times with four-fingered whips, which left permanent scars across their shoulders and backs and, in the worst cases, resulted in death.[40] In one gruesome case, it was revealed that an assistant superintendent had beaten a young boy to death for "not completing his task and not doing it well." Over the course of one workday, the boy was clobbered with a thick cane on three separate occasions and left unable to walk. He was committed to the local hospital and died of his wounds four days later.[41]

After numerous investigations and public outcry, not to mention issues of overcrowding, poor living conditions, and the ailing health of its tenants, the House of Refuge was officially shuttered on May 11, 1935 as alternative reform measures were put into place.

For the newsboys and newsgirls of the 19th century, the horrors of the juvenile asylum presented a great and growing threat. Indeed, it was no easy life for the newsie of the New York City. Poverty, starvation, and incarceration comprised a minefield that the children—the homeless, orphaned, and immigrant among them—had to navigate every morning when they awoke to sell the day's papers. And, by 1883, they would soon learn to recognize the face of their newest adversary: Joseph Pulitzer.

CHAPTER TWO

King of New York

The Rise of Joseph Pulitzer and the *New York World*

It's the simplest solutions that bolster the bottom line.

Across the mahogany desk of the Western Union Railroad headquarters, Joseph Pulitzer stared down Jason "Jay" Gould. In person, Gould's slight frame and mild manner did little to betray his true nature as a conniving, black-souled railroad tycoon, a character so laser-focused on building his empire that Pulitzer's *St. Louis Post-Dispatch* regularly decried him as a liar, a beneficent despot, gluttonous potentate, and soulless monopolist.

It was one thing to lob insults from the safety of a newspaper column distributed some 870 miles outside New York City, and quite another to confront the business magnate face-to-face. And, as much as he may have wished it, Pulitzer wasn't there for a fight.

He was there for a newspaper.

Upon Gould's unexpected acquisition of the *World* in the autumn of 1880, Pulitzer's editorials took on an incredulous tone. "There are many reasons why a great capitalist and speculator like Mr. Gould should own and conduct a Republican organ," he opined, "but the Democratic party, despite its great vitality, can not afford to have its press contaminated by such a vampire."[1]

Three years later, the so-called 'vampire' was hemorrhaging $40,000 a year on a paper that drew a mere 11,000 daily subscribers and offered little more than a slanted view of his personal business dealings. By all measures, the *World* was failing, and everyone—including Joseph Pulitzer—knew it.

That didn't mean Gould was willing to scrap the publication for pennies. He also knew exactly what his nemesis had been up to over the last year: John Cockerill's murder of Alonzo Slayback, the ensuing blowback against the *Post-Dispatch*, its editor's rapidly-deteriorating health. Still, Pulitzer was desperate to stake his claim on New York City's infamous Newspaper Row; Gould knew this, too.

He set the asking price well above $500,000. For more than half a million dollars, Pulitzer would gain the rights to the paper, its equipment, and an Associated Press membership. He could have the building itself for another $200,000.

To anyone else, the *World*'s price tag would have been great fodder for a joke. To Pulitzer, it was a proposition worth serious consideration. He labored over the decision for weeks, consulting both his wife, Kate, and brother, Albert, to gain some clarity. Albert was furious. He was also newly-arrived in New York City and his *New York Journal* was flourishing among bigger enterprises like the *Sun*, *Herald*, and *Tribune*. He didn't think the city could bear two Pulitzers. When business was involved, the men's drive and competitiveness trumped any bonds of brotherhood.

Kate, meanwhile, encouraged her husband to pursue the venture. True, she had seen firsthand the toll that Pulitzer's workaholic tendencies could take—at just 36 years old, he already suffered a chronic cough, constant fatigue, and searing migraines—but she was shrewd enough to recognize that work would always take precedent in their lives. If Pulitzer didn't get the *World*, he would find some other means of securing an East Coast franchise.

Pulitzer listened to his wife. Whatever insecurities he harbored about his ability to resuscitate the *World* in a crowded, cutthroat market, he banished to the back of his mind. He convinced Gould to settle for the sum of $346,000 and negotiated the right to lease the *World*'s offices and gain full control over the paper's staff.

Within months, the city of New York would forget Jay Gould ever owned a newspaper.

From "József" to "Joseph"

Seventy years before his name became synonymous with the most prestigious award in journalism and 36 years before he achieved excellence in that field himself, József Pulitzer was born to Elize Berger and Fülöp Pulitzer of Makó, Hungary on April 10, 1847.

His birth was a fortuitous event for the Pulitzer clan. In the span of 16 years, Elize had birthed nine children; by 1860, she would be left with only József and his younger brother, Albert. Premature death and disease claimed the rest of the family, leaving the young Pulitzer brothers with the burden of continuing their parents' legacy.

In 1847, the Pulitzers had already spent three generations in Makó. József and Albert, had they stuck around, would have been the fourth. A modest farming town of some 35,000 persons, Makó was nestled along the curve of the Magos River, its flat expanse punctuated by the spires of Christian churches and the local Calvinist college. It boasted a thriving agricultural industry, particularly in the seasons when the snowfall was light in the Carpathian Mountains and the dike restricted the swollen river from spilling onto the floodplains. Here, József's great-grandfather, Baruch Simon Pulitzer, first made his living in the grain business, one that was passed down and improved upon by his son, Mihály, and his grandson, Fülöp.

The family trade didn't appeal to young József, who preferred to spend his time nose-deep in biographies and history books. By 1855, it was a moot point: Fülöp had packed up his family and moved to Pest, the merchant-friendly sector of the capital. Every bit the bustling metropolis Makó wasn't, Pest offered the Pulitzers wealth, prosperity, and a prominent place within the city's rapidly-expanding Jewish community. In Makó, Hungarian Jews comprised just five percent of the population; in Pest, they made up nearly 20 percent. At the center of the Pulitzers' neighborhood were the gilded globes of the Dohány Street Synagogue, which stretched a full city block and held the coveted title of the largest synagogue in the world.

As children, József and Albert applied themselves in trade and boarding schools, respectively, studying all manner of foreign languages, history, philosophy, and mathematics. Their parents sought to instill in them the benefits of a well-rounded education, and it was this foundation that gave them the skills they needed to dominate the business world later in life. József saw school as something more insidious than a training ground, however, and his explosive personality was showcased time and again as he staged tantrums during tutoring sessions and refused to learn subjects he found dull or uninspiring.

That temper was undoubtedly inherited from the elder Pulitzer, whose stubbornness and unquenchable need for obedience often alienated his wife and children. On more than one occasion, the boys were forced to forego meals, banished to the outdoor stables after exhibiting what Fülöp perceived as a lack of respect. These were the mannerisms that would one day manifest in an adult József as he structured his publishing empire in the United States.

On July 16, 1858, Fülöp lost a protracted battle with tuberculosis, the same disease that had claimed his eldest son, Lajos, two years prior. Medical expenses ate away at the inheritance money Fülöp had planned to entrust to his children, and Elize quickly remarried in order to make ends meet. Almost as quickly, she was also abandoned by her two teenaged sons, who would never fully recover from the loss of their father. A 14-year-old Albert was sent to live with his grandfather, Mihály, while József made a hasty application to the Austrian Army and hoped that a military career might provide his ticket out of the country.

Alas, it was not to be. József stood six feet three inches tall by the time he was 17 years old, and his thin frame and poor eyesight made him an unappealing choice for a new recruit. The Austrian Army declined his request. So, too, did the French Foreign Legion and the British Army. Even the ships in Hamburg didn't want him, as he had neither the build nor the constitution for a life on the sea.

Before leaving Germany, the gangly teenager found Julian Allen, an American recruiter who was looking for fresh blood to replenish an anemic Union Army. The American Civil War was three years old and in desperate need of strong, able-bodied men to fill their diminishing ranks. They sent agents into the far reaches of Western Europe, hoping to enlist young men with unspoiled dreams of coming to America.

Allen had other motives. Each recruit was eligible for up to $900 for his service in the military—a hefty bounty, and one that put dollar signs in Allen's eyes. According to Pulitzer biographer James McGrath Morris, he offered to cover travel expenses and guaranteed every man a $100 bonus upon reaching the United States, with a $12 stipend for each subsequent month of service. That left a profit of around $650 (or more) on the table, one Allen hoped to grab for himself.[2]

Like so many before him, József took the bait. On July 18, 1864, the 548-ton *Garland* bobbed in the harbor of Antwerp. Several hundred would-be soldiers flocked to its deck, with József was among the last to set foot aboard the ship. He told the officer he was 20 years old, though his scrawny frame must have betrayed him as a teenager. Still, 20 was the requisite age for military enrollment, no matter how desperate the Union forces were to bolster their troops. If the officer suspected the lie, he didn't confront József, and the ship finally pulled away from the glistening Belgian coastline, America in its sights.

In late August, the *Garland* finally reached its destination. József reneged on his agreement with Allen and sought a more profitable venture in New York City, where recruiting booths sprouted like wildflowers across City Hall Park. Overwhelmed with choies, the 17-year-old eventually opted for a cavalry regiment based in Kingston, New York. Twenty-two-year-old farmer Henry Vosburgh was seeking a replacement soldier for the tidy sum of $200—an offer the young immigrant found too good to refuse.

Of course, a lazy streak may also have played a part in helping József make up his mind. "I wanted to ride a horse, to be a horse-soldier," he recounted. "I did not like to walk."[3]

József also liked the name of the regiment—Company L of the First New York Lincoln Cavalry—as it bestowed a certain regal quality on the whole outfit. It reminded him of the way the Austrian Army used the names of kings to distinguish their ranks; a taste of home, as it were.

In order to complete the sign-up process, however, József had to provide the recruiting agents with two vital pieces of information: his age and his name. To the former, he simply repeated what he told the officer of the *Garland*—that he was 20 years old, not the 17 years he looked and felt. Perhaps the long voyage had added years to his appearance, or, more likely, perhaps the agents were grateful for any help they could find. To the latter, he gave the name "Joseph," an anglicized spelling of the Hungarian "József." It was the first time the name "Joseph Pulitzer" became known to the city of New York. It wouldn't be the last.

Battlefields, benches, and an open door

War was long and dreary and cold. Pulitzer played chess to pass the time, a skill that unexpectedly bailed him out of trouble after he decked a sergeant for pulling his nose—an elementary-school prank that incited the teenager's notorious temper. Luckily for Pulitzer, he was chummy with the senior captain of the regiment, a man who also happened to double as a frequent chess partner for the lonely soldier. The captain spared him from harsh punishment for attacking a non-commissioned officer, but the incident only served to further alienate him from his American battle-mates.

All childish fisticuffs aside, there were few real battles for the First New York Lincoln Cavalry to attend. By December 1864, Pulitzer's regiment had engaged Confederate troops at Antioch, Liberty Mills, Waynesborough, Beaverdam Flat, and Shenandoah, never quite getting close enough to take serious fire from the other side. More often than not, they found themselves in an endless trek across the snow-brushed Valley of Virginia, riding for such long stretches that blistered skin and aching muscles became a daily nuisance.

When the war ended, Pulitzer was honorably discharged and given the paltry sum of $135.35. He had served just 270 days in the regiment, well under the full year he promised Vosburgh. Free, war-weary, and newly-homeless, the 18-year-old returned to New York City to seek his fortune for the second time.

Life as a civilian wasn't any easier than it had been as a soldier. American cities were bloated with young soldiers, many of whom were unskilled and unsuited for the jobs they sought. Like Pulitzer, the European recruits who had been so eager to take up a post on the battlefield found themselves at an even greater disadvantage. Only a few spoke English; the rest faced the near-insurmountable task of assimilating into a hostile American society, lest they risked ending up on the streets or worse.

Pulitzer didn't have a job to return to or a steady cash flow from his relatives back home. He meandered through the streets of New York City seeking the occasional odd job, clad in the ragged remains of his army uniform and making his bed on the hard benches of Madison Square. "Every pleasant night until I found employment I slept upon the bench," he told the *Washington Post*, "and my summons to breakfast was frequently the rap of a policeman's club."[4]

By early autumn, it became apparent that there was no fortune to be had in New York City. Pulitzer made his way west to St. Louis, where there was a thriving German community and myriad opportunities to earn a living. He wasn't in a position to refuse any of them. He fired the boiler aboard a ferry boat in order to earn his passage to the city, shoveling coal into the furnace as the fire singed his face and the sleet froze his back. It was thankless work, made all the more difficult as the captain overworked the teenager and berated him for his thick accent.

Over the next two years, Pulitzer took every job he could find. He used his cavalry expertise to tend mules as a hostler at the Benton Barracks, then quit two days later because he could not stomach the mules' stubbornness or the quality of the food provided him. He operated gates for the ferry, dug trenches for cholera victims, loaded and unloaded steamers, managed deliveries, tried his hand at construction work, clerked for Theo Strauss's lumberyard, recorded charters for both the Atlantic and Pacific Railroads, ran small errands for local attorneys, started a small operation as a boss stevedore, and moonlighted as a livery hack for a wealthy family, among other things. The food industry wasn't for him, either—he waited tables at Tony Faust's Oyster House for one day, during which he smashed a plate of beefsteak over the head of an aggrieved diner.

Some mornings, he pocketed a few apples and set out for the Mercantile Library in downtown St. Louis, where he waited on the steps of the building until librarian Udo Brachvogel unlocked the doors. There was a treasure trove of knowledge to be absorbed within the pages of the library's 27,000-some books, and Pulitzer was uniquely suited to the task. His day jobs had given him a crude understanding of the English language, one that he began to refine by poring over books and badgering the other library members to engage in conversation. Never mind that he had to work multiple jobs and 16-hour days to make ends meet. Every spare hour was spent in one of the library's reading rooms or entertaining its patrons during cutthroat rounds of chess. Studious and relentlessly focused, the 19-year-old drew the attention of other prominent figures in St. Louis society: lawyers, journalists, and politicians among them.

In the spring of 1867, Pulitzer's hard work finally paid off. He became an American citizen on March 6 of that year, and within the span of another year, applied for the bar and passed. Life as a young attorney and notary public was ill-suited to his personality, and it wasn't long before he ditched legal work for something more appealing: a post as a reporter for a German daily called the *Westliche Post*.

He could hardly believe his good luck.

"I, the unknown, the luckless, almost a boy of the streets, selected for such a responsibility," he later told biographer Don Carlos Seitz. "It all seemed like a dream."[5]

But if his head was in the clouds, it never showed. Pulitzer quickly proved a tenacious reporter, willing to work harder and longer and smarter than any other staff member on the *Post*. His questions could be "exasperatingly inquisitive," said one rival reporter, but his exceptional work ethic and unflinching ability to push boundaries quickly set him a cut above the rest.[6] Soon, editors of other newspapers were encouraging their own journalists to emulate the young Pulitzer, as they were tired of seeing exclusive stories in the *Post* that they had failed to get for themselves.

The youngest Republican senator

As naturally as Pulitzer gravitated toward journalism, he was inevitably pulled into the adjacent political sphere. His copy was filled with biting remarks against the local politicians he viewed as shady and corrupt, and he was always among the first to illuminate underhanded dealings that put the common people at a disadvantage. Before long, the lines between reporter and politician began to blur.

A 22-year-old Pulitzer found his opening in the winter of 1869, when an election was proposed to fill two vacancies for the Fifth and Sixth districts of the General Assembly. The election itself was held in disdain by the Republican Party, for the sheer number of Democrats elected to the position stretched back a good 25 years. Finding a suitable Republican candidate for the seat and, what's more, engineering a successful campaign to overtake it, seemed to be all but a lost cause.

It was no wonder, then, when presumed Republican candidate and attorney Chester Krum excused himself from the nomination process altogether. Pulitzer, who was attending the convention as a reporter and now-editor of the *Post*, slunk out of the hall. When he returned, his colleagues broke the good news: he had secured a unanimous vote as the new Republican candidate.

Perhaps it was a farce; no one who truly wanted to win would have nominated an underage, foreign-born candidate, especially one with limited political experience and controversial opinions. If Pulitzer's adversaries wanted to discredit him, there were plenty of ways to do so. None of them mattered to the young journalist. Despite the illegality of his nomination, Pulitzer canvassed the area, penned a scathing takedown of his opponent, wrote third-person columns praising his own character, and grew a full beard and mustache to disguise his youthful appearance.

Two things worked in the reporter's favor. First, the Democrats lost their candidate to another resignation, forcing them to back Samuel A. Grantham, a tobacco dealer with no previous dealings in government. Second, it snowed on election day, reducing the number of voters from a potential

1,200+ persons to just over 300. By virtue of his passionate, if illegitimate campaign, Pulitzer had won handily, eclipsing Grantham's 147 votes with his 209.

At last, Pulitzer could put into practice the principles that he so eloquently promoted in the *Post*. Rather than abandon the paper, however, he sought to marry his hard-hitting journalism with his political ambitions. As both a reporter and a newly-minted state senator, he voiced his support for the Fifteenth Amendment, introduced a controversial bill that would eradicate the corrupt St. Louis county court, and exposed the shady dealings of one judge who sought to line his own pockets with leftover funds intended for a new county poorhouse.

Not everyone appreciated Pulitzer's steadfast moral convictions. In the winter of 1870, one lobbyist found himself under fire from the senator: Captain Edward Augustine, who Seitz described as "a huge man with the neck of a bull and the arms of a prize fighter." Augustine was both physically and politically formidable, one of the few who held unchecked power in the county and wielded it exclusively for his own profit and protection. His latest scam involved the construction of a publicly funded insane asylum in nearby Allenton, one whose exorbitant costs had provided the lobbyist with a comfortable, albeit illicit, cash flow.

Pulitzer wasn't buying it. He attacked Augustine in the *Post*, bringing his motives and financiers under intense scrutiny. While such allegations might have been tolerated from a less renowned reporter, Augustine was well aware of the public and political power Pulitzer himself possessed. He resented the implication that he was receiving special consideration from the same court Pulitzer sought to abolish, and he wasn't going to sit idly by as his name was dragged through the mud.

Tensions came to a head on January 27, in a large meeting room of Schmidt's Hotel. Augustine called Pulitzer's latest column into question, claiming that the young reporter was too ill-informed to bring such serious charges against him. When Pulitzer rebutted the accusation, Augustine resorted to insults.

"Nothing but a pup could make such a statement, not knowing them to be facts," he told Pulitzer.[7]

According to the coded language of the day, those were quite literally fighting words.

By the end of the evening, the pair had drawn pistols in a gentleman's duel. Most accounts claimed that Pulitzer fired two bullets: one missed, the other skimmed Augustine's right calf. Augustine responded with full fist and muscle, pounding on Pulitzer's slight frame with the jagged edge of his brass knuckles. When the dust cleared, Augustine walked away with a minor wound and Pulitzer made the trek over to the local police station, where he was charged with disturbing the peace and assault with the intent to kill. The first got him an $11.50 fine; the second, a trial date.

The next ten months brought more challenges. Pulitzer faced overwhelming backlash from the affair and, as he had done many times before, used his platform in the *Post* to defend his own slanted viewpoint. In the House, his opponents were equally combative. One representative recommended a three-person committee to investigate the shooting, a measure that was found so extreme that it was quickly snuffed out lest the other members of the House face additional scrutiny for their own past offenses.

In time, there was plenty to distract the public from the scandal. Pulitzer threw himself into his work once more, protecting the interests of public schools, erecting statues to honor military veterans, and opposing members of the House who were suspected of pocketing bribes in exchange for votes. He ran for re-election in the autumn of 1870, but the elements that worked in his favor the first time around—inclement weather, poor voter turnout, and a week Democratic opponent—had long subsided, leaving a clear path to victory for the Democratic Party.

One year later, the 23-year-old stood trial for his actions against Augustine. His guilt was unquestionable, but his friends were plentiful and their coffers deep. Pulitzer left the courthouse with a $405 fine on his conscience, an unusually light punishment for an allegation as serious as attempted manslaughter. Three of his friends—former mayor Daniel G. Taylor, lieutenant governor Edwin O. Standard, and miller Henry C. Yaeger—paid the debt, and an anonymous ex-lobbyist reportedly strong-armed the rest of Pulitzer's dissenters into silence. "If that boy goes to prison," he told them, "he will not go alone."[8]

The rise and fall of the Liberal Republican Party

As the curtain fell on 1871, Pulitzer gladly stepped out of the spotlight. His primary concern shifted to the future of the *Westliche Post*, where he was free to speculate on the current political climate with unfettered emotion. It was the kind of bliss that lasted just two weeks. Circuit attorney Charles Johnson had exerted pressure on the governor to reserve a vacancy on the St. Louis Police Commission for his former client and friend. After some hemming and hawing, during which Pulitzer needed to be convinced that the post wouldn't threaten his status at the paper, the young reporter accepted the part-time gig.

The job was not unappealing. It required few hours out of Pulitzer's six-day workweek and paid a handsome annual salary of $1,000. Even better, it allowed Pulitzer to wield a more direct authority than he had been accustomed to as a state senator. As one of just four police commissioners in St. Louis, his targeted attacks on local gamblers and seedy politicians were backed up by both the letter of the law and brute force of the extensive 432-member police department.

By late January, a worthier cause had dropped in his lap. An undercurrent of discord was running through the Republican Party, ramping up in intensity as President Ulysses S. Grant neared his bid for reelection. Missouri governor Benjamin Gratz Brown, former Secretary of the Interior Jacob Cox, and charismatic senator Carl Schurz pooled the disgruntled Republicans—wannabe presidential candidates, journalists with axes to grind, and the rare abolitionist among them— into their own faction, termed the "Liberal Republican Party." Together, they opposed Grant's platform on nearly every level, crying corruption, greed, and unchecked federal oversight. Theirs would be a campaign of lofty pre-war ideals and tariff reduction, civil service reform, political amnesty for Southern leaders, and states' rights. It wouldn't just topple Grant from the White House; it would usher in a new era of Republicanism and a new golden age for the country.

A more expertly-calibrated microscope might have identified the molecules of racism that comprised the new movement. According to Grant biographer Ron Chernow, the majority of the party eagerly aligned themselves with the elite, white Southern class in their haste to distance themselves from Grant. Liberal Republicans had not opposed the abolition of slavery or the addition of the Fifteenth Amendment—on the contrary, they had put their weight behind the measure just two years earlier. Now, they felt overwhelmed by the tide of progress threatening to break on their shore. Like Schurz, they decried the Reconstruction as a "horror" and "nightmare" for Southern states and pushed back against what they perceived to be a "Negro supremacy."[9] "Home rule" was the new buzzword in light of the ill-received Civil Rights Act of 1871, which allowed federal troops to overrule states' authority as they dismantled the presence of the Ku Klux Klan in former Confederate territories.

Not a few opponents of Liberal Republicanism pointed out the hypocrisy of the defense of so-called "state sovereignty." As activist Lydia Maria Child put it, "When the Ku Klux [Klan] renew their plans to exterminate Republicans, white and black, they shall be dealt with by Southern civil authorities—that is, by judges and jurors who are themselves members of Ku Klux associations."[10]

In May 1872, the Liberal Republican Party found their mouthpiece. Six ballots eventually secured the nomination of Horace Greeley, the infamous 61-year-old editor of the *New York Tribune*. If the roar of laughter upon Greeley's selection was any indication, they could not have selected a more unlikely candidate. He alienated members of his own party by opposing free trade and endorsing temperance and socialism, and the years he spent ripping into the Democratic Party now haunted him as he tried to make amends in order to strike a much-needed alliance against Grant.

"I don't know whether you are aware what a conceited, ignorant, half-cracked, obstinate old creature he is," *The Nation's* E.L. Godkin warned Schurz.[11]

Schurz may have been well aware of Greeley's poor reputation—his attempts to displace the veteran journalist suggest that was the case—but Pulitzer lacked similar foresight to recognize the Liberal Republicans' losing battle. While holding down the fort for the *Post*, he worked sixteen-hour days on the campaign and stumped for the man through Missouri, Indiana, and Ohio, making 60-some speeches to German voters in the months leading up to the election.

In spite of Pulitzer's best attempts, voters refused to warm to Greeley. The speeches Greeley made were both coarse and unpolished, and he lacked the sincerity and finesse necessary to sway the undecided hearts of a large Democratic base. In November, Grant carried the election easily with 286 electoral votes and a striking 56% of the popular vote. Defeat did not come naturally to Greeley, and in this case, it proved fatal. He had lost his election, his wife, and his newspaper in the span of several months; now, on the brink of insanity, he succumbed to frequent mental and nervous breakdowns born of grief and exhaustion. He died before the Electoral College even had the chance to fill out their ballots.

Greeley's death reverberated throughout a fractured Liberal Republican Party. The campaign had set everyone on edge, even the proprietors of the *Post*. Several months before the election, a few members had approached the 25-year-old Pulitzer and announced their intention to retire. They thought Greeley cast the Republicans in a poor light and would irreparably tarnish the reputation of the paper, and would Pulitzer be interested in purchasing a stake in the publication at "very liberal terms"?

He would.

By September, Pulitzer had a controlling interest in the paper that had once opened the door to his burgeoning career as a hard-hitting journalist and politician. Ownership proved a short-lived joy: Within the span of several months, the young editor was already on the outs with co-owners Carl Schurz and Emil Preetorius. Schurz found he could not use the paper to boost his campaign for reelection as it was too closely associated with Pulitzer's name, instead of his own, while Preetorius publicly opposed Pulitzer's unsuccessful bid for another seat on the police commission. In the spring of 1873, Pulitzer repaid his debts and severed his last tie with the *Westliche Post*, walking away from a toxic partnership with $30,000 in his pocket and a European vacation on his mind.

Disillusioned Republican, restless Democrat

The easy life held little appeal for someone of Pulitzer's ambition and accomplishments. He frittered away several months in Western Europe, imbibing French liquor and drinking in Parisian opera, and eventually returned to St. Louis in November 1873 to a veritable bacchanalia hosted by his friends and former colleagues.

Without a political party or a paper to call his own, Pulitzer took a room adjacent to the offices of his former attorney, Charles Johnson. There, he was tutored in the finer points of the law and soon announced his intention to enter into a practice for the second time in his 26 years. The drama of the courtroom was not unlike the tumultuous ebb and flow of politics, and Pulitzer was nothing if not well-suited for the rigorous hours and study it would require become proficient in legislative loopholes and regulations.

In the end, sacrificing his journalistic ambitions proved too difficult a task for the short-tempered lawyer-to-be. In January 1874, he seized another opportunity to gain control of a newspaper. The local *Staats-Zeitung*, a small German daily, had recently gone bankrupt. Pulitzer put in a winning bid of a few thousand dollars and began transforming the paper into an evening edition.

At least, that's the story he was sticking by. Behind closed doors, Pulitzer had a far more complicated scheme up his sleeves. The *Staats-Zeitung* had been granted a coveted Associated Press membership, which gave them the rights to the flurry of news dispatches that were routinely handed out to top-tier publications in New York City and other major cities across the country. Not all papers could afford the same luxury; the *St. Louis Globe*, for instance, had been routinely denied membership by the disgruntled owner of a rival paper. Pulitzer presented the *Globe*'s editors with an interesting proposition: If they would purchase the now-defunct *Staats-Zeitung* from him, they could convert the publication to English, change its name to the *St. Louis Globe*, and reap the benefits of AP coverage without any underhanded dealings.

The *Globe*'s William McKee and Daniel Houser were all too glad to take Pulitzer up on the offer. They shelled out a cool $20,000 for the newspaper and AP membership bundle while Pulitzer offloaded the printing presses and leftover furniture to another pair of aspiring newspaper owners for a tidy sum. He was once again divested of his interest in the newspaper industry, but considerably richer and ready to make something of himself in the world.

Now a man of some means, it only seemed fitting that Pulitzer return to the political circuit. The Liberal Republican Party had blossomed and withered within the span of the 1872 election, but another was ready to take its place: The People's Party. Colloquially known as the 'Tadpoles,' the People's Party was comprised of the same band of disgruntled former Republicans who sought reform and another opportunity to push back against Democratic forces. They nominated William Gentry for the Missouri governorship, a mild-mannered farmer who possessed wealth but no head for politics and harbored no hope of defeating Democratic candidate Charles M. Hardin.

Pulitzer would not hitch his wagon to a losing ticket a second time. He withdrew from the People's Party and impugned Gentry's name in an interview with the *Globe*:

> "Mr. Gentry is an excellent farmer, but because he is an excellent farmer is no reason why he should make an excellent Governor. [...] I'm a good fellow and I believe you think so; you are a good fellow, I know that; but what an absurdity it would be for either of us to aspire to the office of Governor of the great State of Missouri. The man Gentry is an ass, and he was nominated by asses."[12]

While Pulitzer later disputed the validity of the interview, the sentiment behind it rang true. He saw the party's attempts at compromise as a betrayal of their principles of reform, and jumped ship to the Democratic Party soon thereafter to throw his support behind Hardin.

"Neither the unquestionable personal honesty of Farmer Gentry, nor the ingenuousness of the platform, nor the power of the old associations, the natural reluctance to sever them, the sympathy and admiration for honored friends, nor the participation in the incipiency of the movement before it had any form, unity or aim, can reconcile me to so palpable a result of politics without principle," he told the *Missouri Republican*.[13]

Pulitzer may not have been fully on board with the tenets of the Democratic Party, inasmuch as they ran toward "inflation and repudiation," but he admired the Democrats' ability to stick to their own values in the face of corruption and compromise. Abandoning key principles to secure elections and unite disparate political parties and social classes was not something that interested him.

The next few years passed fitfully. Pulitzer successfully campaigned for a seat in the delegacy in January 1875 and used his new position to pontificate about the freedom of the press and involve himself in the drafting of a new state constitution. The following winter, when *New York Herald* reporter Albert Pulitzer covered the high-profile prosecution of presidential secretary Orville E. Babcock, Pulitzer joined his brother in the courtroom to file his own stories for the humble *St. Louis Times*.

By September, the next presidential election had rolled around again. Pulitzer couldn't resist the pull of another campaign. He backed Democratic candidate Samuel Jones Tilden against the Republican Rutherford B. Hayes, a noted favorite of Pulitzer's former business partner, Carl Schurz. Pulitzer trailed Schurz around the campaign trail, refuting his pro-Hayes arguments and trying in vain to lure his old friend into heated debates. When he wasn't composing witty speeches on the road, he targeted the Republicans in sharp-tongued columns for Charles Dana's *New York Sun*.

Despite Pulitzer's undeniable skill as an orator and journalist, there was no fair fight to be had. The deck had been rigged against the Democrats as Republicans bribed voters, disposed of legitimate Democratic ballots, and switched the final electoral vote to give Hayes the edge—and a seat in the White House.

Disappointed and disillusioned, Pulitzer withdrew from politics a second time. He was 31 years old and had little to call his own: several thousand dollars, a room at the Willard Hotel in Washington, D.C., a couple of now-fading bylines in the *Sun*. On June 19, 1878, he married 25-year-old Katherine Davis, the youngest daughter of Georgetown judge William Worthington Davis and cousin to former Confederate president Jefferson

Davis. The two were smitten as much as a young socialite and a perpetual workaholic could be; Kate had received the journalist's first-ever love letter only months before.

"I am almost tired of this life—aimless, homeless, loveless, I would have said, but for you," the letter read. "I am impatient to turn over a new leaf and start a new life—one of which home must be the foundation, affection, ambition and occupation the corner stones, and you my dear, my inseparable companion."[14]

Even in the throes of wedded bliss, it was only a matter of time before the happy groom returned to his true love: the press.

The *Dispatch* and the man in the chinchilla coat

A frigid winter air seeped through the coats and collars of the 30-odd men gathered by the steps of the Old Courthouse in St. Louis. It was the morning of December 9, 1878, and two bankrupt newspapers were on the auction block.

Skulking through the crowd in a blue chinchilla overcoat, a tall man with a prominent profile and even more prominent reputation kept his eye on the auctioneer. Pulitzer had $5,000 in savings and was ready to sink it in a worthy paper, if one could be had for that price. Reports differed; some said the *St. Louis Dispatch* could fetch as much as $40,000, even though no publisher in Missouri could wring a profit from its pages. Others, *Missouri Republican* editor William Hyde among them, said it wasn't worth a damn.

The bidding began moments after Pulitzer's arrival. The ailing eight-year-old *St. Louis Journal* was quickly disposed of with a winning $600 bid, though it was hardly worth more than the presses that printed its stock.

The *Dispatch*, on the other hand, still held some promise. It was an evening paper bundled with an AP membership, which the auctioneer estimated at a $20,000 value alone. The publication itself certainly wasn't worth boasting about—it had been established in 1862 as the *St. Louis Union* and was intended solely as a political battering ram for U.S. Senator Frank Blair, who hoped to demolish Democratic candidate John Frémont and the *Missouri Democrat* behind him. Failing that, it had fallen into disrepair as a second-rate evening paper.

"Gentlemen, I now propose to sell you the *Evening Dispatch*, a paper that will live when all the other evening papers are dead," cried the auctioneer, rather boldly.[15]

The first bid landed at $1,000, put forth by a Simon J. Arnold, the supposed emissary for Republican city collector Meyer Rosenblatt. From the back of the crowd, a volunteer offered $1,500 on the condition of anonymity. No other bidders dared toss their hats in the ring.

The price for the *Dispatch* continued to climb. Arnold put forth a final bid of $2,900 and was promptly shot down by a counteroffer of $3,000 from the stranger. When it came time to give up his name and stake his claim on the paper, however, the man was nowhere to be found. He'd made a discreet exit into the ice-covered backdrop of St. Louis, and no amount of sleuthing could uncover his identity. Arnold made a quick about-turn as several new bidders rushed to the auctioneer's podium, each eager to put in an additional offer for the paper.

They were too late. For the sum of $2,500—well under the $3,000 price tag the stranger volunteered and abandoned just minutes before—the purchase had been secured in favor of one Simon Arnold—and the man who hired him as proxy, Joseph Pulitzer.

Reviving a paper was no easy business. The *Dispatch*'s assets were negligible, its readership dwindling, its staff insufficient, and its elevator broken. According to Don Seitz, the old flatbed press could barely turn over and the forms had to be slid down the stairs to the press room below.[16]

Three days after Pulitzer acquired the ailing outfit, John Alvarez Dillon paid a visit to the man in the blue chinchilla coat. Dillon's own newspaper, the *St. Louis Evening Post*, was an elegantly-crafted publication that served large portions of society news for the hungry elite. Its circulation outpaced that of the rival *Dispatch* and *Evening Star*, but wasn't widely-read among the lower classes of the area. Where Pulitzer was looking to exploit that weakness to advance his own paper, Dillon presented the opportunity to circumvent an inevitable circulation war.

Even Pulitzer was not above accepting a lifeline. The two merged their papers at once; Dillon remained the president and managing editor and Pulitzer slotted into the dual role of vice president and political editor. An important caveat was tacked onto the agreement, giving Pulitzer free rein to write about anything he chose without censorship.

Dillon wasn't yet familiar with his new business partner's tenacious, take-no-prisoners approach. Armed with that knowledge, perhaps he would have chosen to risk the circulation war after all. Pulitzer didn't know how to share, nor did he have any intention of letting Dillon dictate the course the new paper would take. His first editorial for the new franchise made his intentions clear:

"The *Post* and *Dispatch* will serve no party but the people; will be no organ of Republicanism, but the organ of truth; will follow no causes but its conclusions; will not support the 'Administration,' but criticize it; will oppose all frauds and shams wherever and whatever they are; will advocate principles and ideas rather than prejudices and partisanship."[17]

Pulitzer made good on his word. The *Post and Dispatch* chased down every scandal in the city, exposing tax dodgers, illicit gambling rings, shady committee meetings, lovelorn suicide victims, and rival papers who dared to filch its copy for their own front pages. Pulitzer hired reporters to pursue suspected murderers and investigate insurance companies that folded after defrauding their clients of millions in premiums and benefits. There was no story too grim to attract his attention, nor anyone with pockets deep enough to distract him. He became the master of the righteous crusade, revealing a deep knowledge of current events and an unshakeable passion for the moral high ground while taking the wealthiest and most corrupt society members to task on the front page.

The *Post and Dispatch* seized the public's attention and moral anger from the get-go, but it also drew loud accusations of sensationalism. Pulitzer was an expert in fashioning mountains from molehills, as he did when accusing a Catholic priest of breaking his vow of celibacy to father a child out of wedlock. The priest was removed from his position, the public consumed an extra 1,000 papers to read about the controversy, and the claim went unsubstantiated.

More shocking was the paper's coverage of critical current events, including the shooting and subsequent death of President James Abram Garfield. When Garfield was shot at a railway station in Washington, D.C., Pulitzer laid into the team of doctors who claimed the Commander-in-Chief was on the cusp of a full recovery. "He Is Dying," the *Post and Dispatch* announced. Pulitzer refused to take the medical reports at face value. He lambasted the doctors as "reckless liars" and claimed that Garfield would soon die of blood poisoning. The public may have despised the callous treatment of such a delicate matter, but Pulitzer was not one for tact—and he wasn't wrong, either. Garfield's blood had been poisoned, likely by an infection exacerbated by unsterilized treatment, and his lungs quickly deteriorated. Two long, torturous months after shooting, the president died from his wounds.

Pulitzer didn't seem to care that the public found his stories unduly exaggerated or that his advertisers continued to pull funding. At long last, he had command of his own paper—his own truth-telling machine—and he was loath to loosen his grasp on it.

It wasn't just entitlement that kept the 31-year-old editor invested in his paper. In order to stay ahead of the competition, he immersed himself in every area of publishing. He held political debates while penning editorials; rewrote copy that didn't meet his standards or needed that extra *zing!*; analyzed column inches, salary figures, and profit margins; reviewed page proofs; even joined the newspaper hawkers to hand out copies on the streets of the city itself. He was the first man in the office each morning and the last to leave every night, often poring over each page by gaslight until the late hour forced him to return home for a few hours' sleep. His articles could turn the most complacent news item into a breathless, edge-of-your-seat thriller, his editorials seethed and sizzled with every sentence, and his prose discriminated against no singular social class.

Some were less than pleased by the paper's success. Several months after the merger, a group of *Post and Dispatch* newspaper hawkers mounted a strike against the publication and its charismatic leader. They protested an unexpected half-cent spike in wholesale costs for their stock, which had inflated the price of the paper from two-and-a-half cents per copy to three cents per copy. Instead of making two-and-a-half cents per copy sold, they now made just two cents on each paper. Pulitzer failed to sympathize with the young children.

"It is hard to fight women, but still harder to argue with boys, especially newsboys," he explained. "At the rate fixed by the proprietors of this journal the newsboys would still make *two cents on every copy sold, or more than newsboys make in any other city of the United States or the world*, in fact twice as much as the average profit of newsboys in any of the Eastern cities or in Chicago, where they are only too happy to sell penny papers, which leave them but a profit of from *one-third to one-half of one cent*. [...] This is absurd. However kindly we are disposed toward the little brigades who sell our paper, it is an absurdity which we are fully determined and able to stop—no matter how long the strike may last."[18]

With no other afternoon papers to take up the newsboys' cause, Pulitzer's word went unchallenged. It was as polite and condescending a refusal as he could muster, and one that would set an uncomfortable precedent for the future newsboys and newsgirls under his employ.

By the twilight months of 1880, the *Post and Dispatch*, now termed the *Post-Dispatch*, was not only revived but thriving. Thanks to Pulitzer's brazen tactics and endless crusades, the paper's circulation had swelled from under 2,000 readers to nearly 9,000. It was the biggest English-language evening journal in St. Louis, and, following a quick $790 sale of the *Star* in 1879 (again by proxy bid), only forced to share its customer base with the fledgling *Evening Chronicle*.

Its only loss? That of president and managing editor Dillon, who jumped ship for a cool $40,000 after losing his temper over the targeted attacks on local tax dodgers. Pulitzer appeared unfazed by the dissolution of their partnership. He selected ace war correspondent John Cockerill to replace Dillon as managing editor.

Cockerill was sharp, critical, and volatile, the embodiment of Pulitzer's most striking features. Satisfied that he had chosen the right man for the job, Pulitzer left most of the day-to-day grunt work to his new editor and focused his efforts on politics and travel, including long trips to New York City where Albert was busy setting up the *Evening Journal*.

Left to his own devices, Cockerill continued the paper's crusades against the corrupt and powerful, dressing down their underhanded business dealings in scathing editorials. His most prominent opponent was lawyer and Democratic congressional candidate James Broadhead, who came under fire after he shirked his responsibility to negotiate fair prices between the city of St. Louis and a local gas company. Broadhead took money from both sides—including a $10,000 retainer from the city—and his greed cost taxpayers a hefty $3 million.

"The more one goes into the record of his life," Cockerill wrote, "the more is the truth evident that [Broadhead] is a man shallow in intellect, feeble in grasp, entirely without either deep convictions or principles like those to which other men anchor—in a word, that he is an ephemeral butterfly of politics, ranging aimlessly over the garden of life, blown about by every win of doctrine. A man on whom it is impossible to reckon, a man, in short, whose want of intellectual stability is phenomenal."[19]

Broadhead went on to secure a seat in Congress anyway, leaving Cockerill apoplectic. He threatened to remove the *Post-Dispatch* as a Democratic-leaning publication, instead switching its alliance to reputable Republican candidates. That caught the attention of Broadhead's law partner Alonzo Slayback, who took up the fight against Cockerill and was soon provoked into confronting the editor face-to-face in the paper's offices.

There was a slap—Slayback to Cockerill—and a gunshot—Cockerill to Slayback. The attorney died within three minutes of receiving the bullet in his chest.

While the particulars of the shooting stood in dispute, its effect on the paper was undeniable. During the aftermath of the killing, the *Missouri Republican* ran roughshod over its rival, stoking public fever until frenzied crowds swarmed the entrance to the *Post-Dispatch* building, demanding that justice be served to both Cockerill and Pulitzer. Worse, advertisers began dropping like flies, and with them went the readers. In a matter of weeks, Pulitzer's *Post-Dispatch* had already lost 2,015 daily subscribers to the fiasco.

Pulitzer arranged for a hasty return from a trip to New York and rushed to the defense of his editor, who was cleared of charges after it was determined that he had acted purely in self-defense. The verdict wasn't enough to satisfy the publisher. Many claimed the killing was a direct result of the sensational journalism pedestaled in the *Post-Dispatch*, an idea that he was compelled to repudiate time and again.

It soon became obvious that Pulitzer was going to have to choose between preserving his partnership with Cockerill or his paper. There was no contest. Cockerill was ousted from the *Post-Dispatch* by year's end, and Dillon resumed his old post with his characteristic reserve and grace. After four tumultuous years at the helm of his first successful publishing venture, Pulitzer was ready to chase new horizons.

This time, he had his eyes fixed on New York.

New York-bound at last

On May 11, 1883, a new paper was clenched in the fist of every newsboy and newsgirl in New York City. Rather, it wasn't a *new* paper, but one that had been plumped and polished beyond recognition: Joseph Pulitzer's *New York World*.

Under Gould's care—or lack thereof—the *World* slunk through the city as a pitiful, plain-looking creature. It attracted the sympathy of 11,000 subscribers on weekdays and 15,000 on Sundays. Gould didn't have a single drop of journalistic ambition in his blood, and once the paper had stopped servicing his personal business deals, it had become a burden to him and a bore to its readers.

The newspaper that New Yorkers now held in their hands was a different breed altogether. It looked virtually the same on the outside: six or seven columns squeezed onto the front page, bound by a masthead that shed its New York moniker and simply stated, "The World." It was the only eight-page newspaper in the country that retailed for two cents, its editor boasted, a downright bargain considering the quality of its editorials and the creativity of its copy. Competing journals, like the *Sun*, could only afford to put out four-page papers, and lengthier publications like the *Herald* and *Times* peddled their wares at three to four cents per copy. The *World* endeavored to set a new standard by becoming the biggest, cheapest, and best paper in all of New York.

Pulitzer wasted little time imprinting the paper with his peculiar idealism, hoping to fully convey to consumers that important changes were on the horizon:

> "Performance is better than promise," his first editorial read. "Exuberant assurances are cheap. I make none. I simply refer the public to the new *World* itself, which henceforth shall be the daily evidence of its own growing improvement, with forty-eight daily witnesses in its forty-eight columns.
>
> There is room in this great and growing city for a journal that is not only cheap but bright, not only bright but large, not only large but truly democratic—dedicated to the cause of the people rather than that of purse-potentates—devoted more to the news of the New than the Old World—that will expose all fraud and sham, fight all public evils and abuses—that will serve and battle for the people with earnest sincerity.
>
> In that cause and for that end solely the new *World* is hereby enlisted and committed to the attention of the intelligent public."[20]

No one but Pulitzer could make such lofty claims sound sincere. Actualizing those goals, on the other hand, would take a more talented workforce than the one Gould had left him. He had already filched the *Journal*'s managing editor, E.C. Hancock, as well as his lead columnist and another of his editorial writers, perhaps irreparably damaging his relationship with Albert. He brought Cockerill over from St. Louis and ferreted out the staff members that were more perturbed than energized by his erratic mannerisms and irascibility. He expected every one of his employees to stand ready with an answer for whatever question flitted through his mind, whether he needed to know what time the paper would go to press or how many head of cattle, *exactly*, had arrived in the city yesterday. Anyone who couldn't handle the heat could, as the saying goes, get out of the kitchen.

"It is by argument that I measure a man," said Pulitzer, "his shortcomings, his possession or lack of logic, and, above all, whether he has the courage of his convictions, for no man can long work for me with satisfaction to himself or myself unless he has this courage."[21] Whether Pulitzer could take criticism as easily as he doled it out was another matter entirely.

As combative as Pulitzer could be, his methods got results. He demanded colorful copy to accompany his eye-catching headlines and pressured his writers to deliver succinct paragraphs and sharp, accurate detail. Under his direction, news was never just news. It had to breathe and inspire in the same way that novels and poetry did. He never wanted to have to rely on the day's events to deliver unforgettable stories; instead, he wanted to make every day unforgettable.*

It didn't take long for the retooled *World* to recapture the attention of its local readership. In the first few months of his new regime, Pulitzer peppered the front page with jaw-dropping headlines and perverse tales: "Screaming for Mercy," "Baptised in Blood," "Let Me Die! Let Me Die!" He covered suicide attempts, stampedes, boxing matches, glitzy society balls, and the unveiling of the Brooklyn Bridge. There was no such thing as a slow news day for Pulitzer's *World*, a boon that readers came to depend on as they nearly doubled his circulation over the course of just three months. By August 1883, the *World* was in the hands of over 39,000 subscribers, an increase of 16,239 from the moment he acquired the paper.

Though Pulitzer endeavored to excel in the newspaper circuit, he wasn't singularly focused on putting out the best paper possible. Stylized columns and innovative marketing strategies were important, but the *World* was also designed to drum up support for political candidates and charitable causes. To that end, Pulitzer wrote headline after headline about the development and shipment of the Statue of Liberty, a 151-foot, 225-ton copper sculpture that had to be sent piecemeal to American shores. The various pieces for the statue had been molded and cast, but it had nothing to prop it up. A granite

---

* Pulitzer's snappy columns not only elevated the quality of the newspaper, but they largely succeeded in creating mass appeal. The city's substantial immigrant population still struggled to master the English language, and Pulitzer made sure that his paper was written in a way that would not only be attractive to them, but easily understood.

pedestal would cost a good quarter of a million dollars, and the American committee tasked with completing the chore was still $100,000 shy of their goal.

Pulitzer was appalled. He had lived the immigrant experience. He was intimately acquainted with the mixture of pride and fear that filled his chest when he boarded the *Garland* without knowing if he'd see his family again, if the vessel was sturdy enough for the treacherous voyage, or if his anonymous shipmates could be trusted. He had seen the Manhattan splinter across the skyline, beckoning him to the first American city he would ever step foot in. He had slept on hard benches in Madison Square and learned to scavenge for jobs and make whole meals out of cold, dry apples and, later, raise himself up to a place of prominence within the upper echelon of American society.

Is it any wonder, then, that he attacked this issue with such fervor? Pulitzer planted bold headlines on the front pages of the *World* and penned heartfelt editorials, imploring and chastising his readers by turns. Eventually, he resorted to more straightforward fundraising tactics. Anyone who made any monetary contribution to the statue, no matter how slight, could see their name in print as thanks for their support. Some noted, and rightfully so, that he could have supplied the funds out of his own pocket and washed his hands of the matter, but for Pulitzer it was about the principle of the matter.

"Let us not wait for the millionaires to give this money," Pulitzer entreated. "[The Statue of Liberty] is not a gift from the millionaires of France to the millionaires of America, but a gift of the whole population of France to the whole people of America."[24]

Five months later, the *World* had received well over $100,000 in donations. Even the newsies sent in their pocket change to support the cause.

Charity was good for business. Halfway through 1885, the Sunday *World* was deemed the biggest and most widely-circulated newspaper in the country. Granted, it was Pulitzer himself who was tooting his own horn, stamping the growing circulation numbers in the topmost corner of every sheet, but there was plenty of evidence to suggest that the report was truthful.

Although the summer of 1885 was hailed as a professional success for Pulitzer, his personal life had taken a sharp turn for the worse. Over the remaining 26 years of his life, he would continue to be dogged by myriad physical issues. On the nights when he was able to tear himself away from the office, he spent hours tossing and turning, unable to sleep. Chronic sleep deprivation and overwork had weakened his body, and evenings spent perusing every line of the *World* by the light of a gas lamp had spurred the rapid deterioration of his eyesight. At just 38 years old, he already looked and acted like a man twice his age.

Terrible health exacerbated Pulitzer's terrible temper. Even in his prime, he had a reputation as a hothead, but combined with mental and physical exhaustion, his anger and volatility reached new depths. He began to nitpick every column and decision his editorial staff made and demanded to be sent editions of the paper when he was abroad so he could tear them apart. He blamed his wife, Kate, for lapsing in her marital duties and when she fought back, said he would never forgive her outburst.[23]

His cruelest behavior was reserved for his children. On one occasion, he became enraged when Kate asked him to look after their 14-year-old daughter, Lucille, who was bedridden while recovering from a grisly and complicated throat surgery. "Pity Lucille!" Pulitzer cried. "No! I'm the only one to pity—has no one any pity for *me*!—does no one realize what I suffer! My own house turned into a hospital! Doctors coming at all hours! You rushing upstairs in the middle of meals, without a word of conversation for me. No one pities me and you ask me to pity Lucille!" He finally calmed down enough to order his assistant to fetch a bouquet of flowers for Lucille, then immediately forgot the incident had ever occurred.[†24]

Two years later, Pulitzer was all but infirm. The retina had detached in his right eye, rendering him half-blind, and the left retina would detach within a year or two. In addition to

---

† It's fair to note that the incident was recorded by Pulitzer's personal secretary and pianist, Felix Webber, a man so needled and inflicted upon that he had every reason to besmirch Pulitzer's character in his private letters. Such outbursts were not rare, however, nor was Webber the only witness to them.

his insomnia, he suffered from continual bouts of indigestion and often had trouble breathing due to asthma. Worse still, he became unable to tolerate any noise, from a quiet chuckle to the whisper of cutlery across a plate. In the years to come, every residence he owned would need to be soundproofed, including the rooms of the Chatwold estate in Bar Harbor, each of which were barricaded with foot-thick granite walls and nicknamed "The Tower of Silence."[25] Every doctor he consulted prescribed rest; Pulitzer was not to look at another newspaper if he could help it, which, obviously, he couldn't. Anyone who had spent a minute in his presence knew that Pulitzer's stubborn, relentless temperament would never allow him to give up the *World*—or any foothold in the world of journalism, for that matter. It was only a question of learning how to cope.

Over the next few years, these matters so occupied Pulitzer's attention that he failed to see a bigger threat materialize on the horizon. A new newspaper man had just moved to New York City, and he soon had *New York Journal* in hand for a mere $180,000.

The gentleman's name?

William Randolph Hearst.

CHAPTER THREE

The Chief

William Randolph Hearst Builds an Empire

Every new outcome, it's income for you—
thanks to the bottom line!

The smoke slithered into the billiard room at 11 p.m. Not wanting to alarm the hundreds of guests sequestered in the bedrooms of Monterey's famed seaside resort, the Hotel Del Monte, a few of the men started poking around the old building until they found the culprit: a fire in the battery room beneath the basement, where hotel workers were accustomed to taking their dinner each night.

There was every reason to believe that even the unruliest fire could be quenched within the corridors of the stately hotel. Hallways were outfitted with hoses and fire extinguishers and an elaborate, $500,000 piping system was hooked up to a $400,000 reservoir on a nearby ranch, then threaded throughout the building for just such an occasion. "The force of water was so great," the *Los Angeles Times* maintained, "that if a full head were turned on it would have torn down an ordinary-sized building."[1]

Something foul was afoot, however, and there would be no dousing the flames that night. When the hotel clerk and his assistants rushed to activate the waterworks, they found the massive reserve of water reduced to a dribble, the droplets of water instantly consumed by the heat. The *Times* cried foul play, but in those initial moments of panic and perspiration, no one had time to investigate the cause of the malfunction.

From the lawn outside, local firefighters were equally pressed by the blaze, the twin streams of their long hoses spraying the three-story building at the height of just ten feet.

Inside, rich, pitch-black ribbons of smoke snaked into the hallways, ferreting out men, women, and children as the fire chewed its way through each floor. It gutted the ladies' sitting room and the parlor, singed the reading room and the dining room and the kitchen, and wrapped its ashy, smoldering fingers around the ballroom. Hundreds of guests poured out onto the grounds of the hotel, clad in pajamas, towels, and blankets, clinging to whatever valuables they had managed to secure from their rooms. Their faces were illuminated only by the bursts of fire that sometimes shot out from the windows and roof of the hotel, and by the dense, blood-red plumes of smoke that stretched from the slopes of the 7,000-acre Monterey resort out toward Santa Cruz. Not one life had been lost to the inferno.

By 1 a.m., the water supply had completely given out; by dawn, the brick chimneys stood alone among debris and ash layered over black lawns and gardens. The Hotel Del Monte was gone.

Natural disasters ranked a distant third to murder and political scandals, but that didn't stop the fire from feeding the front page of every newspaper within a 300-mile radius of the now-infamous hotel grounds.

"In Ashes!" the *San Francisco Chronicle* proclaimed. "The Hotel Del Monte Burned. A Midnight Fire at Monterey."

"The 'Del Monte.' Totally Burned in a Midnight Fire. A Splendid Structure Gone," the *Los Angeles Herald* added.

"The Del Monte Fire," said Sacramento's *Record-Union*, a bit blithely. "Total Destruction of the Magnificent Hotel at Monterey."

For young newspaper editor William Randolph Hearst, the ramifications of such an event were even greater. This was the *San Francisco Examiner*'s first big story since it changed hands a month prior, and he wasn't about to let it slip away.

Hours after the first whisper of smoke caught the noses of the hotel guests, Hearst had emptied his offices and commissioned a special Southern Pacific train to shuttle his reporters and artists down to Monterey. Upon their hasty return to the city on April 3, just a day after the fateful fire swallowed the Hotel Del Monte whole, Hearst and his staff crafted a 14-page edition of the paper exclusively devoted to every minute and detail of the disaster. They filled page after page with harrowing first-hand accounts of the pandemonium inside the hotel, accusations of arson and underhanded dealings by "disgruntled workers," and grotesque illustrations that stretched three to four columns wide.

> "HUNGRY, FRANTIC FLAMES," the banner screamed atop the front page in thick, black letters. "They Leap Madly Upon the Splendid Pleasure Palace by the Bay of Monterey, Encircling Del Monte in their Ravenous Embrace From Pinnacle to Pinnacle to Foundation. Leaping Higher, Higher, Higher, With Desperate Desire. Running Madly Riotous Through Cornice, Archway, and Façade. Rushing in Upon the Trembling Guests with Savage Fury. Appalled and Panic-Stricken the Breathless Fugitives Gaze Upon the Scene of Terror. The Magnificent Hotel and Its Rich Adornments Now a Smoldering Heap of Ashes. The 'Examiner' Sends a Special Train to Monterey to Gather Full Details of the Terrible Disaster."[2]

Hyperbolic to a fault, the *Examiner* milked the tragedy for all it was worth, selling the special editions as fast as it could print them. Hearst ordered another press run, then another—those sold out, too. A precursor to the much-maligned form of "yellow journalism" that would sweep through New York City decades later, his extravagant language and reckless headlines arrested the attention of every literate newspaper reader within 100 miles of San Francisco. It seemed the public had an appetite for purple prose, and Hearst was just the man to feed it to them.

"A genius or a gangster"

Almost from the moment he was born, William Randolph Hearst played yin to Joseph Pulitzer's yang. It is unfair to position a pair of great rivals against each other so early in life, inasmuch as it is impossible to resist comparing two larger-than-life personalities: Pulitzer, the fastidious, weak-dispositioned journalist hot on the trail of the American Dream vs. Hearst, the shrewd, perceptive businessman who parlayed his family's immense American-bred wealth into a gilded empire.

All of that was yet to unfold. On April 29, 1863, Hearst busied himself with the grand entrance of his birth in a room of the Stevenson House hotel of San Francisco, California. His father, George Hearst, was supervising the spoils of a silver and gold mine nestled in the Sierra Nevada mountains; his mother, Phebe Apperson Hearst, was alone save for her parents and a wet nurse named Eliza Pike. Like her, they had been transplanted from their native Missouri as George sought his fortunes in the burgeoning bayside towns of the West Coast.

Life in the Hearst household had its swells and recessions, due in part to the volatile nature of George's work and his long absences. Prospecting was not a guaranteed source of income, and when a property rights claim was contested in court or George's real estate ventures went belly-up, as they did from time to time, the family's fortunes rose and fell accordingly.

Only 20 years old at the birth of her son, Phebe was ill-equipped for a life steeped in isolation. Even the decadent trappings of a bay-view house in San Francisco could not distract from her husband's protracted silences and increasingly worrisome business deals. "Willie," as Hearst was often called during his childhood (his father preferred nicknames like "Sonny" and "Billy Buster" for the boy), didn't make things any easier on his young mother. He was tall for his age, and smart, but nursed a wicked streak that bewildered her.

"His forte was an irrepressible imagination," Phebe would later say, though that was a mild way of excusing the frequent, reckless behavior from a child old enough to know better.[3] Desperate for the attention that an absent father couldn't give and an overwhelmed mother was incapable of lavishing, young Hearst developed a knack for cruel pranks: pouring heaping doses of castor oil on his mother's best dress, shattering the window of his dance academy with a large cobblestone, spearing goldfish with bent pins, terrorizing cats, shooting pigeons with miniature brass cannons, puncturing the ceiling of a Parisian hotel with an antique French military rifle, and on one occasion, setting off a handful of Bengal fireworks in his bedroom so he could cry "Fire!" in the middle of the night.[4]

Rare was the occasion that Hearst succeeded in eliciting the rage or focused attention that such schemes deserved. He was first and foremost an only child; more than that, he was often his mother's only companion. His parents would have hung the world on a string for their boy. There was nothing he asked for that he did not receive: rabbits and white mice; riding lessons and fencing lessons and dancing lessons; great stacks of storybooks; beer steins, watches, collector's stamps, and *Bilderbücher* comic books; excursions to art galleries, palaces, churches, and theatres; a cart and pony; a Punch and Judy show; ice cream; fireworks. He was tutored in French, German, Greek, Latin, algebra, history, geography, and English grammar, and what he could not learn in a classroom setting he was taught among the spires and sprawl of Europe itself.

By the time Hearst reached puberty, the family's period of temporary financial instability had come to a permanent end. George had struck the motherlode—this time quite literally, as he was one of the first to unearth a near-endless bounty of gold ore in the Black Hills of the Dakotas. George had always been a man who could "smell gold or silver," and right now, all five senses were on high alert.[5] He snapped up properties in the Dakotas, Utah, Nevada, and Montana, then bought out the land and water rights and erected railroad and makeshift mining towns to support his massive task force.

If the rapid expansion of wealth and success went to George's head, he took pains to conceal it. He had always been austere in style and manner, and chose not to flaunt his money as others in his position might have been tempted to do. That frugality didn't extend to the luxuries and indulgences enjoyed by his wife and son. As in everything, Phebe only wanted the best for her son, and in 1879, the best looked like a Harvard University education.

Years of road trips and European tours had given 16-year-old Hearst a patchwork education. Some gaps had been filled in by tutors, others by his mother's personal fascination for art and history. He dabbled in private schooling as a boy, but never stuck with any one patron for too long thanks to George's fluctuating financial status and Phebe's helicopter parenting. If he was going to earn a spot at Harvard—something even his parents' immense wealth couldn't guarantee—he needed a year or two of formal education first.

In the autumn of '79, Phebe took Hearst on a "farewell tour" of Europe and had him enrolled in St. Paul's Episcopal School of Concord, New Hampshire upon his return. It was the longest the two had ever been separated. St. Paul's was a rigorous, highly religious establishment where students were enjoined to attend church services three times daily and the boys passed their free time with rounds of cricket on neatly manicured lawns. Hearst preferred baseball, the kind played in vacant lots and measured by the arc of a ball through the glass pane of a nearby window.

The teenager was miserable. "I have settled into a state of perpetual homesickness," he wrote his mother, "which although not quite so bad as when I first came, is pretty bad and I think it will continue until I see you again. I never knew how much time there was in two months before and how long it could be strung out."[6]

He'd get his wish. Phebe visited St. Paul's in November and whisked Hearst away for a brief holiday visit to Cambridge. She hoped that the sight of the stately Harvard campus would renew his dedication to his studies; if only he could visualize the goal he was working toward, perhaps the cricket matches and buttoned-up preachers wouldn't get under his skin so easily.

It was a vain hope. By next autumn, Hearst had dropped out of school altogether. He was more comfortable on the sun-graced shores of the West Coast, where private tutors could teach him all the Greek, Latin, ancient history and geography, mathematics, foreign languages, physics, and English composition he needed to pass his university entrance exams. Neither parent objected to the decision.

Some things had changed while Hearst was away. George had his fingers in the mining industry, naturally, but decided to start dabbling with politics on the side as well. As his teenage son moped about New Hampshire, the elder Hearst had occupied himself with the acquisition of the *San Francisco Examiner*, a failing Democratic newspaper that he envisioned as his ticket to the state governorship. He spruced up the publication from top to bottom, shelling out cash for a new headquarters in downtown San Francisco, hiring a bevy of new reporters to fill the desks, and poaching rival *San Francisco Chronicle* editor

Emanuel Katz to oversee the enterprise. While a few historians have suggested that Hearst got his first taste of the newspaper business here, it would certainly not be his last.

Custard pies, champagne-drunk alligators, and chamber pots, oh my!

Nineteen-year-old Hearst cut a peculiar figure at Harvard. He was still tall for his age, with a high voice and an affinity for bright neckties and plaid clothing that would have undoubtedly made him the subject of extreme ridicule were it not for his enormous wealth. George acted as bank and generous lender during Hearst's college days, while Phebe took pains to outfit her son's suite in Matthews Hall with a personal library, maid, and valet. Even among the well-to-do at Harvard, such measures smacked of excess.

More telling was Hearst's attitude. Although he aced his entrance examination, thanks in part to a lax rule that allowed private tutors to peruse the exam material as they prepped their students, he couldn't summon the motivation necessary to excel in his studies. A "gentleman's C" was all that Harvard required and all that Hearst deemed necessary to earn. The rest of his time was spent in frivolous pursuits, from expensive trips to Manhattan to theatre shows in Boston, where the teenager and his friends occasionally lobbed custard pies at the actors.

He didn't always have to go far to make mischief. Hearst was a clown about campus—both in and out of class—and had the wild stories to prove it. He kept a pet alligator named "Champagne Charley," who subsisted on a diet of leftover wine and spent the better part of its days being dragged, half-drunk, around the dormitories. He hosted exclusive poker parties that ran until dawn and over-committed himself to social clubs and informal theatre troupes, only to pull out of his commitments when something more interesting presented itself. Once, after being offended by some incident, he procured a donkey, and delivered it to his professor's office, with a note attached that read, "Now there are two of you."[7]

Between numerous social engagements and lengthy courses of physics, German, chemistry, Latin, Greek, and analytic geometry, Hearst nursed lingering, colds and sore throats. Whether or not these were the results of frequent partying was never formally determined. The biting New England winter kept him sequestered inside, where he began to hallucinate the warm climate of his hometown.

"I hate this weak, pretty New England scenery with its gentle rolling hills, its pea green foliage, its vistas, tame enough to begin with but totally disfigured by houses and barns which could not be told apart save for the respective inhabitants," Hearst wrote Phebe. "I hate it as I do a weak pretty face without force or character. I long to see our own woods, the jagged rocks and towering mountains, the majestic pines, the grand impressive scenery of the far West."[8]

This time, Phebe knew better than to take the bait. Harvard may have shared a coastline with St. Paul's, but her son was not destined to be a lifelong dropout, let alone a *Harvard University dropout*. "It would almost kill me if you should not go through college in a creditable manner," she told him.[9]

In the late winter of his sophomore year, Hearst finally found something to capture his interest. His childhood friend and fellow Harvard undergraduate, Eugene Lent, was in dire need of a co-business manager to help rescue the underfunded *Harvard Lampoon*. The *Lampoon* was one of two prominent papers put out by Harvard students and, when not engaged in a feud with the rival *Harvard Crimson*, prided itself on its satire and legendary beer nights. In order to keep the *Lampoon* afloat, it needed the financial backing of a business manager or that business manager's wealthy parents. While Lent's parents weren't hurting for money, they had wisely capped the allowance their son was permitted to keep at school.

Hearst, with his deep pockets and penchant for mischief, appealed to Lent as a natural business partner. George and Phebe were generous to a fault, supplying their would-be entrepreneur with a liberal stipend of $150 each month—the cost of an entire year's tuition at the university. Shelling out additional funds for a school paper, even one so disreputable by nature, was well within their wheelhouse.

For once in his life, however, Hearst voluntarily cut the purse strings. He would not use his family's wealth as a stepping

stone to success; that is, no more than he had already benefitted from the immense privilege and money they endowed him
with. As the *Lampoon* began to capsize, Hearst used his local
connections with various tailors, haberdashers, and shopkeep-
ers around Cambridge to build a steady stream of advertising
revenue. He enlisted the help of his friends, who helped engi-
neer a circulation drive and pestered Harvard alumni with
requests for $3 subscriptions. He even called on Phebe to pres-
sure the San Francisco Harvard Club for donations. Wherever
he sensed he had leverage, he made it work in his favor.

It didn't take long for the paper to turn a profit, a milestone
that had seemed near-impossible with Lent at the helm. Under
Hearst's devoted care, the *Lampoon* flourished. It doubled its
circulation, expanded its advertiser base, and reaped $650 in
gross profits well before the year's end. Elated, Hearst sent
another missive to his mother:

"Show this to Papa and tell him just to wait till Gene and
I get hold of the old *Examiner* and we'll boom her in the same
way she needs it."[10]

Reforming the *Examiner* would have to wait. By the autumn
of 1884, Hearst was wrapped up in another passion project:
Grover Cleveland's presidential campaign. Few Democrats
littered the Harvard campus, and the 21-year-old was determined to rally the few he could find as Cleveland took on
Republican candidate James G. Blaine. Having proven his
self-sufficiency by sustaining the *Lampoon*, Hearst no longer
harbored any qualms about asking his parents for money. He
eagerly requested "a few hundred" from his father, who was
busy pushing the Democratic agenda on the West Coast.

Cleveland took the White House after defeating Blaine with
48.9% of the popular vote and 219 electoral votes. A more
ecstatic voter than Hearst could not be found. He funneled his
father's money into a blowout the likes of which Harvard had
never seen before. Alcohol flowed freely from "wagon-loads of
beer," banners sporting the faces of Cleveland and incumbent
vice president Thomas A. Hendricks were hoisted above the
streets, as was a giant flag, and the air sizzled with fireworks
and swelled with the jubilant harmonies of a brass band
imported from Boston.[11]

The celebration raged all night. In the morning, those who had the good sense not to party until sunrise were unhappily awoken by the piercing crows of Hearst's flock of roosters. Hearst must have felt the ache of a hangover as well; he stayed up with the crowd and was honored in a speech that credited the efforts of both the elder and younger Hearst in the election. The boy was so embarrassed by the unexpected recognition that he fled the podium.

Unfortunately for Hearst, Harvard's faculty wasn't ready to forgive such an egregious breach of decorum. He was suspended in February 1885, then expelled a month later after it became clear that his focus was still not on the school or its academic programs. There would be no hope of reinstatement.

Never one to take a loss lying down, Hearst quickly devised a revenge scheme. He had personalized chamber pots delivered to each of his professors with their names engraved at the bottom of the vessels.

"I assured the gentleman of the Faculty of Harvard College that I didn't regret so much having lost my degree as having given them an opportunity to refuse it to me," he bragged to his mother.[12]

Phebe didn't see the humor in the prank. Her son was 22 years old, unemployed and academically disinclined, and recently forced out of the most prestigious university in the country. Worse, there seemed to be no amount of money or persuasion that could change the faculty's mind. Hearst applied himself to his studies with the help of private tutors, but was twice denied reentrance to the university. He departed midway through his junior year and never returned to graduate.

'When he wants cake, he wants cake, and he wants it now'

"I want the *San Francisco Examiner*," Hearst told his father.

George was flabbergasted. Only a fool, he thought, would take a failing newspaper over a gold mine. He wanted his son to have something to sink his hands into, some piece of property or business venture that would furnish his own reputation and success independent from the family treasury.

In the year following the explosive expulsion from Harvard, George sent Hearst and his friends away to tour the vast expanse of his Babícora ranch in Chihuahua, Mexico. The ranch stretched one million acres across four high plateaus, splintered by the peaks and valleys of a neighboring mountain range. George all but spread his palms wide and gestured to the rich swath of land before proffering it to the 23-year-old college dropout.

Hearst refused, first Babícora, then another fertile 48,000-acre ranch in San Simeon, the Anaconda copper mines of Montana, and the Homestake gold mine that George had discovered in the hills of Lead, South Dakota some seven or eight years earlier.[13] The only thing he wanted was the paper.

"Great God!" George cried. "Haven't I spent money enough on that paper already? I took it for a bad debt and it's a sure loser. Instead of building it up for my own son, I've been saving it up to give to an enemy."[14]

Luckily for Hearst, there were no enemies readily available to take on a floundering political paper. George fretted over his son's financial situation—did he know, for instance, that even the most successful publisher could not squeeze more than $100,000 per annum out of the best paper in the world?

"Hell!" George complained to Thomas Williams, then-business manager of the *Examiner*. "That ain't no money."[15] A hundred grand must have seemed a pithy amount to someone who spent decades plundering gold mines and scouting million-acre properties. There was no easy way to build wealth, the elder Hearst knew that much to be true, but there were smart ways to do it, and reviving the *Examiner* was not one of them.

Still, no amount of cajoling or bribery could dissuade his son. It wasn't by chance that he fixed his eye on the *Examiner*, nor was he naïve enough to believe that the door-to-door solicitations that buoyed the *Harvard Lampoon* would have the same effect on the developing metropolis of San Francisco.

Shortly after his rise as the business manager of the *Lampoon*, Hearst made an earnest plea to his father. He wrote page after page of detailed observations about the *Examiner* and carefully incorporated his suggestions to resuscitate the paper's popularity and expand its circulation. He wasn't just a boy looking for a business opportunity; he was a boy in love with a newspaper.

"I have begun to have a strange fondness for our little paper," Hearst told his father, "a tenderness like unto that which a mother feels for a puny or deformed offspring, and I should hate to see it die now after it had battled so long and so nobly for existence; in fact, to tell the truth, I am possessed of the weakness which at some time or other of their lives pervades most men; I am convinced that I could run a newspaper successfully."

Sentiment, however heartfelt, came cheap. Hearst pressed on.

"Now if you should make over to me the *Examiner*—with enough money to carry out my schemes—I'll tell you what I would do!

In the first place, I would change the general appearance of the paper and make seven wide columns where we now have nine narrow ones, then I would have the type spaced more, and these two changes would give the pages a much cleaner and neater appearance.

Secondly, it would be well to make the paper as far as possible original, to clip only when absolutely necessary and to imitate only some such leading journal as the New York *World*, which is undoubtedly the best paper of that class to which the *Examiner* belongs—that class which appeals to the people and which depends for its success upon enterprise, energy and a certain startling originality and not upon the wisdom of its political opinions or the lofty style of its editorials; and to accomplish this we must have—as the *World* has—active, intelligent and energetic young men; we must have men who come out West in the hopeful buoyancy of youth for the purposes of making their fortunes and not a worthless scum that has been carried there by the eddies of repeated failures.

Thirdly, we must advertise the paper from Oregon to New Mexico and must also increase our number of advertisements if we have to lower our rates to do it, thus we can put on the first page that our circulation is such and our advertisements so and so and constantly increasing.

And now having spoken of the three great essential points let us turn to details."

The illustrations are a detail, though a very important one. Illustrations embellish a page; illustrations attract the eye and stimulate the imagination of the masses and materially aid the comprehension of an unaccustomed reader and thus are of particular importance to that class of people which the *Examiner* claims to address. Such illustrations, however, as have heretofore appeared in the paper nauseate rather than stimulate the imagination and certainly do anything but embellish a page.

Another detail of questionable importance is that we actually or apparently establish some connection between ourselves and the New York *World*, and obtain a certain prestige in bearing some relation to that paper. We might contract to have important private telegrams forwarded or something of that sort, but understand that the principal advantage we are to derive is from the attention that such a connection would excite and from the advertisement we could make of it. Whether the *World* would consent to such an arrangement for any reasonable sum is very doubtful, for its net profit is over one thousand dollars a day and no doubt it would consider the *Examiner* is beneath its notice. Just think, over one thousand dollars a day and four years ago it belonged to Jay Gould and was losing money rapidly.

And now to close with a suggestion of great consequence, namely, that all these changes be made not by degrees but as once so that the improvement will be very marked and noticeable and will attract universal attention and comment.[16]

Hearst had inadvertently struck on an important truth: All press is good press. It mattered little if Joseph Pulitzer's *New York World* held the *Examiner* in esteem or if, as the young man suggested, it considered the West Coast copycat beneath its notice. Any attention, positive or negative, would directly benefit the Hearst boys.

George may have been impressed with his son's wisdom and depth of perception, but he failed to return a reply. Perhaps he did not consider that Hearst was serious—or, as he made plain several years later, perhaps he simply thought it an ill-timed investment.

Had the letter not exhibited a remarkable business acumen, had it not revealed a pragmatism as well as a grandiose vision for the paper's future, Hearst's overwhelming zeal would have seemed laughable. Only someone with his position and privilege would undertake such a big gamble. As long as the

Examiner had been in the family, it existed solely as a vehicle for George's political leanings. It would never rival the adjacent *San Francisco Chronicle*, to say nothing of the behemoths of the newspaper industry: the *New York Tribune, Sun,* and *World.*

Of course, none of that was about to stop Hearst from carrying out his plan.

He badgered his father for two years: interviewing potential business managers, recommending writers and editors for staff vacancies, devising new advertising techniques, criticizing the paper's shoddy illustrations, and comparing its every aspect with larger, more renown publications in hopes of improving its quality and circulation. There were even rumors that Hearst had taken a temporary position with the *New York World*, where he apprenticed under executive Ballard Smith to get a firm grasp on the ins and outs of the industry.[17]

"I am anxious to begin work on the *Examiner*," he wrote his father. "I have all my pipes laid, and it only remains to turn on the gas. One year from the day I take hold of the thing our circulation will have increased ten thousand. [...] We must be alarmingly enterprising, and we must be startlingly original. We must be honest and fearless. We must have greater variety than we have ever had. We must print more matter than we have printed."[18]

Worn down by his son's constant badgering and preoccupied with his new appointment as a United States senator, George finally relented. "There's one thing sure about my boy Bill," he'd say in years to come. "I've been watching him, and I notice that when he wants cake, he wants cake; and he wants it now. And I notice that after a while he gets his cake."[19]

In the spring of 1887, when the blue gum eucalyptus trees flowered atop Mount Parnassus and the sun pierced the fog of the San Francisco bay, William Randolph Hearst got his cake. The *Examiner* was officially under new management.

The Monarch of the Dailies

The tragic fire at Hotel Del Monte gave the public its first taste of Hearstian hyperbole. Before the *Examiner* could satiate its patrons, however, it had to prove itself capable of brewing newsworthy stories day after day. Hearst expanded the daily edition from six to eight pages, with eight columns and half-inch headlines trumpeting across the front page instead of the nine-column, quarter-inch-headline sheets typically found on the street corner. Sports stories—long considered the bane of respectable newspapers—were promoted to Page One, where they blossomed from two columns to five or six columns and featured every species of group and individual competition: baseball, yacht racing, boxing, and horse racing included. Even the Sunday paper got special treatment, swelling to a full sixteen pages to make room for a flock of new advertisers.

Most importantly, every news story in every edition of the *Examiner* was purposely structured to maximize its shock value. Hearst didn't intend to use his paper to cater to the dry intellectualism of the crusty upper class; what's more, he couldn't afford to alienate the majority of the city's readers if he wanted to grow his circulation. His was a paper for the working classes, the poor, the philosophers and short story lovers, the sports fanatics, and above all, those who naturally gravitated toward a brand of reporting that would later be termed "yellow journalism." According to the creed espoused by rival editor Arthur McEwen, "Any issue the front page of which failed to elicit a 'Gee Whiz!' from its readers was a failure, whereas the second page ought to bring forth a 'Holy Moses!' and the third an astounded 'God Almighty!'"[20]

Rare were the issues that had not been crammed full with the lurid details of local crimes and high-profile infidelities, suicides, divorces, economic crises, and myriad flavors of tragedy and depravity. Nothing made the 24-year-old squeamish. He pitted scantily-clad swimmers against uptight English clergymen, uncovered a band of murderers lurking in the streets of San Francisco, and routinely pried into the motivations of law enforcers and government officials to uproot every last seed of corruption and dishonesty. His reporters, likewise, fell to extreme measures in their haste to get the next scoop: infiltrating insane asylums as afflicted inmates, attending highbrow churches clad in rags, and undertaking ill-advised rescue operations during fierce sea-storms.

To Hearst, as well as the *Examiner's* devoted subscribers, it mattered little that his stories liberally mixed fact with fiction. All that mattered was that the story was worth telling—the more salacious and grisly, the better.

Those who found such sensationalism unpalatable, meanwhile, might instead enjoy the poems, serials, and popular songs dotting the back pages, or else take some comfort in the paper's pleas to improve the streets and schools of the city. Hearst would never really become the champion of the people he imagined himself to be—his gratuitous family wealth prevented him from fully empathizing with the plight of the downtrodden and oppressed, to say nothing of his staunch (and racist) opposition to Chinese immigration—but he made a concerted effort to expose and overturn toxic power imbalances wherever he saw them.

From the lofty headquarters of his offices on Market Street, Hearst sicced his reporters on the politicians, police officers, and bosses who kept the city in a stranglehold. Journalists like Ambrose Bierce, Allen and Florence Kelly, Ernest Lawrence Thayer, Henry R. Haxton, George Bruton, Frank Gassaway, Ned Townsend, and Petie Bigelow took up the cause as well. Together, they railed against a bipartisan city charter that sought to empower the bosses, shamed the city board into reducing its sky-high rates for the local water supply, and went head-to-head against the monolithic Southern Pacific Railroad, which had its noose around the neck of every newspaper in town but the *Examiner*. To Hearst, the corrupt and powerful were merely characters in his enchanted playground, one in which there were "giants and dragons to be slain simply for the fun of the thing."[21]

Slaying giants and dragons eventually paid off. When Hearst first assumed control of the paper in March 1887, its circulation was a paltry 15,000, peanuts to the 37,500 the rival *San Francisco Chronicle* pulled in each year. Two years later, the *Examiner* was bleeding funds as Hearst desperately tried to increase his readership and popularity; some estimated a whopping $232,452 had been drained from his personal and family bank accounts to cover for his regular schemes and promotional gags. A little of the money went toward practical expenses, like the two printing presses that were nicknamed "Monarch" and "Jumbo" and could rattle off a 24-page spread with full lines of text.

Every remaining penny was reserved for some of the most hair-brained marketing ploys the city had ever seen. Hearst spared no expense to make his readers feel cared-for, lavishing them with free admission to the zoo, free books for children, $100 prizes for uncovering clues in a mystery story, a ten-acre parcel of land, a prized thoroughbred yearling, a trip to Paris. He even incentivized child newspaper hawkers with promises of gold watches, violins, books, and bronze mantle-pieces for those who sold multiple subscriptions.

No matter how ludicrous the tack, though, there was no denying Hearst was seeing results. By the spring of 1889, he had attracted an annual patronage of 55,029 for the daily edition and 62,240 for the Sunday pages.

Not one to rest on his laurels for long, Hearst sought to make news where he couldn't find it. He soon introduced the *Examiner*'s loyal patronage to Martha Winifred Sweet Black, better known to the masses as the spirited actress-turned-columnist "Annie Laurie."

Hearst (or, more likely, his managing editor Sam Chamberlain) hadn't made the hire out of any special generosity of spirit, nor was he interested in evening the playing field for aspiring women reporters. He was instead responding to the trend of "stunt reporting," a practice made popular by the top journalists of the day—Pulitzer and his *World* included. A flashier form of investigative journalism, stunt reporting frequently imperiled the health and safety of young women, pushing them to undertake ridiculous and extreme measures in pursuit of stomach-churning exposés.

It was for just such an exposé that Black set out on a rainy winter afternoon: clad in ragged attire, belladonna-dilated pupils mimicking the symptoms of real illness. She got off the streetcar and staggered along Kearny Street in downtown

San Francisco, then feigned a faint on a pile of muddy card-board boxes. Her acting drew a sizable crowd, before which she was dragged away by a pair of police officers and loaded into a makeshift ambulance. ("I could very easily realize then what agony a wounded person would undergo in being brought in that awful prison van to the hospital," she revealed to her readers. "It seemed impossible that a person with a fractured limb could live through the terrible pain that that tumbling, rumbling, jerking, jolting old rattle-trap would cause him.")

After no slight discomfort, her first-hand column was printed in the *Examiner* under the headline, "A City's Disgrace—Sample of the Civilization of the Nineteenth Century.—Brutality of Public Servants." Black's careful attention to the abuses of the local law enforcement, hospital workers, and doctors formed the basis of a scathing report.

"The doctor took two strides and was beside me," Black narrated. "He gripped my neck with both hands, digging his thumbs into the hollows below my ears.

I screamed with pain and rage and managed to push him aside.

This seemed to infuriate him. He grabbed me by the shoul-der with no fierce a grip that my shoulder is lame yet. It took the skin right off. He threw me backward on to the bed with spiteful vehemence and snarled, 'Let her lie there, and if she makes any fuss strap her down.'"[22]

It was just the kind of story that Hearst's readers ate up—one that not only dabbled in sensationalism, but had the power to enact real social reform.*

Several weeks earlier, a new decade began on January 1, 1890. With the turning of the calendar pages came a new worry.

The *Examiner* had flourished within the small San Franciscan market—it had overtaken rival *San Francisco Call*'s numbers and continued to give the *Chronicle* a run for its money—but after three thrilling, expensive years at the editor's desk, Hearst had not yet made his paper profitable.

---

* Black published tens of thousands of articles over her multi-decade career with the paper. Her expansive work had a lasting effect on the nonfiction genre as she challenged class discrimination and mistreatment in fruit canneries, hospitals, law firms, women's prisons, leper communities, and opera houses, among many other locales.

The 26-year-old surrounded himself with like-minded reporters, artists, and photographers who shared his zest for life and his flair for the dramatic. Hearst was quieter and more reserved than his crazy stunts suggested, but his intelligence, unimpeachable work ethic, and dry humor commanded the respect of every staff member. With their help, he believed he could transform the *Examiner* into a self-sustaining, first-rate publication, beginning with a mammoth 44-page edition of the paper on New Year's Day.

It was a ballsy move. Customers had never seen any paper so fat and impressive, and they demanded an excess of 90,000 copies when it first hit the streets that Wednesday. Four months later, with circulation numbers persistently, irritatingly lagging, Hearst rolled out a 50-page paper—this time, with a contest that promised prizes ranging from thoroughbred horses to San Francisco's own $7,000 "*Examiner* Premium Cottage." He stoked public outrage over topics like marriage ("What Is the Ideal Wife?" one article prodded its readers), donated to thousands of underprivileged orphans, and sent his reporters on wild escapades along the sharp crags and perilous waters of the San Francisco Bay. By the end of the year, he had offered patrons a chance to win livestock, personal carriages, leather-bound dictionaries, cottages, barns, parcels of land in Washington, Oregon, and California, reprints of modern and classic art, cookbooks, furniture and household items, and gold-and-diamond encrusted badges, among other valuable perks. If anyone doubted the depth of Hearst's pockets before, they had no reason to now.

For all his trouble and expense, Hearst received a few prizes of his own. At the outset of the 1890s, he *Examiner* was finally profitable, though it had taken a little longer than Hearst's initial two-year estimate. It was the biggest publication among its West Coast rivals, eclipsed only by the giants of the East Coast. And, on December 28, it was hailed as the fourth-best advertising medium in the world by none other than the *New York World* itself.[23]

No sooner had Hearst commanded the attention of the West Coast than another tragedy struck, this one fearfully close to home. George Hearst had fallen ill, likely compounded by chronic fatigue and alcoholism, and died on February 28, 1891.

The aftermath of his father's death brought Hearst fresh pain. Following a lavish funeral, he discovered that the mining mogul had declined to leave a single cent to him in his will. Instead, the family properties and stocks were left in Phoebe's care. The estimated total value hovered somewhere in the vicinity of $15-20 million, though a good portion would need to be reconciled against George's vast debts.

Hearst took the snub as proof of the rejection he had always felt from his father. Although George had outlined specific instructions in his will, asking Phoebe to portion out as much as she felt necessary to their only child, neither parent trusted the junior Hearst to manage the wealth in a prudent manner. His frustration was worsened by the rebirth of his rivalry with the *Chronicle*, which sought to overtake the *Examiner* by emulating its marketing strategies and erecting a stately new brick office building on Market Street. It was becoming more and more exhausting for the young editor to keep ahead of the competition, and as he neared his thirties, he contemplated a more permanent change of scenery.

Bitter, hurt, and restless, Hearst began to look for opportunities to expand his media presence in the Eastern reaches of the United States. As Pulitzer had realized only eight years prior, it was time for Hearst to stake his own claim in New York City.

The "chambermaids' delight"

Shopping for a new newspaper proved more difficult than Hearst expected. First was the matter of his purse-strings; they were held tightly by Phoebe, who had been persuaded not to divide the estate or enter into any formal financial arrangement with her son. Instead, she continued to dole out smaller sums to Hearst as needed, perhaps in the hope that he would exercise greater financial restraint of his own accord.

On the contrary: Hearst's tastes ran toward extravagance, and it was only the small matter of his diminishing bank account that kept him from purchasing the biggest and best New York City had to offer. According to reports from his business manager Charles Palmer, four papers were on the chopping block: the *New York Times*, the *Advertiser*, the *Recorder*, and the *Morning Journal*.

Each paper was struggling, but only one was cheap.[†] The proprietor of the *Journal*, Albert Pulitzer, had run himself out of the newspaper business after raising his prices to compete with the *World*, and recently shed his stake in the publication for the $400,000 that publisher John R. McLean was offering.

McLean couldn't make the paper profitable, either. He reduced the price to a penny per paper and filled the pages with gossip, politics, and other hot news items that were sure to attract the literate New Yorker. What he possessed in eagerness and a can-do spirit, however, he lacked in ingenuity. The paper failed to distinguish itself in an increasingly crowded and creative market, and the price reduction didn't boost his circulation numbers the way he hoped it would. When Palmer swung by McClean's residence as proxy for the absent Hearst, the publisher floated the idea of a partnership, in which Hearst would be able to purchase a $300,000 half-share in the *Journal*. Hearst was in no rush. He dragged out the negotiations for another two months until McClean met his terms: $180,000 for total control of the *Journal*.

On October 3, 1895, Hearst assumed total control of his first New York-based enterprise. Not one of his rivals could have predicted that the acquisition would change the landscape of journalism forever.

It is uncertain if Joseph Pulitzer fully registered the significance of the 32-year-old's arrival in New York City. Rumors abounded: some said *World*'s editor had tried to poach Hearst's staff from across the country, while others claimed that Hearst had made a push to purchase the *World* for himself. Surely Pulitzer knew about the purchase. Though at odds with his brother, Albert, it would have taken a particular kind of willful obtuseness not to notice the paper changing hands from year to year. And Hearst had earned a mention in Pulitzer's paper several years earlier, too, though it was one thing to recognize greatness in a fellow newspaperman and another thing to regard him as a legitimate adversary.

By the end of 1895, all of that would change.

---

† Some reports estimated the Recorder's asking price at $400,000. The Times and Advertiser each retailed for $300,000—every one too rich for both Hearst and his mother.

CHAPTER FOUR

A Crooked Game

The Eight-Million-Dollar Rivalry That Dominated the Newspaper Industry and Started a War

You wanna move the next edition?
Give us an earthquake or a war.

Frederic Remington was bored.

He'd been in Cuba for a week and had yet to get his first taste of the war that had been spilling over the island during the last two years. William Randolph Hearst, the controversial new editor of the *New York Journal*, had sent him there on a month-long expedition with famed war correspondent Richard Harding Davis, and Remington was in charge of supplying battlefront sketches and illustrations for Davis's blood-spattered stories.

Before the pair were able to cross the lines of the Spanish troops, Remington had posted a telegram to New York.

"Everything is quiet. There is no trouble here. There will be no war. I wish to return. Remington."

He might as well have asked Hearst to delay the rising of the sun. The *Journal*'s editor-in-chief was a calculating and pragmatic man, the kind who could draw on reserves of great patience when he knew a good story was on the line.

"Please remain," he cabled Remington. "You furnish the pictures, and I'll furnish the war. W.R. Hearst."[1]

Historians have long disputed the validity of Hearst's infamous missive to Remington. Not only had the war for Cuban independence been raging since 1895, rendering

Remington's claim both head-scratching and inaccurate, but no physical proof of the two telegrams appears to exist. Only one man—former *Journal* reporter and Hearst biographer James Creelman—purported to have witnessed the exchange, and records show that he was traveling in Europe while Remington grew antsy in Cuba. Had Remington, a 36-year-old illustrator Davis characterized as a "firebrand" who needed to be "humored and petted all the time," dared to take such an insouciant tone with Hearst, it seems unlikely that the *Journal*'s leader would have dismissed it in so calm a manner.[2]

Telegram or no telegram, Remington wouldn't have to wait long before things got interesting again. Not a month after his purported missive reached the *Journal*'s offices, an American battleship exploded in Havana Harbor. The destruction of the USS *Maine* sparked an entirely new brand of outrage—one that reverberated from the Cuban harbor to the gilded publishing houses of Newspaper Row itself. Motivated more by greed than a pressing need for truth, the *World* and *Journal* invented all manner of motives, culprits, and methods to stoke the public's imagination. They sent journalists to the front lines of the Cuban rebellion and claimed to have commissioned expert divers to survey the bottom of the harbor for clues.

The more absurd the story, the easier it was for the newsboys and newsgirls to cry the headlines. Espionage, murder, secret missives, underwater mines, and kidnappings provided continual fodder for New York City's daily papers. It was a luxury that did not go unappreciated. During the war, they no longer had to attract customers with their own invented tales, nor did they find themselves embellishing salacious stories of Cuban prisoners being strip-searched, young women imprisoned by their rapists, or American bodies floating, lifeless, in Cuban waters. For once, it was the headlines, not the newsies, that sold papers. And it mattered little to them that the publishers were running on fumes, stretching their purse strings to cover the salaries and travel fees of war correspondents, illustrators, and dispatch ships in addition to their usual printing expenditures. When those publishers then raised the wholesale price of newspapers from 50 to 60 cents a hundred, the newsies' reflexive protestations flickered and died like a match in a tornado. Even they could sense that war was good for business.

This was not always a sentiment shared by the common consumer. Across the United States, more conservative readers continued to malign the newspapers for their overuse of sensationalism and misleading hyperbole. Even as they recognized the hold Pulitzer's *World* and Hearst's *Journal* had on the public's collective imagination, they claimed the journals were more corrupting than creative, an unnecessary blight on an otherwise moral society.

> "How little they know of 'yellow journalism,' who denounce it!" cried Creelman in his 1901 book, *On the Great Highway.* "How swift they are to condemn its shrieking headlines, its exaggerated pictures, its coarse buffoonery, its intrusions upon private life, and its occasional inaccuracies. How blind to its unfearing warfare against rascality, its detection and prosecution of crime, its costly searching for knowledge throughout the earth, its exposure of humbug, its endless funds for the quick relief of distress!"[3]

Whether the publications brought such marvelous benefits to the public was up for debate (among other issues, the purple prose was routinely found rife with factual inaccuracies), but one thing was certain: There were no more powerful newspapers in the country—perhaps even the world.

Vile newspapers put out

"'Sensationalism' is always the cry of the newspaper to the rival which passes it," the *Journal* sneered. "It means that the newspaper to which it is applied prints the news first."[4]

The barb was intended to snag the attention of the *New York Herald*, which had recently printed a little dig at the *Journal* for its self-congratulatory statements on the rescue of teenage Cuban rebel Evangelina Cisneros. In the heyday of sensationalized reporting, however, Hearst might have described any competing paper in the same manner.

The 1890s had ushered in a new era of journalism, one in which the public's appetite for graphic headlines, hyperbolic anecdotes, and ludicrous stunts made Hearst and Pulitzer the tastemakers of New York City. Those who fell behind—the *Herald, Tribune, Sun,* and *Times* among them—comforted themselves by taking the moral high ground, but it wasn't long before they felt the sting of lost revenue and readership.

In petty retaliation, they came up with a new term for such outlandish tactics: "yellow journalism." The phrase was first coined by *New York Press* editor Ervin Wardman in 1897. Pulitzer's *World* took on the character of the "older yellow [journal]" or "senior yellow," while Hearst's *Journal* was nicknamed the "younger yellow" or "junior yellow."[5] Exactly how Wardman invented the term remains a mystery, but it was clearly no label of endearment.

Yellow journalism, itself vaguely defined, became synonymous with cheap gimmicks and exaggerated and untruthful reporting. Yellow journalism was the way Hearst launched an all-out rescue operation to return 18-year-old Cisneros to the United States. It was the way Pulitzer made the assault of a 16-year-old girl a hot news item with the hysterical headline: "For God's Sake Kill Me!"[6] It was Hearst's habit of juxtaposing illustrations of scantily-clad women with descriptions of buttoned-up clergy, and Pulitzer's deep dive on the cannibalistic ending to a failed expedition in the Arctic. It was the way news ceased to be news and was instead transformed into art.

Sensationalism wasn't inherently bad. When used correctly, it arrested the public's attention and drew them to matters of local and national interest. On an extreme level, it even shaped the path of political elections and became a force for social change. Thanks to the *Journal's* relentless coverage of Cuban insurgency during the Spanish-American War, it was able to generate great outrage and sympathy when the teenage Cisneros was captured and jailed for resisting the sexual advances of Spanish colonel José Berriz. Pulitzer's *World* fired off column after column in protest of the police sergeant who walked free after raping 16-year-old Maggie Morris, blazing with indignation until the officer was tried, convicted, and sentenced to a 17-and-a-half year stay in Sing Sing Prison.

According to journalism professor William A. Hachten, there was another, less-publicized benefit of yellow journalism: It increased literacy among the newly-arrived immigrants of New York.[7] Men and women who hoped to make a new start in a new world were often introduced to American culture through the pages of the *World* and *Journal*, which featured easy-to-read headlines, large illustrations, and news items that regularly centered on poor and working-class members of society. The yellow press may have been a secondhand resource given the plethora of foreign-language newspapers that lined the streets of the city, but for the immigrant looking to assimilate, they could provide a valuable trove of information. Pulitzer and Hearst weren't blind to the power of these new readers. The more accessible their newspapers were, the wider their circulation and the bigger their profits would be.

Unsurprisingly, other New York publishers had difficulty spotting the merits of the yellow journals—or, if they did, it only fueled the resentment they felt as they slipped further down in the industry's pecking order.* It wasn't just that the *World* and *Journal* chose not to play by the rules; it was the way their rule-breaking enable them to drive sales and, by turn, threaten the sales of competing papers. Had Pulitzer and Hearst's gory headlines and ridiculous publicity stunts not been so popular, had they not inflated their circulations and profit margins to obscene numbers, it's highly unlikely that their rivals would have bothered raising a fuss in the first place.

An element of classism could also be detected in the backlash. "Better Classes Condemn It," the *New York Times* announced in the spring of 1897, describing how the "so-called new journalism" had been growing among the "better classes in this vicinity."[9] Rival publishers painted the *World* and *Journal* as sensational fodder for the lower classes, but Pulitzer and Hearst weren't in the business of turning away readers in

---

* The *Buffalo Enquirer* fretted over the widespread implications of yellow journalism. "The question that naturally suggests itself to the reflective, is how far may journalism go, how far dare it go?" read its lament in part. "The province of a newspaper is primarily to print news; that is its legitimate business; to tell the public as often as suits the public's convenience what is happening in the world, whether good deeds or bad; to set down as near to truth as may be, and as far from malice as can be, what are the doings of men that interest their fellows. That alone is task enough. To do that alone, and do it properly, will tax all the energy and enterprise and brains and money that are at the disposal of any newspaper owner."[8]

any social strata. It was obvious that their brazen reporting tactics were equally appealing to the upper class, giving them the kind of universal appeal they craved.

This irritated papers like the *Times* and the *Tribune* and the *Sun*. They were happy to leave the blue-collar workers and barely-literate readers to the two publishers, so long as they could be assured that the middle and upper classes would continue to exclusively patronize their own publications. That was no longer the case.

Not long after the initial rise of yellow journalism, the self-appointed moral gatekeepers of New York City decided to mobilize against the newspapers. During the winter of 1896, the New York Ministers' Association proposed a boycott of all newspapers that typified the "pernicious influence" of yellow journalism. They exerted their influence on the nearby Newark Free Public Library and persuaded the librarians and trustees to remove all copies of the *World* and *Journal* from their files.[10]

They weren't the only ones to do so. The *New York Sun* gleefully devoted a portion of its front pages to cataloguing the various establishments that boycotted the journals: the New York City Mission and Tract Society; the Harlem Branch of the Young Men's Christian Association; the Ansonia Public Library; the Broome Street Free Library; the Montauk Club of Brooklyn; the Flatbush Young Republican Club of Brooklyn; the New York Yacht Club; the Union Club; the Harvard Club; the Merchants' Club; the Clergy Club; the Grolier Club; Yale University, and more.

Thanks to the boycott's rapid growth, the two papers were soon despised more than the unfurled centerfold of a *Playboy* in the pews of a church. Less than four months after the Newark Library instituted the ban, the *New York Press* counted over 80 libraries, reading rooms, associations, and universities that had prohibited the distribution and reading of the *World* and *Journal*. The boycott spread as far south as New Jersey and as far east as Connecticut. Even the few organizations that chose to keep the yellow journals on file had taken some measures against them.

"In many institutions where the *World* and *Journal* are still admitted," the *Sun* explained in March 1897, "they are and have been for some time excluded from the libraries and reading rooms, and are kept under lock and key, to be brought out on the express demand of adults only."[11]

A few conservative consumers also took up the cause, some with more vitriol than the publishers who led the attack. State Superintendent of Public Instruction Charles R. Skinner railed against the "flood of revolting brutality [recorded] in the sensational press," though he also noted, not incorrectly, that the "public receives what it is willing to pay for."[12] Brooklyn Reverend Theodore L. Cuyler, who previously blamed bicycles and social visits for the city's moral downfall, was not so temperate in his opinions:

"I can dismiss the character of these papers," he told the *Sun*, "by saying that they are infinitely more repulsive and damaging to the general health of the community than would be the product of the garbage barrel and sewer were it thrown broadcast throughout the city and country. In fact, it is the garbage and sewerage of literature."[13]

Repulsive and damaging though the sensationalized press may have been, it was exactly the kind of thing that whetted the appetite of the masses. Aside from a handful of moral high-grounders, most readers—those young and old, refined and uncouth, religious and skeptical, immigrant and native (or, more accurately, colonizer)—were the ones who elected to purchase the boycotted papers and would ultimately dictate the shape and flow of the newspaper industry itself. Much to Hearst and Pulitzer's satisfaction, they had only to sate the cravings of the public in order to stay ikn business, ban or no ban.

A contest of madmen

Fiercer still was the war waged between the publishers themselves.

From the moment he stepped foot on New York soil, 32-year-old William Randolph Hearst had only one newspaper within his sights. Perched atop Printing House Square in bronze and marble spectacle, the *New York World* set the standard by which every other newspaper measured itself. It championed underdogs and victims against greedy corporations and slick-fingered villains. It was unabashed in its call for reform and its endorsement of those whom it deemed fit to carry out that reform. It dazzled its readers with multi-column illustrations and biting political cartoons. It was a paper for the people. To Hearst, it looked like the Holy Grail.

Where Hearst once saw an idol in Joseph Pulitzer, he now saw a rival. He was no longer the over-ambitious teenager who had coveted Pulitzer's platform while making a mess of things at Harvard University. He had come up in the world, plunged his fists into the newspaper industry, and cultivated a greater understanding of what it took to gain recognition and respect among his peers. The *San Francisco Examiner* had given him a crash course in shaping public opinion and stoking social outrage, but even on its best day, it could never match the scope, readership, and profitability that the *World* had achieved. No, if Hearst was going to make a real name for himself, he was going to have to pack up his life and move back to the bustling metropolises that clung to the icy spine of the East Coast.

If he wanted to be the best, he was going to have to beat Pulitzer at his own game.

There was no way for Pulitzer to anticipate that the anonymous West Coast playboy with the high voice and impeccable neckties was about to become his biggest rival. How could he? Hearst had stealthily observed the *World*'s editor from afar, memorizing his methods and practicing the not-so-subtle art of imitation as he waited for the perfect opportunity to strike.

He didn't need to long. Within the first year of his inauspicious arrival, Hearst's presence in New York City had become virtually impossible to ignore. He had inherited from Albert Pulitzer, by way of John R. McLean, a paper with a lousy reputation and humble headquarters, not unlike the *World* under Jay Gould's thumb. The offices of the *Journal* were spread across the second and third floors of the Tribune Building, a structure so rundown it nearly collapsed under the weight of its own shadow.

Hearst knew better than to judge on appearances alone. It only mattered what readers found between the pages of the *Journal*, not what they might read into the shabby trappings of his offices, several months into his residency as editor-in-chief, he made two drastic attempts to increase the paper's circulation by deliberately cutting into his own profits.

The first thing he did was expand the daily paper to a full twelves pages, giving him ample room to describe, in obscene detail, the numerous crimes and political injustices littering the streets of New York City.

He copied the tone and feel of Pulitzer's bestselling publication with wide headlines and striking illustrations and broadened the paper's scope to include international affairs as well as local gossip. There was something for everyone: smoldering tenement fires and Yale-Princeton football games and Waldorf-Astoria wedding receptions and Homer Davenport political caricatures.

The young editor was spry and headstrong. He kept a schedule that irritated even the most lackadaisical newspaper staff, bounding into the offices after noon to look over the latest editorial changes, then disappearing for a late lunch, a musical comedy or scintillating vaudeville performance, and a fine dinner at Jim's Chop House or Delmonico's (among a number of reputable establishments in which his was a regular face). Still outfitted in the evening's finery, he returned to the office well after midnight, new visions and ideas for the next morning's paper swimming in his head.

"[...] it was always an interesting spectacle to me to watch this young millionaire, usually in irreproachable evening dress, working over the forms," wrote editor Willis Abbott, "changing a head here, shifting the position of an article there, clamoring always for more pictures and bigger type."

Despite his quirks, or perhaps because of them, the paper was doing well. It had already arrested the attention of the city's readers; now, Hearst thought, it was time to hit the *World* where it hurt the most.

Not long after the *Journal* debuted its new look, Hearst shaved the price of his paper down to one cent. He plastered the new price on billboards around town, posting them along elevated railway stations and mounting them in street cars. Many of the city's registered voters received envelopes with pennies from the *Journal*'s enthusiastic publisher, along with the reassurance that the publication offered more value for a single penny than any other form of cheap entertainment could. Those who did not receive money from Hearst were invited to participate in an "Age and Youth Contest," which promised free bicycles to readers who could identify the portraits of famous historical figures and politicians.

"You can't get more than all the news," the *Journal* told its new subscribers. "You can't pay less than one cent."

As Hearst's circulation began to snowball, however, his profits started to melt. Readers wanted the big, cheap papers he was selling, but the subsequent hike in printing costs meant the new editor was losing money on every paper sold. For someone less financially secure, such drastic measures would have been insane. Hearst, on the other hand, continued to reel in profits from the *Examiner* and cash from the generous heart (and pocketbook) of his widowed mother. He could experiment with bolder headlines and expensive promotions in his quest to overtake Pulitzer without once worrying that he'd bankrupt his newfound enterprise.

And he did.

In four months' time, Hearst had achieved the improbable. His reckless spending and captivating brand of journalism had commanded the interest, if not the respect, of New York City's patrons. As the calendar flipped to January 1896, the *Journal*'s subscriber base blossomed from its initial 30,000 readers to over 120,000, some 50,000 beneath the *World*'s 185,000-member audience. It was a remarkable feat for any publisher to pull off, let alone a figure so relatively new to the industry, but anyone who knew Hearst well might have guessed that there were bigger surprises yet in store.

The problem, as always, lay with Pulitzer. Hearst was tired of throwing down the gauntlet again and again while his rival pretended not to notice it. He was ready to discard the protocol befittint a fair fight and go on the attack.

By the end of January, the *Journal*'s head honcho had arranged a meeting with the esteemed Morrill Goddard at the Hoffman House hotel in Manhattan. Goddard was something of a boy genius, if the term could be applied to a man creeping up on 31 years old. He ran Pulitzer's Sunday paper with much of the finesse and fanaticism of his superior, provoking the public with large drawings of naked women and illuminating the talents of illustrator R.F. Outcault, who would soon rise to prominence as the inventor of "The Yellow Kid" comic strips. More importantly, he filled the papers with pages upon pages of advertisements and nearly doubled the Sunday *World*'s circulation to an impressive 450,000 subscribers in the span of two short years.

Staring across the table at Hearst, Goddard felt skeptical. He had a sure thing in the *World*, an established presence within one of the most prestigious newspaper offices in the country.

"Your proposition might interest me, Mr. Hearst, but I don't want to change a certainty for an uncertainty," he said. "Frankly, I doubt if you will last three months in this town."

Hearst was no fool. He understood the young man's doubts; perhaps, at one point, he even shared them. But he knew that money talked louder and more convincingly than any eloquent rebuttal he could give. He offered Goddard the two things he hoped would be irresistible to a man in his position: the editor's desk of the Sunday *Journal* and a raise in the shape of $35,000.

Goddard accepted—with reservations. After all, he hadn't built the *World* on his singular talent alone, and wasn't about to sell himself as a one-man machine. If he was going to transform the Sunday *Journal* into a worthy competitor for the *World*, he needed the full backing of his journalists and illustrators, Outcault among them.

That was no matter to Hearst. "All right," he told Goddard. "Let's take the whole staff."[14]

One by one, the *Journal* filled its ranks with ex-*World* employees, including cartoonists R.F. Outcault and T.E. Powers, arts critic Alan Dale, and comic writer Bill Nye. Pulitzer may have been half-blind, but he could see right through the *Journal*'s schemes. He nudged his business manager, Solomon Carvalho, to buy back Goddard at a higher rate, and, not a day later, was promptly defeated again by Hearst's blank-check approach.

Pulitzer couldn't stop Hearst from pilfering his staff members, but he could control where the transactions took place (or, more accurately, did not take place). In a fit of rage, he booted Hearst and his paper from the *World* building. They would have to conduct their business—be it journalism or thievery—elsewhere.

Before he closed the book on his first year in New York City, Hearst had finally earned the recognition he sought from Pulitzer. Plenty of rival publications and their editors had irked the *World*'s temperamental publisher, but never before had he been the victim of such a blatant case of identity theft. Whatever Pulitzer had, Hearst wanted—and more. He no longer cared to emulate his role model; he wanted to become him. He filched Goddard from Pulitzer's desk, then right-hand man Solomon Carvalho, then the entire staff of the *Sunday World*.† Within months, Hearst's fledgling staff had more than doubled in size, with the expertise and edge necessary to churn out their own über-popular political cartoons and biting editorials.

Pulitzer was furious. He didn't intend to take these losses lying down, but his pockets were nowhere near as deep as Hearst's, and if there was one thing that could buy the loyalty of the *World*'s staff, it was money. And Hearst wasn't just buying out the competition. He had offered Pulitzer's men a working environment free of petty in-fighting and totalitarian control, backed by multiyear contracts that offered the kind of job security Pulitzer was unwilling to guarantee his staff. As Pulitzer's personal secretary and pianist, Felix Webber, once put it, the man had a distinctive way of "keeping all your nerves on the bristle."

"If 100 difficult things are done and well-done and one little slip is made," Webber added, "he will forget the 100 things but remember and rub well in the one slip. Leaving him is just like getting up from the dentist's chair and letting all one's nerves relax again."[15]

What's more, Pulitzer had neither the stamina nor the resources to keep up with his new competitor. The 48-year-old newspaper mogul was already starting to see serious signs of decaying health, including milky-white cataracts that had infected both eyes, chronic fatigue, and a debilitating sensitivity to sound that was borne of his various workaholic tendencies. His emotional outbursts were frequent and

---

† By the end of one of Hearst's bigger raids, the only remaining staff member was secretary Emma Jane Hogg. It's not clear if she stayed out of loyalty or simply because the same offer had not been extended to her.

irrational as the single-minded wrath of a toddler—sometimes directed at his wife's spending, other times at what he perceived to be an editorial misstep or betrayal. Worst of all were the times when he took it out on his ailing daughter, Lucille.‡ In the summer of 1894, the 14-year-old girl was laid up in the upper bedroom of her father's house after undergoing an intensive throat surgery. Her grave condition inspired great concern from her mother, Katherine, but only appeared to trigger annoyance from Pulitzer himself. After one turbulent family dinner, during which his wife had the audacity to question her husband's lack of empathy, the man exploded.

"Pity Lucille!" he shrieked. "No! I'm the only one to pity—has no one any pity for *me!*—does no one realize what I suffer! My own house turned into a hospital! Doctors coming at all hours! You rushing upstairs in the middle of meals, without a word of conversation for me. No one pities me and you ask me to pity Lucille!"[16]

When his rage subsided, Pulitzer tried to make halfhearted amends by ordering Webber to select the biggest bouquet of flowers available—not in order to bring his daughter comfort, but because he had seen flowers littered around the bedroom and was jealous of the attention she had bestowed on her well-wishers.

"[...] jealousy of the most intense kind is the only symptom of anything approaching affection he can feel for anyone, even his own children," Webber mentioned in a brief aside.[17] It would prove a telling statement in the years that followed, especially where the city's young newspaper hawkers were concerned.

Pulitzer's long list of physical and mental ailments was only compounded by the insouciance of a 33-year-old California nest egg baby who seemed hell-bent on one-upping him at every turn. Paranoid and panicked, his back pressed to the metaphorical wall, he did the only thing that seemed prudent in the moment: At the urging of his editors, Pulitzer

---

‡ Lucille was Pulitzer's eldest daughter. She survived her throat surgery, but died of typhoid fever just three years later at age 17. Pulitzer's younger daughter, Katherine, also died prematurely. She contracted a fatal bout of pneumonia in 1884 when she was two years old.

reduced the price of the *Morning World* to a single penny per copy. Now the two dailies were on an even playing field. It would be up to the readers to decide between Hearst's scandals and Pulitzer's dramas—a no-brainer, Pulitzer thought. Who would want Hearst's yellow journals when they could have the *World* for the same price?

As it turned out, a lot of people would. Hearst knew it, too. He extended a formal, if mocking welcome to the *World* when it officially joined the ranks of the penny press in February 1896, while Pulitzer tried to spin the situation in a positive light:

"It Will Be Fuller than Ever. More Independent than Ever. More Truly Popular than Ever," trumpeted the half-page announcement splashed across the face of the *World*. "The power of The World to do good lies in the public confidence and support which it has won for itself. To increase that measure of public confidence and support, it is only necessary to get people to read The World. The readers of The World are the friends of The World. By offering the greatest newspaper for the smallest price, The World expects to double its army of readers and friends."[18]

The horn-tootage continued for another several columns as Pulitzer not-so-modestly referred to it as "the biggest paper in the universe" and the "biggest newspaper at the smallest price." These brags were flanked by several effusive quotes from local postmasters and bankers and non-competing editors of Boston and Philadelphia publications, each of whom envisioned the *World* cresting a readership of one million in the weeks and months to come.

"I do not believe that, as a rule, any of the leading papers of the great cities can afford to print a paper for one cent," the *Boston Globe*'s Charles H. Taylor countered.[19] He quickly walked back the comment, citing the *World* as a rare exception to the rule, but he would have been wiser not to ignore his gut feeling.

Though it was true that Pulitzer was losing consumers to Hearst's immense reserves of cash and limitless generosity by the day, lowering the price of the *World* only decreased its revenue stream further. Pulitzer quickly learned that readers didn't care about saving a penny per paper. The *Morning World*'s ambitious two-cent price tag wasn't the reason why they had stopped reading it. They wanted to see illustrations of the latest trends in novelty bicycle fashion and read about the plight of criminalized homeless women and enter contests that promised gold and horses and cottages in the country-side—in other words, content they could only get from Hearst. And they were only too willing to shell out their hard-earned coinage to get it.

The *World*, meanwhile, fell well short of the million-reader mark it had so confidently predicted. Although it made modest improvements in overall readership right off the bat, it stag-nated as readers insisted on snapping up copy after copy of the *Journal*. Advertisers, too, turned hostile in response to Pulitzer's cost-cutting measures: first, when he clipped the paper's size, then when he hiked the cost of the ads them-selves. Not only did they resent having to pay more for reduced column space, but they believed that the discounted price of newspapers would attract a lower, less spendthrift class of consumers. These tactics may have helped the *World* under-cut the competition over at the *New York Advertiser*, *Recorder*, *Mercury*, and *Press*, but it was failing to make so much as a dent in Hearst's ever-expanding subscriber base.

Hearst was prepared to run Pulitzer ragged. After playing catch-up for years, it finally looked like he was pulling ahead of the heavyweight *World* and its editor, and he wasn't afraid to bend the rules to maintain his lead, either. Now he wanted to stake a claim on the same moral high ground that Pulitzer had built his brand on, the kind of journalism that demands justice for the common man and a voice for the powerless. Perhaps more accurately, he wanted to attract the immigrant and working classes—an as-yet untapped market for the *Journal*.

He had a solid role model in Pulitzer. After 12 years at the helm of the *World*, Pulitzer had shown himself to be a man of mostly-upstanding character, a savvy do-gooder who helped the city as much as he exploited it for his own gain. He funded public parks, provided holiday dinners and medical care to impoverished children, enabled France to ship the statue of "Lady Liberty" for installation in New York Harbor, prevented the uneducated from investing in shoddy insurance companies, investigated the city's food sources, employed the bright, fearless reporter Elizabeth "Nellie Bly" Cochran and sponsored her trip around the world, pushed for reform in insane asylums, and documented illicit gambling dens in New Jersey, among other noble-hearted causes. He was first and foremost a man of the people; at the very least, that's what his carefully curated appearance would have readers believe.

As he did with most things, Hearst took Pulitzer's reform measures to new (and occasionally ridiculous) heights. He posted a vehement defense of Jewish immigrants[§] and spoke out against the Raines Law, which sought to impose more stringent regulations on the consumption of alcohol by prohibiting its sale in saloons and other common watering holes on Sundays. He whipped his press room into a frenzy over every political and social scandal, going so far as to brand a subset of his employees as his very own "Murder Squad." Together, they traversed the slums and alleys of the city to hunt down criminals and brigands, later publishing tales of their vigilante justice in the folds of the daily papers. It was this brand of bullheadedness that would eventually inspire Hearst to involve himself in the Spanish-American War two years later.

First, though, Hearst had to finish the fight he had started in his own backyard. With or without a million subscribers, Pulitzer refused to back out of an industry in which he was widely considered the favorite. Hearst had raided his staff and played copycat and reached a level of success that felt downright alarming to the elder editor, but these were battles he could lose without conceding the war. While tone and intention has often been muddled by misinterpretations of history, no true sense of loathing could be traced in Pulitzer's telegrams to managing editor Don Seitz, whom he cautioned to treat the *Journal* as a legitimate threat.

"If we do not admit that the *Journal* is printed better and so far as pictures are concerned, is better, then we are blind," Pulitzer wrote.[20]

---

§   It's important to note that Hearst's sympathetic portrayal of European immigrants was often juxtaposed against a derisive and racist attitude toward African-Americans. The effect of his racist rhetoric, especially imprinted in something as widely-read and esteemed as the *Journal*, cannot be overstated.

Pulitzer didn't dispute the legitimacy of Hearst's endeavors, but the young editor's confidence and boyish recklessness caused him no end of anxiety. In rare moments of clarity, he realized that the only way to beat Hearst was to do what the *World* had always done: print the most colorful, riveting, and truthful newspaper on the market, at a better price and higher quality than any other competitor in the country.

It was a noble goal, to be sure, but one more easily conceived than executed. Much to Pulitzer's dismay, Hearst had more unpleasant surprises in store for the editor of the bronze-domed empire. In the autumn of 1897, he enticed another handful of the *World*'s highly-coveted editors to join the *Journal*. The greatest coup? Thirty-three-year-old *Sunday* edition editor Arthur Brisbane, a powerful force of nature in his own right.

Brisbane was a man after Pulitzer's heart: tenacious in the press room, fearless in confrontation, and a notorious card sharp. In the five years he'd spent in the *World*'s employ, he applied his gift for sensationalism to some of the most talked-about events in the country, including New York City's first death by electrocution ("The rigor of death came on the instant. An odor of burning flesh and singed hair filled the room. For a moment a blue flame played about the base of the victim's spine."[21]) and the bloody standoff between striking members of Pennsylvania's Carnegie Steel Company and the weaponized Pinkerton detectives who held them off ("The [Pinkerton agents] screamed for mercy. They were beaten over the head with clubs and the butt ends of rifles. You could almost hear the skulls crack."[22]). He surpassed even Pulitzer's penchant for the absurd and overwrought, and was always petitioning his boss to make the headlines wider and the columns more colorful in an attempt to bring in more readers. On the rare occasion when Brisbane wasn't scouring the streets for the next scandal, he was a frequent companion to the ailing Pulitzer on long excursions through Europe and, when Hearst came calling for the *Sunday* staff in 1896, assumed control of the weekend paper with unparalleled savviness and success.

Well before Hearst had caught wind of the talented young journalist, however, the cracks in the foundation of Brisbane's relationship with Pulitzer were beginning to show. Two willful, volatile personalities could not coexist in the pressure cooker that was the *World*, especially when it came to moral philosophies and financial matters. Brisbane had grand visions for himself and for the paper. He wanted his own byline, a concession the crotchety Pulitzer refused time and again. He wanted to pay handsomely for the editorials penned by the *World*'s reserve of great journalists, while Pulitzer preferred a thriftier approach. He may have even entertained the idea of making a name for himself, separated from any affiliation with the leading men of the publishing industry.

Some combination of these factors, likely aggravated by one of Pulitzer's signature outbursts, eventually drove Brisbane straight into the *Journal*'s office. He persuaded Hearst to hire him, then talked his way into the editorship of the ailing *Evening Journal*—and, even more shockingly, voluntarily accepted a lower salary in exchange for more creative control over his own content.¶ Without Pulitzer looking over his shoulder, Brisbane finally had enough space and freedom to prove that his ideas worked. After toiling over the *Evening Journal* for just seven weeks, he matched—then exceeded—the *Evening World*'s circulation. Not only did he have a keen intuition for the desires and opinions of the common man,** but he knew how to spin a story that would sell more papers than any other publisher in town.

By the dawn of 1898, it was clear that New York City no longer had one preeminent publisher in power. Hearst may not have succeeded in booting Pulitzer from the top of the industry food chain entirely, but he had proven his equal in nearly every way.

Pulitzer, on the other hand, felt his patience wearing thin. He had given Hearst every opportunity to beat him on merit alone,

---

¶ More precisely, Brisbane took a $7,000 pay cut, with the provision that he would receive a $1,000 bonus for every additional 10,000 copies sold. In six months, he was sitting pretty with the sum of $23,000.

** "Remember that a newspaper is mostly read by very busy people, or by very tired people, or by very uneducated people none of whom are going to hunt up a dictionary to find out what you mean. And never forget that if you don't hit a newspaper reader between the eyes with your first sentence, there is no need of writing a second one," Brisbane once instructed his fellow reporters.[23]

but the brash young editor and his 'junior' journal insisted on breaking the rules at every turn. Against a lesser paper, with less money and fewer readers at stake, Pulitzer might have turned a blind eye. He could hardly afford such magnanimity now.

Driven by an increasing inclination to pettiness, Pulitzer continued pouring money into the fight to outperform Hearst, and balanced his spendthrift habits with absurd penny-pinching measures at home. His wife, Kate, was chastised for her inability to pay household bills and purchase necessities for $6,000 a month—well beneath the expenditures necessary for keeping up with Hearst's *Journal*. He chewed out his mechanic and coal supplier, he haggled over doctor bills, he invested in little cottages and lavish estates scattered throughout the East Coast, he trimmed the length of the *World* and admonished those who didn't share in his singular vision for the paper.

More often than not, he fretted over Hearst: what his rival publisher was thinking, feeling, plotting, printing, and distributing to the city's day laborers and soft-palmed upper classes. Pulitzer upgraded his printing equipment and paid his workers so generously that Hearst could not help but try to match his prices. He kept his finger on the pulse of the wire service industry and seized the opportunity to shut out Hearst from a much-needed Associated Press membership when United Press went under in 1897.[††] He arranged lunches with former *World* employees and attempted to gauge how Hearst's reckless spending was affecting his bottom line, hoping that Phoebe Apperson Hearst was nearing the day when she would tighten her purse strings for good.

In perhaps the most telling sign of paranoia yet, the *World*'s 50-year-old editor devised an elaborate code for anyone associated with the *Journal*. He was already half-convinced that Hearst had planted a spy among his ranks; absurd, yes, but not inconceivable given the depths to which the West Coast newspaper mogul had already deigned to stoop. Pulitzer instructed

---

[††] Not surprisingly, Hearst found a creative workaround to subvert Pulitzer's tactics. He purchased the *New York Morning Advertiser*, which, like Pulitzer's acquisition of the *World* some 14 years earlier, came bundled with the coveted membership.

his staff to treat the code with the utmost integrity. Every telegram and message was to be scrambled with the approved aliases: William Randolph Hearst became "Gush," while Pulitzer himself was referred to as "Andes."‡‡ The *Morning World* was the "Senior," the *Evening World* the "Junior," and the *Journal*, simply "Geranium." Those who fell out of favor with Pulitzer (or were never in favor to begin with) were saddled with still more unflattering terms: "Glutinous" for Theodore Roosevelt, "Mediocrity" for one-time Vice President and Governor of New York Levi P. Morton, "Rotund" for William Howard Taft, and "Malaria" for the whole of the Republican Party.

By the late 1890s, the feud had swelled to epic proportions. The lesser newspapers of New York City could not ignore the yellow journals' pointed marketing campaigns and competing headlines, nor could they refrain from commenting on them. They frequently tried to discredit the *World* and *Journal* with implications of pettiness, duplicitousness, and a self-serving quality that any discerning reader was sure to find distasteful. (Of course, if those readers then turned their attention—and pocket money—toward New York City's smaller presses, that was a welcome bonus.)

> "These two papers are bitter rivals," the *Sun* told its readers in the summer of 1897. "Each is trying to cut the other's throat, for neither has any competitor except the other, and each is struggling to make the more provocative and more seductive appeal to the same audience. They stand by themselves, actually and in public estimation, wholly outside the field of decent and self-respecting journalism. In all sinister and subtle ways, with pen and pencil, they are pursuing industriously their feverish competition to monopolize the forbidden field in which they are rivals."[25]

The *Fourth Estate* offered a more succinct critique of the rivalry: "[...] when two newspapers find their time chiefly occupied in exaggeration of one another's faults it is then time to consider whether journalism is doing due justice to its high estate."[26]

---

‡‡   Hardly a modest moniker, as the Andes represents the longest stretch of continental mountains in the world. According to Pulitzer biographer James McGrath Morris, the identity of "Andes" was hardly a secret and soon became one of the most popular nicknames for the *World*'s esteemed editor.[24]

Doing justice to the high estate of journalism wasn't exactly at the top of Pulitzer and Hearst's to-do lists. As a temperate New York spring congealed into the thick heat of summer, the *World* and *Journal* had greater concerns than their social standing among the city's journalists and culture connoisseurs.

In fact, they had what just so happened to be the best fodder for sensationalized journalism and public outcry: A war.

The *Journal*'s war

Even the solemn business of war was not exempt from the media's predilection for unchecked speculation. Though much has been made of the way the yellow press inflamed public sentiment during the Spanish-American War of 1898, the three-month conflict was but an offshoot of a decade-long struggle for Cuban independence.

In the autumn of 1868, sugar mill owner and self-proclaimed abolitionist Carlos Manuel de Céspedes spearheaded the Ten Years' War, at the end of which the Cuban rebels forfeited their right to fight for independence and settled for limited manumission of their slaves and greater representation in Spanish parliament, among other minor advantages. The following year saw the continuation of the war, albeit on a much smaller scale. This time led by revolutionary Calixto García, the "Little War" flowered and wilted from the summer of 1879 to the autumn of 1880 with little progress made. It was all too apparent that Cuba now lacked the resources, foreign aid, and public support that helped drive their previous battles against Spain.. The final push for independence began in the winter of 1895, when Cuban insurrectionists José Martí and Máximo Gómez presented their countrymen and women with the Manifesto of Montecristi. The document—both an instruction manual for the revolution to come and a rhapsody of long-hoped for liberty and equality—intended to awaken the Cuban people to the necessity of autonomous rule and separation from the overreaching arm of the Spanish government.

"We Cubans are starting the war, and Cubans and Spaniards will finish it together," it read in part. "If they do not mistreat us, we will not mistreat them. If they show respect, we will respect them. The blade is answered with the blade, and friendship is answered with friendship."

Not everyone agreed with Martí's call to sever ties with Spain. More than a few rebels preferred partial rule to total separation; in fact, it was this kind of dissension that had weakened the movement in the first place. Pressed by his longsuffering idealism and sense of *patria*, Martí persisted. He recognized the threat looming on the horizon, not just the one where Cuba failed to extricate itself from Spanish control, but one where Cuba was forcibly allied with and annexed by the neighboring United States.§§ Neither situation, he feared, would lead the country down a path of true autonomy.

Martí would not survive to see his premonitions come to pass. More skilled with the pen than the sword, the Cuban revolutionary was ill-equipped for the rigors of war and perished in the Battle of Dos Ríos not three months after the revolution began. In his stead, Máximo Gómez and Antonio Maceo pushed forward, divesting the civilian population of their right to remain neutral during a time of increasing volatility and, more importantly, undercutting the efforts of the Spanish army through various tactics of guerrilla warfare.

The United States, meanwhile, appeared to have little interest in involving itself with Cuba's affairs. On June 12, 1895, President Grover Cleveland issued a proclamation of neutrality that effectively forbade the U.S. from lending military support to either side in the war. Whether rooted in measures of diplomacy or more self-serving interests, it hardly mattered. The resolution lasted less than a year before Cleveland was forced to retract it.

Just eleven months after the inception of the Cuban War for Independence, Spanish captain-general Arsenio Martínez

---

§§   In the aftermath of the Ten Years' War, Cuba's sugar boom resulted in a skewed partnership with its primary investors in the United States. Some estimated the U.S. had sunk as much as $50 million in the sugar industry, in addition to substantial gains in land ownership. According to historian Ted A. Henken, Cuba may have belonged to Spain in name, but it was economically dependent on the United States long before the Spanish-American War began in 1898.[27]

Campos resigned his post.¶¶ He was swiftly replaced by General Valeriano Weyler, a man whose reputation for brutality preceded him—and undoubtedly played a crucial role in his selection to the post as well. The 56-year-old veteran was routinely villainized in the press ("Weyler the Terrible" and "the man of blood and iron" were but a couple of his nicknames) and in the months that followed, did his best to live up to his well-deserved reputation.

As Spanish troops became increasingly frustrated by the insurgents' unpredictable guerrilla tactics, Weyler turned to more severe measures in order to shift the momentum against the rebels. One of his most outrageous approaches called for the involuntary regrouping of the Cuban people into *reconcentración* camps. Civilians who made their homes in rural areas were forced to relocate to larger cities, while those who insisted on remaining in the countryside were soon branded "insurgents" and treated as such. Within the borders of the camps, however, scant resources were provided for the thousands of men, women, and children who needed proper food and clothing to survive. By the outbreak of the Spanish-American War in 1898, the camps lost an estimated 150,000 to 200,000 Cubans to famine, malnutrition, and disease.***

As Weyler piled up human rights violations in the Cuban countryside, Hearst and Pulitzer circled each other like feral dogs in the street. The *Journal* boasted a combined circulation of 750,000, affected as that number might have been from Hearst's endless promotions and the inclusion of his German-language

---

¶¶ Campos was forced to step down after he refused to carry out certain orders against the Cuban rebels. He hinted at the dispute in his resignation announcement, saying in part, "[...] I have not been able to follow out the war policy which, in the opinion of the conservatives and reformists, it was desirous I should follow, but which my conscience forbade me to adopt."[28] Some have suggested that he was morally opposed to the idea of ethnic cleansing, an atrocious practice that his successor, Valeriano Weyler, appeared to endors.

*** Weyler's primary design reportedly was not to punish civilians, but rather to ferret out Cuban insurrectionists by cutting off their supplies and identifying their supporters. Still, there has been nothing to suggest that he made any attempt to address the inhumane conditions of the *reconcentración* camps or took any strides to prevent the unnecessary deaths of thousands of innocent Cubans.

edition. Pulitzer, on the other hand, watched the *World* lose an estimated 67,000 subscribers as the sun broke over the first morning of 1897, bringing its total circulation down to 743,024. War—as a Shakespearean drama and endless outrage machine—was just what New York's hungriest editors craved.

Hearst, in typical Hearst fashion, deployed as many as eight *"Journal* Commissioners." Plied with medical instruments and a $2,000 gold-plated sword (a needlessly extravagant gift intended for Cuban army leader Máximo Gómez), the men traversed the country in an attempt to add their number to the insurgents. The most famous of the troupe, former fiction writer Richard Harding Davis, took a $3,000 stipend and agreed to a month-long stay in Havana, where he was still too far removed from the heart of the battlefield to offer any meaningful insights.

That didn't prevent him from making his mark. By February 1897, the young reporter had his first real wartime front-pager: the humiliation of three Cuban women at the hands of male Spanish detectives. The girls were apprehended under suspicion of espionage and had been stripped and searched aboard the *Olivette*, an American ship bound for Tampa, Florida.

"Does Our Flag Shield Women?" the *Journal*'s headline cried; Davis asserted that it did not.

More striking was the illustration that brought his story to life. *Journal* illustrator Frederic Remington had covered most of the front page with a graphic illustration of one of the girls, Clemencia Arango, standing naked in front of three Spanish officers. The alleged victims later clarified the situation: they hadn't been detained by men, but searched in private by another woman. Davis, for his part, severed ties with the *Journal* on claims that his original report had been errone-ously and extravagantly spun out of context.

Even in the face of incontrovertible evidence, Hearst was slow to retract the story, and Pulitzer, ever-ready to exploit his rival's weaknesses, pounced on the window of opportunity it presented. "The Unclothed Women Searched by Men was an Invention of a New York Newspaper," the <i>World</i> trum-peted in the days following the *Journal*'s blunder.

Perhaps given more spare time, Hearst would have penned his own scathing rebuttal, but as luck (or misfortune) would have it, scandals continued to roll in from Cuba at an alarming rate.

At the end of the month, Pulitzer had a bone to pick, not just with Hearst, but with Weyler himself. The yellow journals weren't just interested in covering Spain's controversial tactics against the Cuban rebels, even as they made easy and plentiful fodder for the front pages. Their editors had skin in the game, too. The brutal Spanish general was disinclined to accommodate any American journalists looking to cover the war, particularly as those journalists made use of the Cuban insurgents as sources and points of interest. Long before the conflict limped to its conclusion, Weyler restricted the efforts of all Cuban-sympathizing reporters by way of censorship, with harsh penalties awaiting those who dared violate his policies. To the extent that he could control the press coming in and out of the country, he did, hoping to eradicate any kind of sympathetic coverage of the rebels' efforts against Spain.

As the last days of the month petered out, Spain found yet another way to aggravate the *World*. This time, they arrested Pulitzer's war correspondent, Sylvester Scovel. Scovel had been traveling through Cuba with a fake police pass and tried to pass himself off under a different name. The plethora of American journalists crawling over the Cuban landscape was impossible to ignore, though, and Scovel was imprisoned soon after the offense was discovered, prompting outcry from the New York press back home.

An attack on insurgents was one thing, but the personal affront to one of Pulitzer's own would not be borne by the editor. Much as the *Journal* had done with the incident aboard the *Olivette*, the *World* blew Scovel's imprisonment out of proportion. As far as the American public was aware, the journalist wasn't just detained in a prison, but sequestered in the basest conditions of a "vile jail, in a filthy and small-pox infected town," where he faced "imminent butchery by a decree of a drumhead court-martial." Dramatic? Yes, but Pulitzer's flair for drama was paired with unquestionable influence among members of the state and federal government. His relentless campaign to free Scovel was eventually backed by the U.S. Senate and State Department.

Thanks to Pulitzer's relentless campaign and hyperbolic headlines, Scovel was no longer confined to a hellish hovel (if he ever had been)—his cell was decorated with all manner of lavish furniture and gifts, and he was permitted visits from several admiring supporters, one of whom managed to smuggle out a daily record of his treatment in prison. Even Weyler paid a visit to the reporter, though he did little to hide his disdain for Pulitzer's man. His personal opinion of the American press held little weight in this particular case; by March 10, the Spanish government had freed Scovel and returned him to New York City. Not by coincidence, the *World*'s circulation had risen by 8,000 subscribers.

Scovel was hardly the first to be wrongfully imprisoned, nor would he be the last. Among the controversies spawned by Weyler's take-no-prisoners approach to the insurrection, a dentist by the name of Dr. Ricardo Ruiz was lionized by the *Journal* after he was found dead in his jail cell. It was an easy death to pin on the Spanish troops, though the truth was a bit more complicated: A native Cuban, Ruiz ducked out of an earlier rebellion and obtained U.S. citizenship, then got caught up in another rebel cause upon returning to his homeland. He spent two weeks in jail for his involvement in a raid, then allegedly committed suicide.[†††]

Aside from a few glancing blows here and there, the *World* and *Journal* appeared content to trade off scandals during the war. That all changed in the summer of 1897, when 18-year-old Evangelina Cosio y Cisneros got caught in the crosshairs of the rebellion. The daughter of Cuban insurgent leader Augustin Cosio, Evangelina landed on Spain's radar after imploring Weyler to reduce her father's sentence from execution to life imprisonment. Together with her sister, the three were confined to Isla de Pinos, the second-largest island in the country, and lived there in relative security until Evangelina began plotting escape.

[†††] There was some disagreement over the nature of Ruiz's death. The Spanish guards insisted that he had ended his life by pounding his head against the wall of his cell; Hearst, among other members of the press, believed Ruiz had been murdered.

Exactly how that escape attempt unfolded remains unclear, but as was so often the case in a war-torn country with a strict gag order, whatever facts existed were soon tainted by wild speculation. In one version, Evangelina invited Spanish governor José Berriz to her home, where he was waylaid by Cuban rebels and beaten until reinforcements arrived. In another, more insidious account, Berriz had become unnaturally obsessed with the young girl and attempted to rape her. Given this context, the subsequent ambush attempt was not some desperate ploy to allow Evangelina and her family to escape, but a revenge plot against the military commander. His cries caught the attention of a passing patrol, who came to his rescue and arrested the Cosio-Cisneros family.

When reports of the arrest reached the offices of American presses, it was of little surprise that Hearst chose to run with an embellished accounting of facts. Two months later, word came that Evangelina had been sentenced to a 20-year imprisonment for her role in the attack at Isla de Pinos. Biographer James Creelman claimed that, the news whipped up a frenzy in the *Journal* offices, the likes of which had never been seen before.

> "We've got Spain, now!" Hearst cackled. "Telegraph to our correspondent in Havana to wire every detail of this case. Get up a petition to the Queen Regent of Spain for this girl's pardon. Enlist the women of America. Have them sign the petition. Wake up our correspondents all over the country. Have distinguished women sign first. Cable the petitions and the names to the Queen Regent. Notify our minister in Madrid. We can make a national issue of this case. It will do more to open the eyes of the country than a thousand editorials or political speeches. The Spanish minister can attack our correspondents, but we'll see if he can face the women of America when they take up the fight. That girl must be saved if we have to take her out of prison by force or send a steamer to meet the vessel that carries her away—but that would be piracy, wouldn't it?"[29]

Whether or not Hearst actually made such an eloquent and impassioned plea is doubtful, especially given Creelman's bias (and, later, his fictionalized account of Remington's time in Cuba). The publisher still made good on every promise, soliciting help from the Queen Regent of Spain and inspiring notable women—Mrs. Jefferson Davis, Julia Ward Howe, Frances Hodgson Burnett, even President McKinley's mother, Nancy—to sign a heartfelt petition in support of Evangelina's release. It wasn't enough.

If his hunger truly had been for war, he would have left the teenager in prison, where her harsh sentencing would have continued to stoke the outrage of American politicians and government figures. Hearst was first and foremost a journalist, however, and his plan to break Evangelina out of Cuba made for a far more interesting—and marketable—story.

Pulitzer wasn't about to be scooped by his rival, and certainly not on an event that was sure to capture interest far beyond the perimeter of Park Row. He sent Scovel to Cuba ahead of Hearst's man, Karl Decker, but lost the race to rescue the "Cuban Joan of Arc" after Scovel was recognized and re-deported. It's unlikely that Scovel's designs were much different than Decker's. The *Journal* reporter bribed the guards and brought the young girl back to the United States, where she was treated like a prodigal daughter: plied with expensive gowns, a suite at the Waldorf, a feast at Delmonico's, a parade through Madison Square Garden, and a reception with President McKinley, most of it on Hearst's dime.

"Evangelina Cisneros Rescued by the *Journal*," proclaimed the ceremonious headline. "An American Newspaper Accomplishes at a Single Stroke What the Red Tape of Diplomacy Failed Utterly to Bring About in Many Months," the subheading added.[30] Two columns' width was devoted to portraits of the teenager in pre- and post- states of imprisonment: the first marked by plump cheeks, fine dress, and a demure expression; the latter by plain clothes, unkempt hair, and a look best characterized as hopelessness.‡‡‡

In multiple accounts of Evangelina's rescue, the *Journal* conveniently left out any mention of a bribe, choosing instead to swap dull facts for colorful prose.

---

‡‡‡ However dramatic in nature, the portraits may not have scandalized the *Journal*'s readers as much as expected, given that they had been used for another of Cisneros' front-page stories several months earlier.

"I have broken the bars of Recojidas and have set free the beautiful captive of monster Weyler," Decker wrote in the column that followed, "restoring her to her friends and relatives, and doing by strength, skill and strategy what could not be accomplished by petition and urgent request of the Pope. [...] To-night all Havana rings with the story. It is the one topic of conversation; everything else pales into significance."

The plight of a downtrodden Cuban girl wasn't enough to motivate President McKinley to send his country to war, nor was that Hearst or Pulitzer's intention. The yellow press feasted on scenes of carnage and injustice between Cuba and Spain, but Hearst was caught up in a sob story too far-fetched to be credible, and Pulitzer insisted on balancing the most ludicrous reports with a modicum of caution. With Evangelina safely plucked from her prison cell, there was little impetus for American troops to go tramping on Cuban soil anytime soon.

Scarcely three months later, in the winter of 1898, the landscape of the war had shifted yet again. This time, there was precious little ambiguity about the United States' role in the Cuban revolution. On January 25, the American battleship *Maine* glided into Havana Harbor for the first time...and the last. Three weeks later, on an otherwise placid evening, the ship exploded. An estimated 264 American sailors and two officers were killed in the explosion.

Hundreds of bodies littered the harbor as Scovel ran toward the scene. He had been permitted to return to Cuba in the wake of Weyler's departure from the Spanish forces, and had witnessed a new bitterness begin to fester as Weyler's replacement, the mild-mannered Ramon Blanco, tried to offer autonomy to the Cuban people. Most insisted on holding out for total self-government, while a separate and far more vocal contingent spoke out against both the Cuban extremists and meddling Americans.

Scovel didn't fear the threats (or, if he did, he didn't let on), and his columns assured the American public that war wouldn't touch their shores. In Havana, staring at fragments of ship and sailors bobbing in the water, that confidence evaporated. He hastily wrote home, dashing off a few half-formed theories about the nature of the attack: a secret plot to destroy the ship, the conclusive word of a "dynamite expert" who cried foul play, a torpedo.

"*Maine* Explosion Caused by Bomb or Torpedo?" the *World* asked its readers on February 17.[31]

The *Journal* wasn't content to sit and speculate. They needed answers. Five days after the explosion, on February 20, Hearst ran a front-page sure to stir up controversy:

"How the *Maine* Actually Looks as It Lies, Wrecked by Spanish Treachery, in Havana."[32]

Implicating the Spanish troops in the attack was no slip of the tongue—or the pen. Hearst perpetuated the idea that Spain was behind the attack—specifically, that they had planted the submarine mine that was found responsible for the explosion—and sculpted each column around that belief.[§§§] He claimed to have definitive proof of the submarine mine that sank the *Maine*, furnishing elaborate illustrations of the "sunken torpedo" and a supposed map of every other mine lurking in the depths of the harbor. He told the public that the Spanish had not buried the sailors at all, but out of spiteful feeling toward the United States, left the American bodies on the wharf as plentiful carrion for the vultures. He printed a cable from Captain Charles D. Sigsbee to the Secretary of the Navy Long, the contents of which suggested that the explosion was deliberately orchestrated. When that proved false, he circulated an interview with Theodore Roosevelt in which the Assistant Secretary of the Navy praised the *Journal* as a newspaper of "great influence and circulation," one that insisted on "telling the facts as they exist." This, too, was exposed as false and gleefully ridiculed by Pulitzer.

That's not to suggest that Pulitzer possessed all the common sense and prudence missing from Hearst's approach to the war. He was guilty of reprinting the falsified cable from Charles Sigsbee in the *World* and lost his managing editor, Ernest

---

§§§   Hearst ignored the facts that didn't fit within this belief: the fact that General Ramon Blanco wept upon learning of the *Maine*'s fate, the way Spain offered to suspend their fight against Cuba, the temperance with which President McKinley treated the tragedy, etc. In reality, there had been no conclusive evidence to suggest that the explosion was either deliberate or accidental, let alone perpetrated by Spain in a fit of anti-American feeling.

Chamberlin, to a fit of war-crazed madness (and soon afterward, a fatal bout of pneumonia). He also commissioned a tugboat and a team of "expert divers" to poke around Havana Harbor for evidence of mines, but was denied access by Spanish officials.¶¶¶

For this and more, *New York Evening Post* editor Edwin Godkin roundly condemned both of the yellow journals:

> "Every one who knows anything about 'yellow journals' knows that everything they do and say is intended to promote sales," he wrote. "No one supposes a yellow journal cares five cents about the Cubans, the *Maine* victims, or anything else. A yellow journal is probably the nearest approach to hell, existing in any Christian state. It is a crying shame that men should work such mischief in order to sell more papers."[33]

There was no doubt the *World* and *Journal* were making a pretty penny off of every scandal and misfortune that made its way from Cuba to the U.S. In the first three days following the *Maine*'s explosion, the *Journal* totaled an unprecedented 3,098,825 subscribers. Two months later, the twin journals were raking in 1.3 million daily subscribers apiece. It was a good time to be in the newspaper business.

What effect the yellow press had on the American government is difficult to say, but no concrete evidence has linked Hearst and Pulitzer's relentless warmongering with the beginning of the United States' involvement in the Cuban rebellion. It seems far more credible that, rather than a slew of exploitative yellow editorials, it was the atrocities faced by the Cuban people—wrongful imprisonment, tragic and preventable deaths, the appalling conditions of Weyler's *reconcentración* camps—combined with the deaths of hundreds of American sailors that finally compelled President McKinley to take action.

On April 25, 1898, the United States went to war with Spain.

The war lasted ten weeks. Hearst reveled in each one, sparing no expense to get a front-row seat to the carnage and craze. While his paper attracted millions of subscribers by the day,

---

¶¶¶   The lack of access didn't prevent Hearst from utilizing his own team of expert divers, each of whom miraculously found whatever proof was needed to validate the *Journal*'s absurd claims.

he squandered his profits left and right: half a million dollars toward an undisclosed list of "essentials," eleven seafaring vessels (including two yachts, a Red Cross boat, and a Brazilian cattle boat), the salaries of nineteen writers and illustrators to cover every hill that had seen so much as a drop of blood, and a 138-foot steam yacht that was temporarily accepted as an honorary vessel in the U.S. Navy (sans its giddy, boyish owner).

"How Do You Like the *Journal's* War?" the paper crowed. For all the money Hearst had poured into the conflict—that is, the money he poured into furnishing his staff with the best access and resources—the war may as well have been his.

It wasn't for lack of motivation that Pulitzer fell behind Hearst as the war staggered toward its inevitable conclusion. Like his fellow yellow journalist, he had racked up quite a bill in order to stay on the front lines, including the $27,000 he sunk into three dispatch boats**** and the eighteen correspondents he paid to cover the war itself.

Desperate to keep pace with his spry 35-year-old rival, Pulitzer began to pilfer Hearst's stories. It wasn't the first time the yellow journal had been accused of playing copycat—in fact, both papers were often guilty of reprinting the other's material without credit or much care to rephrase the stolen content—but now the stakes were bigger than ever before. There was no way Hearst was prepared to share the spotlight or his ill-gotten spoils of war, especially with his biggest rival.

No stranger to a good prank, Hearst had the *Journal* draw up a story about Colonel Reflipe W. Thenuz, an Austrian artillerist who allegedly died in battle as he defended the Aguadores. The piece was immediately poached up by the *World*, who ever-so-slightly tweaked the copy, slapped a false attribution at the end of it, and passed it off as their own.

The setup couldn't have been easier; the execution, more flawless. With no small amount of glee, the *Journal* spelled out the con for their competitor: "Reflipe W. Thenuz" was not only a fictional ally to the Cuban insurgency, but an anagram for "We Pilfer The Nuz [sic]." The whole thing had turned into an

---

**** These he ordered to circumvent the censors and ferry dispatches to and from the *World's* headquarters in New York City.

unintentional admission of guilt on the *World*'s part—given Pulitzer's continual scramble to catch up to the *Journal*'s latest gimmicks, it doubled as a total humiliation of the elder yellow journal. Hearst wasn't about to take sympathy on his archenemy now. He milked the moment for all it was worth, even printing a full-page cartoon to better illustrate Pulitzer's questionable editorial decisions.

For every headline Hearst devoted to the war, he found another opportunity to outdo the aging Pulitzer. When the *World* criticized the acclaimed 71st Regiment for retreating in the face of battle, then praised the efforts of Theodore Roosevelt and his infamous "Rough Riders," the *Journal* rushed to the regiment's defense in an exuberant display of patriotism. Pulitzer realized his faux pas (not illuminating the truth, but targeting beloved public figures), but his attempts to rectify the situation were rejected.

"Slurs on the Bravery of the Boys of the 71st," Hearst's headline proclaimed, in smaller letters scolding the *World* for crying cowardice where there was none. To further emphasize his point, Hearst furnished the report with a falsified eyewitness account of the battle—from his own perspective.[††††]

President McKinley didn't need Hearst or Pulitzer to keep the war alive and present in the public's imagination, but given the sheer volume of their vainglorious headlines and larger-than-life anecdotes, it's easy to see why the two journalists were given such a place of prominence in the history books. Whether or not the public fell for their antics is another question altogether; recent research points toward a decline in dependence on print media during the turn of the 20th century, and for the few discerning readers who had the time and inclination to peruse the entirety of the *World* or *Journal*, it seems plausible that they would have learned to take each overblown account with a grain of salt.[‡‡‡‡]

[††††] It didn't matter to Hearst that there was no conceivable way either he or supposed eyewitness Edward Marshall could have been in Cuba on the dates provided. It also didn't matter to him that Roosevelt later backed up Pulitzer's claims and expressed his profound disappointment over the desertion of the 71st.

[‡‡‡‡] "We haven't the time to read it all if we wanted to," a report in the *Fourth*

After three months, against a Spanish army debilitated by yellow fever and the unyielding efforts of Cuban insurgents, the United States came away victorious.§§§§ They had entered the fight in the final round and delivered the knockout punch. Their reward came in the form of the Treaty of Paris, which saw the Philippines, Guam, and Puerto Rico signed over to the U.S. for the tidy sum of $20 million. Cuba still wasn't free, not in the way José Martí once envisioned his country's freedom. Instead, it became a protectorate under the United States, with a leash slightly longer than the one afforded them by Spain.

Press revealed in 1899. "In the morning the paper is scanned while going to business, and in the afternoon while going home. In this short space of time we can do little more than read the headlines, and take a sip here and there of the news that interests us individually."[34] Customers were not only limiting their consumption of the dailies, but unlike the vastly more influential publications of rural America, they remained a skeptical audience. "Nothing could be more curious than the contrast between the wild aspect of the first pages of our [yellow journals] and the calm of the persons who are seen reading them," E.L. Godkin remarked in *The Nation*, citing the lack of visible reaction as proof that most readers knew how to tell a tall tale from a real one.[35]

§§§§ Tactical victory notwithstanding, American troops were similarly struck down by a combination of disease, malnutrition, inadequate shelter, and lack of proper clothing. According to the U.S. Department of Veteran Affairs, approximately 2,061 men died from non-combat factors, and an additional thousand returned home in terrible physical condition, partially due to the consumption of "embalmed beef."[36]

A return to peace...
but not prosperity

No one rejoiced more in the triumph of the U.S. over Spain than Pulitzer and Hearst. As public outrage ebbed and the press once again turned its attention to local affairs, the editors used the conclusion of the war to hog the spotlight a little longer. For once, Pulitzer was the first to make a grand gesture. He decked out Park Row in vibrant swaths of red, white, and blue bunting and was among the first to welcome home the parade of warships returning from Cuba in August.

In peacetime, as in war, Hearst refused to take the backseat to any of his rivals. When he caught wind that the Navy was preparing its parade up the Hudson River, he petitioned city mayor Robert Anderson Van Wyck to issue an official holiday in honor of the Navy's success in making "America a bigger country and the American nation a bigger nation." The idea was nixed. Wyck told the energetic editor that such matters were well outside his jurisdiction, so Hearst settled for the next best thing: An unofficial holiday sponsored by the *Journal*, during which the paper would celebrate the recent success of the Navy in the Spanish-American War with balloons, an abundance of shimmering rainbow confetti, and a special escort from the paper's own dispatch ship, *Anita*.

"*Journal*'s Plan for Full Holiday Adopted," the paper exclaimed. "All New York May Greet Our Heroes." It was close enough. Hearst hadn't needed permission to invent half of the stories he told during the war, and he didn't need any help garnering applause for his philanthropic efforts at home, either.

By the autumn of 1898, talk of Cuba and Spain had all but faded from the foremost pages of the press. The newsies lamented the end of the war; it had been a summer of prosperity, of juicy headlines and juicier illustrations, of papers that could sell themselves better and quicker than the most creative newsboy on his most inspired day. When the winter chill began to wind its way through City Hall Park once more, the newsies fished for pennies to settle their debts at the lodging houses and warmed themselves in booze-soaked, breath-warmed saloons as they pawned off the last of their evening editions.

Within the newsrooms of the twin yellow presses, Pulitzer and Hearst took stock of their gains and losses from the war. Pulitzer's *World* was still held in higher regard than the *Journal*, due to its superior credibility and circulation, but the younger journal was gaining ground quickly.

It helped that Hearst remained connected to family money. Every cent Pulitzer sunk in his fight against Hearst was coming out of his own pockets. As the war fizzled out in the summer of '98, Pulitzer was forced to trim his budgets for the paper and his own personal expenditures. He sold stock and kept an even closer eye on his wife's accounts, frugal as she claimed to be. It was the only way he could afford to keep his head above water, and, what's more, extend his dispute with the *Journal*.

The wartime circulation boom had been a great boon for the *World* and *Journal*, but it wasn't nearly enough to cover the exorbitant bills they had racked up during the crisis. Other, less sensationalized papers regained their equilibrium fairly quickly once the war was wrapped, but they didn't have the dozens of reporters, fleets of dispatch ships, and elaborate parades to pay for, either. Unfortunately for the city's child work force, the publishers' inability to climb out of the red also meant that they couldn't afford to return the wholesale cost of their newspapers to pre-war prices anytime soon. While the price around town dropped back to 50 cents per hundred papers, Pulitzer and Hearst refused to part with even a tenth of a cent per paper, claiming they needed the extra cash to cover the costs of producing the two best papers in the city.

It was true, to a point. The two editors had lost buckets of money in the war thanks to their reckless spending patterns and inexhaustible need to outdo each other. Now, they weighed limited options as they tried to recoup their losses: reducing the size and price of their papers, slashing salaries across the board, or taking a cut from the middlemen. The first solution was a non-starter. Reducing the scope and sale price of either the *World* or the *Journal* would have given the other man a definite advantage. Cutting salaries, especially those of the publications' editors and journalists, would also have backfired on the yellow journals. As they had already proven on several occasions, their employees stood ready to jump ship whenever they sensed a better deal was dangling in front of them. Stiffing the newsies an extra dime per hundred papers didn't require any additional action on the publishers' part—the prices had already been hiked up during the war for the express purpose of covering additional printing costs—and it stood to increase their profit margins by as much as a million dollars in annual revenue.

Perhaps Pulitzer and Hearst didn't think the newsies would notice if they maintained their wartime prices or, more likely, they simply didn't care. Had they been paying closer attention, they might have gotten an inkling of the trouble to come.

Back in early May, just two weeks after the United States declared war on Spain, the *World* and *Journal* made the initial bump in their wholesale prices from 50 cents per hundred papers to 60 cents a bundle. It was a common tactic used by papers who found themselves floundering for one reason or another, and never one that was well-received by the young children compelled to eat those losses. The newsies of Park Row turned on the yellow journals in an instant. They went on the offensive against the delivery wagon drivers, newsstand owners, and any boy or girl who insisted on hawking the offending papers. After getting nabbed by the cops for roughing up one of the smaller newsboys, 18-year-old striker Alfred Quinn made an impassioned plea to the court:

> "Say, this arrest is dead wrong," Quinn protested. "Shouldn't us newsboys git a chance to live? We're goin' to fight for our rights and I guess we'll get them if them fly-by-night kids that ain't newsboys as a business can be shoved out of the way. We've struck against the *Journal* and *World* and we're not sellin' no more of their extras. Why? Well, you see, they've put up the price. It began this morning. We used to get them for 50 cents a hundred, but to-day they put up the price to 60 cents and we don't handle them no more. There's 500 of us and we are going to make a fight for it."[37]

So serious were the newsies in their strike that they appealed to the local metal polishers' union for aid. The men put their faith in the children's cause, but when a delegate raised the topic at a much larger meeting for the city's Central Labor Union, it was unilaterally dismissed as "too small a matter" for them to take up.[38] Left unassisted, even 500 newsies could not maintain a strike against the two yellow papers. They lacked the manpower, stamina, and organization to grow the boycott—furthermore, they recognized the very real threat of losing their jobs during such a prosperous time. War was perfectly suited to the business of selling newspapers, and if the newsies refused to do their jobs, there would be no shortage of scabs to take their place.

A year later, that had all changed. The editors of the *World* and *Journal* may have been struggling to stay in the black, but their misfortunes paled in comparison to those of the impoverished children who patrolled the streets of New York City. The newsies, safe to say, didn't have the luxury of lending a sympathetic ear to their millionaire bosses.

At the peak of a fierce Manhattan summer, the kids' frustration had reached its natural boiling point. If the yellow journals needed a sensational story to tell, it was a sensational story they were going to get.

CHAPTER FIVE

Strike!

Newsboys vs. *The World*

*Mr. Hearst and Pulitzer, have we got news for you! See,
the World don't know but they're gonna pay. 'Stead of
hawkin' headlines, we'll be makin' 'em today…*

There was a change in the air that morning, a kind of kinetic energy that pulsed through the streets of the city. Anyone strolling along Park Row or peeping out of the windows of the *World* building might have noticed a shift in the breeze, the distilled heaviness that crept up on the tenants of Printing House Square as the newsboys and newsgirls left their homes and boarding houses, rolling out of stairwells and alleyways to make their way to the newspaper distribution depots on Frankfort Street.

Six small newsies clustered around their leader, a boy known only to the press as Jack Sullivan. The group had fashioned an informal arbitration committee and sent off a few of their ambassadors to represent the interests of all disgruntled employees of the *New York World* and *New York Journal*.

"Well, my brave men, what news?" Sullivan asked his coworkers.

The spokesman of the committee hedged. Neither Joseph Pulitzer nor William Randolph Hearst had conceded the wholesale price reduction the newsies were seeking. It was July 1899, eleven torturous months after the Spanish-American War had drawn to a close, and much to the distress of the newsies, the two publishers remained too preoccupied with their own petty feud to consider the welfare of their child laborers. There was only one recourse left.

"Its [sic] dis a way," the boy told Jack. "We went to de bloke wot sells de papers and we tells him dat its [sic] got to be two fer a cent or nuthin'. He says, 'Wot are yer goin' to do about it if yer don't get 'em?' 'Strike,' sez I, and Monix, he puts in his oar and backs me up. The bloke sez 'Go ahead and strike,' and here we is. Dat's all."

It wasn't as if the idea of a strike had never crossed the children's minds. There had been other movements in other cities, little pockets of unrest that flourished and faded with the fluctuating supply and demand of local papers.

Few were successful.

The strikes fattened editorials and gave publishers something to gripe about on slow news days, but rare was the child-led movement that inspired real panic in the newsroom. Most affairs were regarded as an unnecessary nuisance to the journalists, editors, circulation managers, and delivery wagon drivers who regularly serviced the papers. In the eyes of the editors and publishers who ran the major presses of the day, the boys and girls who circulated their publications on the streets were expendable, fickle, and prone to exaggeration. This was the portrait they offered the public: one where the newsies cared more for cards, theatre excursions, and games of crap than a fair wage. Strike leaders, if any could be singled out from the masses, were branded as rowdy and pugnacious; ill-mannered kids who couldn't appreciate the advantageous hand life had offered them.

It was a sly trick, and one that worked on a soft-hearted reader more often than not. Papers like the *World* and *Journal*, may not have had the power to start and end wars, but they were certainly capable of manipulating public sympathy when it served their bottom line. What could be easier than convincing a customer—especially one already prone to aggravation and annoyance through the newsies' regular marketing ploys—that the boycott they passed on the street corner was one borne of greed and childish emotion?

It is unknown if Jack Sullivan and his newsies knew that such strikes were usually doomed to die a quick death. Maybe they were veterans of the previous year's strike against the yellow journals, when the newsies first protested the wartime price hike. Maybe the outcome mattered little to them—maybe, even if the newsies of New York City had an inkling of the direction in which this strike was headed, they would have mounted it on principle alone.

The origin of the strike of 1899 remains shrouded in mystery, obfuscated by the lack of knowledge the newspapers had about the private formation of a newsboy-led committee or the whispers that had been passed along as the newsies gathered at the wagons and distribution offices. Still, there were theories. In a memo to Joseph Pulitzer dated July 27, 1899, Don Carlos Seitz described an unusual incident that he believed had provoked widespread unrest:

> "The strike started in Long Island City where a dishonest Journal driver stuffed sample copies in his bundles and sold his surplus, then refused to pay the boys when they complained. They tipped his wagon over and drove him out of the town and fired by their success decided to make a stand against the WORLD and Geranium [Pulitzer's code word for the *New York Journal*] for 50 cents per hundred. The news travelled over here and a young fellow named Morris Cohen, who sells about 300 *World*s a day in City Hall Park got hold of the boys and got them to strike without any formal demand, pulling the little fellows away from the windows and the newspapers did the rest."[1]*

While the real genesis of the strike may only be known to a select few, the *World* and *Journal* could agree with the newsies about one thing: By Thursday, July 20, a new strike had been mounted—and this one wasn't going away anytime soon.

---

* Seitz's story was never corroborated by any publicly printed account of the strike, and given his obvious bias in favor of the *World*, even private correspondence could not be trusted to be entirely truthful. The *Journal*, too, appeared confused about the origin of the strike; as Seitz told Pulitzer, "[Solomon Carvalho] called me up and accused us of inciting the strike."[2] Seitz also (incorrectly) suggested that the "street railway people" were the ones backing the newsies' efforts. This was far from the only instance when the narratives put forth by the newsies (via multiple non-struck newspapers) were directly countered by those of the *World* and *Journal* employees. Both had ample motivation to give biased accounts—the *World* and *Journal*, to promote themselves as fair and balanced minds under siege from greedy children; the newsies, to drum up still more sympathy from the public—further obscuring the true nature of the protest and its ensuing fallout.

"They tink we're cravens, but we'll show 'em dat we ain't," Jack told his crew, a scowl wrinkling his face. "De time is over-ripe fer action. De cops won't have no time fer us. What is de sense of de meetin'? Is it strike?"

It was, the newsies shouted.

"Well, den, de strike is ordered," the newsboy decided. "Der must be no half measures, my men. If you sees any one sellin' de 'Woild' or 'Joinal,' swat 'em."

A voice piped up from the crowd. "You mean swipe de papes?"

"Sure—tear 'em up, trow 'em in de river—any ole ting. If der's no furder bizness de meetin's adjoined."[3]

The newsies had their marching orders. Each boy and girl carried bravado and spunk in spades, but they would need more than sheer moxie alone in order to ignite a battle against some of the most powerful figures in New York City, figures who cared little that their new opponents were also young and fragile. Taking on the *World* and *Journal* meant taking on every person in the papers' offices and back pockets: the newsdealers, the police, even the mayor of New York himself.

They were impossible odds, to be sure. It would require something truly remarkable to outwit and outmaneuver New York's most influential businessmen, and soon, the newsies found exactly what they were looking for—not a handful of smooth stones, nor the elastic arm of a young shepherd boy, but something just as improbable and lucky: a rare window of opportunity.

Trolley strike sparks inspiration

Several weeks before Jack Sullivan and his crew got the idea to go up against Pulitzer and Hearst, another strike brewed across the river in Brooklyn. The streetcar operators of the Brooklyn Rapid-Transit Company and Metropolitan Street Company had long been dissatisfied with the pay cuts and labor violations exacted by their bosses. Their daily wages were slashed from $2.40-2.50 to just $2 a day, and they were not paid for time spent taking meals or waiting for trolleys throughout the workday, a clear violation of the ten-hour law that required workers to be fully compensated for a maximum of 10 hours in a 12-hour period. Assuming a worker was assigned to a 10-hour shift and spent an hour or more waiting for their trolley to arrive at the depot, the transit company was only obligated to pay them for nine hours of work and could not legally offer them more hours to make up for their lost wages.

Three years earlier, in the winter of 1895, the streetcar operators and brakemen had struck for similar reasons. Management refused to budge on the ten-hour law, inspiring a city-wide strike that involved over 5,000 workers and effectively brought the city to a grinding halt. Chaos reigned supreme; the strikers swarmed the police officers and militiamen and replacement workers, pelting them with coal and stones whenever they attempted to get the transit system back up and running. After nearly a month, the strike was quelled, but no substantial gains had been made by the trolley workers' union and their relationship with the transit companies had all but disintegrated.

By mid-July 1899, that sense of discontent had only grown stronger. Even the idle chatter of the city's operators and brakemen provoked unrest; following whispers of an impending strike, the company's stock plummeted and the local papers scrambled to report that such drastic measures would never come to fruition.

Had the two sides engaged in any genuine attempt to work out a compromise, those predictions might have eventually proved correct. There was too much bad blood between them, however, and they inched no closer to an agreement that summer than they had several years earlier. On July 13, 1899, eighty-one disgruntled District Master Workmen assembled to discuss the collective rights of over 50,000 employees.

The consensus? Strike.

Before dawn broke on July 16, over a thousand trolley workers took to the streets. They adopted the same ferocious tactics of their predecessors: cutting wires, ripping up the lines, heaving large boulders and chunks of granite onto the tracks, and pitching rocks at the cars that tried to run and the police officers who stood guard over them. According to the *World*'s estimate, their efforts curbed the number of active trolley cars from 1,250 to just 750. The workers lost a collective

$4,750 during the first day of the strike, peanuts compared to the projected $22,500 losses the companies had taken.[4]

The only problem, it seemed, is that they had forecast greater numbers of strikers than those who initially went out. General Master Workman John N. Parsons attributed the mistake to the fact that the first day of the strike coincided with payday, and many of the workers wanted to collect their wages before staging their rebellion. There was no way of knowing how long the strike might last or how long they'd forfeit their daily earnings, if they had jobs to return to at all.

Nevertheless, newspapers like the *New York Sun* and *Times* ridiculed the protestors and accused rival publishers of collusion with strike instigators. They rattled off the names of the lines that were kept open throughout the first round of demonstrations as proof that the strike was on the cusp of petering out.

"The 'great' trolley strike ordered by the Knights of Labor in Brooklyn at 2 o'clock yesterday morning fizzled. It fizzled like a yellow journal dream," scoffed the *New York Sun*.[5]

"There is, moreover, no evidence of any considerable sympathy with them in the public mind," the *New York Times* added. "There can be none when so many of the workmen themselves are openly opposed to the strike as needless and foolish."[6]

The last strike had ended in a bloody fight between the striking workers and the bayonet-wielding militia, who ended up skewering a few poor souls during one tense stand-off. This time, the strikers knew they'd have to adopt more extreme measures—and convince more of their ranks to join arms and fists for the cause—if they were to secure a concession of any kind.

Two days after the strike began, the *World* ran a half-page illustration of a great fire licking the sides of a streetcar and its terrified operator. It was a grisly sight. One motorman had directed his streetcar straight through a bonfire, the *World* claimed, scattering burning boxes and barrels rather than facing the angry mob of strikers.[7]

Worse was yet to come.

The day after the bonfire, a hundred police officers were summoned in the middle of the night when a loud explosion rattled a switch tower in Brooklyn and collapsed a few sections of elevated railroad tracks. During the day, protestors swarmed the replacement conductors, beating them so badly that many were hospitalized as a result. Women were the primary instigators of the attacks on the police; they directed the crowds to bombard the officers with stones and debris and paid children a penny for each missile they threw, confident that the men would refrain from retaliating with their clubs and guns. The courtrooms of the city filled to capacity with belligerent youths who had taken up the cause on the strikers' behalf. Other workers sabotaged the remaining trolley cars by plugging their switches and greasing the rails, and only the conductors' quick reflexes prevented serious harm to their passengers as they maneuvered onto safer stretches of track.[8]

The strikers' antics persisted day after day, spreading to Manhattan, Long Island City, and Staten Island. Despite the general inconvenience they caused local police and passengers, though, they had yet to gain the upper hand in the fight for workers' rights. Not only did the transit companies refuse to meet their demands, but Metropolitan Street Railroad Company President H.H. Vreeland pretended that there was no strike happening in the first place.

"There is no strike, and there will be none to-morrow," Vreeland announced. "We will carry all our patrons as usual. There will be no danger."[9]

It was a ridiculous line to trot out, especially given the hordes of police officers that had long been engaged in fending off the protestors—and, as workman Parsons alleged, instigating unprovoked attacks on the striking workers, too. A few officers had even brought their pistols to the gatherings and fired into the crowds of men, women, and children.

"[It] conclusively proves that President Vreeland depends on [the cops] to settle the strike," Parsons told the World.[10]

If there was one subset of New Yorkers who benefitted from this melee between the cops and strikers, it was the newsies. The newsboys and newsgirls of New York City had their own strike in mind, and they could sniff out an opportunity better than anyone. With the cops tied up in the trolley strike, no one would be watching them as they plundered the newsstands and distribution centers that served the *World* and *Journal*.† No one would care if they ripped up some papers or knocked the heads of a few scabs and deliverymen; and if they did, the newsies were sure that they would easily outnumber their detractors.

On the eve of July 20, 1899, the stage was primed and ready for a new performance. Hours earlier, newsboy Lawrence Weggenman had been spotted hawking the two yellow journals at the Long Island City train station. It wasn't to be tolerated for a second. When news of the event reached Manhattan, the newsies sent a delegate to reason with Weggenman—by way of several closed fists.

Who then mobilized the thousands of newspaper hawkers working in New York City? When did the children's frustration over lost profits and a poor compensation structure finally become unbearable? The details are still a bit fuzzy. After all, it's not as if the papers chronicling the strike were given advance notice of the movement; at least, none appeared to take the children up on such an offer. And, days before the papers realized what was happening, the newsboys and news-girls had already organized a strike committee and started spreading the news from borough to borough. Printing House Square was vacant, the cops distracted, and the *World* and *Journal* oblivious to the hit they were about to take.

The summer was ripe for protest.

In other words, the newsies were ready to seize the day.

The strike begins

"Dey put up prices to six papes fer a dime w'en de war began," 11-year-old strike leader Boots McAleenan told the *Sun*. "Den de war quit an we wanted to git 'em two fer a cent again, but dey wouldn't. Dat's what we're goin' on strike 'er now. We're doin' it now because de cops is all busy, an' we can do any scab

---

† In fact, it was this strategy that worked to both the benefit of the newsies and the ill of the trolley workers. As the children's strike grew in scope and magnitude, less public attention was devoted to the adult strikers and the yellow journals were kept off of the trolley cars altogether. For this reason, strike leader "Blind" Diamond confided in the *New York Sun*, the newsboys and newsgirls expected no help from the adult unions.

newsboy dat shows his face without police interference. We're here fer our rights, an' we will die defending' 'em. At de rates dey give us now we can't make only four cents on ten papes, an' dat ain't enough to pay fer snipes."[11‡]

It was an eloquent argument, if unfairly caricaturized by the *Sun*. After their first unsuccessful attempt at negotiations, the newsies had officially declared war against Pulitzer's *World* and Hearst's *Journal*. Their dissatisfaction over the publishers' ten-cent price hike had simmered long enough—now, with most of the city's policemen tied up in the trolley workers' strike, it had started to boil over.

Pulitzer and Hearst's rivals reveled in the newsies' protest. It was a fortuitous moment for any paper looking to expand their customer base or boost their sales. For too long, the yellow papers had highlighted the scandals of socialites and plutocrats, wars fought on distant shores and the broken promises and party lines of would-be politicians. Rarely, if ever, was that critical lens turned inward. The newspaper industry often had a rough time convincing the public of the evils of the yellow press, but only the cold-hearted consumer would side with two wealthy, influential newspaper moguls over the poor and earnest newsies.

It wasn't as if the newsies were asking for the world. They had no designs to further cripple the profits of the *World* and *Journal*, as the publishers' ongoing feud had already done a fine job of that all by itself. The newsies didn't demand kindness from the distributors and delivery wagon drivers, more pleasant selling conditions, snazzier headlines, shorter hours, compensation for unsold newspapers, or annual perks like the Thanksgiving turkeys and theatre tickets that were often distributed by the proprietors of local papers who wanted to appear charitable in the society pages. They weren't asking for a raise or even, though they deserved it, a livable wage.

All they wanted was a fair shake of the leg. The ten-cent hike barely scratched their profit margins in the spring of 1898, when the presses were hot and the news so explosive it

---

‡ A "scab" was a replacement worker who assumed the daily responsibilities of the strikers and declined to join their union or cause.

could have sold itself on merit alone. Now, with Pulitzer and Hearst digging in their heels at the thought of relinquishing even a tenth of a cent to their adolescent workforce, a strike not only became necessary, but inevitable.

By 9 a.m. on the morning of July 20, 1899, over 300 child newspaper hawkers surrounded the distributors of the *World* and *Journal*. Most brandished sticks, staves, and clubs, their weapons dangling on strings around their wrists like a those of a miniaturized police force. Others carried crudely-made banners and advertised placards in their caps: "We don't sell scab papers," "Down with the Yellow Journals!" "Down with the *World* and *Journal*!" "Now is the Time to Arbitrate!"

When the first delivery wagons turned onto Frankfort Street, the children began their assault. The drivers were pelted from all directions, so fiercely and constantly that they appealed to the nearby police station, which could only procure two cops as the rest were tied up with the trolley strike on the other side of the East River. The strikers jeered the police officers. *Go to bed*, they said. *Sleep it off.*

The newsies were ferocious in their crusade. There was no debate to be had within the throng the protestors, no fair trial for the dissenter who chose to carry the *World* and *Journal* under their arm. Any newspaper seller caught with either of the offending sheets could count on a swift sentencing in the form of a fist aimed at their face.

"Ye don't sell no more *Woild* 'r *Joinal*, 'r ye get yer face punched in, see?" the strikers shouted.[12]

By mid-morning, whispers of a concession began to trickle through the crowd like the fine smoke of a morning cigarette. There was a rumor that the distributors of the *World* were offering papers for three cents a sheet, well above the newsies' initial asking price and a bargain far too tempting to be true.

Another strike leader, 11-year-old Moses Burris, investigated the claim himself.

"Say, is dis a charity game or does it go all de time?"

"Don't know," came the answer. "The price is three for a cent now."

"Do we git any wroten [sic] agreement from youse guys dat it keeps down to union rates?"

There was no satisfactory answer to be given. It was a thin-ly-veiled ploy to assuage the newsies' hurt feelings and entice them to pick up their papers and resume their posts for the day. Burris scoffed at the offer, saying "Don't touch the scab papes! Dey're tryin' to work us."[13]

The rest of the crowd was not so easily convinced it was a con. Across the street, the *Journal* advertised a five-for-one deal so sweet that the office was soon inundated with the eager faces of the striking masses. Pandemonium reigned on Frankfort Street; Burris rushed to stop the protestors from accepting the deal, while 15-year-old John Gallupo and 13-year-old Louis Kirlow tried in vain to enforce the ban.

The *World* would not be outdone by its fiercest rival. It tossed free papers to the children, several of whom grabbed frantically at the merchandise and began heading for their customary street corners and selling spots. Burris, Gallupo, and Kirlow were incredulous. The strike was only hours old, and already it had been threatened by the underhanded deal-ings of the very papers that inspired the ruckus in the first place. The boys enlisted the help of a dozen strikers and began to wail on the deserters, snatching the papers from their arms and filling the air with jagged scraps of newsprint.

A police officer materialized in the midst of the chaos and plucked the ringleaders from the fight. He kept a firm grasp on the newsies as he marched them over to Centre Street Court, where the magistrate proved less forceful, but no less forgiv-ing. Burris and Gallupo were charged with disorderly conduct and committed to the care of the Gerry Society, based in part on the officer's complaint that Burris was a "perfect demon" who had tried to maim one of the scabs.

Kirlow was even unluckier. He had not only helped scare off the scabs, but was accused of barging into the *Journal*'s distri-bution offices and clubbing the newsies who had lined up to receive the day's edition. The magistrate recognized Kirlow as a repeat offender and ordered a six-month confinement in the Juvenile Asylum, no minor sentencing for a boy so far below the asylum's requisite age limit for release.

The arrests had a sobering effect on the strikers. They proudly rebuffed the *World* and *Journal*'s disingenuous offers and marched on to Wall Street, purging the sidewalks and stoops of scabs, bloodying the noses of those who needed convincing, and scattering the carcasses of fresh newspapers wherever they went. It was a veritable parade that descended on the Financial District, bringing brokers and businessmen to the windows and doorways of the buildings as the boys and girls passed by. They showered the children with pennies, nickels, dimes, and quarters, and down in the streets, banana pushcart sellers and newspaper stand owners scrambled to avoid the oncoming mob. Those who were larger and stronger than the newsies tried to stand their ground, but even "The Squealer," a stout newswoman whose piercing cry the *Sun* characterized as that of an "enraged elephant," was forced to give way when a band of newsboys stripped her of her skirt after catching her with new copies of the *Journal* in tow.

"Dem papers is boycotted an' we don't allow none t' be sold," warned the strikers' spokesman. "See? If you wasn't a lady ye'd had yer face poked in. Now git!"[14]

"The Squealer" didn't need to be told twice. The boys exchanged her skirt for her guarantee that no more boycotted papers would be found among her wares.

Harsher measures were applied to the male newspaper hawkers who defected from the strike. A pair of older newspaper sellers, 23-year-old A.J. Klock and Bertha Saffe, were spotted trading *Journals* at the foot of the Brooklyn Bridge and arrested after engaging in fisticuffs with a band of strikers. Fifteen-year-old newsboy Emil Kahune, meanwhile, was turned over to the Gerry Society when an onlooker witnessed him applying a severe beating to 15-year-old defector Milo Green.

Rudderless and spent, the strikers put down their sticks and pamphlets for the day and retired to the cool shade of the alley to shoot craps. Their faces were painted with blood, sweat, dirt, and ink as they mulled over the events of the day and plotted their recourse for the next morning.

Elsewhere in the city, alarm bells sounded in the publishing offices along Newspaper Row. News of the newsies' strike had arrived at Pulitzer's newsroom well before the first wave of strikers clogged up Wall Street, and both the *World* and *Journal* were considerably rattled, loathe as they were to admit it.

Emory Foster, then-editor of the *Evening Journal*, insisted that both papers acquiesce to the strikers' demands of 50 cents per hundred papers, for which he was swiftly remanded by dissenters within the Publishers' Association. The price, they told him, had been fixed by mutual agreement and could not be adjusted. Seitz, meanwhile, denied all rumors that the *World* was secretly going for the strikers' preferred rate in certain areas of the state.[§]

While turmoil reigned behind the scenes, a public concession was out of the question. Still, the *New York Herald* noted that a few employees had started to dust off volumes of arbitration advice in preparation for a compromise with the newsies. Had the children been aware that they had so unnerved their opponents, they may have relaxed their grip and lost the war they were so desperate to wage.

For now, however, they had gotten their first heady, intoxicating sip of victory on the streets...and were soon thirsting for more.

An unlikely alliance

Joseph Pulitzer made a striking Goliath to the newsies' David, but unlike the club-wielding Philistine, he could not be bothered to show up to battle such a miniscule opponent. The 52-year-old publisher was not, as some might have surmised, silently fuming in the copper-domed offices of the *World* building, nor was he putting the finishing touches on a calculated revenge. In fact, he wasn't in New York at all. He had retired to the seaside town of Bar Harbor, Maine, spent from a recent European excursion and not yet recuperated enough to return to the daily grind that his empire demanded.

True to form, Pulitzer was at his unhappiest when he felt others had kept him the dark, particularly on matters of his own business. He demanded that Seitz send him with frequent

---

§ In a hastily-scrawled note to Pulitzer, Seitz confided the most persistent and egregious rumor of all: that Hearst himself had considered yielding to the newsboys' initial terms of settlement. "I cannot believe he will be so foolish," Seitz assured Pulitzer.[15] It was a premonition that would be fulfilled only days later, when Hearst did an about-turn and resolved to "stick it out to the end of time."

reports, often delivered in telegrams and memos, on every-thing from the titles of newspaper columns to the circulation numbers for every rival publisher in Manhattan. By July 20, nothing was more pressing nor pertinent to his interests than the newsies' boycott.

Seitz couldn't send the telegrams fast enough. The move-ment had quickly infected the Bowery, the Bronx, Harlem, Jersey City, Newark, Hoboken, Long Island City, and Brooklyn, and was growing more contagious by the day. As the first day of the strike drew to a close, 14-year-old District Master Workboy of the Brooklyn Union, Spot Conlon, donned a pair of pink suspenders and crossed the Brooklyn Bridge to meet with the Manhattan newsie delegation and their General Master Workboy, "Blind" Diamond.

"We bring youse greetings a' promises of support," Conlon told the contingent. "We have tied up de scab sheets so tight dat y' can't buy one fer a dollar in de street. Hold out, me gallant kids, an' to-morrer I meself, at de head of t'ree t'ousand noble hearts from Brooklyn, will be over here t' help youse win yer noble scrap fer freedom an' fair play."[16]

A roar erupted from the crowd, who clung to Conlon's promise that support would arrive in the morning. They agreed to limited the violence to a "poke in de jor" against the scab workers, a vow none of them ever intended to keep.

Spot Conlon wasn't the only one to pledge his support to the newsies' efforts. Blocks away from the center of the strike, a pair of small newsboys collapsed on a stoop and wept. They didn't have the manpower to overpower the bigger newspaper strikers who ran that neighborhood and had received blows even more painful than the ones they hoped to inflict.

"If we only had de right kind of a leader up here we'd be all right," they wailed. "But Jack [Sullivan] is too busy in Wall Street."[17]

What happened next, according to the *New-York Tribune*, appeared to the children as miraculous and awe-inspiring as an act of God. A red-haired newsgirl named Jennie, looking for all the world like a vengeful Joan of Arc, charged into the fray against the newsies who dared peddle the forbidden papers. The newsboys' oppressors didn't wait for another fist to bloody their ghost-white cheeks. They took one look at her and fled in all directions, their yellow papers dropping like corpses on the streets behind them.

Only two days into the strike, Seitz was worried. He'd witnessed Pulitzer weather similar newsie-led strikes in St. Louis, but nothing of this magnitude had ever rattled the publisher.

> "The newsboy's strike has grown into an extensive and menacing affair," he wrote Pulitzer, "encouraged by other newspapers and backed, [*Journal* business manager Solomon Carvalho] believes, by street railway people. It is proving a serious problem. Incendiary circulars are being distributed and the boys so far have sent two *Journal* men to the Manhattan Hospital and have scared three *World* men so that they have disappeared from their posts. A call is out for a Mass Meeting of the boys in front of the Pulitzer Building and we have just been compelled to ask the police for assistance in the matter."

If this seemed strange to Pulitzer, stranger still was Seitz's next plan of action. He had paid a visit to Carvalho and agreed to hire a posse of adult men to peddle both the *World* and *Journal* when the distribution offices opened on Monday morning. Any kind of alliance between the two rivals was suspect, naturally, but Seitz recognized that the newsies' strike could cripple both papers' circulations if it was allowed to run unchecked.

> "We ran out but 281,000 [papers] yesterday," the memo continued, "a drop certainly of 60,000 while the returns will probably be very large. [Carvalho] did not state their losses, but said that they were very, very heavy. He did not show any signs of weakening, however, but on my way out I met Gush [Pulitzer's code word for Hearst] and a group of newsboys who ran away from him with cheerful smiles and calling out, 'Goodbye, Mr. Gush.'"[18]

For Pulitzer and Hearst, opposing the newsies wasn't just a matter of retaining readership, but of preserving the delicate relationships they had with their advertisers. Yellow journalism attracted public interest, but it was advertising that kept the papers afloat and financed the bloodthirsty competition between the two editors. The businesses and organizations that had been so keen to place their copy in the pages of New

York's most prominent publications were the first to detect the dangerous ramifications of the strike. As soon as the children's movement gained traction, the advertisers went to Pulitzer and Hearst to demand refunds.

Together, Seitz and Carvalho puzzled over dropped ads and dwindling sales figures, but more troubling still was the effect the boycott was having on the rest of the city. Public feeling was with the protestors, not just among the throngs of common men and women but among a variety of newspapers, too. The *Commercial Advertiser* picked on the *World* and *Journal* without reserve, as did the *Telegram*, the *Daily News*, the *Mail and Express*, the *Sun*, and the *Tribune*. Seitz privately complained that those sitting on the editorial desks had let their sympathies flow unchecked. Any reasonable business dealer, he figured, could be counted on for discretion and loyalty—to the Publishers' Association, if not the business of publishing itself—inasmuch as it served their own self-interests. If it occurred to him that the lesser New York papers were thriving off the popularity of the city's newest scandal, he didn't care to admit it.

Down on the streets below Newspaper Row, the strike raged on. Sentiment ran high and wild as the newsies paraded through the city, their hats and jackets adorned with signs that protested the yellow papers and their use of scabs. No newsstand on Wall Street (or any other street, for that matter) was safe from the rap of their sticks and fists as they passed by.

"Dere's t'ree t'ousand of us, and we'll win sure," one newsboy boasted to the *Times*.[19]

The kid had every reason to feel confident. Even as New York City cops continued to arrest armfuls of children for their merciless treatment of "scabs and traitors," it was proving near impossible to rein in each chaotic outbreak. On Saturday, July 22, the newsies distributed pamphlets advertising the boycott, with the words "World" and "Journal" drawn up in special yellow lettering. Within their own circle, there were whispers of a formal meeting of the strikers at the intersection of Park Row and Frankfort Street. As the police were busy protecting the delivery wagon drivers, it was getting increasingly harder to intercept the wagons each morning. The newsies decided to turn their attention to the scab workers: anyone caught with the papers would receive a club to the temple.

"Yer clubs ain't made fer toot'picks," "Blind" Diamond reminded the newsies. "If dey's any scab papes sold on dis row to-day an' somebody don't git hurted dat means deat' to our union. Remember dat an' do yer duty an' de scabs."[20]

Cross-Eyed Peters, a newsboy representative from the uptown troops, echoed Diamond's heartfelt statement and vowed to catch every scab above Fourteenth Street and put them in the "horspital."

In the afternoon, a dozen such incidents played out in front of the distributors and cops. The *Sun* painted the scene thusly:

> "These little street dramas were usually in two short acts filled with action. First act: The seller of the scab papers dealing with a customer: scouts approaching from the wings: sharp signal whistles: customer unconscious, dealer nervous. Second act: A cry, "Sock it to de scab:" a rush, the thwack of sticks on the dealer's head and shoulders: dismay and flight of the customer, pursued by shouts of "Scab!" capture of the contraband papers: police somewhat belated: curtain."[21]

It was more curious and compelling theatre than any Broadway had to offer. The newsies were wise enough to scatter their attacks over a wide enough vicinity that a few policemen could do little good, and reconvened for a jubilant celebration when enough of the papers had been confiscated and ripped up.

Foolproof though that plan may have been, the newsies could hardly boast the same bravado in a man-to-man fight against the cops. The officers had clubs, too, and they swung theirs "low and scythe-like" as they took careful aim at the children. On occasion, an offending newspaper seller would find themselves surrounded by a small guard of cops, then encircled again with several dozen newsies. No customer found the setup appealing, and while the scabs and rogue sellers may have kept their yellow sheets, no one else dared touch them.

'Kill any gye what sells a scab extry'

Support from Spot Conlon and his Brooklyn contingent was still forthcoming. The group of "three thousand noble hearts" had failed to show up by Saturday morning, and a message soon arrived to inform the Manhattan newsies that Conlon had too many Brooklyn-based scabs to lend a hand to his brothers and sisters elsewhere in New York.

Frustrating as it may have been for those on the front lines of the Bowery and Printing House Square to hear, it was no bluff. The Brooklyn newsies were indeed in the thick of their own battles. They plucked the yellow newspapers from the laps of trolley passengers and dogged the route of every newsie who concealed a *World* or *Journal* under their coats, even tossing one such rule-breaker into the river. They organized 200 newsies in a back alley and formed their own union with their own leaders and flyers. According to various reports from the *Sun* and *Tribune*, most of the newsie strikers had outfitted themselves with table legs and red sticks that looked as if they had been fashioned from "fat wheel spokes"; these the children brought down on the heads of unsuspecting violators without reserve or discrimination.

One strike defector, Michael Romeo, crossed the Brooklyn Bridge with a supply of the forbidden papers. How he escaped the wrath of the Manhattan newsies was unclear, but there was no mistaking the fury of the group awaiting him on the other side. The boy met the newsies' red clubs with a knife, taking swipes at the crowd as he pushed his way through them.

Another of the smaller fellows, a newsboy by the name of "Eddy" Murphy, fended off the rogue with the red club, bringing it down on the boy's wrist and head over and over again. The club won; the knife slipped into the gutter and Murphy's comrades kicked and punched the scab before fleeing the scene, leaving him with a smattering of deep bruises and a head wound for his troubles.

The scabs weren't the only ones who felt the painful ramifications of the boycott. Wagons full of *World* and *Journal* papers were sent back to New York City at the end of the day, their wares unpurchased and unwanted. An anonymous newsdealer told the *Sun* that the combined losses of both cities amounted to 100,000 papers a day. Whatever the toll the violence was taking on the children of New York, it was seeing results.

"De papes has got ter come down ter two fer a cent an' dey gotter put de agreement out on der bulletin boards," Diamond told reporters.[22] The children had no interest in arbitration, but some feared that the publishers would eventually renege on any proposed solution to the strike.

They were right to be concerned.

The strikers organize

The portly police officer standing on the street corner and the reporter scrambling to make deadline may have found the pandemonium of the children's strike both overwhelming and perplexing, but within the ranks of the newsies, there was a controlled chaos to their movement.

The newsboys and newsgirls appointed leaders, at least one per district, who also served as representatives within the larger body of strikers. They formed committees that determined where and when the scab beatings would take place, how much violence to inflict on the police officers and rogue newspaper sellers, and what form of punishment best fit crimes like petty thievery and outright betrayal. When one newsboy was caught filching a peach from a grocery stand, the newsies forced him to return the stolen fruit and withstand ten sharp blows from a flat stick as penance. The newsies' committee then took the matter to a nearby officer and reported the crime, promising that there would be no further illegal activity from their group.

The policeman just stared blankly. It was impossible to separate the newsies' battle cries and warmongering from real crimes, and he couldn't be bothered to punish a boy who had likely split the day's activities between stealing a peach and braining countless scabs.

"Wot de hell can yer do wit' dat kind of a cop agin yer?" strike leader McAleen complained.[23]

More serious was the case of the newswomen who sold papers at the entrance to the Brooklyn Bridge. They smuggled copies of the barred publications under their shawls and skirts and offered them to passersby upon request. Perhaps the newsies had learned their lesson with "The Squealer." Perhaps they realized there was nothing to gain and no respect to be earned by disrobing the women in order to prevent them from hawking their wares. Perhaps, as "Kid Blink" later explained, it was just a matter of newfound chivalry.

"A feller can't soak a lady, and yer can't get at them women's scab papes without soakin' them," he said. "We'll have to let them alone, I guess! Anyway, we've got Annie with us. Yer can bet there ain't no *World*s or *Journal*s under her skirts."[24]

The newsboys needn't have worried too much about the rogue newswomen who flaunted scab papers and issued empty threats. The few women who remained on their side had no such qualms about "soaking a lady," as newswoman Annie made perfectly clear to a rival seller when she told the *Sun* she could "tie seven Mrs. Corcorans in a knot [...] and invited Mrs. Corcoran to come up to her stand and take a licking."[25] The request was understandably refused.

Chasing down every defiant strikebreaker and distributor was difficult work, but it didn't exempt the newsies from their day jobs. They simply couldn't afford to take a protracted leave of absence from newspaper hawking, even in pursuit of fair treatment from the vendors they depended on. Many children had families to support, parents to help, and brothers and sisters to feed. Those who were homeless used their daily earnings to purchase lodging and food at charity houses throughout New York City, necessities too precious to forfeit even as they felt compelled to take a moral stand against their employers.

Thankfully for the working children of the city, New York boasted more daily papers than most American metropolises. None of the rival papers had quite the pull and pizzazz of the *World* and *Journal*, to be sure, but readers were often sympathetic to the children's plight and didn't need much convincing to patronize other publications, if only as a temporary alternative.

The *New York Evening Telegram* was a favorite of the newsies—so much so, in fact, that newsdealers were soon required to triple and quadruple their usual orders for the paper. The newsboys and newsgirls gladly advertised the paper, plastering the name of the *Telegram* on their banners and signs as they moved from street corner to street corner.

If there was one thing that reached an easy consensus among the children, it was the necessity of inflicting violence on those who stood in their way. Most of the newswomen may have gotten a pass, but the scabs and hired workers did not.¶ On Friday afternoon, as many as five hundred protestors thronged about Columbus Avenue, draping the newsstands and lampposts with signs that read "Help the Newsboys," "We Will Fight for Our Rights," and "Our Cause Is Just." They charged the incoming wagons and assaulted the men who attempted to muscle their way through the crowd to sell the papers.

One man refused to give in to the strikers. When the newsies blocked his path, he placed his bundle back on the street and sat on it, determined to hold his ground. He was heavyset, with a big red nose that grew even bigger and redder as the newsies inflicted their blows with clubs and barrel staves. When the police finally stepped in to quash the attack, the man was red all over and quite subdued, his papers splashed with blood and shredded like confetti over the road.[27]

By the end of the afternoon, every newsdealer in the area had gladly abandoned their post. It was clear the newsies ruled the streets of New York City—and, in due time, it would become equally obvious that the real strike decisions weren't being made among the wagons and distribution depots of Frankfort Street, but in the shiny offices of the yellow journals themselves.

'We're the strikers, Mr. Hearst'

After three days of marches, fights, rallies, and arrests, the newsies finally got an audience with someone who mattered: William Randolph Hearst himself. Over the weekend, a small crowd of newsboys ambushed the editor as he stepped out of a cab and made his way to the entrance of his building.

¶   The newsies made a rare exception for the scab who renounced his ways and took up the strike banner, as one small fellow learned to do the hard way. He solicited the protection of a police officer as he traipsed down to the distribution center to collect his yellow papers, but Young "Mush" Myers quickly distracted the cop and another fifteen newsboys chased the boy down and pummeled him into submission. When the scab was sufficiently swollen and bruised, blood gushing from his nose and tears streaming down his face, the newsies offered him a position within their ranks. The boy hastily accepted the offer. Not an hour later, the boy was spotted wailing on another scab.[26]

"We're the strikers, Mr. Hearst," one of the newsboys said.

"Well, boys, what can I do for you?" Hearst said. He had appeared content to let Carvalho handle the counterattacks against the protestors for the last several days, but now that he was looking at the children face-to-face, he at least had the good grace to apply a thin veneer of tact.

"Well, we want 100 papers for 50 cents," the boys replied. "We get it from the other papers except the *World*."

Hearst invited the newsies to accompany him to his office. It was quite literally the chance of a lifetime, and one the children knew wouldn't come around again. They assembled an impromptu committee featuring strike leader "Kid Blink" and newsboys Jim Seabook, Jim Gady, and Dave Simon, and went in.

Their hopes were dashed soon enough. If it was a concession the newsboys were hoping for, the editor-in-chief was in no position to give one. Rather, in true Hearstian fashion, he wanted to know exactly how the newsies had managed to damage the *World*'s profits.

> "He wanted to know what the *World* was goin' to do," Blink told the rest of the newsies after the meeting. "I told him that we was dealing with the *Journal* now, and that if he cut [the wholesale prices of the newspapers] the *World* would cut quick enough. He says he had to talk it over with some other guys before he'd give an answer, and then I asked him if he wouldn't arbitrate, like his paper says. He laughed and said he'd give us an answer Monday right here, and that if he decided to arbitrate he'd meet us at the Broadway Central Hotel."[28]

The newsies erupted in shouts and cheers. Surely, such an amicable conversation signaled the end of the strike, they thought.

If only it were that simple.

Hearst's words had resurrected their hope of reaching a satisfying resolution, but there was plenty of reason for caution—not the least of which was the way the two papers continued deceptive practices like offering three- to five-paper bundles for a single cent. Their editors also sent emissaries to the lodging houses of the city, seeking able-bodied men who would take a 40-cent-per hundred deal and an additional $2 per day to combat the newsies' efforts.

On the morning of July 23, 1899, a man with the brashness of a lifelong drunk and the disheveled appearance of an insomniac showed up at the office of the *New York Sun*.

> "I'm a Bowery bum, and one of about a hundred that's signed to take out *World*s and *Journal*s to-morrow," he revealed. "But say, we ain't a-going to do it. It's all a bluff. We told them scouts that we'd do it when they offered $2 a day, but every one of us has decided to stick by the newsboys and we won't sell no papers. Put that in the pape and tell the public that it's on the level."[29]

The gesture was greatly appreciated by the children. They had fought long and hard for their rights, and now that the initial novelty of the strike was beginning to fade, they needed public support more desperately than ever before. In the high offices of the *World* and *Journal*, meanwhile, the men's decision was carefully noted by the yellow journals.

If Pulitzer and Hearst were going to beat the newsies once and for all, they were going to have to get creative.

CHAPTER SIX

Once and for All

Bribery, Betrayal, and a Concession

Finally, we're raising the stakes, this time whatever it takes! This time the union awakes—once and for all!

The newsies of New York had the city in a chokehold. There wasn't a street corner or newspaper stand that hadn't felt the fist of a newsboy or newsgirl, nor a non-struck paper that had yet to benefit from the plummeting sales of the *New York World* and *New York Journal*. Public sentiment was with the children, if not out of sympathy for their plight then certainly out of fear for their own well-being. The strikers weren't prone to excusing the behavior of readers who dared to crack open the front page of a yellow journal on street corners and trolley cars.

After four days of demonstrations and revolt, the publishers still refused to budge. Neither the *World* nor the *Journal* had given a single drop of ink to cover the strike in their editorials, and the hasty promises that William Randolph Hearst made to the newsboys at the start of their boycott had gone unfulfilled. There would be no arbitration and no compromise, not as long as the children insisted on clobbering scab workers and running roughshod over each delivery wagon that crossed their path.*

On July 24, strike leader Kid Blink assembled 500 of his companions outside of the *New York Tribune* building. It was

---

* *World* business manager Don Seitz informed the *Brooklyn Daily Eagle* that the yellow journals were resolute in their decision not to arbitrate with the newsies, as the children's demands had not been taken in private to the publishers first.

time to take more drastic measures, he told the newsies, not just for the pleasure of sticking it to Pulitzer and Hearst, but to drum up more support for their cause. They would organize a parade and wave their banners through every major street and thoroughfare in New York City.

> "De bigger dis p'rade is, de bigger success it is," he said. "If we p'rade in de morning we kin all go out, 'cause it's before de evening papes come out and nobody can't be detained by business. Den again d'yer remember what happened when a few of us went down into Wall Street de oder day? Didn't we get more nickels and dimes in than we've had since? We want de business men with us if we're goin' ter keep dis fight up, and ter git 'em we must p'rade down their way."[1]

The newsies took their parade seriously. It wasn't a preemptive celebration, but a strategic marketing tactic designed to pull in as many supporters as possible. They carefully charted a route from City Hall Park up through the Bowery and Fifth Avenue to Washington Square, hired a band and carriages, and pooled $11 to furnish 11,000 flyers, on which was printed the heartfelt slogan "Help the Struggling Newsboys." They weren't looking for handouts, the newsies explained to strike sympathizers, but assistance in boycotting the two yellow papers. (As the New York Sun observed, they weren't above scooping up the spare change that fell at their feet, either.[2]) Cleverer still were the homemade signs the strikers had fashioned from newsprint and scraps of wood. They had collected bundles of the illicit papers and carefully cut out a trolley strike headline from the World, leaving only the words that spelled out "Strikers Still Firm" and ignoring the part that read, "But Cars Still Running."

Had the strikers more foresight and less enthusiasm, they might have realized that the city had no intention of allowing them a parade. Staging one would require authorization from both city mayor Robert Anderson Van Wyck and police superintendent William "Big Bill" Devery; the former of whom gave them a "song and dance" and the latter of whom was miffed by the previous day's events, when a hundred newsies dared to march past the great newspaper offices of Park Row without a permit. The next day, with four of the strike leaders already locked up by the Gerry Society after failing to procure a cumulative $20 in court-ordered fines, Chief Devery told the newsies that he couldn't fulfill their request for another parade, with or without a official permit from Wyck. The official reason: They hadn't given him the requisite six-hour window to prepare his men to scope out the parade route and prepare for such a large assembly. Off the record, however, the cops had no vested interest in protecting the strikers, nor were they eager to sanction anything that would cause such a protracted commotion in their neighborhood.[†]

Behind the scenes, something more nefarious had started to unfold. As the newsies worked on their petition for a parade, the *Journal*'s Solomon Carvalho held a private meeting with Mayor Wyck. In yet another memo directed to Pulitzer, Seitz revealed that the mayor had all but expressed his support for the papers' efforts to quash the strike.[‡] Whether Carvalho had twisted his arm, hinted at a bribe, or simply needled the man into supporting the newspapers' cause is unclear. Needless to say, this was a different side to the mayor than the newsboys and newsgirls had seen in the hours following their rally at Irving Hall.

It was a crushing blow to the children's efforts. The strike, by its very nature, was intended to disrupt local business, but the newsies needed permission to stage any kind of mass meeting lest they risk further arrests and unwanted delays. What's more, they needed the support of local consumers and readers in order to stand strong against Pulitzer and Hearst— or else risk the death of their revolution altogether.

Luckily, there was still one person who believed in the newsies.

---

† According to the children, the Chief's words went something like this: "I wouldn't sign that thing for a thousand dollars."

‡ It should be stated once again that the contents of Seitz's memos may not be regarded as unbiased fact, as he was solely responsible for keeping Pulitzer abreast of any situations involving the *World* and may have downplayed or exaggerated the circumstances in order to to allay the publisher's anxieties or paint a more flattering picture of business operations.

The rally to end all rallies

Timothy Daniel Sullivan was no stranger to the rigors of the newsboys' trade. Native to the slums of the infamous Five Points neighborhood, he spent many a school night peddling papers and shining shoes along Park Row, and his compassion for the working class informed his politics during his rise to prominence as a Tammany Hall leader and state senator in the late 1880s and 1890s.

By the time he was 37 years old, Sullivan had amassed a small fortune from atop his perch in the Bowery. His investments spanned the practical and fanciful (real estate, local theatre, horse racing) to the criminal (prizefighting, boxing, gambling), and the yin-yang of his philanthropic endeavors and dirty politics made him a controversial yet respected character throughout the city.

At the zenith of that year's summer, when the streets ran hot and the newsies splashed under the bronze candelabra of the City Hall Park fountain, Sullivan's eye turned toward the children. The memory of his impoverished childhood was never a distant one, and he felt something akin to empathy for the boys and girls who made their petition for equal rights and fair pay. Before their protest was five days old, the senator had written a heartfelt letter to the newsies' executive committee in support of the boycott, then backed up his words with the sum of $100, to be placed in a newsboys' fund and given over to strike matters. On July 24, as the strikers made hopeful preparations for their parade, Sullivan rented out New Irving Hall and invited the newsies to fill the venue floor to ceiling.

The night was soon given over to sheer mayhem. At 8 p.m., 5,000 newsies from the Bronx to the Battery and Brooklyn to Jersey City flooded the streets outside the hall. Two thousand Brooklyn strikers were led by Racetrack Higgins, who bore a floral horseshoe that had been gifted to the strikers by the *Brooklyn Eagle* and was to be awarded to the boy or girl who delivered the best speech. Another hundred hailed from Jersey City, while the remaining 2,900 newsies were split between Manhattan and the Bronx.[3] Too impatient to wait for the meeting to begin, the group howled and sprinted and smashed their way past the doors to occupy every chair and windowsill with "compressed young humanity."[4] Only 2,000 managed to cram their way into the narrow hall, leaving the other 3,000 to mingle with a pitiful army of 15 police officers in the streets below.

Inside, joyful pandemonium reigned supreme. The newsies climbed on their chairs to see better and a few were so overcome with excitement that they fell to impromptu wrestling matches on the floor of the hall. Newsboy chairman Nick Myers introduced several adult strike speakers, each of whom made a brief exhortation in support of the children's cause.

"You are only the rising generation," former newsboy and assemblyman Philip Wissig told the crowd, "and if the older ones can't support you, they can at least treat you fairly. Now keep up the fight. Don't violate the law; don't use dynamite, but stick together and you will win."[5]

The feeling of invincibility grew stronger when the newsboys themselves were permitted on stage. The floral horseshoe was trotted out as a prize for the striker who gave the best speech; this, too, the children cheered.

A plain-looking newsie by the name of Dave Simons was the first to appear on his comrades' behalf. He had been appointed the President of the Newsboys' Union and quietly reminded the assembly that the *World* and *Journal* had yet to demand arbitration for the newsies in the same way that they advocated it so fiercely on the trolley strikers' behalf.

"We're goin' to win this fight, boys, only we must stick together and hold firm," he admonished the crowd. "The *Journal* and *World* has got the money, but we got the situation in our hands, and they know it. Now, I'm goin' to ask you not to use no more violence. Let up on the scabs."

The cheers turned to boos. Let up on the scabs? Had Simons been directing the strike with a blindfold over his eyes? It was unfathomable to imagine carrying out any kind of successful boycott without the assistance of clenched fists and clubs, especially as many of the scabs were sturdy-looking men between the ages of 25 and 50 years old and didn't take kindly to more peaceful methods of persuasion.

"Oh, *soytenly*," came the sarcastic reply.

"Now, I mean it," Simons warned the children. "We can't gain nothing by banging these fellers around. Let's fight on the level, and see if we can't win out that way."[6]

The hall erupted in laughter. They'd never heard a better gag.

Following Simons was Bob "Indian" Stone, a newsboy characterized in the papers only by his war-like cry on the street corner. Stone had sobering words for the newsies. He was one of the few strikers who scored a face-to-face meeting with Hearst, but had found the publisher reluctant to return to pre-war prices, claiming that he could only afford the 10-cent rollback if Pulitzer did it first.

"Just tink wot dey makes on der ads," Stone said. "And dey wants our 10 cents profert, too. I went to see Mister Hearst, and he just as good as run me outen his offiz. Let's not do nuthin' wrong. Let's tend to business, and not trow no sticks and stones, and not hit nobody over de head. Just let's sell dose papers wot treats us right."[7]

The newsies gave "Bob Indian" a five-minute round of applause. Perhaps Simons and Stone were on to something after all. Soaking the scabs had been the most effective way of clearing the city of the yellow journals, but it was also working against the children. The more violence they inflicted, the more reason Pulitzer and Hearst had to dismiss their demands.

As the adults wrapped up their admiring remarks and the newsboys gorged themselves on stories and speeches, they suddenly spied the red shock of Kid Blink's hair as the boy made his way to the stage. The walls quaked with the shouts of every newsboy and newsgirl in attendance; out in the street, the children took up the cry with wild feeling.

"Yer know me, boys!" Kid Blink shouted. "Well, I'm here to say if we are goin' to win this strike we must stick like glue and never give in. Am I right? Ain't that 10 cents worth as much to us as it is to Hearst and Pulitzer, who are millionaires? Well, I guess it is. If they can't spare it, how can we?"

"Soak 'em, Blink," cried a newsboy who had not yet taken the earnest words of the previous union members to heart.

"Soak nothin'," Blink told his colleague. "I'm tellin' the truth. I'm tryin' to figure out how 10 cents on a hundred papers can mean more to a millionaire than it does to a newsboy, an' I can't

see it. Now, boys, I'm goin' ter say like the rest: No more violence. Let up on the drivers. No more rackets like that one the
other night where a *Journal* and a *World* wagon was turned over
in Madison Street. Say, to tell the truth, I was there myself."

"You bet yer was," the crowd retorted.

"Well, never mind, we're goin' to let up on the scabs now and
win the strike on the square. Kid Blink's a talkin' to yer now.
Do yer know him? We won in 1893 and will win in 1899, but
stick together like plaster."[8]

There was hardly more to be said. Keep the peace, cooperate
only with the newspapers that offer a square deal, and hold
fast for a resolution—these were the primary tenets of the
newsies' movement. Newswoman Annie Kelly and Brooklyn
strike leader Racetrack Higgins each tacked on their own
words of encouragement, and Higgins reassured the audience
that the yellow papers were losing money faster than the
strikers themselves.

"I think we'll win this fight all right," he boasted. "I ain't
made 20 cents this week, but I can stand a heap of that and so
can all the Brooklyn boys. Don't you touch *World*s or *Journal*s
until they give us a decent deal. We're putting them out of
business fast and they know it."[9]

The newsies rejoiced. Newsboy mascot "Hungry Joe" Kernan
climbed on the Chairman's table and belted a song about
a one-legged newsboy, the horseshoe wreath was placed in the
hands of Kid Blink, and the two-hour meeting adjourned with
the battle cries of 5,000 newsboys and newsgirls as they once
again swarmed the streets of New York, each feeling giddier
and more invincible than ever before.

The bribed and the betrayed

Victory was sweet and brief. The next night, two hundred
Brooklyn newsies constructed a makeshift stage from empty
dry goods boxes and staged a second rally. They passed around
an empty cigar box for contributions and appointed speakers.

This time, there were no floral decorations, good-natured
fistfights, or rousing singalongs to be had. The children listened intently as strike orator Walter Murphy took the stage

to inform the crowd that the *World* and *Journal* had made their first offer: a five-cent reduction that would bring the cost of papers down to 55 cents per hundred.[10]

Word began to spread that the strike was over. It was a feeling that *World* business manager Don Carlos Seitz seemed to share; he had put forth similar news to Pulitzer in a telegram earlier that day. "Strike broken," he scribbled across the page. "Much work required to restore curate [Pulitzer's code word for 'circulation'] and rehabilitate paper with public. Shall have strong ten page paper for several days regardless of potash [Pulitzer's code word for 'advertising']."[11]

The newsies who circulated papers among the suburban areas of New York refused to accept the news, and the rest insisted that they had declined the initial offer in hopes of getting a reduction to 50 cents per hundred papers.

Further complications were yet to come. Over in Manhattan, the rest of the newsies gathered in a saloon on Park Row to settle a concerning matter. Strike leaders Kid Blink and Dave Simons had been accused of betraying the cause and turning profits on the scab papers. The newsies apprehended Blink, who clutched a roll of bills and was outfitted head-to-toe in a new suit, the kind the children claimed had never before been seen in the history of their profession and one that could not have been purchased except by the generosity of the yellow journals. He resisted the accusations for as long as he could, but eventually copped to hawking the *World* and *Journal*—and promptly made a run for it.

All hell broke loose on Park Row. The strikers, acting as both judge and jury, chased their leader through the streets until they collided with a pair of detectives, who wrongly concluded that Blink was leading the charge and immediately placed him under arrest.

At the courthouse, Blink pleaded his case to the magistrate.

"I'm de leader of de strike of de newsboys," he insisted.

"What?" the magistrate snapped. "You the leader of a strike? What nonsense."[12]

He issued a five-dollar fine, an impossible charge for the recently dethroned newsie to repay. A representative from one of the yellow papers quickly offered to repay the fee, but

Blink's mother appeared with a bondsman and settled the matter herself. The newsboy, once hailed as the champion of the underdogs and great orator of the strike, would not be tolerated among the ranks of striking newsies again.

No less dramatic was the fate that had befallen Newsboys' Union President Dave Simons. Mere days after he presided over the great rally at Irving Hall, the strike leader was spotted among a group of scabs exiting the *Journal* offices, stacks of the yellow papers balanced precariously atop their shoulders. Each scab now stood to receive the handsome sum of $1 per day from the *World* and *Journal*, an offer that was proving more irresistible to the newsies with every day that passed.

Not all strikers were fooled by the papers' cheap ploys, however, and it was 500 of these determined free-thinkers who intercepted the scabs at Frankfort Street. Enraged by the betrayal of their union president, they descended on the workers in droves, using the smaller newsies to occupy nearby police officers while they attacked the other boys.

Simons escaped the fray and later paid a visit to the local saloon to prove his innocence to the strikers in a more peaceable manner. He emptied his pockets and lifted his shirt. There was nothing concealed on his person and no evidence to suggest corruption or betrayal, but the newsies remained dubious. They allowed him to trade his title as president for the more modest responsibilities of union treasurer and enlisted newsboy Morris Cohen to take his place at the head of the union. "Young Monix," another strike leader, assumed the prominent position that once belonged to Kid Blink.§

---

§   Both boys were eventually acquitted by a panel of their peers. On July 27, Dave Simons and Kid Blink stood trial in front of the newsies as Racetrack Higgins charged them with "being bribed wid four hundred bones." Kid Blink swayed the hearts of his fellow compatriots with a passionate speech: "Most potint, grave and reverint Higgins, my very nobul and approved fellow strikers: Rude am I in me speech, and I'll be blessed ef I know wot you're gettin' at. Fer since dis voice uf mine had any kind er squeal, 'till now some nine moons wasted, I have used it in de uxtra fiel'. More dan pertains ter feats of broil and battul, and derefore little shall I grace me cause in speakin' fer meself. Since early yout' I've sold de papes. De battles, spolsons, prizefights wot has passed I've shouted till me troat was hoarse. I do beseech youse here me cause. Take me to 'De Joinal' office and if you find I took de bribe, not

It was the beginning of the end for the newsies' strike. Every morning, more newsboys and newsgirls traded in their strike placards for *World*s and *Journal*s. Scabs grew bolder; so, too, did cops and wagon drivers. Even the local editors were starting to grumble about the support the children received in the press, blaming publications like the *Sun* and *Telegram* for riling up the newsies and making them believe they could browbeat Pulitzer and Hearst into submission.

In the newsrooms of the yellow papers, the *Journal* made frantic reparations with the city's police force in order to secure their help in quelling outbreaks around their distribution centers.¶ When an outspoken delegation from the National Newsdealers and Stationers' Association arrived to throw their weight behind the children's cause, Hearst—millionaire, media mogul, and savvy entrepreneur that he was—cried poor.

"In the first place, there is, as you know, no 'strike' against the *Journal*. This is simply an attempted boycott," one of the lesser *Journal* editors relayed to the Association.

"Not a man employed by the *Journal* has gone out or presented any demands. Every employe [sic] of the *Journal* is a union man, paid union wages or better. The demands come not from employes [sic], but from merchants—men and boys who buy our papers and demand that we reduce our selling price."

According to the *Journal*'s calculations, a newsboy made 66 cents profit on every dollar and was permitted to make returns at full price.** The terms and conditions put forth by other papers were not as generous: the three-cent *New York Herald* and *Tribune* offered a 25-cent profit on the dollar, while the *Morning Sun* guaranteed a 32-cent profit. Even strike leader Dave Simons, the *Journal* claimed, had admitted to raking in

---

only take me papers, but let de sentence even fall upon me life."¹³

¶   The *World*, too, was sent into a tailspin over the number of newsdealers and employees who had been roughed up by the strikers. Of particular concern was their inability to hire adequate police protection, as 1,400 officers had already been called away to duty on the Brooklyn trolley strike.

**   This appears to directly contradict later claims that the strike was resolved after the yellow journals agreed to purchase unsold stock for full returns.

daily profits of $1.20 per 300 *Evening Journals* sold while only making seven cents off of 14 *Evening Telegrams*.††

These numbers provided the newsies ample compensation, argued Hearst and his men, as the children had already been living with the 60-cent costs for some time.

> "Something has been said of war prices," said the *Journal*'s editor. "There was and is no war price. The price 60 cents per hundred is the price that the *Evening Sun* and *Evening World* sold for ten years before the *Evening Journal* was issued. At that time, as you are aware, we cou'd easily have increased the price of the paper both to the dealers and to the public and without protest. But instead of that, we published all the news and stood all the loss, leaving the profit to the newsboys and the newsdealers."

In fact, he continued, the *Journal* financed all expenditures: white paper subscriptions to news associations; salaries for editors, reporters, correspondents, artists, pressmen, stereotypers, and compositors; a $33,000 wire to the Pacific Coast; and the general costs of printing and distribution.

And what did the boys and girls of the city bring to the table?

"The newsdealer puts the paper on his stand, the newsboy holds it out at arms' length, and for that part of the work gets four-tenths of a cent," the paper scoffed.[15]

The *Journal* had made its stance clear, both on the boycott and on its opinions of its labor force. It didn't see the children as an extension of the paper or as valued employees. It didn't take into consideration the homeless immigrants sleeping in ash-coated stairwells or the six-year-olds wandering through saloons after dark or the newsgirls tending to weeks-old infants while passing out papers in the middle of a City Hall Park winter. It didn't value the investment their school-age newspaper hawkers had made in the paper: the rigorous

---

†† Simons had reportedly demanded the *Journal* reduce its selling price to that of the *Telegram*, while fellow newsie leader Morris Cohen suggested lowering the quality of the newspaper to match its competitor. Hearst was reluctant to adopt either tactic given the lesser popularity of the *Telegram*. "[...] we are not here to produce anything but the best paper," his employee told the Newsdealers Association. In a column published on July 30, the *Journal* also blamed the *Telegram* for inciting the newsboys to strike.[14]

12-hour shifts they kept, the ingenuity they practiced in shouting headlines and wringing tips from customers' hands, the continued threats of kidnappings and bodily harm they sustained from pedophilic clients and careless crowds.

No, to Hearst and his staff, the newsies had overstepped their bounds, thinking themselves a more vital component of the industry than they really were. There would be no concession made, either in the prices charged to the newsdealers[‡‡] and customers or the quality of the papers itself. A compromise between the parties was out of the question.

How could the newsies possibly win now?

A bitter end

The final nail in the coffin was delivered soon enough. On the afternoon of July 30, four newsboys—Edward Fitzgerald, Henry "Butts" Butler, Jack Harney, and Jack Seeley—were admitted to the *World*'s circulation office and proposed a compromise. For the easy sum of $600, they said, the strike would be brought to a peaceful end. Of course, should the *World* and *Journal* fail to comply with the demands, the newsies would strengthen their ranks and solicit monetary support from rival papers.

"Compromise" wasn't the word that *World* circulation manager Patrick Duff would have used to describe the meeting. He accused the newsies of attempted extortion, a claim that was backed up by *Journal* employee Edward Harris and local detective Mr. Distler, who had eavesdropped on the conversation, seized three of the four suspects, and promptly hauled them off to court.

Extortion was a serious charge. Magistrate Mott, the very same who had presided over Kid Blink's hearing only days before, ordered a formal trial and set bail at $1,000 per child.[§§]

---

‡‡ According to the same editorial, several anonymous newsboys suggested that the *Journal* sell the paper at 50 cents per hundred copies to the newsies and offer a higher, albeit unspecified price to the newsdealers. Another unnamed strike leader allegedly told the paper to sell to the downtown newsies at 50 cents per hundred while charging Brooklyn, Harlem, and uptown newsies a 60-cent-per-100 fee.

§§ As no one could pay up, the three newsboys were committed to the nearby Tombs Prison.

He was unsympathetic to the newsies' protests; according to their account of the meeting, they had been lured to the office by none other than Kid Blink himself, who claimed that the *World* and *Journal* were prepared to offer a permanent five-cent discount on their papers and accept all returns for half-price. The newsboys followed Blink to the *World* office, where Edward Harris tried to bribe the kids to voluntarily end the strike.

"Now, boys, this strike is hurting both you and us, and we want to settle it," Harris told the crew. "Will you take $300 to stop it by 6 o'clock to-night?"

The strikers told Harris they would not. They could no more control the thousands of striking newsies than a ship captain could command an oncoming thunderstorm. They declined to sign a written agreement, but were told that the *World* had authorized $10 payments for the first ten boys who took up the offer. Harris thrust a bill in one of the boy's palms, leaving it there just long enough for Distler to barge in and make his arrests.[16] Butler and Seeley jumped out of the window; Seeley slid down the water pipe and was gone in a jiff, but cracked the pipe in his haste and left Butler on the roof, where he was quickly snatched up by the detective.

It was a colorful story, though no more believable than the one put forth by the adults. The truth of the situation mattered little. Whether innocent or guilty, the boys had been beaten. Theirs was not the side of power, money, or influence. Though the newsies drove the action on the streets, they wielded precious little authority in the courtrooms and jails of New York City—and everyone knew it.

Pulitzer and Hearst didn't need to outmuscle or outwit the newsies; they only needed to outlast them. It was an expensive strategy, one that cost the publishers countless subscribers and thousands of dollars of advertising revenue. As a direct result of the strike, the *World*'s press run had been reduced from 360,000 to 125,000; factoring in returns, which skyrocketed from 15-16% to 35%, the paper's circulation had plummeted 73% from approximately 304,200 to a measly 81,250.[17]

Several competitors estimated the strike had spread to a 100-mile radius from its home base on Park Row. Still, the yellow journals knew that the children's crusade came with a short shelf life. It didn't matter that the newsies had plenty of other publications to patronize; most of their days were spent rioting and breaking up scab efforts. They didn't have time to work full days hawking papers and were losing more money and support by the day.

By August 2, 1899, the strike appeared to have reached its natural end. As far as the members of the New York press were concerned, no final convocation was held by the newsies, nor any formal declaration given by any of the informal unions stationed across Manhattan or Brooklyn.¶¶ There was no explosive standoff between the strikers and the distributors, no tense meeting with Pulitzer within the ivory pillars of the *World* building. Union leaders no longer forbade the sale of the yellow journals and the strikers were mounting fewer attacks against the wagon drivers who carried them. Like the white-hot cartridge of an erupting firework, the newsies' strike crackled and popped, capturing the country's attention for a fleeting moment before it fizzled into the night sky.

When pressed, some of the children admitted a compelling reason for changing their minds: The *World* and *Journal* had decided to accept all unsold papers for full refunds, issued not in the form of cash, but as credit toward future purchases.[18]

The next day, the *World* broke its silence on the strike. On the back page of the paper, an editorial stretched halfway across the page: "Plain Statement of Facts for Public Consideration."

> "There is no 'strike' of newsboys at present," the column read. "The unorganized movement led by those who hoped to gain public confidence by lying about their successful rivals long ago collapsed. While this 'strike' was in progress *The Evening World* deemed it wise to continue its own business in its own way. Now that *The Evening World* is for sale everywhere, as usual, it is only fair that the public should know all the facts in the case.
>
> Not knowing the facts, it was only natural that the public should sympathize with the boys. So does *The World*—so long

---

¶¶ There was some debate over the legitimacy of the newsies' unions. Ultimately, Seitz pointed out to Pulitzer, the newsies had managed to do "colossal damage" to the two papers over the course of their two-week strike, unionized or not.

as the boys are reasonable. But sympathy must be based on common sense and justice."[19]

That "common sense" was outlined in a breakdown of the *World*'s various expenditures, each another reason to discredit the newsies' complaints. Pulitzer claimed that the 50-cent price had been a temporary experiment that was found to be unprofitable given the enormous size and quality of his paper, not to mention the recent and exorbitant costs of cablegrams and illustrations. It was a claim no other publication, save the *Journal*, had ever made.

By the *World*'s estimation, it was pocketing five-tenths of one cent per newspaper while the newsies pocketed four-tenths of a cent per copy. Was it fair that the newsboy or newsgirl stood to make "almost as much simply for holding the paper in [their] arms as *The World* [had on hand] to pay its Union workers, editors, artists, photographers, pressmen, and for white paper, ink, news, cable and telegraph tolls"? The editors of the *World* didn't think so.

Pulitzer was a professional contortionist, able to twist his words to suit any message he pleased—in this case, to discredit thousands of young, homeless children who had the audacity to demand a fair wage from the millionaire. It's not apparent whether the *World*'s readers managed to see through the self-serving editorial. Certainly, the public had placed their support behind the newsies during the strike, motivated as they were by a potent combination of sympathy and fear. To the average passerby, the newsboys and newsgirls of the city were largely regarded as a piece of the landscape: at best, pitiable victims of poverty and circumstance; at worst, a necessary evil to be avoided or eradicated.*** When the newsies went on strike, many of their

---

*** In a letter to the editor of the *New York Sun*, one disgruntled customer insisted on harsher punishment for newsboys who insisted on breaking the law. "I am moved to ask the Wall Street brokers who have lately applauded the riotous newsboys and messenger boys to look a little further toward the future before watching with enjoyment their performance," the letter began. "What will these same brokers think of it when, ten or fifteen years from this, or probably much sooner, these same boys, then grown men of 25 or 30, attack trolley cars or steam cars, or storehouses or banks or brokers' offices to secure

customers began patronizing the smaller rivals of the *World* and *Journal*; concerned, rightfully so, that future attempts to purchase the yellow papers would place an unwelcome target on their backs. Those who did not fear retaliation from the newsies doled out generous tips and exhorted the children to stay strong in their fight against Pulitzer and Hearst.††† Well-intentioned though the newsies' customers might have been, however, they had no real skin in the game—and, crucially, no real way of forcing the papers' editors to treat their young workers in a more ethical manner.

News of the children's efforts had slowly waned over the last week of the strike. Even the *Sun*, often the most enthusiastic supporter of the strikers, had significantly decreased its coverage.††† Only the *New-York Tribune* offered up a pithy eulogy:

> "Once upon a time a dog with a piece of meat in his mouth, was crossing a river. Seeing his reflection in the water, said, 'That dog has a bigger piece of meat.' He thereupon opened his mouth to make a snatch at the other dog's meat, whereupon his own fell into the water. 'And so the poor dog had none.'

> There were once a number of newsboys who went on a strike. Things were coming their way. They had received offers of papers at five cents less a hundred than before. Then one of them said, 'Our leader has gotten a large sum of money.' So all of the little boys grabbed for free papers that were being

---

what they shall then regard as their rights? Yet just this sort of result will be the natural outcome of these deeds of violence by these boys if they are treated as many men of the press, and even the Magistrates on the bench, seem inclined to treat them."[20] No ink was devoted to the harsh sentences that befell the newsboys who were arrested and tried for their lawless behavior, nor did the letter-writer consider the impetus behind the strike itself.

††† Strike sympathizers may have been influenced by the positive strike coverage in pro-union columns from the *New York Sun* and *Brooklyn Daily Eagle*, among other papers, or else they were spurred to action after personally witnessing the violence which often befell the children.

‡‡‡ This may have been due in part to Seitz's threats. As he wrote to Pulitzer in a memo dated July 27, 1899, "*The Sun* suddenly got some sense and daylight after I saw the reporter and told him that they would come next and would be wiped out if he gave in to the boys." He also enlisted the help of the Publishers' Association in discouraging further stories from New York publications and threatened to have both the *World* and *Journal* pull their membership if other publishers did not fall in line.[21]

distributed. And now they pay the old price for their stock. All of which goes to show that fables are not really fables, and that history repeats itself."[22]

Perhaps it was an unfair assessment, but there was no way of knowing how Pulitzer and Hearst would have reacted if the newsies had been able to hold their ground a few days or weeks longer. Would the publishers have bent to the will of the masses? Could they have afforded greater losses in advertising revenue and circulation? Might the newsies have negotiated a more advantageous compromise after resisting the papers' initial offers?

Those were questions that would haunt every newsboy and newsgirl who found themselves back in the employ of the *World* and *Journal* that summer, digging through their pockets every dark morning for another 60 cents to pay for another hundred papers.

The newsies' last word

The children of New York City didn't get the fairytale ending they deserved, but they had still accomplished something magnificent. No other body of strikers before or since had succeeded in crippling powerful newspaper magnates the way the 1899 newsies did.

In two weeks, they had organized and led thousands of newsboys and newsgirls in a firm protest against the *World* and the *Journal*, not only squaring off against the papers' news-dealers and scab workers, but standing up to the city's corrupt and powerful police force as well. They organized rallies, parades, and mass meetings, and gave a fair chance to every scab who proved willing to tear up the boycotted papers and take up the strike banners instead. They captured the hearts and pocket money of New York City's consumers and became powerful allies to the non-struck newspapers, increasing the readership of their allies by leaps and bounds while the yellow journals scrambled to retain both advertisers and subscribers. They proved they could not be easily dismissed or undervalued, inspiring fellow newsies, messengers, and bootblacks in neighboring counties and cities to take up the fight for their own rights and setting a strong precedent for additional child labor reform movements in the decades to follow.§§§

Most importantly, the children had sent an unmistakable warning to their employers. Big headlines, fancy illustrations, eloquent editorials, bloody wars, and high society gossip were all fine facets of a good newspaper, but they didn't sell papes.

Newsies sold papes, and without the newsies, their publishers had nothing.

---

§§§   Child labor reform was slow to develop in the United States over the 20th century, and it would come at the hands of adult activists and legislators, not the adolescent workers themselves. In January 1918, the newsies of New York went on strike again to protest yet another price hike by the city's papers. This one was far worse: Instead of raising the cost of wholesale papers from 50 to 60 cents per hundred to finance wartime expenses, the publishers unanimously decided to raise the sale price of afternoon papers from one to two cents. The newsies—as well as any other independent vendor servicing the papers—would be left to pocket just 30 cents of every 100 they invested in their daily stock. The children may have won the battle against Pulitzer and Hearst in 1899, but they were about to lose the war. Newspaper hawking was a dying profession, replaced by newsstands and subscription services that had all but rendered the children obsolete during the new century. The papers temporarily resolved the 1918 boycott by issuing full returns to the newsies, just as they had nearly two decades earlier, but the policy was soon ruled unlawful as it supposedly encouraged the children to purchase more product than they were capable of unloading in a day's work.[23] After eight months, during which the newsies tried in vain to solicit support from politicians, lawyers, and adult unionizers, they finally admitted defeat.

CHAPTER SEVEN

The Story Behind the Story

The Making of Walt Disney's *Newsies*

If the life don't seem to suit ya, how 'bout a change of scene—
far from the headlines and the deadlines in between?

History, famously, is written by the victors.

It is one of the indisputable spoils of war, the medal hung around a neck, the icing on top of the already-devoured cake. Those who win get to decide *how* they won: how the battle unfolded, how pitiful their opponents looked, how many insurmountable odds were stacked against them, how righteous their cause was, how well-deserved their victory.

For centuries, history has proven itself no great arbiter of justice, and history-makers, no great excavators of the truth. Those who land on the "wrong" side of history are often doomed to be misrepresented, maligned or obscured by it. And, for nearly 90 long years after the strike of 1899 dragged to its unsatisfactory conclusion, so were the newsies.

During the spring of 1985, screenwriter Bob Tzudiker cracked open a copy of the *New York Times*. Tucked away in the back pages was a brief description of David Nasaw's *Children of the City: At Work and at Play*; then, at the bottom of the page, an eye-opening coda:

"In 1899, an event took place that would have been perfect for film use by the Dead End Kids, but as Mr. Nasaw points out, it has been a neglected episode. Unhappy with a raise in the wholesale price of Joseph Pulitzer's *World* and William Randolph Hearst's *Journal*, New York newsboys, copying the methods of grown-ups' unions, organized a successful strike against these titans of journalism, with devastating effects on the newspapers' circulations. 'The publishers conceded defeat in the second week of the strike,' Mr. Nasaw writes, 'by offering the boys an advantageous compromise.'"[1]

Tzudiker was intrigued. It was the quintessential story of the underdog, made more sympathetic by the young age of the newsies and the power wielded by their personal Goliaths. Better yet: It was a story that had yet to attract the public's eye, and though he may not have been aware of it in that moment, a story that had only recently been excavated from the annals of 19th-century American history.

Years passed. Tzudiker took part-time acting gigs and eventually circled back to the screenwriting sphere with his first screenplay, a romantic comedy written on spec with his writing partner and wife, Noni White. *Mrs. Faust* was hardly the commercial and critical breakthrough Tzudiker and White were waiting for, but it was just successful enough that it could open other doors for the pair—including one that led to the development of a little passion project known as "Newsies."

As they threw themselves headlong into the creative process, it quickly became apparent that the newsboys' story would require a unique and thoughtful treatment. Not only was there an innate richness to the source material, teeming as it was with a cast of characters both prominent and relatively unknown, but it required the writers to cultivate a deeper understanding of the history surrounding the newsies' pivotal decision to boycott he two newspaper tycoons.

Together, the two hunted down a copy of Nasaw's study in a little bookshop in Berkeley, California and asked Tzudiker's parents to postmark boxes of documents that had been squirreled away in the recesses of the Library of Congress in Washington, D.C. There was a fount of information to draw from: telegrams between Don Carlos Seitz and Joseph Pulitzer, meticulous accounts from a variety of period-appropriate newspapers, carefully-researched studies of child labor practices, and more.

Soon, however, Tzudiker and White were tasked with telling their own interpretation of the newsies' story. Could they bring long-awaited justice to the newsies of 1899 New York

City without sacrificing historical accuracy or nuance? More importantly, would anyone want to watch that kind of a film? They were about to find out.

The story they wanted (and needed) to write

The first thing they needed to do was pick a villain for their story. Which newspaper mogul would the newsies stage their battle against: the frail, bitter Pulitzer or the brash, innovative Hearst? Tzudiker and White settled on the former. Orson Welles had already selected Hearst as the focal point for *Citizen Kane* (1941), while Pulitzer's history as an immigrant and self-proclaimed champion of the poor made his betrayal of the newsies all the more gut-wrenching to watch.[2]

For the protagonist, they fashioned a boy named "Jack," an orphaned newsie who was mostly a composite of historical strike leaders Louis "Kid Blink" Ballatt and Morris Cohen. They saddled Jack with a tragic backstory, one in which the orphaned newsboy lost his younger brother to the orphan train* and suffered post-traumatic stress disorder after inadvertently causing the death of another newsie. Throughout the protracted war against Pulitzer and Hearst, the only thing Jack clung to was the dream of moving to Santa Fe, New Mexico* and reuniting with his family at long last.†

The remaining cast of characters was fleshed out from stories of children that had surfaced in newspaper columns

---

* From 1854 through the late 1920s, the "orphan train" was largely operated by the Children's Village, Children's Aid Society, and New York Foundling Hospital. The overarching goal was to alleviate issues of orphanage crowding in metropolitan areas by relocating orphaned children out West; however, these measures were not always seen as compassionate, and were often compounded by controversies like compulsory conversion to Protestantism, the forced fracturing of immigrant families, and indentureship. The movement was eventually nullified later in the 20th century as states began to establish more stringent protocols and compensatory measures for families looking to bring local foster children into their homes.]

† In an essay for *Newsies: Stories of the Unlikely Broadway Hit*, Tzudiker revealed that he was inspired to use Santa Fe as a potential destination for Jack after living there himself for several years.[3]

and history books. "Boots," for instance, was based on a young boy who began working the streets as a bootblack before joining the strike as a bonafide newsie. In the script, he was given a fictional set of parents and an uncle who ran a honky-tonk called "Boots' Place." The juke joint was an early prototype of the New York jazz club and was intended to be a rallying spot for the young strikers.

Tzudiker and White didn't intend to ignore the newsgirls, either.

"We had read somewhere during our research that one out of 10 newsies were girls," White said.[4]

They created "Charlie the newsgirl," a tomboyish newspaper seller who lived in a house of ill repute with her aunt, Louise, and harbored an unrequited crush on Jack. By the end of Tzudiker and White's story, the pair left New York City behind and they boarded the train to Santa Fe together.

Eventually, the writers returned to their agent, Caren Bohrman, with a script that they felt captured the beating heart of the newsies' struggle. Pulitzer was a nuanced, troubled character whose morals were brought into sharp contrast against his cutthroat business practices; Jack, David, Charlie, Boots, and Les brought life and diversity to the New York class of newsies; and the events of the 1899 strike had been interpreted in varying shades of historical reproduction and Hollywood drama. It offered everything the public already loved about rags-to-riches stories like *Annie* and *Oliver!*, with a dash of intrepid salesmanship and social justice-laced warmongering thrown in for good measure. All it lacked was an enthusiastic buyer.

Bohrman arranged nine pitch meetings for *Newsies*. The first eight development executives passed. Period dramas, particularly those that centered on century-old debates about children's rights, hadn't really been done since *Oliver!* (1968). The biggest blockbusters of the 1980s skewed toward science fiction (*The Empire Strikes Back*, *Return of the Jedi*, *E.T.*, *Ghostbusters*), superhero schmaltz (*Batman*, *Superman II*, *RoboCop*), and time travel and faux-historical action-adventure flicks (*Back to the Future*, *Raiders of the Lost Ark*, *Indiana Jones and the Last Crusade*). The treatment of a child labor strike was both unprecedented and unexpected—and no one could say for sure how successful it would be.

Luckily, there was one person who found *Newsies* as moving as Tzudiker and White did: Marianne Sweeny of Finnell/Dante Productions. She finessed two meetings with Disney film executive Donald DeLine and Stephen Spielberg's Amblin Entertainment. Spielberg never got a chance at the film. After 45 minutes, DeLine was smitten with the newsboys, and the handshake deal he struck with the writers was soon solidified in writing.

Newsies was coming to Hollywood.

Finding a cast for *Newsies*

In 1991, 17-year-old actor Christian Bale needed a new gig. He had charmed critics with a heart-rending portrayal of Jamie Graham in Spielberg's *Empire of the Sun* only four years earlier, but audiences didn't take to the film and the rapid acceleration of puberty meant that the fresh-faced teen would need to remarket himself to stay relevant. After some bit parts in TV movies and creative strategizing by his father David, who billed his son as a versatile Ethan Hawke-type, Bale landed a three-picture deal with Disney. The projects themselves had not yet been decided on, but David wanted the teenager to go out for a lead role in *Hard Promises*, a film that treated the newsboys strike of 1899.[‡]

Bale was dubious. He saw himself as a serious actor and wanted to pursue opportunities that would allow him to emulate leading men like James Dean and Steve McQueen. He didn't fit the mold of the brooding heartthrob or class clown, and was skeptical that Disney could deliver the kind of Oscar bait that he needed to build his reputation in the industry.

From the outset, *Hard Promises* certainly didn't look like one of Hollywood's run-of-the-mill teen romances. It appeared to be a straightforward historical treatment of child labor rights in turn-of-the-century New York City, and one that featured

---

[‡] *Newsies* was re-titled *Hard Promises* during its lengthy development in the studio. It finally reverted to *Newsies* prior to its cinematic debut in 1992.

a strong male lead at its core. Perhaps more crucially, the casting call coincided with the Bale family's strategic shift toward Hollywood-based roles. Bale's father, David, was ready to see his son move in the California circuit alongside other up-and-comers like Ethan Hawke and River Phoenix. And Disney's newest endeavor would undoubtedly give the kid some rising star power to leverage into bigger and better roles.

Bale complied with his father's wishes. He went in for a reading of *Hard Promises* and enchanted the creative team with his strong acting and passable 19th-century New York twang. The role was proffered, university plans were temporarily shelved, and before long, both Bale and his father were on a plane to the sunny, billboard-littered hills of Los Angeles, California for good.

In the heart of Hollywood, meanwhile, Disney studio head Jeffrey Katzenberg was having second thoughts about *Hard Promises*. The material, while compelling on its own, lacked some of the over-the-top production value that had become a hallmark of previous Disney films. The studio was gradually approaching the zenith of its Renaissance movement with animated darlings like *The Little Mermaid* (1989), which had boomed to over $6 million in its opening weekend and won two Academy Awards, including one for Alan Menken and Howard Ashman's catchy Calypso number, "Under the Sea." Plans for another animated musical, *Beauty and the Beast*, were already well underway, and it required no great stretch of the imagination to predict that the elegant French fairytale and its sweeping ballads would follow in *The Little Mermaid*'s footsteps.

Katzenberg wanted to go even bigger. Disney had always prided itself on thinking outside the box, and what would be more outside the box than the resurrection of the live-action musical? Others disagreed. DeLine believed that *Hard Promises* would fit well within the musical genre, but doubted the studio had the ability to execute it with the same care and skill they had poured into their animated features.[5] Executive music producer Chris Montan agreed.

"Most of the senior executives at the studio had never made a live-action musical, so it was natural that there was a big learning curve," he recalled. "*Newsies* was trying to walk that really uncomfortable line between realism and musical comedy. I think that was its undoing—it just wasn't unified that way."[6]

Nevertheless, the studio pushed forward with their new plan. *Hard Promises* the historical drama became *Newsies* the musical, with 20 minutes of song-and-dance work shoehorned into Tzudiker and White's script.[§] Danny Troob took on the arrangements, orchestrations, and vocal coaching for a posse of young actors that had little to no formal vocal training whatsoever. Following the devastating loss of Howard Ashman in March 1991, Alan Menken tackled *Newsies'* musical numbers with lyricist Jack Feldman, whose biggest hit to date had been Barry Manilow's 1978 showgirl showstopper "Copacabana (At the Copa)." Renowned choreographer Kenny Ortega grabbed the reins of the production; alongside Katzenberg, he was the only person who appeared to truly believe in the project.

"[Musicals] offered hope and a beautiful place to go to," the first-time director said. "When I read the 'Newsies' script, I could hear music."[7]

In the meantime, Bale was set to undergo a screen test for the film, the last step before he could officially ink his name to a contract. Then, Ortega broke the news: The film was going to be rewritten as a musical and would require no small degree of singing and dancing—some of it across a rooftop, no less.

"I met the director [Ortega] and told him I wasn't comfortable with the dancing and singing," Bale later complained to *Seventeen Magazine.* "I didn't want to be a bloody Artful Dodger in a remake of *Oliver!*, jumping down the street with a smile on my face." Ortega tried to steady the young actor's nerves. He reassured Bale that *Newsies* was nothing like *Oliver!*, that it was a serious project, that even Al Pacino himself had embraced some musical roles early in his career. In other words: a lie.

Bale still wasn't convinced that Disney was steering the production in the right direction. He asked if his character, the renegade newsboy leader and wannabe-cowboy Jack Kelly,

---

§   Bob Tzudiker and Noni White were lifted from the project shortly after turning in their fifth draft of the script, while writers David Fallon and Tom Rickman were tasked with finding a place for the music. The transition from drama to musical was so quick, Tzudiker noted, that many new hires had no idea of the drastic changes to the film until they began working on it.

would be permitted to duck into a nearby building on set to avoid participating in the musical numbers. No such luck, he was told. Much as he might despise it, it would have been unthinkable to omit the lead actor of a musical from every scene that featured singing and dancing. Bale's hesitations were never fully assuaged—if anything, they multiplied when the film was released in theaters—but some additional pressure from his father helped seal the deal.

"Even then," the teenager said, "I knew I'd never do anything like that again."[8]

Luckily for Disney, the rest of the cast quickly fell into place. Robert Duvall signed on as the cigar-puffing Pulitzer and Ann-Margret accepted the role of Medda Larkson, the charismatic "Swedish Meadowlark" of the vaudevillian Irving Hall. Bill Pullman, whose previous film credits included *Spaceballs* (1987) and *The Accidental Tourist* (1988), was cast as *New York Sun* reporter and strike sympathizer Bryan Denton. Kevin Tighe and Michael Lerner filled in the background roles: Tighe as the menacing Mister Snyder and warden of the House of Refuge, and Lerner as Wesel, a gullible circulation manager for the *New York World*.

Even more crucial was the casting of the newsies themselves. Significant changes had been made to Tzudiker and White's original script, eliminating "Charlie the newsgirl" and replacing Jack's love interest with Sarah Jacobs, the shy sister to newsboy brothers David and Les Jacobs. No other female character took Charlie's place among the boys. In fact, by the time the cast list was solidified and principal photography wrapped, there were only seven women in a cast of 86, and only four who were given named characters to play.¶ There was no Annie Kelly, no "Aunty" Cochran or vengeful "Squealer," no red-headed Jennie tearing around the corner to rip up scab papers and scatter the strikebreakers.

¶   The female characters of *Newsies* include Medda Larkson, Sarah Jacobs, Esther Jacobs, Patrick's mother, and three nuns, as well as several hundred unidentifiable extras. Of the first four on that list, Medda Larkson and Sarah Jacobs are the only female characters to appear in multiple scenes. They share a combined 32 spoken lines of dialogue—most of them monosyllabic answers that fail to advance the plot or flesh out their own inner monologues.

Whether Katzenberg and his team were genuinely ignorant of the roles that girls and women played in the 1899 strike or whether the studio believed the film would possess more universal appeal with an all-male ensemble is unclear. By the end of the casting process, nearly 60 boys had secured roles as the striking newsboys. A few were already established TV show regulars and feature film stars—Max Casella ("Racetrack Higgins") played a womanizing sidekick to Neil Patrick Harris' prepubescent medical genius on *Doogie Howser, M.D.*, David Moscow ("David Jacobs") earned some recognition as a young Tom Hanks in *Big*, and Gabriel Damon ("Spot Conlon") voiced the precocious Littlefoot on *The Land Before Time*—but most others were young actors still waiting for their big Hollywood break.

As it turned out, acting would be the least of their worries. Not one of the boys resembled anything close to a triple threat, and production couldn't properly begin until Ortega knew if they'd be able to handle the rigors of choreographed musical numbers and elaborate stunt work. The boys' collective inexperience may have been a harbinger of the critical and commercial failure that awaited *Newsies* at the box office, but the first-time director saw it as a unique and thrilling challenge. He rolled back the start of principal photography and arranged a 10-week boot camp, during which his adolescent cast (a reluctant Christian Bale included) kept round-the-clock schedules of voice and dialect coaching, physical conditioning, scene studies, choreography rehearsals, stunt lessons, gymnastics and martial arts training, and private academic tutoring.**

"It was torture," Max Casella said of the experience later. "It got easier after awhile [sic] but the first month and a half was horrible."

David Moscow put it more succinctly: "I thought I was going to die."[10]

** As was typical of the child actor experience, the minors in the cast—spanning a range of ages and grades—met in an empty trailer to continue their studies in between set calls. Head teacher Sharon Sacks was always on the lookout for projects that could engage students of varying needs and expertise, and she eventually found an activity that was not only relevant to their studies, but the film itself: putting out a newspaper of their own.[9]

For ten months, the boys tumbled and barrel rolled and punched and kicked and scrapped together. They laid down the tracks for Alan Menken and Jack Feldman's rousing group numbers and soulful ballads in the recording studio where Frank Sinatra once crooned "It Was a Very Good Year" and "Strangers in the Night." They took pointers from choreographers Peggy Holmes and William Holden Jr. (and, once, the inimitable Gene Kelly himself) as they memorized high kicks and tap dance routines. Some, like Casella, ventured out to the Los Angeles Public Library, where they pored over microfilm articles and the photographs of renowned social reformer Jacob Riis in order to better inform their on-screen personas.

At the end of the program, Disney was no longer dealing with a few dozen amateur actors, but a wild, tight-knit posse of rabble-rousers not unlike those once found on the streets of turn-of-the-century New York City.

"We feel like we're a bunch of Newsies," Casella said.

From *Newsies* to "Snoozies"

By mid-April 1991, Disney had outfitted the production with all the trappings of a modern movie musical. The choreography was set, the soundtrack recorded, the period buildings and sets meticulously reconstructed. The only thing left to do was shoot it—a process that took roughly three months in the 100-degree shade of the Valley. The boys slicked back their hair with some combination of hairspray and perspiration while the costume department struggled to patch every tear and repair every seam that unraveled during hours of somersaults and riots. Christian Bale embraced his character as the down-on-his-luck dreamer, lasso-twirling and vaulting onto stray pinto horses as he belted the film's lone solo, "Santa Fe." Slowly but surely, the cast was doing justice to the vision set forth by Tzudiker and White, one in which every triumph and downfall of the 1899 newsies came to vibrant, melodic life.

"There was such excitement on set," Casella remembered later, "with everyone really believing that the movie was going to be a huge hit."[11]

There was still one problem, albeit nothing the film's young cast had recognized yet. *Newsies* had too many cooks in the kitchen. Even for a studio that had singlehandedly created a market for feature-length animated films, a studio whose various cinematic endeavors had been decorated with 46 Academy Awards in a 60-year span—a studio that, come to think of it, had frequently and expertly broken more ground and bucked more trends than any of its competitors to date—it was too ambitious a project. It couldn't possibly epitomize all the hopes Bob Tzudiker and Noni White and Michael Finnell and Jeffrey Katzenberg and Kenny Ortega and Christian Bale had foisted upon it. It couldn't simultaneously be a touching period piece, a groundbreaking live-action musical with seamlessly-choreographed dance breaks and earnest yet polished musical numbers, and the kind of serious film one could imagine a young Al Pacino pulling off. In that kind of pressure cooker, it could only become one thing: a heartfelt, well-intentioned, shambolic mess.

On a balmy weekend the following April, moviegoers might have noticed *Newsies* perched atop the marquee next to *FernGully: The Last Rainforest*, *Sleepwalkers*, *My Cousin Vinny*, *Beethoven*, and *Howards End*, among a few others. As Katzenberg predicted, *Newsies* was unlike anything audiences had seen in decades, if ever. It didn't look like any of Hollywood's latest releases: a charming, if preachy cartoon flick about rainforest preservation, an underrated Stephen King piece (shapeshifting psychic vampires! Bipedal werecats! A Mark Hamill cameo!), a comedy built on the mishaps of an inexperienced personal injury lawyer, the PG-rated shenanigans of a lovable St. Bernard, or an Oscar-winning romance centered on the politics of class and wealth in 20th century England.

No, *Newsies* was in a class of its own. It followed the charismatic 17-year-old newsboy, "Cowboy" Jack Kelly, who puttered around the streets of Manhattan by day and dreamed of traveling West every night. Jack and his crew ran the streets of New York City, hawking copies of the *New York World* and paying their dues to the prestigious, apoplectic *World* editor, Joseph Pulitzer. When Pulitzer decided to jack up the price of papers and further inflate his own profits, Jack and David organized a youth-led strike to boycott the newspaper and demand fairer working conditions. Backed by soft-hearted journalist Bryan Denton and the righteously indignant of then-governor Theodore Roosevelt, the kids forced Pulitzer's hand and won the day, setting a new precedent for beleaguered and overworked child laborers across the United States.[††]

Newsies was the last film the public expected—or wanted— from Disney. It carried a decidedly pro-union message, an interesting choice given the bitter five-week strike that had fractured the studio's workforce some 50 years earlier. It depicted underage children drinking alcohol, taking bets, and puffing on cigarettes (common habits for the average 19th-century newsboy, less so for the youth of the '90s). It indulged in copious amounts of singing and dancing with nary a talking candelabra or Jamaican crab to make the whole thing palatable. Its only recognizable stamp of Disney branding was its signature happy ending, which strayed so far from historical events as to appear entirely ludicrous.

Neither audiences nor critics were quite sure what to make of the campy newsboy musical. The first 1,223 theaters to debut the film grossed $1,232,508 during its first weekend and a measly $520,925 the second. Disney panicked. Just two days after the film tanked at the box office, the studio's marketing department called an emergency meeting—one with all the gravity and desperation of a prayer meeting, an anonymous source later told the *Los Angeles Times*' David J. Fox.[12]

From there, a veritable breeding ground of complaints and poor reviews festered and multiplied. Distributors accused Disney of misrepresenting the nature of the film during its theatrical trailers, claiming that it was not apparent from the promo material that the movie was a full-length musical or that it intended to showcase two-time Oscar nominee Ann-Margret. Theater-chain owners harangued Disney until they were granted early releases from their distribution contracts, allowing them to excise *Newsies* from their marquees and theaters and open up the space for films like *White Sands* and *Diary of a Hitman*. By

---

†† A complete synopsis of *Newsies* (1992) can be found in the back of this book.

the end of its theatrical run, *Newsies* had grossed just over $2.8 million against a production budget of $15 million.

However bad the box office totals, the reviews were worse. Roger Ebert rated *Newsies* 1.5 stars, the kind of faint praise that damned movies like *Sleeping with the Enemy* (1991) and *The Karate Kid Part III* (1989) before it.

"*Newsies* is like warmed-over Horatio Alger," Ebert observed, "complete with such indispensable clichés as the newsboy on crutches, the little kid, and of course the hero's best pal, who has a pretty sister." [13]

His laundry list of objections made scarce mention of the film's treatment—except to call Menken and Feldman's material "forgettable"—and instead detailed its perceived historical inaccuracies: 10-year-old newsboys chugging beers in local saloons, the philanthropy of a scantily-clad vaudevillian star, corrupt orphanage owners pocketing charity money, street waifs organizing a miniature army to protest a one-tenth-cent price hike, and the like. Instead of putting in the work to fact-check the historical background of the film (he dismissed the idea with a pithy, "Yes, Virginia"), Ebert wrote off *Newsies* as out of touch and out of character for a studio that boasted such a rich and decorated résumé.

Others were less forgiving of the way Disney's team imbued a straightforward historical drama with schmaltzy musical elements. To the steely-eyed press, Ortega's choreography choices were decried as "clutzy [sic] dance numbers" that "never reached the high points," [14] performances that had a "wretched sameness" and evoked "a fleet of dancers in an Army P.E. formation performing a kind of macho stampede [...] a syncopated tai chi to the boomboomboom of a drum."

"When dance numbers remind you of the Gladiator School in *Spartacus*, something's wrong," the *Baltimore Sun*'s Stephen Hunter warned. [15]

Tzudiker and White took most of the flack for a story that was, by turns, "bland and meandering" [16] and "tedious when it [was] without a melody," [17] one that, while rooted in fact, was "defeated by the short-hit format of MTV, where the aim is not to advance a plot line but to showcase a star." [18] Never mind that their original story had been sliced *en chiffonade* by the inexorable powers-that-be at Disney and left as a garnish atop a hastily-assembled big book musical. Never mind that the grittier and more colorful elements of life in 19ᵗʰ-century New York City—the way sex workers utilized the newsies as errand-boys, the daily rigors and perils of homelessness, the violent methods the children used to depose strikebreakers—had been carefully omitted from the final script, forcing the writers to frame the newsies' strike from a decidedly anti-violence, family-friendly angle. All the critics could see were the missteps, the soft-focus lens on a hard piece of history.

"As much as the film may try to peddle warm and solidar-ity, it remains disturbingly cold and impersonal," griped Dave Kehr of the *Chicago Tribune*, "limited by the formulaic writing of Bob Tzudiker and Noni White and stymied by Ortega's apparent distance from his cast."[19]

Showtune veteran Alan Menken drew tepid reactions for his soundtrack; it was nearly impossible for reviewers to assess his latest collaboration with Jack Feldman without comparing it to the esteemed (and more successful) partnership he once shared with late lyricist Howard Ashman.†† A few raised their eye-brows at the songs, which skewed heavily toward "pure, naïve nostalgia" and leaned on one too many inspirational group numbers to carry the newsies' message with the gravitas it required. Still others believed that the musical breaks, though cheesy, were the only thing preventing *Newsies* from sinking into oblivion altogether. The songs were both too formulaic and not formulaic enough; rather than fleshing out characters' internal monologues and external struggles, as is so frequently seen in musical treatments, they turned on a variety of generic platitudes that could have as easily applied to any 21st-century union dispute as the newsies' strike in 1899. "The movie just about fetishizes its own squareness," one critic complained.[20]

As critics groused and box office numbers plummeted, *Newsies* suffered a fate worse than failure: It became a joke.

---

†† Menken and Ashman composed hit songs for *Little Shop of Horrors* (1989), *The Little Mermaid* (1989), *Beauty and the Beast* (1991), and *Aladdin* (1992), among several other films. Ashman died of complications from AIDS on March 14, 1991.

Those within the industry compared it to 1989's widely-panned live-action *Howard the Duck*.§§ The few theatergoers who bothered to purchase a ticket found it exceedingly difficult to emphasize with the newsies' plight.

"No effort is made to show their lives in a way today's kids can identify with," Ebert claimed, adding that the "hundreds of kids" who attended a screening of the film didn't seem to be all that emotionally invested in the outcome of the street waifs' strike. "The fact that old man Pulitzer once tried to cheat newsies out of a tenth of a cent must represent, for many of them, the very definition of underwhelming."[21]

The frigidity of *Newsies*' critical reception also struck a nerve with its young cast. The boys who spent nearly six months tap-dancing and high-kicking and honing their *New Yawk* accents on the backlots of Universal Studios had invested something real and tangible in the film. Unlike the adults who ran the show, they didn't see the writing on the wall or recognize the gamble being made on the film. They didn't know that the majority of the studio's executives had never before tackled a live-action musical, that Katzenberg had been forced to make substantial cuts to the original footage, or that the film was already testing poorly across the board. To executive music producer Chris Montan, the film "felt like a production by a team of people who didn't have a great deal of experience doing [movie musicals]."[22] To the cast, *Newsies* felt like a sure thing.

"There was such excitement on set with everyone really believing that the movie was going to be a big hit," Casella reflected in the decades following *Newsies*' initial release. "It was a real shock to witness the movie bomb when it premiered the next spring. A crushing disappointment, actually."[23]

No one felt the disappointment of *Newsies*' ruination more acutely than Christian Bale.

By the spring of 1992, the 18-year-old had already wrapped production on another Disney project. *Swing Kids* was a quasi-historical treatment of anti-Nazi youth in pre-World War II Germany and a counterculture movement that hinged on

---

§§ According to Christian Bale biographer Harrison Cheung, the film was aptly nicknamed "Flopsies" following its quick demise.

a love of Jewish-American jazz, English fashion, and the jitterbug. Bale was cast as Thomas Berger, a self-proclaimed "swing kid" whose passion and defiant nature is eventually and regrettably manipulated by the brutish ideologies of the Hitler Youth.

Swing Kids didn't depend on plaintive solos or synchronized union anthems to balance out its frenetic pacing and frequent melodrama. It was, more or less, the kind of serious film that had attracted Bale to the studio in the first place. At long last, he was making art on his own terms—at least, closer to his own terms than *Newsies* had been.

Neither film garnered the widespread public support and critical acclaim that were the necessary hallmarks of great cinema, however, and it wasn't long before Bale began to distance himself from the studio altogether.¶¶ In 1995, he returned to voice Thomas in the animated musical *Pocahontas*, thereby completing his three-film obligation to Disney. While his career gradually expanded to include roles in acclaimed films like *American Psycho* (2000), *The Machinist* (2004), and *The Dark Knight* (2008), among many others, he never seemed comfortable reminiscing about his experience as the dashing and devil-may-care newsboy that was Jack Kelly.

"At 17, you want to be taken very seriously—you don't want to be doing a musical," he told *Entertainment Weekly* in 2007. "Time healed those wounds. But it took a while." [25]

There was no way around it: *Newsies* had stumbled into critical and commercial failure. For the second time, it seemed, the newsies' story was dead in the water.

The birth of "Fansies"

There was one thing the critics didn't get quite right: Kids loved *Newsies*. The film may not have been appropriate Oscars fodder, and no one was about to argue that it deserved a place among acclaimed period dramas like *Citizen Kane* (1941) or *Once Upon*

¶¶   Case in point: *Swing Kids* ranked even lower than *Newsies* with a one-star rating from Roger Ebert. "There are moments here where the movie seems to believe Hitler was bad," he wrote, "not because he mapped genocidal madness, but because he wouldn't let the Swing Kids dance all night." [24]

a Time in America (1984). It was true, too, that adults balked at the film's lengthy runtime and moralizing tone. It was corny and cloying and sentimental for all the wrong reasons, they thought. And while they clucked and sputtered and complained about what constituted "true cinema," the children who went to see Newsies developed their own take on the film.

Kids—even those who grew up among cushy American suburbs of the 1980s, not the overfull tenements and street corners of 1899 New York City—were the only demographic capable of fully understanding the intricacies of adolescent longing and defiance. Three days after critics printed their profound disapproval above the crisp folds of the local papers, twelve-year-old Cari Gelber's letter to the editor was published in the *New York Times*:

> "I am 12 years old, and I am writing because I feel that the reviewers are wrong about children's movies," Gelber began. "They usually say the movie is bad or stupid. I think those critics should only review R-rated movies. And you should get a kid to review PG or PG-13 movies. I know I would love to!
>
> Adults don't have the same opinions as kids do, and when they said that a movie isn't good, I always end up loving it. For instance, this weekend I saw 'Newsies' and thought it was excellent though the reviewers didn't."[26]

Gelber wasn't the only one who saw value in the newsies' story. On October 14, 1992, months after the last brick-and-mortar theater purged the last reels from its projection booths, the studio released *Newsies* on VHS and Betamax home video. It was a last-ditch effort to recoup some of the $12 million they lost on the film; in a more optimistic sense, it also gave *Newsies* story a wider audience, one Disney hoped would be more receptive to a musical about child labor rights.

Still, it was slow going. *Newsies* wasn't exactly an instant hit on home video, either, and in the spring of 1993, Disney tried another tack. The Disney Channel was nearing its 10-year anniversary and had recently reached a threshold of seven million subscribers, each of whom were regularly treated to a smorgasbord of vintage Hollywood flicks, historical documentaries, concert specials, and Disney's original animated and live-action films and cartoons. Finding enough programming to run during each 24-hour cycle was proving an arduous task, though, and the programming chief was always looking for more family-friendly material to fill multi-hour blocks.

Enter: *Newsies*. The oft-overlooked film may have failed to stimulate theatergoers, but it was perfectly suited for the average home viewer looking to while away a couple of hours on a Sunday evening. *Newsies* was initially included in a "Free Spring Preview" on March 28, 1993 as part of Disney's ongoing efforts to attract additional subscribers. Exactly how and when it first caught fire among Disney fans has been lost to the passage of time, but by the mid-1990s two things were abundantly clear: The Disney Channel had shown *Newsies* to the point of excess, and the public was eating it up.

Like Bob Tzudiker's fortuitous encounter with David Nasaw's research on the newsies' strike, *Newsies* needed only to be placed in front of the right audience to become relevant again. For fans of the film, the self-dubbed "Fansies," it didn't matter that the film treated historical events that had little relevance or importance in 1990s America. *Newsies* was about more than a strike over a one-tenth-cent price hike; it was about the politics of brotherhood and friendship, the heartfelt camaraderie formed between underdogs, the way kids could muscle their way into the adult world and make an impact against near-impossible odds.

Among a certain subset of vocal, earnest viewers, *Newsies* was irresistible. Kids taped the movie off of their television sets and emptied the shelves of the local video stores. They donned their own newsboy caps and rehearsed the choreography to hits like "Seize the Day" and "The World Will Know." They tried to perfect Jack Kelly's overwrought New York accent and memorized the cadence of Patrick's mother's plaintive howls in "Carrying the Banner." They appreciated Spot Conlon's swagger and David Moscow's convictions and had strongly-held opinions about the kiss Jack Kelly shares with Sarah Jacobs in the film's penultimate moment.

From a critic's perspective—that is, to those who even bothered to give *Newsies* a second thought—the abrupt shift in public opinion was inexplicable. Disney, on the other hand, didn't go looking for the reason behind the sudden spike in home video sales. It was enough that the movie had finally found its niche, especially one that allowed the studio to recoup its initial investment with a cool $18 million in video sales alone.

With *Newsies* newly profitable and thriving on the company's cable channel, Disney turned its attention to other projects. The idea of the live-action movie musical was put to bed as animators churned out guaranteed award-winners like *Aladdin* (1992), *The Lion King* (1994), *The Hunchback of Notre Dame* (1996), *Hercules* (1997), and *Mulan* (1998). Tzudiker and White's work on *Newsies* opened the door to further opportunities with the studio, including a Phil Collins-infused version of Edgar Rice Burroughs' classic 1912 novel, *Tarzan* (1999).

Deep in the recesses of the pre-2000 Internet, on forums and chat rooms and rudimentary HTML pages, *Newsies* lived on. Children who grew up belting "Santa Fe" and memorizing the toe-tapping rhythm of "King of New York" created websites like NewsiesFreak, The Refuge, and 4 a Buck I Might; others scripted lengthy sequels to the film on FanFiction.net,[***] most sprinkled with more than a dash of smut and impropriety. Teenage girls—and, to a lesser extent, boys—were captivated by the tender, carefree relationships between the characters.

"*Newsies* [...] quietly changed the hearts and minds of a generation of schoolgirls," longtime fan and author Sarah Marshall wrote in an essay for *The Baffler* in 2018. "It helped us find each other. It asked us to think about politics. And it inspired us to write a *lot* of gay erotica."[27]

Whether Disney was aware of it or not, their little historical drama had outgrown the vision Kenny Ortega and Jeffrey Katzenberg had for it. Its complex choreography, heartfelt showtunes, and kind-hearted clan of underdogs had provided the pillars for a real-life community. Eager young fans and burgeoning writers jumped into the gaps left in the film, fleshing out friendships and romantic relationships between the characters and inserting their own experiences and dreams into the film's narrative. For many young women, including Marshall, *Newsies* provided the framework for them to confront issues of

---

[***]   As of 2019, over 7,300 *Newsies*-related stories, or "fics," have been logged during the site's 20-year lifespan.

gendered exclusion and the subtleties of sexist social coding—
the idea that girls couldn't or shouldn't hang with the boys,
that they were naturally at a higher risk of being physically
threatened or excluded, that they were subject to fade into the
background as seamlessly and cheerfully as Sarah Jacobs and
only trotted out when the hero needed emotional support or
a physical reward for his endeavors.

> "It's a movie that worked in my life, and in the lives of so
> many girls I knew and loved, not as a story but a space, a
> set of characters and sets we could use to explore our de-
> sires, our creativity, our fears, our sexualities, ourselves,"
> Marshall said. "There was something, at least to me, that felt
> particularly liberating about a *world* of boys, and the idea of
> not just watching that world but being within it: a world you
> could walk fearfully and joyfully within, freed from a life in
> which your body was a dangerous object that could, at any
> moment, cause someone to suddenly wish to dominate or
> destroy you. This was what the culture I grew up in told me
> that girlhood was, and I know that *Newsies* felt freeing to me
> not because of the when and where of it, but because it was
> a loving ode to fearless boyhood, and there was no freedom
> I wanted more."[28]

Adolescent fiction writers weren't the only ones who felt
drawn to the musical. Aspiring dancers were heartened by
the positive masculine portrayal of young male dancers; as
some confided in lyricist Jack Feldman, *Newsies* became the
springboard that propelled them to pursue their dreams of
professional theatre and dance.[29] Many a musical theatre
prodigy cut their teeth on the *Newsies* soundtrack, too, including future Broadway stars Jeremy Jordan and Ben Fankhauser.

"I tore through that VHS so hard that my mom ended up
having to buy multiple replacements," Jordan wrote in 2013.
"Jack might as well have been the older brother I never had.
In fact, I'm pretty sure that even as a kid growing up in South
Texas, I had mastered the 'New Yawk' accent by the time I was
10. I had newsie running in my blood."[30]

Watching *Newsies* gave its young viewers a sense of belong-
ing and freedom. They lived vicariously through Jack Kelly and
Crutchy and Racetrack, imagining a mostly-fictitious world in

which children wriggled out from under the thumbs of their parents and caretakers, enjoying all the pleasures and perils of adulthood with reckless abandon. (Less attention was paid to the very real-life consequences of poverty, hunger, abuse, and homelessness—all burdens borne by the newsies of 19th century America.) Within the pristine streets and cafés of Hollywoodized Manhattan, the boys belonged only to each other.

At age eight or nine, Fankhauser became captivated by the world of musical theatre during summer camp, where the kids were recruited for an informal production of *Newsies*.

"I loved that I got to be somebody else onstage," Fankhauser remembered. He was assigned the role of "Crutchy" and assigned the musical's opening monologue. "In this particular production, (this is terrible!) we added some random songs from other movie musicals. We had a set of girl twins, so the counselors aptly cast them as the Delancey 'sisters.' Bullies oftentimes feel lonely, and in our production the Delancey sisters sang 'Out Here on My Own' from *Fame*."[31]

While Fankhauser's camp counselors may have made some unorthodox casting and song choices, they weren't the first— or the last—to adapt *Newsies* for the stage. In the decade following the film's theatrical release, the newspaper-hawking, headline-hollering newsboys began crying their wares in school auditoriums, community theatres, and acting camps across the country. Unlike other Broadway classics like *Les Misérables*, *Rent*, and *Phantom of the Opera*, among a variety of others, *Newsies* was the perfect choice for young casts of inexperienced actors, as its subject material dealt directly with the aspirations and accomplishments of youth, rather than adults struggling to live with HIV diagnoses or love-struck French phantoms and revolutionaries. As music teachers and drama directors could well appreciate, its music and choreography required no expert training to play in a convincing way, either.

For those who intended to stage *Newsies* on a more professional level, however, there was a small problem:: Disney had still not licensed the stage rights to the script. Following the film's quick demise at the box office and subsequent resurgence on cable and home video, the studio hadn't given *Newsies* another thought. Resuscitating it would require time, effort, and money, none of which they were prepared to pour into a production that had flopped so publicly and thoroughly.

That hardly deterred the musical's rapidly-growing fanbase. Fans pieced together the script from repeated screenings of the film and transcribed each of its nine songs. They designed turn-of-the-century newsboy attire and began casting girls as newsies and villains alongside their male counterparts. They petitioned Disney to license the musical; then, spurred by their love for the film, asked the studio to bring it to Broadway.

Disney may have given up on *Newsies*, but its fans refused to follow suit. By sheer willpower, they managed to do more than revive the musical—they made it their own. If anyone was going to keep the newsboys' story alive, it was going to be the fans.

CHAPTER EIGHT

Newsies Forever

From the Razzies to the Tony Awards

Newsies forever, second to none! One for all and all for one!

March 31, 1981 was a strange day for celebration. In the twi-light hour along South Grand Avenue in Los Angeles, California, the red carpet blanketed the edges of the Dorothy Chandler Pavilion as the stars began poking through a periwinkle sky. The crowd fidgeted in the metal bleachers overlooking the tangle of reporters and filmmakers; they had lined up hours before the first Oscars nominees emerged from their stretch limousines, and now, on the cusp of the event itself, a subdued air quelled the usual hullaballoo surrounding the festivities. Eileen Brennan beamed under a cascade of faux red fur, Loretta Lynn shimmered in a bedazzled silver number, and the two supernovas of the evening—Diana Ross and Michael Jackson—smiled bigger and glowed brighter than any other celestial bodies of the silver screen.

Inside, removed from their spotlights and shrouded in deep shadow, the attendees listened intently as perennial Academy Awards host Johnny Carson forewent his usual monologue of snappy one-liners. There were more pressing matters at hand. Less than 24 hours before the opening ceremony, 25-year-old John Hinckley Jr. had opened fire on Ronald Reagan at the entrance of the Washington Hilton Hotel, striking the presi-dent in the lung and injuring several others nearby.

"I'm sure that all of you here and all of you watching tonight understand why we delayed this program for 24 hours," Carson told the audience. "Because of the incredible events of yesterday."

"That old adage, 'The show must go one,' seemed relatively unimportant," he added.

But go on it did—eventually, and with a gravity not often felt during Hollywood's glitzy soirées. Twenty-year-old Timothy Hutton became the youngest-ever Best Supporting Actor following his captivating portrayal of the suicidal Conrad Jarrett in Best Picture winner *Ordinary People*; 82-year-old Eva La Gallienne commanded recognition as the last living nominee to be born in the 1800s, though she lost the Best Supporting Actress trophy to 27-year-old Mary Steenburgen of *Melvin and Howard*; makeup artist Christopher Tucker's transformative work with lead actor John Hunt on *The Elephant Man* inspired the creation of a brand-new Oscars category the following spring. By every measure, the show was a success.

At least, that's how some saw it. In a less-celebrated neighborhood of Los Angeles, within the recesses of an apartment building that had seen better days, film school graduate John Wilson was throwing an Oscars party of his own. This one didn't have quite the sheen of the official event, nor did it celebrate the innovation and emotion behind Tinseltown's latest moneymakers. Instead, Wilson focused on pronounced cinematic missteps and gaffes, performances gone askew and moments too hammy to be taken seriously.

From a painted cardboard podium in his living room, Wilson's party guests sifted through the worst films of 1980 and awarded "dis-honors" to seven films: fumbling Village People movie-musical *Can't Stop the Music* (Worst Picture and Worst Screenplay); soft-focus roller disco travesty *Xanadu* (Worst Director); the outrageously outdated and emotionally unavailable Neil Diamond in *The Jazz Singer* (Worst Actor); Brooke Shields' awkward, albeit iconic performance in *Blue Lagoon* (Worst Actress); eight-year-old John Adames in *Gloria* and 73-year-old Lawrence Olivier in *The Jazz Singer* (co-Worst Supporting Actors); the frustrated and lovesick Amy Irving, whose explosive affair with Willie Nelson's character became a peculiar backdrop for *Honeysuckle Rose* (Worst Supporting Actress); and George Dunning and Andrew Fenady's not-quite-earworm "The Man with Bogart's Face," as featured in *The Man with Bogart's Face* (Worst Original Song).

The mock awards show ended with neither a bang nor a whimper, but a rousing singalong to a parody version of "That's Entertainment."[1] He dubbed the whole affair the annual "Golden Raspberry Awards," colloquially referred to as the "Razzies," and just like that, a new tradition was born.

Wilson didn't need to put forth extraordinary effort to attract the attention of the Hollywood elite. Within 15 years of the inaugural Golden Raspberry Awards show, CNN and *USA Today* had given the event national attention, while director Paul Verhoeven became the first to accept his award (Worst Director, *Showgirls*) in person and Bill Cosby demanded a handful of 24-karat gold statuettes* for landing Worst Picture, Worst Screenplay, and Worst Actor in the universally-panned spy flick *Leonard Part 6*.[2] Some, like Cosby, reacted well to their new titles as Razzie award-winners, but a far greater contingent took umbrage over the perceived slight. (Of course, that was the entire point of the ceremony, but it didn't lessen the sting at all.)

In 1993, another film entered the inner circle of Razzies award-winners: *Newsies*. The campy Disney musical was nominated in five of nine categories: Worst Picture, Worst Supporting Actor (Robert Duvall as Joseph Pulitzer), Worst Supporting Actress (Ann-Margret as Medda Larkson), Worst Director (Kenny Ortega), and Worst Original Song ("High Times, Hard Times" by Alan Menken and Jack Feldman). It won Worst Original Song, beating out Enya's bilingual ballad "Book of Days" (*Far and Away*) and a Whitney Houston dance club bop, "Queen of the Night" (*The Bodyguard*).

In 1993, *Newsies* composer Alan Menken had just secured his third and fourth career Oscars when he received word of the Razzie that had been fashioned in his name.†

---

* Cosby was no great fan of the film himself, and insisted that his Razzie Awards be immortalized in gold and Italian marble. Fox Television footed the $27,000 bill, while the network's *Late Show* gave him a platform to receive his awards in the weeks following the official ceremony.

† Alan Menken and Jack Feldman were the first nominees to net both an Oscar and a Razzie in the same year. They earned two Academy Awards for *Beauty and the Beast* (Best Original Score and Best Original Song) and one Razzie for *Newsies* (Worst Original Song). Others soon followed suit, including

"It was a very emotionally draining night, because Howard [Ashman] was gone," Menken told the *New York Times'* Dave Itzkoff some years later. "And then in the press room, they said, 'Oh, you won the Razzie for worst song.' I just took that. It was an acknowledgment that 'Newsies' was a big fat flop, and isn't that funny? It was not a particularly great song."[3]

As had become customary, the Razzies were announced the day before the Oscars played out, nearly a full year after *Newsies'* ill-omened debut. it would be another several months before the film caught fire on the Disney Channel and home video, and another decade before it strong-armed its way into Times Square as a full-fledged Broadway production.

This was rock bottom. Luckily for both Menken and *Newsies*, the only direction left to go was up.

The spark that started it all...again

By the dawn of the 21st century, Disney had to do something about *Newsies*. The film, a poetic, if heavy-handed interpretation of the newsboys' strike of 1899, had collapsed upon its arrival at the box office in April 1992. Critics mutilated the good intentions and earnest efforts of the cast and creative team, spearing the head of the production (renowned choreographer and debut director Kenny Ortega) and holding it up as a deterrent to other would-be movie-musicals.

It worked for a while. Pooh-poohed by cinephiles and ignored by the masses, the film pocketed just $2.8 million in theaters, well below the $15 million budget such an elaborate period piece required. It took *Newsies* the better part of a year to find its own devoted fanbase—and what a fanbase it found. Kids across the country tuned into multiple airings of the film on cable TV, then cajoled their parents to buy it on VHS tapes and Betamax video cassettes. As a fledgling World Wide Web took on substantive form and scope, teenagers pedestaled the characters and songs on fan-made websites, spurring the

---

screenwriter Brian Helgeland in 1998 (Academy Award: Best Adapted Screenplay, *L.A. Confidential*; Razzie: Worst Screenplay, *The Postman* and leading actress Sandra Bullock in 2010 (Academy Award: Best Actress, *The Blind Side*; Razzies: Worst Actress and Worst Screen Couple, *All About Steve*).

frenzy to new and impressive levels. Fans didn't just want to enjoy the newsies' story—they wanted to recreate it. More than a few of them had already been moved to stage their own performances of "Seize the Day" and "Carrying the Banner" in school auditoriums and camps and living rooms in order to bring the newsies of New York City back to life.

To Disney, *Newsies'* fan-driven resurgence was a heart-warming, if belated response. It was touching to watch kids and young adults embrace the story (seeing it, for the first time, as it was truly intended to be seen), but the company felt no impetus to do anything further with the material. Landing a failed movie-musical on Broadway to play in front of a fanbase that, for all they knew, counted no more than a few hundred or thousand in its ranks, would have been futile at best and an utter disaster at worst. Let the summer camps and amateur theatres have their pirated newsboy musicals. There was little, if anything, that Disney stood to gain from it anymore.

In 2006, the viability of the live-action movie-musical was tested with another Kenny Ortega production. *High School Musical* had nothing to do with newsboys or union disputes; as its title suggested, it focused on a group of young high school jocks and drama enthusiasts who were tasked with putting on a spring musical. Like *Newsies*, it gave a platform to young adults who were struggling to find their voice—the basketball star who develops an appetite for musical theater, the shy math whiz who needs to break out of her shell, cliques of geeks and athletes who find they share a unique kinship—and made its point with Ortega's slick choreography and catchy group numbers.

More importantly, at least as far as Disney's bottom line was concerned, *High School Musical* was single-handedly responsible for reviving a genre that had died with *Newsies* back in 1992. Over 7.7 million viewers tuned into its U.S. cable premiere on January 20, 2006. It wasn't just an instant hit; it would go on to become one of the company's most profitable and popular franchises, too. The soundtrack landed at No. 2 on *Billboard*'s year-end chart and, according to Disney's calculations, was the fastest-selling DVD release of a made-for-TV film to date.[4] Within its first three years in circulation,

High School Musical had been seen by over 255 million people worldwide and spawned two immensely successful sequels. Maybe there was something to this youth-based movie-musical business after all.

As the Disney Channel's ever-expanding cable viewership began stanning star-crossed lovers Troy Bolton and Gabriella Montez, the company took another long look at *Newsies*. Over at Disney Theatrical Group, headed by Thomas Schumacher, a project was in the works to develop and license a new batch of professional stage shows. Instead of pouring time, money, and talent to take each individual show to Broadway, Disney found they could reap faster rewards by skipping a preliminary pit stop in Times Square and shipping the scripts straight to schools and small professional and community theatre groups instead.

"One of the lists generated on an annual basis is the top-requested titles for stage adaptations," creative development vice president Steve Fickinger wrote in 2013. "Year after year, one title made its appearance either at the top or near the top of the list: *Newsies*."[5]

It seemed foolish not to try. Sure, *Newsies* had flatlined when it first premiered in front of audiences, and even taking into account the undeniable popularity of *High School Musical*, it was conceivable that the public at large wasn't ready for a new stage adaptation of the singing newsboys ill-advised strike. On the other hand, Disney reasoned, it wasn't as if they had Broadway within its sights. At most, they sought to appease *Newsies*' massive fanbase by giving them what they really wanted: not a sequel or a Broadway show, but licensing rights to seize the day in their own cities and hometowns.

After 14 years, it seemed Disney was finally ready to return to *Newsies*. Little did they know what they were in for.

Recipe for success or formula for failure?

"How about a stage version of that?"

"It's never going to work. Forget it."

Harvey Fierstein stared at the sunset-colored DVD atop Alan Menken's piano. The silhouette of a young Christian Bale leaping atop a mountainous pile of discarded newspapers had given him an idea. The two were supposed to be collaborating on a score for the upcoming musical *Kinky Boots*, but suddenly Fierstein's mind was elsewhere. *Newsies* was among Menken's less notable works—in his own words, a "disaster" that lacked the vision and direction to survive a jump from the silver screen to the stage. It was just the kind of challenge that gave Fierstein a thrill.

"Let me take a whack at it," he told Menken. "I'll watch the movie again and see if there's something I can do to get it to work. If I come up with an idea, we can try. If not, no harm done."[6]

The raspy-throated actor-turned-playwright made a compelling point, albeit one Disney had already explored. Around 2007, Menken had received a call from his agent. Disney was interested in converting *Newsies* to the stage. It was a no-strings-attached deal for the musician, who wouldn't be required to touch the material twice.

"[My agent] told me: 'You don't have to get involved,'" Menken revealed to the *New York Times*. "'They'll take your songs, and someone else will come and write new ones. I just want to let you know.'"

That wasn't going to fly with Disney's most prolific composer.

"Oh, no," Menken protested. "No, no, no. It's my baby, no."

"Alan, there's not going to be any money."

"I don't care. I don't care, this is my baby."[7]

After some preliminary tweaks and two underwhelming table reads, however, Disney was no closer to shaping *Newsies* into a stock and amateur production than they had been 16 years ago. Bob Tzudiker and Noni White had imbued the 1992 film with heart and wit, but their script fell flat on the stage—owing, perhaps in part, to their lack of familiarity with the pacing and structure of musical theatre. Eventually, the creative team had to face the music. Following a final work-shopping session in October 2008, they collectively agreed to table discussions of a *Newsies* stage musical. Whoever handled the project next, if anyone, would need to take the kid gloves off and start digging deep into the story, especially if they intended to sidestep the widespread criticism and financial pitfalls that cursed Disney's original production.

Several months passed. Disney Theatrical had bigger concerns than the fate of a musical about orphaned newsboys. Four Broadway shows had shuttered within the last two years—including *Beauty and the Beast* and *Tarzan*—and Disney was looking for a sure thing. Over at the Lunt-Fontanne Theatre, meanwhile, an ambitious production of *The Little Mermaid* suffered a protracted and painful death as it failed to command the same critical acclaim that followed its animated source material. Academy Award-winning musical numbers, extravagant sea-toned set pieces and the magic of hidden wires (rigged to enable its ocean ensemble to "swim" above the stage) failed to captivate crowd after crowd of landlubbers. After 22 long months, the $15-million musical closed its doors for good on August 30, 2009.

Only two Disney musicals refused to relinquish their hold on New York City. *The Lion King* proved unexpectedly and undeniably successful when it made its puppet-heavy Broadway premiere on October 15, 1997. Where Ariel and Sebastian lost some of their animated joie de vivre in the transition to a live-action production, the lion-sized *Hamlet* adaptation came to life in new and refreshing ways in the theatre. Rather than imitating the acclaimed film beat for beat, *The Lion King* used tasteful pageantry and elegant costumes to improve on the story without sacrificing its most iconic moments. Audiences still wept over Mufasa's death-by-fratricide and bopped along to "Hakuna Matata" and felt chills electrifying their spine as the first notes of "Circle of Life" broke upon the rows of the Minskoff Theatre. In time, it would become the third-longest-running show in the history of Broadway's legendary inner circle.

Two blocks away, under the gilded canopies of the New Amsterdam Theatre, *Mary Poppins* played out its third season on Broadway. Disney wouldn't disclose its earnings on the show, but it was clear the no-nonsense flying nanny and her whimsical world of imagination (suspension wires notwithstanding) were destined for a long run—though it would never attract the notoriety or profits that *The Lion King* continued to rake in year after year. Notably, it was the only live-action Disney film to make a successful transfer to the stage, and one that aged gracefully before capping its six-year lifespan on March 13, 2013.

Flash forward to that pivotal meeting between Fierstein and Menken in 2009, one that neither the composer nor playwright initially recognized as a turning point for the company. Fierstein lit the fuse that would ignite *Newsies the Musical*, even as Menken cautioned him that Disney had already tried and failed to do anything meaningful with the material.

The inherent risks of tackling a failed show didn't seem to matter to the librettist. He was already smitten with *Newsies*, thanks in part to a few nights he had spent rewinding the tape for his young nephews, and immediately saw potential lurking behind Jack Kelly's "adorable ineptness" and the boyish athleticism that punctuated the musical's stirring anthems.

Neither the film's poor critical reception nor Menken's well-intentioned warning could dissuade him: Fierstein was going to bring *Newsies* back with or without Disney's help. He took the good news straight to Disney Theatrical president Thomas Schumacher, who seemed equally delighted to find someone both capable and willing to deliver the newsies' story to the masses.

"Harvey," he said," if you could come up with a stage adaptation, you would make a lot of people happy."[8]

It helped that no one expected much out of *Newsies the Musical*. The film may have caught fire with a particular subset of a particular generation, but the public at large couldn't have cared less about the outdated period piece. What's more, the average rate at which Disney and non-Disney Broadway shows failed hovered around 75 percent, costing the company no small chunk of change, especially as should-be classics like *The Little Mermaid* ceased to gain traction.[9]

This worked in Fierstein's favor. Together with Menken and Feldman, he would have total creative control over the revival of *Newsies*. The worst outcome, he told Schumacher, was that they wasted some time fiddling with the lyrics to a few old melodies. It was the other side of the coin that he was more interested in, the one where they finally did justice to a story about children seizing control of their own destinies against cruel and indefatigable forces. (And if *Newsies* became an immensely profitable outfit for Disney and lived up to the hype generated by thousands of rabid teenage fans, all the better.)

Schumacher didn't hesitate. He gave Fierstein the green light to do with *Newsies* as he saw fit. What could happen?

Revisiting the newsies of 1899

At last last, *Newsies* was getting a second look; more than that, it was getting a full-blown makeover. In the words of Alan Menken, art had finally met the right moment. But what was next for the show? How could they pull off something that had already failed so many times before?

Fierstein, Menken, and Feldman knew they couldn't replicate every beat of the old movie on the stage, nor did they want to. The structure of a compelling story was in there somewhere amid modern dance choreography and old-fashioned costumes and Jack Kelly's never-say-die dream of moving out West, but it would require a little finesse to turn an almost unbelievably successful child-led strike and the peculiar theatricality of 19th-century vaudeville into a polished script fit for school auditoriums and community theatres across the country.

Before Fierstein touched a single line of the script, he lingered at the metaphorical crossroads. What kind of story was begging to be told? Did the film do enough justice to the newsies of 1899? Would the audience expect a faithful rendition of their favorite cult film? Would they balk at a more artistic interpretation of the strike? How could Disney make the newsies relevant to the kids of mid-2000s America?

There were as-yet unplumbed depths of the newsies' experience, to be sure—their complex ongoing relationship with myriad rivals of the *New York World* and *Journal*, the presence and power of the young newsgirls in their ranks, the exploitative quality of the strike coverage itself—but neither

Fierstein nor Disney were fishing for a more historically accurate version of the newsboys' tale.

"Facts are not what drama is," the playwright said. "I don't care that Pulitzer was in Maine [during the strike]."[10]

Fierstein made it clear that he wasn't interested in the minutiae of turn-of-the-century New York City. Instead, he wanted to approach the production with even broader brush-strokes, creating a portrait that captured the raw spirit of the newsboys' movement without getting hung up on every period-specific fleck of paint. It took a while for him to find a genuine point of connection with the newsies' story, and when he finally did, it manifested in the most obvious place: between the folded pages of a newspaper.

Flipping through the pages of a local paper, *Newsies'* newest book writer had a revelation.

"I wanted to make at least one cogent argument defending print media to a culture that doesn't seem to care if the daily paper disappears altogether," he wrote in an essay for the *Huffington Post*. "[...] And then I came face to face with an item whose attributes cannot be quickly scrolled through. It's a newspaper stronghold that demands attention and participation: The political cartoon."[11]

He had picked up on something that even Tzudiker and White had missed in their original treatment. Although the history of the 1899 strike was important to tell (and tell *well*), it was just as important that modern audiences find a way to relate to it, too. Aspiring Broadway dancers and budding historical fiction writers found plenty of inspiration in the earnest performances from Christian Bale and his posse of urchins and self-made salesmen, but the film's tepid reviews suggested, with all the delicacy of a bullhorn, that the majority of audiences didn't find the period drama relevant to their own lives in the slightest.

By Fierstein's interpretation, Jack's art became a seamless blend of the personal and political, from his sketches of pitiful scenes in the House of Refuge to the cartoon of a boot crushing the children gathered at Newsie Square. When placed in the right hands—in this case, those of *New York Sun* reporter Katherine Plumber and state governor Theodore Roosevelt—they provided the young newsboy with a gateway to lasting social change. It's his sketches that inspire Katherine to expose the Refuge's myriad abuses and his mural that becomes a rallying point for the strikers all across the boroughs of New York.‡

While Fierstein hoped that the audience would recognize the power of the political cartoon to confront current political and social issues, he also allowed the newsboys to speak through both art and literature as a way of signaling to Joseph Pulitzer that a new generation was ready to rise up and claim their place in the world.

"If I've done my job right, it makes a statement that's bigger than the newsies," he told the *Times*. "It's about a bunch of kids changing the world, about handing over the world to a new generation."[12]

Figuring out how to get the newsies' message across without resorting to the feel-good campiness that infected the 1992 film presented another hurdle, however. He turned to Menken and Feldman, who had been itching to tinker with the songs that once earned them a Razzie.

"I grabbed the chance to go back and make improvements in any number of areas: clarity, storytelling, character, gracefulness, etc.," said Feldmane.[13] He excised the line, "We need a good assassination!" (and its accompanying pelvic thrusts) from the musical's opening number, "Carrying the Banner," and replaced it with a tamer query. Gone, too, was the forlorn wail of Patrick's mother as she wandered through a gaggle of newsboys to look for her missing son.

Elsewhere in the script, Disney's creative team revamped its supporting cast. Medda Larkin was no longer the simpering, curly-hair Swedish Meadowlark who flirted with the newsboys and cooed her way through saccharine solos. Instead, she called to mind a combination of the talent and theatricality of famed African-American vaudevillian star Aida Overton Walker and starlet-turned-sex-symbol Mae West. Medda offers Jack, Davey,

---

‡ In a fairly on-the-nose moment in the musical's final scene, even the villainous Joseph Pulitzer mentions to Jack that he might use his rudimentary skills as a political cartoonist to expose corrupt political dealings in local government.

and Les welcome refuge in the theatre—where she is now not only the marquee performer, but proud owner of the mortgage—insisting, in one of the show's few meta moments, "Where better to escape trouble than a theatre?[14] Unlike the plot of the 1992 film, where Medda plays witness to a harrowing ambush at Irving Hall, the Bowery's biggest star is not present for any of the altercations between the newsboys and strikebreakers, though it's later suggested that her intimate familiarity with Theodore Roosevelt plays a part in getting the governor to exert pressure on Pulitzer and end the strike for good.

The villains of the story—Warden Snyder, Mr. Wiesel, the Delancey brothers, and a handful of minor antagonists—were largely left as is, while the "big baddie," Joseph Pulitzer, got a facelift and a new outlook on life. No longer the infirm editor of a paper about to go belly-up, he transformed into a spry, conniving business mogul with a flair for condescension and a knack for self-preservation. Pulitzer was also given a big reveal to deliver in Act 2,[§] as well as an expository solo in which he lays out his evil master plan to rob the newsboys of a one-tenth-cent profit per paper.

The biggest change was the addition of *New York Sun* columnist Katherine Plumber. An 18-year-old girl longing to break out of the society pages and report "real news," Katherine was established as the newsboys' biggest ally in their stand against Pulitzer and the *World*. Quick-witted and sharp-tongued, her playful banter with Jack soon turns romantic, and any trace of objectivity goes right out the window as she becomes more and more invested in the newsies' cause—even helping the strikers draw up their own newspaper to expose the injustice of both the strikers' circumstances and the corruption and mistreatment within the Refuge.[¶]

The decision to add Katherine to a full roster of toe-tapping

§   Pulitzer informs Jack that *New York Sun* reporter Katherine Plumber is his daughter, adding yet another obstacle for the lovers to overcome by curtain call.

¶   Headstrong women were hardly in short supply during the 1899 strike, if interviews with the spirited Annie Kelly and her rival Brooklyn Bridge newswomen can be believed. Still, there are plenty of moments throughout *Newsies the Musical* when Katherine's inclusion in the newsboys' strike doesn't feel

newsboys and mustachioed super-villains was an easy one for Disney's creative team. Early in the development process, they realized that Jack's former love interest, Davey and Les' sister Sarah, was all but superfluous to the plot of *Newsies*. She was unceremoniously cut from the script, as was veteran *Sun* reporter and newsboy mentor Bryan Denton. Katherine filled both sets of shoes with more polish and verve than either had managed on their own.

"Creating the main character of Katherine—a sparring partner and love interest for Jack—was huge. And it made Jack smarter to have a smart girlfriend," said executive music producer Chris Montan. "Because we didn't have any romance in the movie [...] And a musical comedy without romance really has a gun to its head."[16]

Katherine represented the first major female character in *Newsies*' history, but Disney was very clear about one thing: They weren't going to pivot from a male-centered story to a period romance (or, to a lesser extent, devote much time to Katherine's particular character arc as a burgeoning young reporter with a conscience—that is, not outside of her romantic connection to Jack).**

"The romance doesn't overtake the piece," Montan added, "which is about young men dancing and singing viscerally. If you

---

very progressive. From the moment she first bumps into Jack on the street, she is framed almost exclusively as an object of desire and affection. Jack crosses boundaries with her in a way that is meant to feel flirtatious—the will-they, won't-they sexual chemistry that drives their inevitable union at the end of the show—but often comes off as creepy: offering to lock himself into a private box with her, dismissing her interest in the strike as an attempt to stalk him, making suggestive overtures to her when she tries to get a serious quote for her front-page piece, and invalidating her ambition to become a "real" reporter. Only when she begins to show an evident bias in favor of the newsies (and relents to his advances) does he take her seriously. Taking their cue from Jack, the rest of the newsboys are similarly disparaging of Katherine's ambitions and person—"Methinks the lady needs to be handled by a 'real man,'" Romeo asserts, and Davey adds, "I'd say we save any exclusive for a real reporter"— in a way that their characters never treated her predecessor, *Sun* reporter Bryan Denton, in the 1992 film.[15]

** Even Katherine's solo, "Watch What Happens," catches her daydreaming about Jack's physical allure and agonizing over the right way to tell the newsies' story. She doesn't question if her bias in favor of the children makes her fit to publish an objective front-page piece about the strike.

take what is entertaining about *Newsies* at its core, it is those boys doing 'Carrying the Banner' or 'King of New York.' It's thrilling."[17]

Menken approached the story from a different angle. "For me, it was a matter of just, 'Get out of the way and let *Newsies* speak,'" he said.

As it turned out, they had plenty left to say.

Jack Kelly 2.0

After months of trimming lyrics and sharpening banter, Disney's creative team was finally ready to move forward with its first developmental reading of *Newsies the Musical*. They rented out a skyline-view studio at Ballet Hispanico on the Upper West Side—not quite a penthouse perch, but tall enough to peer over the lower rooftops of the city—and called in their three bigwigs. Fierstein, Menken, and Feldman had already pored over the material countless times before, but even as they prepped for the 29-hour presentation, they couldn't be quite certain that Disney was moving toward a flesh-and-blood stage production of their own. As far as anyone from Disney Theatrical Group was concerned, the sole goal of the reading was to lay the groundwork for a licensable version they could market to regional theatres in the season to come.

It couldn't hurt to put out feelers for a few principal roles, however, especially when it came to casting the star of the show. The Jack Kelly of Fierstein's new book was talented and calculated, savvy without veering on smarmy, a natural-born leader whose ability to thrive in chaos was tempered by a passion for justice and equal rights. If *Newsies* stood any chance of surviving a revival (even just in script form), they needed to sell the reading audience on exactly that kind of strike-leading, Santa Fe-dreaming protagonist.

Still, the studio was all too cognizant of its missteps with the surly Christian Bale some 17 years earlier, missteps they were actively preparing to avoid their second time around. They didn't need another Hollywood hotshot to drive the story, just someone who could step into the well-worn shoes of an ebullient leader, sensitive artist, and heartstring-tugging turn-of-the-century ragamuffin. Whoever played Jack would have to easily embody all facets of his character, and more importantly, make the material *sing*—literally, yes, but also in such a way that the higher-ups in Disney Theatrical could envision the young newsboy bursting from the ballet studio and onto the streets of 1800s Manhattan itself.

It might have proven a near-impossible task had 25-year-old Texan native Jeremy Jordan not crossed paths with the company in the months leading up to the reading.

"I had never worked for Disney," Jordan recalled, "and I got cast as the lead. That was great, and I loved the movie as a kid so I immediately connected with it and knew what I wanted to do."[18]

With limited time remaining to prove the script's viability, Disney hastily patched together a cast from new recruits and former employees and new recruits and gave them a week to flesh out the show. Staff associate director Jeff Lee arranged what little choreography he could under the Actors' Equity specifications, hoping to infuse the reading with the kind of physicality and passion that was so apparent in Fierstein's dialogue and Menken's music.[††]

When Ballet Hispanico opened its doors at 2:30 p.m. on May 14, 2010, it was as if the final piece of the puzzle had just snapped into place.

"The great thing about Jeremy Jordan was that he walked in the room and he was Jack," said Lee. "Everything that came out of his mouth was pitch-perfect. There was an energy about him that you didn't want to mess with."[21]

Disney didn't have to take a second look at the young actor. It didn't matter that the biggest role Jordan had played to date was a temporary alternate for Tony in the Palace Theatre's multi-season revival of *West Side Story*, or that he didn't carry a natural "New Yawk" accent, or even that he was on the cusp of accepting another lead role in Frank Wildhorn and Don Black's

---

†† According to meticulous guidelines set forth by the Actors' Equity Association, the rehearsal and performance period cannot exceed 29 hours during a staged reading. Actors are not permitted to participate if the reading is intended to solicit backers—not an issue for Disney, Lee pointed out[19]—and no sets, props, wigs, makeup, costumes, excessive choreography, or script memorization is allowed.[20]

Depression-era musical, *Bonnie & Clyde*. The luckiest directors know what it's like to stumble across the rare actor born to the play the part, and for the heads of *Newsies* (and, later, show director Jeff Calhoun), Jeremy Jordan was it.

In December 2010, a second developmental reading was arranged at the New 42nd Street Studios. Fierstein, Menken, and Feldman were working through a laundry list of issues with the show, from the fine points of Joseph Pulitzer's solo to the best way to double up roles among the company.[‡‡] As the last details fell into place, another thought occurred to the cast and creative team. *Newsies* was in fine shape for a stock and amateur release, and there was no doubt it had distinguished itself from the campiness of the 1992 film, but might it also be able to survive a limited run prior to its widespread distribution?

Menken certainly thought so: "Wheels began to turn. Expectations had to be managed. It was a balancing act of extraordinary proportions."[22]

Developing a script for small-market playhouses was one thing—one manageable, low-risk thing—but attempting to make *Newsies* a commercially-viable production was an endeavor of far greater proportions. There were arguments to be made on both sides. On one hand, Disney couldn't simply brush off the overwhelming critical and commercial failure that dogged the 1992 flick. They had been confident in that project, too, and subsequently disappointed by nearly every audience member and box office return. On the other hand, everyone agreed that *Newsies the Musical* was a beast of an entirely different breed. Fierstein's writing was crisp, Feldman's lyrics impeccably edited, and Calhoun's cast comprised of characters both mesmerizing and fully fleshed out.[§§] This was their

---

[‡‡]   In the stage version of *Newsies*, Mr. Wiesel moonlights as the Stage Manager, Mr. Jacobi, and the Mayor; Nunzio later appears as Theodore Roosevelt; Hannah is spotted elsewhere as one of the three charitable nuns, a Bowery Beauty, and on occasion, a newsboy; and many of the Manhattan newsboys double—and triple—as scab workers, Brooklyn newsies, and the (heavily-fictionalized) sons of *New-York Tribune* owner Whitelaw Reid and *Journal* owner William Randolph Hearst.

[§§]   It's worth noting that while Jordan did secure the lead role in the Paper

opportunity to prove that *Newsies* deserved another moment in the spotlight—and they didn't intend to waste it.

On September 25, 2011,¶¶ the early morning light came up on the metal towers of the Paper Mill Playhouse in Millburn, New Jersey. Crutchie, played by the soft-spoken Andrew Keenan-Bolger, hobbled about the moon-softened tenement rooftop as Jeremy Jordan's Jack Kelly pontificated about building a life out West.

"They say folks is dyin' to get there," Jack crooned. "Me, I'm dyin' to get away to a little town out West that's spankin' new. And while I ain't never been there, I can see it clear as day...if you want, I betcha you could see it, too."[24]

Jack gestured out across the shadowy expanse of the 1,200-seat theatre, painting sweeping pictures of clay cities, galloping palominos, and afternoons spent lazing along the Rio Grande. Out in the audience, Disney's creative team was watching a dream of a different sort unfold before their eyes. Every guttural roar from the crowd, every hand lifted in applause or cupped around a cheer served to reinforce what the studio already suspected: This was *Newsies* at its finest.

Humble beginnings in New Jersey

It's not as if Disney snapped their fingers and—*presto!*—*Newsies* was placed in a Broadway house straight out of its second developmental meeting. The reading had sparked something in the show's creators, but the logistics of arranging a professional staging had to be worked out before they could even think about putting the newsies in front of an audience again.

As far as the public was concerned, *Newsies* was being fast-tracked for licensing; anything beyond that was pure

---

Mill Playhouse production of *Newsies the Musical*, as well as its Broadway iteration, a different cast was selected for the December workshop. Principals included Jay Armstrong Johnson as Jack Kelly, Meghann Fahy as Katherine Plumber, Jason Michael Snow as Davey, Matthew Gumley as Les, and Shuler Hensley as Joseph Pulitzer.[23]

¶¶   Performances of *Newsies the Musical* began as early as Thursday, September 15, but the official press opening was scheduled 10 days later on September 25.

speculation. Behind the scenes, however, there was a flurry of decisions to be made. Where would the production be hosted? Could choreographer Christopher Gattelli update Ortega's high-energy dance numbers in a way that felt fresh and modern without detracting from the show's old-fashioned setting? How would set and lighting designers Tobin Ost and Jeff Croiter evoke the atmosphere of 19th-century New York City onstage? Would costume designer Jess Goldstein outfit Jack Kelly in another quasi-Western getup or something more period-appropriate? More importantly, would anyone want to see *Newsies* again?

The first question resolved itself as soon as Steve Fickinger reached out to Mark Hoebee, the artistic director of New Jersey's acclaimed Paper Mill Playhouse. Paper Mill was no hovel; by 2011, Jersey's most famous regional theatre had already benefitted from the worldwide releases of *Harold and Maude* (2005) and *A Wonderful Life* (2006) and captivated audiences with an array of stars from Liza Minnelli and Carol Channing to Kristin Chenoweth and Patrick Swayze. Nestled on the banks of the Rahway River, some 23 miles from the dazzling marquees of Manhattan, it was in close enough proximity to the Great White Way that it could pull from Broadway-caliber talent while preparing its own slate of shows to make the jump to Times Square. Its capacity, estimated at a cool 1,200 seats, also rivaled that of Broadway's more capacious houses and could give prospective shows some inkling of how well-received they'd be in the city—assuming, that is, that they made the transition at all.

"[Fickinger] called and said, 'I have a project, and I want to talk to you about it. Would you come in?'" Hoebee said. "I didn't know what it was. And when he started talking about *Newsies*, immediately my eyes lit up and I thought, 'I cannot believe that we are having this conversation!' He said, 'We're looking for a home to test it. Is this something you'd be interested—' I didn't let him finish."[25]

It wasn't the first time Hoebee had dreamed of bringing the 1992 cult classic to Paper Mill's stage,*** and once Disney

---

***   The idea, he said, had been floated by the theatre's former CEO

Theatrical reached out about the possibility of turning *Newsies* into a full-fledged musical, he didn't need any extra convincing to sign on to the project. One very emphatic 'yes' later, *Newsies the Musical* had its first temporary home.

Little by little, the creative team began to dismantle the hurdles blocking their path to opening night. Tobin Ost, aided by Jeff Calhoun and Thomas Schumacher, crafted a modern moving "jungle gym" out of two-ton, 24-foot-tall metal towers that could not only pivot and shift to accommodate elaborate group dance routines, but stand in for various locations around the city as well: Jack Kelly's rooftop home, the *World* distribution center, Katherine Plumber's office, the Refuge, the cellar of the *World* building, Newsie Square. Full screen projections and minimal set pieces were carefully layered in to flesh out the lavish interior of Joseph Pulitzer's office, the tables at Jacobi's Deli, and the stage and theatre boxes of the Burlesque House, but it was the towers that framed the newsies' split leaps, flips, back handsprings, and double tours in both intimidating and impressive fashion.

With the mammoth metal towers juxtaposed against the newsboys' more traditional 19th-century garb, Disney had finally settled on a perfect marriage between edgy and classic elements of the stage musical. Then came the sticker shock: The towers would cost over $500,000 to construct, well beyond the outer limits of Disney's budget for set design.

"We were faced with going back to Tom, then returning to Jeff and Tobin to come up with something vastly cheaper...or figuring out a way to make this design viable," said associate producer Anne Quart. "With three big towers that come downstage and rotate to create various atmospheres, you couldn't just go to one tower—it's not quite the same."[26]

The towers may have been indispensable to Ost's vision for the show, but there was no way they could scrimp and save enough to make it a reality. It was starting to feel like a near-impossible task when, in an inspired moment, Quart decided to construct them in such a way that they could be easily collapsed, transported, and erected at various regional theatres across the

---

almost a decade earlier in 2002.

country. Nothing as grand as a Broadway run or official North American tour was in the works, but the possibility of renting out the towers would allow Disney to cover the initial costs of construction. Better yet, it would lend an even more professional feel to future productions of the show.

Both Schumacher and managing director David Schrader agreed to find an extra $250,000-300,000 to put toward the massive set pieces. Barring a complete redesign, which they had neither the time nor the inclination for, it was the only option that made any kind of practical sense.

From the dappled shadows falling across the rooftops of Manhattan to the newsboys' signature caps and Lycra-lined trousers, every aspect of Paper Mill's newest show was designed to enhance the newsies' story. Disney just needed one more piece to fall into place: the newsboys themselves.

Casting a professional stage musical required an entirely different yardstick than casting a Hollywood drama. Back in 1992, the studio selected dozens of young, amateur actors and put them through a rigorous, 10-week training process so they could fight, dance, and sing with some measure of believability. Their performances were gritty and unpolished, and it was that relative inexperience that lent a much-needed air of authenticity to the project.

On stage, Disney wasn't looking to mold another gaggle of inexperienced child actors into something resembling the orphan troupe of *Oliver!* Choreographer Christopher Gattelli, who had wormed his way into the production after a fortuitous run-in with creative development manager Jane Abramson,††† had an entirely different concept in mind.

Nostalgia had already proven valuable currency. *Newsies the Musical* had a venue and choreographer; soon, it would attract an unprecedented number of veteran and amateur dancers to fill the roles of the leaping, tap-dancing, backflip-and-newspaper-pirouetting newsboys. It didn't matter

---

††† Like Hoebee, Gattelli had fond memories of the 1992 film and wasn't about to take 'no' for an answer once he found out Disney had plans for a stage production. "I'm doing that show," he told Abramson over and over again.[27] Luckily, Disney also felt it was a perfect match.

that the show had yet to make it to Broadway—that, at this point, it wasn't even clear how its four-week run in New Jersey would be received—everyone wanted the chance to be part of such an iconic and dance-focused piece. When the casting call came in for the Paper Mill production, over one thousand dancers showed up.

"People were there who had done principal contracts before, or a thousand Broadway shows, but it didn't matter," said Aaron Albano, who would eventually be cast as "Finch." "We were all willing to take whatever we could get because *Newsies* meant so much to us. We got the chance to be a part of a phenomenon that we grew up with in such an influential way."[28]

This was all music to Disney's ears. They could pick from the cream of the crop and, considering that Gattelli's vision for the show was essentially "*Billy Elliot* times 20," that's exactly what they'd need to do.

By the time Gattelli, Calhoun, Schumacher, Fierstein, Menken, and Feldman had exhausted the hundreds of dancers who advanced through multiple rounds of auditions and callbacks, they had amassed enough talent to cast multiple shows and then some. It was obvious they weren't working with the baby-faced first-timers that had challenged Kenny Ortega and choreographers Peggy Holmes and William Holden, Jr. nearly two decades earlier. Gattelli's newsies were the real McCoy.

The choreographer, and, by extension, the rest of Disney's creative team, didn't just need good dancers to flesh out the fight scenes and passionate rallies around New York City. They needed to get at the heart of the striking newsboys' clan, the way Ortega had managed to do with Christian Bale and David Moscow and Max Casella and Marty Belafsky and Luke Edwards. The audience that had so faithfully dogged the film wasn't going to make the trek out to Millburn, New Jersey to watch a newsboys-themed revue pass itself off as the second coming of *Newsies*. Menken and Feldman had already orchestrated the musical's stirring soundtrack, but it was up to Gattelli to advance the story by blending expert dance technique and masterful choreography with the newsies' old-fashioned charm and innocence.

It was easier said than done. Gattelli had to convey the newsies' character arcs while seamlessly integrating more elaborate group numbers and tap dance sequences in an homage to—or restructuring of—some of the film's more iconic scenes. After working and reworking bits of choreography with the cast, the end result was a series of subtle shifts that stretched from "Carrying the Banner" to "King of New York."

At the outset of the show, each of the newsboys were given individualized combinations and routines to perform, with rough, unstructured movements that evoked the spontaneous and carefree romps the children often took through the city. As the plot advanced through the formation of the union during "The *World* Will Know" and the violent clash between the strikers and *World* employees in the middle of "Seize the Day," the boys' movements became more unified and polished, a reflection of their increasing maturity.[29]

"For me, the dance in the show, aside from pushing the story forward, is also a metaphor to the story the boys are telling," Gattelli told CBS Boston's Adam Rothenberg. "In the show, the newsboys were at an age where they wanted a seat at the adult table, and didn't mind how hard they had to work to get it. And in our show, you actually see that happen in real time."[30]

The real test was yet to come. Everyone who worked on *Newsies the Musical*, from the ensemble to the stage managers to Schumacher himself, was confident in its impending success. Internally, it was hailed as "magical" (Christopher Gattelli) and "special" (Thom Gates), something "wicked cool" (Tommy Bracco) and "major" (Ben Fankhauser) and "terribly rewarding" (Mark Hummel). Each person had their own come-to-Jesus moment during the development of the show, whether it came on the back of a high G4 as Jeremy Jordan belted "Santa Fe" or during the first synchronized double tour en l'air of "Seize the Day."

The proverbial lightbulb clicked over dance arranger Mark Hummel's head during the first round of rehearsals, when even the cast's unpolished dance routines inspired frequent bursts of applause.

"To get the reaction in the middle of the number, you stop and say, 'Gosh, I guess we're doing something right,'" he confessed.[31]

But *Newsies the Musical* wasn't just for the cast and crew, no matter how deeply the film had resonated with them in 1992 or how lovingly they had treated the source material. It was for the fanbase that had blossomed out of the film's box office collapse and buoyed the newsboys' story for the past two decades. *Newsies* was for the kids who rewound their VHS tapes to watch Spot Conlon sling pebbles at beer bottles and strikebreakers. It was for the storytellers who took solace in their craft and kept Jack Kelly and David Jacobs alive on the page in lively, if non-canonical tales. It was for the 'Fansies' who petitioned Disney to license the musical in the first place and, on occasion, even dared to transform the material on the stages of their own schools and theatres.

Newsies was also for first-timers, and it was that demographic that had Hoebee feeling nervous as previews rolled around in the autumn of 2011. Paper Mill's subscriber base skewed heavily toward retirees and senior citizens,[‡‡‡] many of whom weren't well-versed in the particulars of 19th-century labor politics and were unbound by the nostalgia that was driving younger customers to the theatre in droves.

He needn't have worried.

"At our first Thursday matinee, which is our heavily sub-scribed senior audience, I thought, 'This is going to be a test,'" Hoebee admitted. "When they stood up at the end and loved it, it was a real eye-opener, a huge turning point in the potential of this musical."[32]

It was difficult to say what the audience connected with most: the blend of new and old musical traditions, the stirring melodies that connected one dance number with the next, or, as Hoebee suspected, the alluring "testosterone-built engine" of a predominantly male cast. Whatever the prevailing reason, there was no doubt that *Newsies the Musical* had instantly endeared itself to a new audience—and, much to Disney's relief, a more sympathetic pool of critics. The reviews rolled in hot off the presses, each more enthusiastic than the last.

"'Newsies' has a stirring, old-school sincerity that's hard to resist," the *New York Times*' David Rooney gushed. "In its call

---

[‡‡‡] According to Hoebee, the median age of Paper Mill Playhouse sub-scribers was 62 years old.

to arms, its refusal to back down to big business, its fight for basic human dignity and its skepticism toward politics, the show also has themes that resonate in our new depression."[33]

Vulture agreed. "This is, at bottom, a children's musical about a children's crusade, but it's got some fairly sophisticated flourishes and never stoops to flaccid self-ironizing," critic Scott Brown decided. "There are worse things in life, and onstage, than an old-fashioned fairy tale about the triumph of the Exploited, where the powerful are back-sassed with pot a bourées [sic] and legitimate grievances are registered not just nonviolently, but in tap shoes."[34]

"This is the rare stage show that dramatically improves upon its source material. [...] Broadway could use a fresh burst of good newsies," suggested *Entertainment Weekly*.[35]

Entertainment Weekly wasn't the only one who pictured a bigger platform for the plucky little show-that-could. Company manager Eduardo Castro had Broadway on the brain as soon as the curtains rose on *Newsies the Musical* for the theatre's first 1,200 patrons. There were myriad problems to solve—budget configurations to be made, sales and marketing strategies to be developed, audience interest to be gauged, not to mention improving on Disney's hit-or-miss record with previous movie-to-musical treatments—but as soon as the first positive reviews landed, it didn't seem like there was any other option for the toe-tapping, paper-slinging newsboys of northern New Jersey.

Fast-tracking the development process to secure a spot in Times Square (and, for the lucky few, a handful of Tony nominations) was ill-advised for almost any show in almost any circumstance, but *Newsies the Musical* had several things working in their favor. The story of scrappy underdogs-turned-champions was already a bonafide hit with Jersey audiences, many of whom represented just a fraction of the devoted following that embraced the 1992 film. There were no guarantees in show business, but it seemed like more fans were bound to emerge from the woodwork if *Newsies* made a successful jump to one of Manhattan's esteemed playhouses.

It didn't hurt, either, that there appeared to be no decided frontrunner for the upcoming 2012 Tony Award designation of 'Best Musical.' Desperate for something to offset the widely-panned *Spider-Man: Turn Off the Dark*, theatre companies had already pegged two Off-Broadway productions for last-minute transfers: : *Once*, a heartfelt musical based on the 2007 indie darling of the same name, and an irreverent and gruesome superhero spoof titled *The Toxic Avenger*, also based around a pre-established cult classic.[36] Even against a fistful of new-to-Broadway musicals—*Bonnie & Clyde*, *Ghost*, and *Rebecca*—there was ample room for another newcomer, especially one with *Newsies'* dynamic staging, fresh choreography, and crowd approval.

Rumors abounded that the Nederlander Organization had its eye on the newsboys, but Schumacher gave only the most cautious assurances to the press.

"It's only natural that we want to try to bring this show to Broadway now, when its message is so timely," he was quoted in the *Times*.[37]

There were no two ways about it, though: Neither *Tarzan* nor *The Little Mermaid* had generated the kind of revenue and accolades the company was hoping to receive over the last decade, and the last time *Newsies* had been put in front of a wide audience, it tanked. The potential for spectacular failure far outpaced the musical's potential for success, and Disney couldn't pretend they weren't taking a risk by expensing another move to Broadway.

In the end, the company took a page from the books—er, *newspapers*—of their beloved newsies. Even a failed run on Broadway could boost licensing sales, Schumacher conceded, and the fans had given him no reason to doubt *Newsies'* ability to hack it in the big leagues.

"Am I happy 'Tarzan' and 'Mermaid' didn't run? No," he said. "But the average failure rate for Broadway shows is 75 percent. I can't stop producing out of a fear of failure."[38]

By November 15, 2011, the move was official. A 12-week, $5 million run at Manhattan's 91-year-old Nederlander Theatre was ordered for *Newsies the Musical*, with the Tonys within its sights. The newsboys of Lower Manhattan were going home at last.

Newsies invade Broadway

You could have asked Noni White. You could have asked Harvey Fierstein or Jess Goldstein or Eduardo Castro or Emily Powell or Michael Cohen. Among the skeptics, there were always those who believed *Newsies* would end up on Broadway.

> "There was just something in the air," Jeff Calhoun said. "I think the actors, certainly Chris and I, Ricky, everyone in the room felt: 'My god, [...] I think there's something very special there. This is above and beyond.' And you hope that happens for every show, but sometimes it's just out of your control—[the moment] when it's going to ignite. And it was clear early on to all of us that it was gonna ignite and that we were working on something very special."[39]

Even those who weren't directly involved with the show could sense its potential, as one Broadway theatre owner told Disney Theatrical vice president David Schrader.

"Why aren't you transferring this?" he wondered aloud as the boys seized the day and tossed papes into the first few rows of Paper Mill's auditorium. "Look around. It is a real musical. People actually really like it."[40]

Deciding to stage *Newsies* on Broadway was simple. Making that decision a reality was far more complicated. Even with a venue in place and portable, if enormous, set pieces, there were a million little things left to get right: reassembling the Erector set towers, reconfiguring the staging and choreography to fit a new space, mixing the sound to better accommodate every nook and cranny of the Nederlander's peculiarly-shaped house, and most importantly, figuring out how to attract the same manic crowds that had made *Newsies*' abridged run at Paper Mill such an arresting and explosive event.

The final wrench in Disney's plans: The show would need to be loaded into the theatre in a week's time. They couldn't spare the cash for the customary three-week load-in period, as they didn't know if they would be able to recoup those expenses when *Newsies* made its debut in late March. Impossible constraints had never before stopped Disney from forging ahead with their plans, however, and this would be no exception. Technical supervisors Anne and Geoffrey Quart coordinated the logistics for lighting, sounds, and sets, while Gattelli added the final flourishes to the show's dance routines, Menken and Feldman composed three new songs for Pulitzer, Medda, Katherine, and Jack, Goldstein streamlined elaborate costume pieces and remade props and accessories to withstand a more rigorous show schedule, and Jeremy Jordan officially severed ties with Clyde Barrow to take on Jack Kelly's persona full-time.§§§

With the last newspaper stacked and the last projection screen unfurled, Disney waited for the crowds to come flocking in through the double doors. Luckily this wasn't 1992. The Internet had advanced past basic HTML fan pages and rudimentary online forums, and advancing along with it was a passionate, involved fanbase that was larger and louder and hungrier than the company could have ever anticipated. The advent of rapid-fire, real-time social media platforms allowed Disney to glimpse the mounting enthusiasm for the show's impending move to Broadway, but even the most earnest believer in the show couldn't have predicted the lengths to which fans would go to see their long-awaited dreams come true.

"We could see them interacting on Facebook and Twitter—and they actually bought tickets," Schrader said. "[...] That might happen for a famous title that hadn't been revived in 20 years. But no one had ever seen *Newsies* as a legitimate stage show before. To them it was just an idea. Before long, fans from all 50 states were flocking here—like Woodstock!"[41]

He wasn't exaggerating. From the first preview on March 15, 2012, the Nederlander brimmed with the energy of 1,200 *Newsies* enthusiasts, some of whom had waited 20 years to see the curtain rise on a Broadway production of their favorite campy, once-failed '90s flick. Waves of applause coursed through the theatre after every paper-stomping, spoon-clacking performance of "Seize the Day" and "King

---

§§§   Jordan originated the role of the eponymous Clyde in Jeff Calhoun's *Bonnie & Clyde*, which transferred from the Asolo Repertory Theatre in Sarasota, Fla. to Manhattan's Gerald Schoenfeld Theatre in December 2011. He juggled leading roles in both shows for several months, but poor sales and lukewarm reviews downed *Bonnie & Clyde*'s chances of finishing their open-ended run, freeing its escaped-murderer-turned-folk-hero to jump four blocks downtown and join the newsies for their Broadway debut.

of New York." And applause wasn't the only thing the show received in spades.

The first six preview performances generated a gross of $735,991, easily eclipsing the theatre's long-standing record for profits-per-preview.¶¶¶ When tickets went on sale for the musical's scheduled 12-week engagement, then firmly capped at 101 performances, they began selling so quickly that Disney was forced to reconsider the possibility of an open-ended run before *Newsies* had even made its official debut. Four days after the show's first preview, and just 20 days before opening night, the producers announced a two-month extension of *Newsies*.

Almost overnight, *Newsies* had become *the* hot ticket in town, and there wasn't a balcony perch or orchestra seat that went unfilled from night to night. Still, Disney's marketing team kept fretting about the show's niche appeal. Nostalgia made a fine hype man, but what was going to happen once the show's most dedicated fans had already come to New York City, seen *Newsies*, and bought the newsboy caps? Would anyone be interested in a family-friendly musical that catered more to aspiring dancers and historical fiction buffs than the average Broadway theatergoers?

Disney wasn't about to wait around to find out. Using methods William Randolph Hearst and his headline-hollering newsies would no doubt have approved, they spearheaded aggressive social media and marketing campaigns, plastering snippets of the most rapturous reviews on every bus station and billboard around town: "The Perfect Musical For Our Times!" "A Triumph!" "New York's Smash-Hit!" "An Exhilarating Jolt Of Energy! This Is A Musical Audiences Can Believe in."

Twenty years after *Newsies* warbled and wobbled its way into cinemas for the first time, its critics were scarce to be seen. Then again, it may not be entirely fair to compare the abysmal ratings foisted on a static film with those of the living, breathing animal of live theatre. Any film pundit's viewing of

---

¶¶¶   According to the *New York Times*, *Rent* was the Nederlander's previous best-seller after it grossed $864,321 over eight preview performances in 1996, which averaged out to $108,040.13 per preview. By comparison, *Newsies* averaged $122,665.17 per preview.42

the 1992 movie could only inspire so many interpretations of Robert Duvall's cartoonish tirades and Christian Bale's put-on New Yawk drawl, whereas the quality and content of a live performance might be witnessed again and again through new lenses.

That said, there was no denying the seismic shift in public and critic approval alike. Lackluster *Newsies the Musical* was not, and the reviews were plentiful and kind-hearted—often improving even on the warm reception of the musical's run at Paper Mill.

"Like *Oliver!* and *Annie* before it, *Newsies* delivers the news that on Broadway, orphans can be irresistible," *Entertainment Weekly* raved, crediting Gattelli's "tap-tastic showstopper" and "aggressively acrobatic choreography" as the driving force behind the show's urchin appeal.[43]

Others were quick to agree.

"Theater insiders are calling it the boys' answer to *Annie*, and while that description might sound snarky, it's not entirely off-base," said the *Hollywood Reporter*. "[...] You can call the show brashly formulaic, sentimental or simplistic, but *Newsies* adheres to a time-honored Disney tradition of inspirational storytelling in the best possible sense. It woiks."[44]

The highest praise came from *Variety*: "Sparked by a star-making performance from Jeremy Jordan, a tunefully friendly score from Alan Menken and Jack Feldman, and high-leaping choreography by Christopher Gattelli, 'Newsies' is Disney's happiest outing since 'The Lion King.'"[45]

The final stamp of approval wouldn't be found in the entertainment sections of local newspapers or printed on box office receipts. On May 1, 2012, four weeks after *Newsies the Musical* premiered on Broadway and six weeks after Disney announced the show's two-month extension and seven months after *Newsies* caught fire at the Paper Mill Playhouse and three years after Harvey Fierstein fronted the movement to bring the newsies' story to the stage and 19 years after Alan Menken was the unlucky recipient of a Golden Raspberry Award for Medda Larkson's heavily-accented showstopper, "High Times, Hard Times," Jim Parsons and Kristin Chenoweth stood behind a glass podium at the Dorothy and Lewis B. Cullman

Center and read out the list of Tony Award nominees.

There, under the auspicious headings of "Best Scenic Design of a Musical," "Best Orchestrations," "Best Original Score," "Best Choreography," "Best Book of a Musical," "Best Direction of a Musical," "Best Actor in a Musical," and (most coveted of all) "Best Musical," the same title flashed in blue and black on the screen over and over again: *Newsies*.

The sky congealed into a thick, deep blue above the Beacon Theatre on June 10, 2012. The 66th Annual Tony Awards swept through the city, clad in red carpet and the tarped walls of ads for Broadway's most celebrated event. Dressed to the nines, theatre's finest playwrights, actors, composers, and technicians glittered and gabbed on the way to the Beacon, dodging questions from overeager reporters about their nominations and impending EGOT statuses. Inside the theatre, only 24 things mattered, and they all looked more or less the same: three-and-a-half pound, nickel-plated bronze medallions bearing the names of the true masters of their craft.

Of course, there was more at stake here than a title or short-lived accolade. A designation like "Best Actress" might give an ingénue more bargaining power in her next gig, while something like "Best Musical" could catapult a show from moderate popularity to long-term moneymaker. The medallions were more than reminders of past success; they were stepping stones to future victories.

In the end, almost everything went to the other dark horse of the season, indie festival favorite *Once*. It was nominated 11 times and won eight awards; *Newsies* garnered eight nominations and two wins—one for Chris Gattelli's superb choreography work and one for Alan Menken and Jack Feldman's collaboration on the score.

"It's been such an incredible, improbable journey for *Newsies*," Menken told the audience. "From poor *Newsies*, the movie that made nothing at the box office, that won us the Razzie for Worst Song of the Year, which we did cut from the show."[46]

There was nothing in the gilded marble-and-mahogany halls of Beacon Theatre to evoke the raucous razzing of John Wilson and his cardboard podium and "That's Entertainment" parody in the living room of his L.A. apartment. The Razzies were a distant memory, one made far less vivid by newer, shinier, kinder awards. This was the real deal.

If only the newsies could see their fictional contemporaries now: making a public mockery of the Scrooge-like Pulitzer every evening, victorious at last, their fists curled around the shimmering silver half-moon of a Tony Award instead of a shabby floral horseshoe. They would be hard-pressed to imagine anything more thrilling.

Newsies hits the road

The Tonys was a delightful pit stop for *Newsies the Musical*, but it was hardly the end of the road. While the production missed the big award—Best Musical—which might have otherwise transformed their open-ended run into something bigger and brighter, they were still able to head home to the Nederlander and slap "three-time Tony Award winner" on a fresh batch of posters.

It was a good feeling, and one that was compounded by news of a different, albeit no less welcome, variety. Six months after *Newsies* got their long-anticipated Tonys bumps, the show recouped its initial $5 million investment and became the fastest Broadway production to turn a profit in Disney's history.**** According to the *Times*, *Newsies*' approximate $7.9 million gross was also one of the highest profits turned by any show that landed in Times Square during the 2011-2012 season.

Eventually, though, the sheen of awards season had to wear off. *Newsies* retained its status as a fan favorite through multiple cast changes, including that of Jeremy Jordan, Kara Lindsay, Andrew Keenan-Bolger, and more. Recasting was part and parcel of running a show, and the overturn never seemed to give Schumacher pause.

"I don't know if the broadest audience closely follows which actor plays which roles, unless it's a really big-name star,"

**** Granted, *Newsies*' accomplishment came with two substantial caveats. In the years leading up to its debut in 2012, only four other Disney musicals were financially successful on Broadway: *Beauty and the Beast*, *The Lion King*, *Aida*, and *Mary Poppins*. *Newsies* also had the smallest financial backing of the four.[47]

he told the *Times*. "What's most important to me is having someone who can play the role beautifully."[48]

Beautiful performers cycled in and out of principal and ensemble roles constantly, but it wasn't long before Disney was forced to face the music: sales were down, and it wasn't looking hopeful that they could get them back up in time to save the newsboys of New York.

The Fansies had done all they could to buoy the production. Even their unstemmed tide of love letters, cosplays, fan videos, tweets, Facebook posts, and repeat stage door visits couldn't single-handedly keep the newsies afloat. For one thing, there was an ever-revolving carousel of new, thrilling stories to be converted into Broadway attractions (read: competitors)— *Matilda*, *Kinky Boots*, *Matilda*, and Rodgers and Hammerstein's *Cinderella* were among the newest, with Disney's own *Aladdin* close behind in 2014—and the newness of *Newsies* had long worn off. For another thing, ticket sales hit a typical lull in autumn. In summertime, the show easily turned profits of $1+ million a week, which dropped down to $800,000 when the leaves began to crisp in Central Park in September 2012 and dropped down again to $600,000 the following autumn.

The announcement came on June 22, 2014: *Newsies* was leaving Broadway, for good this time. Once the cast sang the last refrain of "King of New York" ("Victory! / Front page story / Guts and glory / I'm the king / Of New York!") and Jack Kelly performed his last heel click and Race executed his last flip (cigar still intact) by the stated closing date of August 24, 2014, there would be no fan petition or sudden box office surge grand enough to make Schumacher and Disney Theatrical reconsider their decision. The change wasn't without a silver lining: In lieu of a continued run on Broadway, the newsboys of the Nederlander would be packing up their large metal towers and stacks of newspapers and heading out on a 25-city, 43-week North American tour.

Disney hadn't lost track of its endgame. The goal was, as it always had been, to license *Newsies the Musical* to theatres and schools, to put their beloved newsboys in the hands of those who had clamored to tell the children's story for years—and clamored even now. But there was no harm in drumming up a bit of extra support for the show, and if message boards and Instagram hashtags could be taken at anything more than face value, there were thousands of eager Fansies ready to carry the metaphorical banner across the country.

The only issue? Disney had never treated *Newsies* as *just* a musical to be licensed and performed in high school gyms and community college theatres, despite the lines they kept feeding the media. While it was customary for Broadway tours to cut corners when it came to production value and overall quality, hemmed in as they were by smaller budgets and hit-or-miss crowds, Tom Schumacher couldn't bear the idea of sending a poor man's version of the newsies' rambunctious, gripping story into the world. He worked with his team to develop a version of *Newsies* that could easily travel with their mobilized towers, while Gattelli focused his energy on retooling the show's dance routines to better reflect the strengths and specialties of the new cast, and Menken and Feldman once again set to the task of scripting a riveting new number, this one for Crutchie.

After two years, 63 cities, and well over 700 performances, the tour ground to a halt in Southern California for a full week.†††† The Pantages Theatre sparkled with art deco flair amid the who's who and what's what of Hollywood, and in the wee hours of September 11, 2016, Fansies began to stake out their spots along Vine Street in nervous anticipation for that evening's performance. The ticket booths were closed to newcomers; only those who had been personally invited were permitted a seat inside, while hundreds of hopefuls lingered outside the theatre in case there was an advantageous connection to be made or spare seat to be won.

This was no ordinary showing of *Newsies*. Disney, it seemed, had something else up their sleeves.

---

†††† The final tour count: Two years, 65 cities, and 784 performances over 70 engagements.

From the screen to the stage to...the screen

It happened when Tom Schumacher watched *Billy Elliot* for the first time. Not the classic 2000 British drama or the musical adaptation semi-permanently situated in London's West End or the Broadway production or the U.S. National Tour or the Australian Tour, but the taped live recording of *Billy Elliott The Musical* that premiered in 2014. There was something elegant and refined in director Brett Sullivan's vision, an element that transcended the typical stationary view of a live recording. The story also lent itself to film, devoid of fantasy, elaborate costuming, onstage quick changes, special effects, or props too puppet-like to be believed, even by a well-exercised imagination.

In other words, it was the kind of treatment that might also fit something like *Newsies*. Schumacher floated the idea to Sullivan.

> "I wanted to make sure it was great," Schumacher says. "One of the things that makes *Newsies* work well in this environment is that it's a show that does not have a huge fantasy or magic component. Most of our shows in close-up wouldn't look that great. This wouldn't work with *Lion King* or *Beauty and the Beast*, but when that camera pushes in on Jeremy Jordan, you'll be moved."[49]

It was simple enough to envision on paper, but once the ball started rolling, it quickly became evident that any taping of *Newsies* had more than one obstacle blocking its path. Sullivan and his crew cleared the theatre for a week and brought in nine cameras, each of which had to be carefully maneuvered to fit the 24-foot towers on the screen. Calhoun, meanwhile, busied himself by assembling a hodgepodge cast of original Broadway vets and their touring counterparts. Jeremy Jordan, Kara Lindsay, Andrew Keenan-Bolger, and Ben Fankhauser reprised their roles as Jack Kelly, Katherine Plumber, Crutchie, and Davey, respectively, and six more ensemble members were added to beef up the show's already-impressive musical numbers. After months of prep work, added rehearsals, last-minute-cast changes, and seven straight days of filming, the cast of *Newsies* was ready to put the finishing touches on their last performance at the Pantages.

The projection screens lifted above Jack Kelly's penthouse in the sky, and an audible buzz rose from the orchestra to the balcony. This was no ordinary performance; neither was this an ordinary crowd. Some of the magic that infused *Newsies the Musical*'s inaugural run in the little theatre in Millburn, New Jersey had returned. After 24 years, *Newsies* would finally be immortalized on film the right way—the way, some might argue, it should have been done long ago.[‡‡‡‡]

When the towers emptied and the applause receded for the last time, one question still lingered in the mournful echo of "Santa Fe": When, over the course of *Newsies*' meteoric ascension through the world of theatre and film, had Disney drawn attention to the actual newsboys and newsgirls of 1899? What debt did they owe them to get their story right? What had *Newsies* given them the justice they marched and bled and struggled to achieve all those years ago?

That would be left for future generations to decide.

[‡‡‡‡] Far from a box office bomb, *Newsies the Musical* soared on screen, breaking Fathom Events' records as it raked in $3.47 million over its limited three-day release in February 2017.[50]

CHAPTER NINE

The Story They Needed to Write

How Disney Films Interpret and Influence Our Understanding of History

This is the story we needed to write, that's been kept out of sight—but no more!

After nearly 60 years of animating European fairy tales and anthropomorphized animal-based folklore, Disney was ready for something new. They'd had their fill of sketching pale princesses like Snow White and Cinderella, of telling stories that hinged on century-old spells and curses, cauldrons and the crisped skin of poisoned apples. It wasn't that the public didn't enjoy a good fairy tale—the resounding approval and critical acclaim with which *The Little Mermaid* (1989) and *Beauty and the Beast* (1991) was met said otherwise—but rather that the studio wanted to continue pushing the envelope as they careened through their latest Renaissance period.

"In 1991, I pitched to Michael Eisner, Roy E. Disney and Jeffrey Katzenberg the following story idea: 'Pocahontas: A beautiful Indian princess falls in love with a European settler and is torn between her father's wishes to destroy the settlers and her own wishes to help them,'" recalled Mike Gabriel, the eventual co-director of the 1995 animated film *Pocahontas*.[1]

The studio's executives didn't have to think twice. By the end of the pitch meeting, they had already committed to the film. Historical events were an as-yet unexplored resource for the company, which preferred to dabble almost exclusively in diverse mediums of fiction, and Pocahontas' story appeared to strike just the right balance between compelling historical narrative and romanticized cinematic drama.

Animator Glen Keane had a different take. "Disney's been in such a—I don't want to say a 'rut,'" he told *Entertainment Weekly*'s Jason Cochran in 1995. "But we've been doing mainly Caucasian faces."[2]

Until the raven-haired Jasmine began entertaining royal suitors in 1992's *Aladdin*, Keane and his posse of animators drew from a narrow pool of vanilla features. Their female characters, exclusively of the petite, feminine, and white variety, were often relegated to bit parts in their own stories: the damsel in distress, the overlooked servant, the comatose princess, the headstrong captive, the mute mermaid. The angle of a cheekbone or length of an eyelash may have varied from film to film, but there were no real risks to take as long as Disney insisted on churning out faithful adaptations of Anglocentric fairy tales. It was clearly time for a change.

Breaking the mold, both as storytellers and animators, required more finesse and cultural sensitivity than Disney realized. They couldn't take the same creative liberties with the historical figure of Pocahontas as they could with the fictional heroines who preceded her. For better or worse, the film had to be guided by an element of truth.

In the early 1990s, Disney sent a team of writers, researchers, and artists to scope out Jamestown, Virginia, where colonizer John Smith once staked his claim on the New World. And it was there, between the archeological remnants of 17th-century architecture and the lush natural vistas of Virginian rivers and forests that Disney's perfect, mold-breaking plan began to show a few cracks. Jamestown may have made a compelling backdrop for the young lovers of Gabriel's reimagined Shakespearean spectacle, but the real settlers and Native Americans who once walked its streets told a different story, one bloodied by war, kidnappings, disease, and starvation. In other words, a story that was just a touch removed from Disney's PG-rated brand.

History holds that Pocahontas was born around the mid- to late-1590s and was known to her people as Amonute.* She was the presumed favorite among dozens of children fathered by native leader Wahunsenacawh (or Powhatan), who boasted a chieftainship of more than thirty Algonquian-speaking tribes. Some of his chiefdoms had been acquired through crises of widespread disease, others by war, still others by strategic alliance and intermarriage. As the surviving settlers from the Virginia Company weathered fire and famine through their first icy winter in the Jamestown settlement, they could not have been unaware of Powhatan's unassailable power and prosperity.

By the time Pocahontas and John Smith crossed paths in 1607, she was no more than 10 or 11 years old to his 27 years. According to historian Camilla Townsend, the two shared a kinship that, at least on the outside, was perfectly befitting an adult and child.† When Smith was held captive by Powhatan and his cousin, Opechankeno, in the winter of that year, he bonded with Pocahontas as they attempted to teach each other the nuances of the English and Algonquian languages.[4]

The idea of a half-naked child coaching a clothed English-man on his Algonquian pronunciation didn't exactly fit with Disney's proposed adult romance, however. Nor did the fact that the incident for which Pocahontas and John Smith are most famous—her purported rescuing of the stranger from the death blow of a club wielded by her own father—never happened.‡

---

*   As she reached adolescence, she was more commonly referred to as Poca-hontas ("playful one" or "spoiled child"). After her migration to England, she revealed a third name: "Matoaka." By that point, she had already been bap-tized and christened "Rebecca Rolfe," the name she held until she died in 1617.

†   Smith's published works in 1612 and 1624 painted a different, more sexualized picture of Pocahontas. He even asserted that he had been the welcome recipient of sexual advances from thirty naked native women at once, Pocahontas among them. It is almost entirely certain that these claims were fabricated.[3]

‡   Smith wrote extensively about his time in captivity, but failed to mention the alleged rescue until 1624, long after the deaths of any potential eyewit-nesses—including Pocahontas. Travelogues of his exploits in Turkey and France boasted suspiciously similar stories of young women falling in love with him and delivering him from barbaric punishment.[5]

Pocahontas was never smitten with the man 15 years her senior, nor did she spare his life in a touching moment of spontaneous empathy and fevered longing. In the years following her meeting with Smith, she wed Kocoum, a warrior with whom she likely fell in love. The marriage lasted only a few years before the girl was kidnapped by English captain Samuel Argall and transferred to Jamestown while the colonists conducted lengthy hostage negotiations with Powhatan. Around age 18 or 19, Pocahontas was eventually released to marry wealthy tobacco planter John Rolfe and shipped off to London, England, where she gave birth to a son and died at age 21, most likely due to illness.

Smith, on the other hand, was returned to Jamestown for a small ransom. He then lost whatever good standing he had gained with the native Virginians after holding them at gunpoint in order to restock his settlement with food and supplies. The brief meeting he arranged with Pocahontas in London before her death did not go well.

It wasn't as if Disney hadn't cracked a history textbook in half a century. They knew what historical constraints were placed upon the story, which details (Pocahontas' young age; John Smith's homicidal tendencies) might interfere with the fairytale-like script they had in mind. And they had no intention of pushing the envelope on cultural matters, either.

During the fall of 1992, the company provoked a swift public outcry following the release of *Aladdin*, in which Arab-presenting characters spoke in thick foreign accents and exhibited dishonest and violent tendencies. By contrast, Aladdin and Jasmine (the hero and heroine of the movie) adhered to a stricter moral code and were marked by lighter complexions and Americanized accents.[§] At the behest of the American-Arab Anti-Discrimination Committee, Disney altered the most offending line from the film—"Where they cut off your ear / If they don't like your face"—but did little else to rectify a tense situation.

---

§   Aladdin's features purposefully mirrored those of Caucasian actor Tom Cruise and live-action model Rob Willoughby, and Jasmine was patterned after live-action model Robina Ritchie and animator Mark Henn's sister Beth.[6] Both characters, presumably of Middle Eastern descent, were brought to life by white voice actors.

Disney animators found themselves straddling an even finer line. The company had already committed several serious faux pas with *Peter Pan* back in 1953, where the movie's only Native American characters donned large feather headdresses, puffed on a ceremonial pipe, and threatened to burn white children at the stake.¶ Not only did Disney strive to avoid such offensive caricatures the second time around, but they intentionally hired Native American voice actors to record lines for the characters of Pocahontas, Powhatan, Kocoum, and other members of Powhatan's clan, hoping to bring some semblance of authenticity to the film.

"The picture was politically correct," story developer Joe Grant said, later admitting, "We lost out on some great opportunities for caricature, especially with the Indians. We didn't want to be offensive in any way."[7]

Good (albeit problematically phrased) intentions and accurate casting aside, there was still the problem of the story itself. Disney had invested too much time and research into the project to simply scrap it now. Instead of walking away from an R-rated chapter of American history, one that had long been shrouded in urban legends and filtered through an overwhelmingly white perspective, Disney chose to scavenge bits and pieces of Pocahontas' life to fashion a colorful fictional narrative.

Flanked by cheeky forest creatures and the wizened spirit of her grandmother, the Disneyfied character of Pocahontas was no longer presented as a prepubescent child, but an overly-sexualized teenager.** John Smith's racist and violent tendencies were downplayed so he could better fit the part of

---

¶   The only song devoted to the Native Americans, who are identified by John Darling as the "Blackfoot tribe from the Algonquian group," is a racist number entitled, "What Made the Red Man Red?"

**   Native American historian and Powhatan descendent Shirley "Little Dove" Custalow-McGowan stood in as a character model for the eponymous heroine, as did Filipino college student Dyna Taylor. Animators also referenced historical paintings of Pocahontas herself and magazine photographs of supermodel Christy Turlington. Glen Keane described the animated Pocahontas' look as that of a "tribal Eve" with "Mongolian features." "We're doing a mature love story here, and we've got to draw her as such," he told *Entertainment Weekly*. "She has to be sexy."[8] McGowan, meanwhile, stepped away from her role as a consultant and character reference after Disney made it clear that they did

the noble adventurer and sympathetic lover. Add to that the simmering tension between the restless settlers of the Virginia Company (nary a peckish or sickly soul among them) and the battle-hungry warriors under Powhatan's rule, throw in a scheming villain and his simpering first mate, and top it off with Kocoum's murder, Pocahontas' dramatic rescue of John Smith at the moment of his would-be execution, and Smith's even more dramatic last-minute sacrifice to save Powhatan, and the studio had what it considered cinematic gold.

Disney had strayed so far beyond the bounds of history that it was a stretch to say *Pocahontas* was anything resembling historical fiction, let alone an accurate portrayal of the woman herself. But giving adolescent moviegoers a history lesson wasn't necessarily its goal.

"You have to approach it carefully," supervising animator Glen Keane explained. "The Disney version becomes the definitive version."[9]

Keane made an interesting point. For years, films like *Snow White and the Seven Dwarfs* (1937), *Cinderella* (1950), *Sleeping Beauty* (1959), *The Little Mermaid* (1989), and *Beauty and the Beast* (1991) had become the definitive versions of the centuries-old fairy tales they were based on—stories that had been told and retold long before Walt Disney dreamed up his first feature-length animated film.

Pocahontas put into sharp definition what had been an oft-overlooked issue with Disney's fictional stories. The studio wielded a unique power in Hollywood: Almost without exception, each of its film adaptations had taken root in the collective imagination and memories of the American public, supplanting whatever original material they drew from.[††] Now that Disney had chosen to turn its attention toward historical

---

not intend to make an accurate representation of historical events.

†† Case in point: The Grimm Brothers were renowned for their gory fairy tales, many of which were intended for mature audiences. In the 1930s, Walt Disney carefully pruned the story "Little Snow White" of its more objectionable content (attempted strangulation, murder by enchanted red-hot shoes, etc.) and repackaged it with cutting-edge animation and special effects to create the unforgettable classic, *Snow White and the Seven Dwarfs* (1937)—a film that not only became a model for future feature-length animated films,

events, the weight of a new responsibility fell across the shoulders of its animators and story developers. Was it possible to mix the disparate elements of history and entertainment? Could a Disneyfied Pocahontas offer a refreshing and empowering angle on a story that was so dominated by the desire of white colonizers? Or were there some lines that shouldn't be crossed, lest they distort the truth and significance of history itself?

And what did all of this mean for the newsies?

What Disney got right about the newsies

While *Pocahontas* broke ground as the first animated Disney film to borrow extensively from American history, the studio already had a long tradition of pilfering elements from real-life events for their live-action features, from the bloody battles of the Creek War to the harrowing rescue of Lipizzaner horses during World War II to the strike of a few thousand newspaper hawkers on the streets of New York City.

Unlike Pocahontas, Disney didn't owe the same conscientious consideration to the newsies of 1899. The newsboys and newsgirls of turn-of-the-century America may have done a great deal to further workers' rights and child labor reform, but as far as a 21st-century audience was concerned, they were virtually inseparable from Charles Dickens' clowder of pickpocketing urchins. No one was going to hold the studio's feet to the fire over historical inaccuracies, the way they might with a more well-known story, and Disney knew it.[‡‡]

That wasn't to say Disney chucked all historical accounts of the newsies' strike out the window, or that they would have been wrong to do so. Poetic license is permissible—preferable, even—when it illuminates the truth that lurks behind our

---

but helped usher in a new era of the modern, sanitized fairy tale.

‡‡   Granted, a great deal of the criticism lobbed at Disney over *Pocahontas* had to do with the inaccurate portrayal of Native American characters; *Newsies* (1992) and its musical adaptation largely steered clear of racial issues by virtue of omission.

understanding of history. If properly utilized, it can allow us to redress biased accounts of the past, particularly those told by people in positions of racial or socioeconomic power.

By placing *Newsies* firmly in the hands of the striking newsboys, Disney managed to do just that. Both the 1992 film and its 2012 musical adaptation center the children's experiences in a way that no newspaper columnist ever did, pushing Pulitzer and Hearst to the fringes of the narrative as Jack Kelly and David Jacobs and Spot Conlon wage a veritable war against the city's newspaper moguls (and, in doing so, deliver Disney's first overtly pro-union message). Make no mistake: *Newsies* doesn't offer its viewers a fair and unbiased treatment of historical events. Pulitzer's monologues about cutting costs and outselling Hearst come off as the ravings of a madman, and Hearst's role in the strike is all but omitted from the script. Mr. Snyder is cruel, Mr. Wiesel a miserly coward, and Judge Move-along Monahan resolutely unsympathetic toward the plight of the children. Any adult who doesn't care to align themselves with the newsboys' cause is necessarily cast on the subtly-shaded spectrum of villainy.

Thanks to Disney, these retellings actively amplified the children's voices above those of biased reporters and crotchety, half-blind publishers, giving them the agency and audience they were denied by Pulitzer, Hearst, and the New York press.[§§] At long last, the newsies were invited to share their side of the story: freely, noisily, and without interference from even the most well-meaning adults.

What *Newsies* lacks in historical specificity, however, it compensates for by drawing viewers into the heart of the newsboys' fight for respect, fair wages, and the chance to earn a decent living. In particular, it uses four elements to accurately highlight the crux of the children's struggle: the persona of fictional strike leader and newsboy Jack Kelly; the visible bias of *New York Sun* columnists Bryan Denton and Katherine Plumber; New York's corrupt judicial system and,

---

§§   Non-boycotted papers devoted considerable time and energy to strike coverage during the summer of 1899, but they didn't always present a truthful or balanced account of the newsies' efforts.

by extension, Warden Snyder's exaggerated wickedness; and the unswerving idealism behind the strike itself.

JACK KELLY AND THE DREAM OF SANTA FE. Far above the brownstones and ridged fire escapes of Manhattan, a pale blue dawn slinks toward Newsies Square as a 17-year-old newsboy dozes on a nearby rooftop. He has little more than a pair of quarters to his name, scarcely enough to secure a hot meal and a night's sleep in a real bed, and the few minutes he has to himself are squandered on thoughts of traveling out West.

It's a picturesque tableau, though one that smacks more of a Norman Rockwell painting than 19th-century reality. While the person of Jack Kelly may not have existed in 1899, there were plenty of others just like him: young children and teenagers standing at the intersection of premature adulthood and unrealized childhoods, each one dreaming of making a better life for themselves. Bernard Flaherty dreamed of life as a thespian, touring around the great cities of the world as he delivered acclaimed performances on the stage. Mary Welter hoped to leave her trade and get a first-rate education, one that would allow her to set her own career path and better support her elderly parents. Anna Flaherty aspired to run her own newsstand, where she could improve on the three-dollar sum she collected from her customers every afternoon. With perhaps the exception of the enterprising Flaherty and the well-established Horn family, few were content to "carry the banner" their entire lives. On the contrary, most were already searching for a viable escape route well before they reached adulthood.

In the 1992 film, Jack's fixation on cowboy hats and paperback Westerns comes off as a little frivolous, but his longing for a peaceful life out West—one in which he is reunited with his family¶¶—occupation—is hardly out of the ordinary among those of other homeless youth in New York City.

¶¶   In the 1992 film, Jack Kelly tells David Jacobs that he plans to move out West once his parents send for him, though this is heavily implied to be a lie. In the musical, no such reunion (false or otherwise) awaits him in Santa Fe. Both productions end with his decision to stay among the newsboys in New York City.

Of course, this kid is more than a newsboy. He's a leader, too, and one who embodies all the charisma and verve of Louis "Kid Blink" Ballatt and Moses Burns before him. Like the newsies of 1899, his thick accent and lack of formal education occasionally complicates the forward movement of the strike, inasmuch as it endears him to the audience.

Jack, clad in cowboy attire (or, as in the musical, a more traditional newsboy cap, vest, and trousers), is the driving force behind the boycott. It's his passionate outpouring of emotion that rallies the newsboys and compels them to take a stand against the powers-that-be. He orchestrates a peaceful alliance with Spot Conlon and the Brooklyn newsie contingent in order to add a little muscle to the strike. Despite his apparent betrayal of the cause,*** he storms into Pulitzer's office and demands fair compensation—a moment that never happened in the real strike, but one that speaks to the newsies' willingness to put everything on the line for the sake of getting justice and protecting their families.

In a way, Jack Kelly doesn't just stand in for the leaders of the strike, but for every newsie who lived through the 19th century: the half-child, half-adults who learned how to fend for themselves and fight for each other, and ultimately changed the landscape of American publishing forever.

BRYAN DENTON, KATHERINE PLUMBER, AND THE BLA-TANT BIAS THAT BOUND THEM TO THE NEWSBOYS. It's a strange but simple fact: Were it not for the journalists of the *New York Sun*, *Times*, *Tribune*, and *Herald*, among a glut of smaller publications, the newsies' strike might have faded into oblivion. The boycott, though fierce and spectacular, lasted just two weeks. It likely had a profound effect on the activists who were pushing for child labor reform on a state and federal level, but its significance in the wider scope of American history was, well, if not non-existent than certainly of lesser importance.

*** In the film and musical, Jack Kelly is blackmailed into taking a bribe and peddling the boycotted papers after Pulitzer threatens to commit the other newsboys to the Refuge.

In 1899, Pulitzer and Hearst's petty rivalry had yet to run its course. Other publishers—from the fringes of Park Row to the heights of Brooklyn and beyond—took note of the financial toll it was having on the two papers. As soon as the first newsies marched en masse into Printing House Square, enterprising rival reporters began to circle like sharks in bloodied waters.

Wherever the children went, the journalists were close behind: demanding clarification on their strategies, sitting in on private gatherings and recruiting sessions, and documenting every punch thrown and eye blackened during the never-ending brouhaha between the strikers and scab workers. It was a win-win situation for everyone (that is, everyone *not* in the direct employ of the feuding newspapers). The newsies got column space and free advertising, while New York's publishers seized the opportunity to rag on their biggest competitors, and in doing so, boosted their own circulation and profit margins.[†††]

Newsies took things one step further. In the 1992 film, Bill Pullman portrays *New York Sun* journalist Bryan Denton, a former war correspondent with a soft spot for the newsies' cause. It's been a full year since the conclusion of the Spanish-American War, and Denton is hungry for fresh news to sink his teeth into. His interest is piqued after he watches Jack direct the newsboys to spread news of the strike to the remaining boroughs of the city, and it's not long before the reporter has abandoned all semblance of objectivity to defend the cause himself. After getting involved in several small skirmishes, he loses his nerve when Pulitzer suddenly issues a ban on strike coverage, reneging on his deal with the newsies and breaking the trust he built up with Jack and David. Disney's stereotypical happy ending delivers a redemptive twist in Denton's character arc as he returns to aid the newsies in printing their own banners and even takes a copy to New York governor Teddy Roosevelt.

By contrast, Katherine Plumber assumes the role of the headstrong *New York Sun* columnist in *Newsies the Musical*.

[†††] This kind of behavior did not go unchecked by the *World* and *Journal*. As most publications belonged to the Publishers' Association, Seitz used his influence to threaten to quash each rival in turn, and may have successfully bullied a few into killing would-be columns that painted Pulitzer and Hearst's papers in a negative light.

Plumber is young, just 18 years old and already an established writer for the *Sun's* society pages, but she longs to improve her reputation as a serious reporter. Unlike Denton, she doesn't take up the newsies' cause out of boredom or a lack of professional inspiration. Instead, she uses it as a springboard to launch herself into the male-dominated arena of 19th-century journalism, one that values hard news stories more than theatre reviews and gossip columns.

Over the course of the musical, her interest in the newsboys' story begins to cross into an ethically gray area—not only because she falls in love with Jack, but because she's the daughter of Pulitzer himself. As the musical barrels toward its predictably peaceful resolution, Plumber is blacklisted from "every paper in town" and puts her full weight behind the boys, drawing up an article that exposes the horrors of the Refuge and helps convince Teddy Roosevelt to intervene on their behalf. Whether or not she decides to resume her career in journalism is left for the audience to decide.

While both Denton and Plumber make for compelling character studies, there's no evidence to suggest that the journalists of 1899 took such drastic measures when they covered the children's strike. It seems plausible that if a reporter had joined the ranks of the strikers, they would have been swiftly exposed by a fellow colleague or rival.

Bias, on the other hand, ran rampant through the pages of every newspaper in the country. Any publisher who cared about their bottom line knew better than to express outward sympathy for Pulitzer and Hearst, and most New York-based papers delighted in the children's efforts to bring the two giants to their knees. They devoted lengthy columns to the crusade, detailing the battle wounds of every delivery wagon driver and newspaper distributor and taking down quotes from the children. At best, we can safely say that most reporters acted in a sympathetic manner toward the newsies. At worst, they used their articles to cast doubt on the sincerity of the newsies' movement[‡‡‡] and almost exclusively took down

---

[‡‡‡]   This was most plainly seen at the end of the strike, when the *New York Tribune* and *Times* printed alleged accounts of newsboys trying to extort

quotes in "eye dialect," which made the strikers sound child-ish and uneducated.

It's not inconceivable that one of these reporters resembled Denton and Plumber, but chances are, that kind of blatant willingness to sidestep the paper's agenda and assist the striking newsboys and newsgirls would have prevented them from earning the right to write front-page stories—and 21st-century audiences would never have known they existed.

A BROKEN JUDICIAL SYSTEM AND THE HORRORS OF THE REFUGE. At first glance, the pasty-faced, black-hatted man skulking among the crowds at boxing matches and lurking in shadowed alleyways seems no more threatening than a mus-tachioed cartoon villain. Warden Snyder engages in a game of cat and mouse with the newsboys, one that is spurred by his personal vendetta against delinquent (and runaway) newsboy Jack Kelly and grows ever more sinister as the story unfolds. No Disney musical is complete without a comeuppance of some kind, though, so it's hardly surprising when Snyder is condemned by Teddy Roosevelt and led away in handcuffs (or, as in the 1992 film, a cage-like paddy wagon) while the news-boys jeer and holler after him. If only life were as satisfying.

Even taking into account his exaggerated mannerisms and apparently unlimited budget for chasing teenage boys through New York City, Snyder's callous behavior was far surpassed by that of the adult men who ran New York's House of Refuge in the late 1800s.

The first juvenile reformatory in the United States, the House of Refuge teemed with homeless and vagrant youth. Its founders, James W. Gerard and Isaac Collins, initially conceived of the program as an extension of basic prison reform. Within the reformatory, children and teenagers were separated from adult prisoners and made to correct their behavior through hard work and religious instruction. At the end of their sentencing period, equipped with an education and skilled in trade, they would be released as better, more productive members of society.

---

money from Pulitzer.

Within the span of just 35 years, however, that vision had been all but lost. Boys and girls who loitered on the streets of the city—especially those who were poor and of Irish descent—were easy targets for the leaders of the reformatory, who began clearing the streets of "unwanted" youth. Inside the House of Refuge, a fate worse than poverty and petty crime awaited the children. They were subjected to long hours of hard labor and farmed out as indentured servants, made to recant religious beliefs that fell outside the umbrella of Protestant Christianity, and physically and emotionally abused at the hands of their superiors. Release from the prison was no longer a guarantee, and for a few poor souls, resisting disciplinary measures or attempting escape led to certain death.

None of this would have been fitting material for a family-friendly film. Disney wasn't about to show its young viewers horrific scenes of Snyder whipping Crutchy for insubordination or hanging Jack from his thumbs. In the 1992 version of *Newsies*, Crutchy's singular beating happens off-screen (following a harrowing shot of the Delancey brothers dragging the lame newsboy away by his arms), while Jack is relentlessly pursued and mocked by Snyder and finally forced to serve time in the blackened confines of a jail-like cell.

In *Newsies the Musical*, Snyder's role is considerably toned down. Crutchie sings "Letter from the Refuge" while sitting atop a bunk in the reformatory, but there are no scenes inside the House of Refuge that explicitly show Snyder mistreating the inmates—only a fruitless chase scene through the back streets of Manhattan as Jack, David, and Les try to evade capture in Act 1. In fact, the primary proof of Snyder's abuses are Jack's sketches of the rat-infested quarters the boys are forced to sleep in. His one act of violence spills forth during the boys' protest, when the Delancey brothers throw Crutchie to the ground as Snyder beats the boy with his own crutch.§§§

Disney may have spared its viewers the worst of the Refuge's sordid history, but Snyder's character serves as a reminder that the newsboys had a lot to lose if their strike went south. They

---

§§§ While a highly disturbing moment in the show, this incident is not presented as the main reason for Snyder's eventual capture and arrest.

weren't just fighting for higher wages; they were fighting to make a livelihood that would keep them out of the clutches of the reformatory. In other words, they were fighting to stay free.

THE UNWAVERING OPTIMISM AND RIGHTEOUSNESS OF THE NEWSIES' CAUSE. It's the day after the strike, and Jack Kelly has all but given up on the newsboys. Afternoon sunlight streams through the windows of the Burlesque House, empty now save for the sulking teenager, his pots of paint, and a mural that looks something like the mauve hills and ruddy sunsets over Santa Fe. When Davey, Les, and Katherine show up to re-recruit their leader, it's Davey who reminds Jack of all the newsboys stand to gain by continuing their fight.

"Here's how it goes," he tells Jack. "Once we win (and we will be winning, make no mistake—we're already winning), we'll tell 'em straight out: They let Crutchie go or they keep getting pounded!"

"Dave, what the hell?" Jack retorts. "Did they bust up your brains or somethin'? As I recall, Dave, we all got our asses kicked. They won!"[10]

This tête-à-tête continues until Jack concedes Davey's point: Pulitzer and his goons are spinning out of control. They're terrified of the newsboys' as-yet unrealized power (if they weren't, Davey points out, why would they send a veritable army of cops and strikebreakers to target the newsboys?) and appear to be on the verge of a concession. Wracked with guilt over the disastrous results of the previous day's protest, Jack realizes that while he can't atone for his past errors, he can still help the newsies forge a new path to victory.

It's a pivotal moment in the musical, one that expertly highlights the tension between the newsies' incorrigible idealism and the harsh reality of the strike itself. Davey, patterned after strike leader Dave Simons, is convinced that theirs is a winnable war. He can't conceive of a scenario in which Pulitzer doesn't bend to the newsies' demands, intimidated by their vast numbers and strategic attacks on newsdealers and scabs alike.

The self-appointed moral backbone of the movement, Davey is the one who buoys the boys' optimism and appeals to their sense of justice and fair play. When Spot Conlon balks at the

suggestion of a strike, it's Davey who strokes his ego in order
to forge an alliance between the factions of Manhattan and
Brooklyn newsies. When Jack flees the scene after a dirty fight
against Mr. Wiesel and the cops, it's Davey who tracks him
down and convinces him to keep fighting for the cause. When
Jack then takes a bribe from Pulitzer, it's Davey who calls his
moral character into question and assumes responsibility for
the remaining strikers, then helps Jack and Denton print and
distribute hundreds of strike flyers.¶¶¶

The real Dave Simons behaved in much the same manner
as his fictional counterpart. Next to fellow strike leader Kid
Blink, Simons held the *World* and *Journal* accountable when
they refused to deal directly with the newsies. He challenged
the publishers to arbitrate with the strikers, as they had with
the Brooklyn trolley workers, and entreated the city's readers
to abstain from patronizing the two papers until the strike was
fully resolved. At the mass meeting of newsboys and newsgirls
in Irving Hall, Simons' was the calm voice of reason against
the explosive reactions of the crowd. He instructed the strikers to take a less forceful approach to the strike and refrain
from using excessive force against the scabs—a moment that
was met with overwhelming derision from the audience until
Kid Blink backed him up.

Given the volume of injustices that piled up against the
newsies of 1899, it's tempting to throw on a pair of rose-col-
ored glasses whenever we take a peek into the historical
records of the strike. This does the newsboys and newsgirls a
greater disservice than favor.

Like most of the children who counted themselves among
the striking ranks of newsies, Simon was far from perfect.
Just three days after the rally reignited public feeling for the
strikers' cause, the newsboy was spotted entering Frankfort
Street with Kid Blink, each balancing impressive stacks of the
Journal on their shoulders. Simons eventually reconciled with
the strikers—losing his title and credibility in the process—
but his unexpected betrayal revealed him for what he really

¶¶¶   In the stage production, it's Katherine who assists Jack and Davey
with the newsies' banners, not Denton.

was: not a paragon of virtue, but a fallible human capable of both great strength and great weakness.

The character of Davey has relatively few faults by comparison. He doesn't betray the newsies, or cheat Mr. Wiesel out of newspapers, or accept bribes from Pulitzer, or even invent extravagant headlines to earn better tips. In fact, his distinct lack of foibles is precisely what makes him such an interesting subject.

Rather than using Davey to hold up a mirror to the person of Dave Simons, Disney uses him to mirror the innocence, moral conviction, and childish naïveté of the strikers themselves. Davey embodies everything good about the strike of 1899: the newsies' unwavering commitment to see it through, their ability to stand strong against the manipulative efforts of the two papers, the belief that the world owes them some measure of justice and fair play. Even during the moments in which Davey is forced to confront reality—when, for instance, Denton declines to provide further strike coverage in the *Sun* and Jack takes a bribe to work for Pulitzer again—his moral resolution persists, eventually rewarded by Pulitzer's concession and the newsies' victory.

At the end of the story, Davey and Jack saunter into Pulitzer's office, armed with nothing more than a handful of their own strike pamphlets and the surety of their convictions. Davey informs Pulitzer that his circulation has dropped by 70 percent, while Jack admits that the kids used Pulitzer's own printing press to defy his ban on strike coverage. The publisher is staggered by the revelations (and, in the musical, by Teddy Roosevelt's threats of a Senate investigation into his business practices) and easily caves to the newsies' demands.

In true Hollywood fashion, the good guys win out. The newsies get their discounted newspapers and generous compensation for unsold stock and Pulitzer is left to sputter and fume in his bronze tower. It's a comforting idea, one that suggests that those who possess the moral high ground will inevitably win because they're in the right.

There's a compelling argument to be made that the newsies of 1899 were also in the right, but while they may have shared Davey's convictions, it had little impact on the outcome of their own struggle against Pulitzer and Hearst. For better or worse, *Newsies* gives the children the one thing they couldn't get for themselves: a happy ending.

What Disney got wrong about the newsies

There are many accurate ways of framing history that have nothing to do with the truth. It would be accurate to say that the newsies received a concession from Joseph Pulitzer that ended the strike for good, but untruthful to dismiss the effects of the power imbalance between the children and publishers, the growing dissension in the strikers' ranks, or the fabricated accusations of extortion that cast doubt on the purity of the children's convictions and lost them key support from the press and public. It would be accurate to say that the newsies' strike marked a critical turning point in the history of child labor reform, but untruthful to claim that they mounted their protest in order to defend the rights of New York City's boot-blacks, messenger boys, and sweatshop workers.[****]

Disney didn't get everything right about the newsboys and newsgirls of 1899, nor could they have. Even if complete objectivity had been their goal, they were working from a variety of biased sources, including the selective eyewitness reports of the *New York Sun*, *Times*, *Telegram*, and *Tribune*, among so many others, as well as Seitz's confidential anti-strike telegrams to Pulitzer. Remember, too, that 19th-century reporters would have gravitated toward eye-catching events and histrionic headlines above all else, leaving the more mundane and non-violent moments of the strike to fall by the wayside. In a crowd of thousands, a newsboy shaking his strike banner in front of the *World* building wasn't anywhere near as exciting a subject as the one introducing his closed fist to the nose of the nearest delivery wagon driver.

[****] The newsies' strike inspired local bootblacks and messenger boys to protest the meager wages and poor working conditions of their own industries in the summer of 1899, but the movements were otherwise unconnected and had little bearing on each other's respective successes and failures.

Historical fiction, as a rule, deviates from the events and persons on which it is based. Disney never pretended that *Newsies* was a documentary of the 1899 strike; it was always and firmly in the realm of fiction. Like *Pocahontas* after it, both the film and musical gloss over a few key players in the strike as they take excessive liberties with a few of their best-known historical figures.

Tampering with history in this way can do more to mislead than entertain, and there are four major missteps here that merit closer examination: the total omission of newsgirls, both as influential characters in the strike and vital components of the publishing industry; the inherent violence of the strike; the one-dimensional portrait of Joseph Pulitzer and his seldom-seen nemesis, William Randolph Hearst; and the mischaracterization of New York governor (and supposed champion of child labor reform) Theodore Roosevelt.

WHAT ABOUT THE NEWSGIRLS? Newsboys weren't the only ones who had the chutzpah to take on Joseph Pulitzer and William Randolph Hearst. Newsgirls and newswomen played smaller, albeit equally important roles in the strike. Though the specific number of working newsgirls in the 1800s was never officially recorded, their existence was consistently documented by local papers as they competed with the boys for turf and customers.††††

Newsgirls were no less hardy, cunning, and recognized than their male colleagues, but their presence was routinely dismissed and diminished by those who preferred to see the girls adopt more conventional gender roles, both at home and in society at large. Newspapers, even those who depended on the newsgirls for regular promotion and distribution, railed against the corrupting influence of street work on girls while ignoring its supposedly pernicious effects on boys. Publishers

---

†††† Newsgirls generally attracted less attention than their male counterparts, due in part to their inferior social status. It's entirely possible that there were far more newsgirls involved in the 1899 strike than the press let on; on the other hand, it's difficult to believe that any violent crusades involving the newsgirls would have been glossed over by publishers who made a habit of singling out and condemning the young girls for their "immoral" career choices.

claimed newsgirls had an innate purity and innocence that would be tainted by rough work on the streets and accused them of using their "feminine wiles" to steal customers that rightfully belonged to the boys.

Disney may not have adopted such overtly sexist attitudes toward the newsgirls, but by choosing to omit them from the casts of their movie-turned-musical, they did something far more inexcusable: They erased the girls from history altogether.

Of course, this is a slight exaggeration. One fictionalized newsgirl—a tomboy named "Charlie"—played a significant part in Bob Tzudiker and Noni White's original script for *Newsies* (1992), though she was eventually cut from the final draft and replaced by non-newsie Sarah Jacobs. It's doubtful that Disney's creative team ever sat down and decided to take an anti-newsgirl stance, as if they had suddenly morphed into some yakety, misogynistic cartoon villain. It's far more likely that Charlie's particular character arc (including her not-quite-PG-rated upbringing in a brothel) simply didn't fit the studio's vision for the movie, and it never occurred to them to stick a few girls in the ensemble among the likes of Skittery, Boots, and Pie-Eater.

It's harder to make the same claims for *Newsies the Musical*. In a 2011 interview with the *New York Times*, composer Alan Menken revealed that he was aware of the public demand for newsgirls to be included in the musical's narrative.

"My daughter [Nora] went to a girl's camp where they did 'Newsies,' and they invented a character of Swifty for her to play," Menken said. "She said, 'Dad, if you ever do 'Newsies' on stage, you've got to let Swifty be in the show.' I'm still working on that one with Harvey [Fierstein]."[11]

Whether or not those intentions were good, neither Menken nor Fierstein decided to create space for the newsgirls in their new show. Instead, strike leader Jack Kelly's timid love interest and strike sympathizer Sarah Jacobs got a spunky makeover, this time as the opinionated *New York Sun* columnist Katherine Plumber. In the musical, Plumber works a kind of hybrid role between the film's meek Sarah and outspoken reporter Bryan Denton, but make no mistake: Her work on the strike and relationship to the newsboys is frequently overshadowed by the budding romance that develops between her and Jack. And even if she is a more fun token female character to root for than Sarah ever was, her presence does nothing to alleviate the lack of non-male representation in the ensemble.

When *Newsies* finally landed on Broadway in 2012, Laurie Veldheer understudied Katherine Plumber and rotated in and out of the roles of Hannah, a nun, a Bowery Beauty, and Smalls the newsboy. As Smalls, clad in a vest and trousers with her hair pinned under the brim of a newsboy cap, she was just one of the boys.‡‡‡‡ Later, after the show shuttered in Times Square and went on the road, Becca Petersen cycled through the roles of Katherine, Medda Larkin, Hannah, and Sniper, another newsboy in the tour's ensemble. It was the smallest step forward for Disney.

No matter how well-written or compelling, one minority character does not good representation make: nor does one girl disguised among two dozen newsboys.§§§§ Many of the original newsgirls who distributed papers in turn-of-the-century New York City were clad in long dresses and flowered hats and veils when they trafficked their wares. They presented as girls to the public and made little if any effort to mask their identities in hopes of attracting more customers.¶¶¶¶

---

‡‡‡‡   Toward the end of *Newsies the Musical*'s run at the Nederlander Theatre, Veldheer was replaced by Liana Hunt. Hunt told Disney on Broadway that she had developed an elaborate backstory for Smalls, one in which the newsgirl was raised with all brothers and had to become "one of the guys" in order to make a living.[12] Despite her inclusion in the throng of newsboys, however, Disney never drew attention to the fact that female-presenting newsgirls were a vital part of the newspaper hawking industry—and, when it came time to film the stage production in 2016, the "female newsboy" characters of Smalls and Sniper were portrayed by two male ensemble members, Julian DeGuzman and Daniel Switzer.

§§§§   While Sniper's character was originally styled with pigtails—the most feminine aspect of her presentation and a clear indication that she was not just "one of the guys"—she was eventually made to pin her hair beneath her cap in the same way that Smalls had on Broadway.

¶¶¶¶   This observation is not without exception: In 1904, the *New York Sun* noted that 14-year-old newsgirl Josephine Beck cut off her blonde curls, donned her father and brother's garments, and passed herself off as "Joseph 'Joe' Becker, the brush maker." She sold papers alongside the boys from the Newsboys' Lodging House, where she outsold those who mentored her in the trade. "Say, she had us conned all right, all right," said one of the newsboys upon the discovery. "But I wouldn't ha' bullied her so much ef I'd ha' knowed

During the strike of 1899, both women and girls were active proponents and opponents of the newsies' cause, from the girl who took it upon herself to thrash troublemaking scabs to the newswoman who became infamous for her distinctive shriek whenever the strikers caught her dealing yellow journals. As the newspapers were already prone to lend more credibility and column space to the newsboys of the city, their strike coverage likely skewed in favor of the boys' exploits and triumphs as well.

While the newsgirls of New York may not have been as plentiful or prominent as their fellow male protestors, their presence did not go entirely unnoticed. It is both inaccurate and untrue to pretend that Annie Kelly and red-haired Jenny and Mrs. "Beauty" Myers and Hannah Kleff and Mrs. Fenton and "Aunty" Cochran did not play pivotal roles in the boycott that summer, just as it is irresponsible to ignore the selective focus and anti-newsgirl bias that infected many reports of the day.

Disney may not have capitalized on the opportunity to educate audiences about the newsgirls of the 1800s, but that didn't stop smaller productions of the musical from righting past wrongs. Theatre arts choreographer and director Marcos Santana decided to deviate from traditional casting when he brought Disney's *Newsies* to the Axelrod Performing Arts Center in June 2018.

"In the original Broadway production, they dressed the female ensemble as boy newsies. When we were originally casting the show, I asked the choreographer, and myself, 'Can't we just have them as girl newsies? Why do we have to dress them up as boys? There must have been female newsies at the time, right?'" Santana explained to Wendi Maloney and Benny Seda-Galarza of the Library of Congress' Office of Communications.[14]

After delving into the backlog of Lewis Hine photos, several of which depicted young newsgirls working the streets, Santana committed to the idea of making newsgirls more visible in

---

she wus a girl."[13] Along with runaways like Josephine, it's also possible that more girls chose to disguise themselves as newsboys in the early 20th century, when gendered age bans were more strictly enforced in American cities.

Newsies. Early photos of the production revealed ensemble members clad in period-appropriate frocks and dresses alongside the suspender-and-newsboy-capped newsboys.

"[The newsgirls] helped reshape the stereotypical, misogynistic behavior of the era by balancing it with the presence of equally able, committed, independent female figures," Santana added. "As an immigrant, as a minority, I experience the narrowed-minded [sic] process constantly. Diversity is not a priority for most when it comes to building a show. It feels more like an obligation, something they have to do to 'look good.' Thankfully, this archaic way of thinking is evolving, not as fast as I would like, but at least we are making strides forward. Diversity is what makes us evolve."

Representation is what makes us feel seen and heard, that echo of a shared experience that helps us connect with each other across time periods and cultures. As essential as diverse casting is to any theatre production, casting more girls as newsies—specifically, as news*girls*—did more than bring balance to the musical. It returned the newsgirls of 1899 to their rightful place in history and, perhaps for the first time, ensured that their memory would be preserved and honored for generations to come.

SANITIZING THE STRIKE. The newsies of New York City were no stranger to violence. Like a swarm of pesky shepherds pitted against a gargantuan Goliath, they had both the experience and the nerve to face down Pulitzer and Hearst, and enough youthful bravado to believe that they would win.

Although the strike of 1899 is often regarded as the largest and most successful child-led movement of the late 19th century, it was far from the only one of its kind. The newsboys and newsgirls who serviced New York's thriving press had mobilized at least six times, first in 1886***** and then again

---

***** In March 1886, a contingent of Eastern District newsboys and newsgirls struck against the *Brooklyn Times* after they discovered the Western District newsies were receiving the papers at a better rate.[15] Over the course of three or four days, as many as one hundred newsies participated in the strike, blocking delivery wagons and beating up the few who attempted to hawk their wares. The strike had wrapped up by April 2, though conflicting

in 1889,[†††††] 1890,[†††††] 1892, 1893,[§§§§§] and 1898, and always in response to an untimely price hike. Every strike followed the same blueprint: Kids turned out in dozens, if not hundreds, to make their voices heard against the papers, and were invariably found overturning delivery wagons, tearing, scattering, and burning newspapers, hurling clubs and stones at the heads of scabs and strikebreakers, and generally making a ruckus that could not be ignored by a would-be customer or distributor for miles around.

Unlike the fictional characters they inspired, the newsies of New York city were experienced enough to realize that no publisher would make a concession through civilized negotiation. It didn't matter if they had exhibited measures of sympathy to the children in the past, if they had issued rewards for meeting

---

reports credit both the newsboys and the publisher for bringing the boycott to its resolution. No matter the instigator, the result was the same: The *Brooklyn Times* agreed to sell the paper at the same rate to newsies from both districts.[16]

[†††††] Ten years preceding the infamous strike of 1899, the newsies of New York City staged a boycott against the *New York World* and *New York Sun* for exactly the same reason: raising the cost of their wholesale papers from 50 to 60 cents per hundred.[17] Several hundred newsies marched on Park Row, scattering papers and tangling with local police officers while their Brooklyn brethren took a match to a pile of 500 of the banned newspapers. The strike did not resolve in their favor, but set an important precedent for the newsies who would eventually turn on Pulitzer and Hearst in 1899. Interestingly enough, the *Sun* would prove an important ally to the children's cause in the years to come.

[‡‡‡‡‡] An editorial in the *Buffalo Evening News* revealed that the newsboys of the region had boycotted the publication after the wholesale price was raised from 50 to 60 cents per hundred papers. "*The News* has been at great expense making the most perfect paper to be had and has sold the paper below the cost of production—very near the cost of white paper," the *Evening News* insisted, while claiming that the "honest" newsboys in their employ had been conned into striking by "a mob of roughs, mostly bootblacks and idlers who have never sold and will never sell papers."[18] The price was not reduced to match the newsies' demands.

[§§§§§] The newsies struck in 1892 and 1893 against the *Evening News*, requesting that the paper put their wholesale prices back to half a cent per paper and buy back unsold copies at full price. In '92, some 40 or 50 children took up the cause and formed a union, though their efforts proved futile against an able-bodied police force and ample numbers of scab workers.[19] The following summer, the strike commanded even less attention in the press. Neither movement ended with a concession on the *News'* part.

certain quotas or financed lavish holiday dinners or organized trips to the theatre. When it came to matters of business, the publishers refused to acknowledge the newsies' bargaining power or engage with their self-made unions.

The only way the kids could make their demands heard was to go on the attack.

The striking child workers of 1899 didn't do anything by half-measures. It wasn't enough to snatch the newspapers from the hands of would-be customers and newsdealers; they had to rip apart the papers headline by headline, scattering the remnants of Pulitzer and Hearst's yellow journalism across the wide thoroughfares of the city. Two newsboys, John Armstrong and Samuel Wolinsky, were arrested after the strangled cries of a non-striking boy caught the ear of a local police officer. The boys had torn off large sections of the boycotted newspapers and were trying to force the scab to swallow it by the mouthful.[20]

Other newsies resorted to more drastic measures, brandishing an assortment of clubs, sticks, staves, wagon wheel spokes, and knives as they went head-to-head against those who showed plain disapproval of the strike. They persuaded non-strikers to join their ranks, not by illuminating the ongoing need for workers' rights or appealing to their sense of morality and justice, but by ganging up on smaller boys and pummeling them into submission. One unlucky fellow earned a pair of black eyes and a bloody nose before he agreed to put his lot in with the newsies, and was later found wailing on another scab worker some minutes after his own violent conversion.[21]

Even those the *Journal* hired to outmuscle the newsies found themselves overpowered by the forceful and unrelenting nature of the protestors. Popular prizefighter "Johnny" Reagan stepped into the fray around Grand Central Station, fully intending to put his weight behind the adult vendors who dealt in yellow journals, and was immediately besieged by a flurry of small fists and less-small clubs. By the time the police intervened, Reagan was almost unconscious; according to the *Evening Telegram*, "one of [his] cheeks was cut open from the mouth to the ear and his face was so bruised as to be unrecognizable."[22]

The newsies of 1899 were children, yes, but much of their wide-eyed naïveté had been sanded down by years of living and working on the streets. Pulitzer and Hearst's 10-cent price hike may have come as a surprise to them a year ago, yet they had since acquainted themselves with the rigors of labor strikes, both the ones they initiated in the 15 years leading up to the summer of '99 and those perpetrated by men, women, and children in equally exploitative industries. Violence, too, was nothing new. If they weren't duking it out with the publisher and deliverymen for fair treatment and a pay raise, they were clashing with each other over turf and tips.

These hardly seemed like the innocent faces of Disney's newsies. In the 1992 film, veteran newsboy Jack Kelly seems as taken aback by Pulitzer's price hike as anyone, despite the fact that he's lived most of his life as a working newspaper hawker in New York City and would likely have seen or heard about previous protests. Crucially, Disney makes it clear that the worst of the violence is not initiated by the newsboys themselves, but by the story's villains: Pulitzer's goons, dirty cops, Warden Snyder, the Delancey brothers, the strikebreakers. It's not that Disney's newsboys don't fight back, but that they only resort to aggressive tactics when they're painted into a corner, making it much easier for viewers to sympathize with them as the true victims of the strike rather than bloodthirsty hooligans or opportunistic bullies.¶¶¶¶¶

The same holds true for the 2012 musical. Here, the tempestuous nature of the strike is bottled into a single scene at the *World* distribution center. The newsboys go toe-to-toe with the scab workers until Jack makes an appeal to them on behalf of the kids in every sweatshop, factory, and slaughterhouse in New York.

"If we stand together, we can change the whole game," he tells them. "And it ain't just about us. Yeah, all across the city, there are boys and girls who ought to be out playin' or going to school. Instead, they're slavin' to support themselves and their folks. Ain't no crime to bein' poor. No, not a one of us

---

¶¶¶¶¶ This isn't to insinuate that the 1899 newsies fell into either of the latter categories; on the contrary, the public appeared to frequently sympathize with the young boys and girls despite the violent tactics they often resorted to.

complains if the work we do is hard. All we ask is a square deal."[23]

He makes a stirring argument, though it's one that diverges completely from the skull-cracking methods of persuasion used by the real newsies. Victory comes cheap and easy to the newsies as they take on the Delancey brothers, shredding papers and pausing for a requisite—and lengthy—dance break. Only when Mr. Wiesel shows up with the publishers' hired men and cops do the newsboys finally grasp the seriousness of the situation. Weaponless and vulnerable to the clubs and batons aimed in their direction, they finally begin to disperse, fearing arrest or worse.

Given the constraints of the film's PG rating and the family-friendly nature of the stage show, it's hardly surprising that Disney chose to tone down the gruesome events of the newsie/scab conflict. In doing so, however, they unnecessarily simplified the newsies' complex relationship to their business partners and society as a whole. Without absolving the newsies of their violent actions during the strike, it is possible to view them as a product of their environment: one in which the well-being of the young and homeless population was often devalued, children were expected to shoulder the responsibilities and consequences of adulthood far too early in life, and violence was considered less a social faux pas and more of a means to an end.

THE TRAP OF THE ONE-DIMENSIONAL VILLAIN. History does not always give us stories that are readily digestible. It is the playwright, the historian, the author, and the storyteller who curates our collective past in order to break down the most important moments into unforgettable morsels: the discovery newly-made, the climax of a tide-turning battle, the inspirational speech delivered under duress, the victory secured for individual and country. Away from the battlefields and podiums, the minutiae of day-to-day events are often glossed over, even more so when that history is repurposed into film or literature.

Here's the uninteresting thing about the newsies' strike: While Joseph Pulitzer and William Randolph Hearst opposed the children's efforts to lower the price of wholesale papers, they were essentially fighting a war by proxy. Pulitzer was nowhere to be found on Park Row that month; after a leisurely trip through Europe, he boarded a White Star Line steamer in Liverpool, England and set sail for New York on July 12, then hopped the *Afternoon Express* up to Bar Harbor, Maine a week later.

Hearst, on the other hand, entertained the newsies just twice during the strike. In the days leading up to the mass meeting at Irving Hall, a gaggle of newsboys spotted the editor emerging from a cab in front of the *Journal* offices.

"We want 100 papers for 50 cents," they told Hearst. "We get it from the other papers except the *World*."[24]

It took some nerve to name-drop the *World* to its biggest competitor, but the children's earnest request appeared to be met with sincere curiosity from the *Journal*'s proprietor. He invited them inside for a longer chat and, when strike committee leaders Kid Blink, Jim Seabook, Jim Gady, and David Simons emerged from the building later that afternoon, Blink only had positive things to say about his supposed nemesis:

> "He wanted to know what the *World* was goin' to do," Blink told the newsies. "I told him that we was dealing with the *Journal* now, and that if he cut the *World* would cut quick enough. He says he had to talk it over with some other guys before he'd give an answer, and then I asked him if he wouldn't arbitrate, like his paper says. He laughed and said he'd give us an answer Monday right here, and that if he decided to arbitrate he'd meet us at the Broadway Central Hotel."

Three days passed with nary a word from the yellow journals. The newsies were preoccupied with other pursuits: the widespread effect of their rally, plans for an impending parade, and the ongoing fight against Pulitzer's "two-dollar-a-day" strikebreakers. Monday came and went, and Hearst had yet to make a formal appearance at the hotel.

By the time the newsies caught up with Hearst again, the newspaperman had changed his tune.

"Scabbooch, he seen Mr. Hearst getting' into a coupy," Kid Blink told the *New-York Tribune*, "and he went up and asked him wot he wuz goin' to do about [the increased cost of newspapers]. He sez he'll go outen business and close up de shop before he'll give in to us."[25]

The children wouldn't get a third opportunity to plead their case in front of the owner of the *Journal*.****** Back on the streets of New York City, from the stronghold of the Brooklyn Bridge down to the frontlines on Newspaper Row, they tangled with delivery wagon drivers, strike defectors, circulation managers, scab workers, hired goons and detectives, and the occasional cop. Pulitzer may have been too feeble and Hearst too preoccupied to take the newsies on face-to-face, but that didn't mean they were too proud to hire others to do their dirty work for them.

It wasn't that the strike didn't concern the editors of the prized yellow journals—given the desperation with which both men were trying to attract advertisers and outsell their competitors, nothing could have raised more alarm than a city-wide boycott—only that they didn't view the adolescent newspaper hawkers as worthy adversaries. Pulitzer, in particular, could be downright boorish when faced with resistance; as he told Seitz some time later, "I will never negotiate under threats."[27] Hearst may have done what his rival could not (humor the newsboys for an afternoon or two), but he had no serious plans to engage in salary negotiations or retract the price hike, either.†††††† A protest of this magnitude was something to be suppressed, not grounds for opening a conversation about workers' rights.

Though they kept relatively distant from the newsies' war on the streets of New York City, Pulitzer and Hearst still cut

---

****** According to the *Evening Telegram*, considerable efforts had been made on the part of the *World* and *Journal* to reach a compromise with the newsies in advance of their parade, but the children firmly insisted on a reduced wholesale price the journals could not match. "Negotiations were entered into by some of the leaders," the *Telegram* alleged, "but the boys stood firm and declined to make any terms unless there was a distinct promise that papers should be sold hereafter for fifty cents a hundred."[26] The paper declined to identify the newsies who were sent to deal with the papers and did not provide further insight regarding the circumstances or tone of the meetings. It is highly unlikely that Pulitzer or Hearst were directly involved.

†††††† Even when playing "nice," Hearst was laser-focused on maintaining his advantage over Pulitzer. The newsboys noticed as much and constantly referenced the questions Hearst had asked them about Pulitzer's response to the strike. To the *Journal*'s owner, it was simply a matter of competition. If the *World* refused to lower its prices, well, then so would the *Journal*.

imposing figures within the industry they had helped redefine over the last half-decade. Their continued influence over advertisers and competitors, not to mention their uncanny ability to impact public opinion, bespoke a power far greater than that of the beefed-up delivery wagon drivers or pocketknife-wielding scab workers the newsies contended with. They had the time, money, and willpower to outlast the children's best efforts— and, even though it came at the steep cost of hundreds of thousands of subscribers, that's exactly what they did.

The publishers directly and indirectly menaced the newsboys and newsgirls of 1899, but conveying that kind of nuanced threat on the silver screen proved harder than expected. When it came time for screenwriters Bob Tzudiker and Noni White to script their own version of the strike, their antagonists fell flat on the page. There simply wasn't enough room to flesh out the storied rivalry between the yellow journals and explore their complicated, fluctuating relationship with the newsies; as Tzudiker put it, the film demanded that "history [...] be set aside at some point" in order to fit the story to Hollywood standards.[28]

In fact, there was so little room for complex character development in the script that Tzudiker and White decided they couldn't carry two villains. After some discussion, Pulitzer emerged as the newsies' singular adversary, if only by dint of Orson Welles calling "dibs" on Hearst's character when he debuted the acclaimed semi-biopic *Citizen Kane* back in 1941. Welles' interpretation of Hearst was already well-established in modern cinema; Pulitzer's character, on the other hand, could be taken in any number of directions.

In some respects, he was the perfect choice. By 1899, Pulitzer had done far more to change the landscape of print media in 19th-century New York City than Hearst ever had or would. The *Journal*'s young editor played the imitation game all too well, and was indeed on the verge of overtaking the *World*'s subscription numbers by the turn of the century, but it was Pulitzer who had ushered in a new era of unprecedented sensationalism and journalistic power. If the newsies were going to make a compelling stand against any one publisher in New York, it was going to be Joseph Pulitzer.

Even more intriguing, at least to the screenwriters, was the juxtaposition between the publisher's pro-union principles and his callous treatment of the children in his employ—a puzzling character flaw that is exposed in both the film and stage musical.†††††† Still, they bore Pulitzer no debt of impartiality. Tzudiker and White weren't writing a story about the children who got caught in the crosshairs of one of the most famous rivalries in the history of journalism (true as that might have been); they were sculpting a narrative that was wholly centered around the experiences, struggles, and triumphs of New York City's child laborers. If anything, the writers intended their audience to see Pulitzer through the eyes of the newsies, bias notwithstanding.

In the transition from script to screen, something got lost in translation, and whether it was due to what Tzudiker termed the "ruthless compression of film story" or acting choices outside their control is difficult to say. Under the direction of a 61-year-old Robert Duvall, the cigar-puffing, spectacle-squinting Pulitzer appears both petulant and clueless, as if it is not his body that has deteriorated prematurely, but his mind.

"I know we need to make more money," the *World* editor squawks at his staff when forced to examine the paper's recent expenditures. "That's why we're here, to make more money."[30]

Disney's Pulitzer has but two things on his mind: making money and outselling Hearst. To be fair, those were real-life hurdles for Pulitzer in 1899, too, but his Hollywood doppelgänger lacks the industry knowledge, ingenuity, and tenacity to see it through. Duvall plays a healthy, mustachioed grouch who reduces his motivations and methods to the lowest common denominator. When his bookkeeper and business manager—Jonathan and Don Carlos Seitz, respectively—point out that the *World* needs to adopt cost-cutting initiatives or risk financial ruin, Pulitzer splutters in

---

†††††† During Act 2 of *Newsies the Musical*, the city mayor confronts Pulitzer as the newsies prepare to stage their first rally at the Burlesque House. "I've read your editorials, Mr. Pulitzer," he tells the disgruntled editor. "How can you express so much sympathy for the trolley workers and yet have none for the newsies?" Pulitzer scoffs. "Because the trolley workers are striking for a fair contract," he says. "The newsies are striking against me."[29]

half-hearted agreement, imitating the click and whir of keys spinning on the rotary wheel of an adding machine.

"It definitely adds up, sir," Bunsen reassures his boss. It's hard to tell if Duvall has chosen to play the moment for laughs or if his character is simply incapable of mentally calculating the annual profit margin for a 10-cent increase on the wholesale price of the *World*'s penny papers.

Pulitzer proves no more articulate in his confrontations with the newsies, nearly all of which seem to devolve into juvenile shouting matches. During the film's gripping finale, thousands of newsies, bootblacks, messenger boys, and factory workers flood Newsie Square in protest and Pulitzer crams his fingers in his ears to escape the noise.

> Pulitzer: "Close the windows! Close the windows! Go home, go home, go home!"
>
> Jack Kelly: "I don't hear you, Joe!"
>
> Pulitzer: "Go home! Go home to your mothers and fathers! Go home!"
>
> Jack Kelly: "Didn't hear you!"
>
> Pulitzer: "Now, you listen to me!"
>
> Jack Kelly: "Maybe you should listen to me for a change!"
>
> Pulitzer: "No, no! You listen to me!"
>
> Jack Kelly: "No, *you* should listen!"[31]

Pitting Jack Kelly and his newsboys against a toothless Pulitzer does little to underscore the importance of their victory. In 1899, it was no small matter to bring the newspaper magnate to his knees in the span of two weeks; a triumph even William Randolph Hearst couldn't pull off with his harebrained promotional schemes and tabloid fodder.

Against Disney's version of Pulitzer—a man who appears to spontaneously break out into *Fiddler on the Roof*-esque dances, who decrees impossible ultimatums,§§§§§§ who fritters away valuable time picking apart a handful of the thousands of newsboys who hawk his paper, who finishes a complete

---

§§§§§§   Frustrated by the losses he can no longer afford to absorb, Pulitzer tells his staff, "There's lots of money down there in those streets, gentleman. I want to know how I can get more of it—by tonight!"[32]

sentence not two dozen times over the span of the film's 121-minute runtime—the boys' success feels like less of a coup and more of an inevitability.

Thankfully for Disney, they got a do-over—and a pretty good one, at that. Almost 20 years after *Newsies* debuted in theaters, playwright and actor Harvey Fierstein transformed a mediocre treatment of the newsies' strike into something spectacular: ambiguous lyrics rewritten, dispensable characters tossed out the window, every half-finished sentence punctuated with a zinger. With the transformation of Jack Kelly from aspiring ranch hand to skilled cartoonist and nosy journalist Bryan Denton to intrepid activist Katherine Plumber came a similar revamping of Pulitzer's character.

Post-makeover, Fierstein's Pulitzer is no longer the bumbling, numbers-challenged fool of the early 1990s, though he isn't quite the self-made millionaire, inventive publisher, and half-blind workaholic who once ruled Newspaper Row, either. No, this Pulitzer swings hard toward the opposite end of the spectrum as a smug, level-headed businessman who takes perverse pleasure in exerting his dominance over his employees, even when it comes at great expense to his precious bottom line. Where Tzudiker and White's Pulitzer might have grumbled and groused through a disagreement (and the real Pulitzer flown into a tempestuous rage), Fierstein's Pulitzer bristles with a controlled anger that feels both sinister and out of character.

Take the climax of the musical, for example: Jack, Davey, and Spot confront Pulitzer in his office, informing him (with no small measure of glee) that, in their words, "New York is closed for business." The child laborers responsible for the city's daily news, shiny shoes, timely packages and telegrams, and working elevators are on strike indefinitely, pending a price reduction from the *World*'s head editor. It's a meeting that would never have taken place in 1899—the newsies never made it as far as the lobby of the *World* building, let alone up to the 16th-floor office¶¶¶¶¶¶ to speak to its higher-ups—and

---

¶¶¶¶¶¶ Pulitzer's office was under the copper dome of his 309-foot publishing plant, a full six stories above any surrounding structure and so near

one that seems more a reluctant meeting of the minds than a territorial standoff between the publisher and his newsboys. Only after Governor Theodore Roosevelt barges into the office, flanked by the city mayor and mumbling something about a state Senate investigation does Pulitzer express anything more than mild annoyance toward the newsies' ambassadors, and even then he manages to settle the strike with Jack in a prompt and civil manner.

As with the 1992 film, the quick resolution of the strike serves to remind us that this story isn't about its villains. In order to give a voice to the newsies (and limit the production to a palatable two-and-a-half hours), the show writers kicked Pulitzer—with his myriad motivations, character development, endless circulation war with Hearst, and veritable stranglehold on New York City—to the curb...just like yesterday's paper. The result is a one-dimensional depiction of New York's most enterprising editor, ungenerous by necessity as the audience grows to know and sympathize with the child workers who have been cheated out of fair pay and play. It's an interpretation that may not hew close to historical events, but it is one that remains faithful to the version of history that Tzudiker and White and Fierstein felt compelled to tell.

THEODORE ROOSEVELT: GOVERNOR, CHILD LABOR REFORM CHAMPION, AND SAVIOR OF THE NEWSIES? "Give 'em the good news." Governor Theodore Roosevelt peers out of the topmost window of the *World*'s offices, a smile stretched underneath the bushy expanse of his auburn mustache. The faint hum of the newsies' refrain echoes in the square below, and Roosevelt warns Pulitzer to make up his mind quickly, lest the children's song drone on forever.

"What good news?" Pulitzer sneers.

"That you've come to your senses and rolled back prices," the governor says. "Unless, of course, you want to invite a full state Senate investigation into your employment practices."

---

the heavens that Reverend Charles Henry Parkhurst reportedly said he felt like "Christ being tempted by the devil" when he peered out the windows to the postcard-sized sprawl of City Hall Park below.[33]

"You wouldn't dare!"

"After the pressure you wielded to keep me from office? I'd do it with a smile!"[34]

Pulitzer seethes. With his back against the wall, he has no choice but to concede to some of the newsies' demands. He offers to lower the distribution price to 55 cents per hundred papers and, at the urging of strike leader Jack Kelly, buy back all unsold copies of the *World*. The strike, helped along by a well-timed threat from Teddy Roosevelt in the eleventh hour, is over at last.

It's a satisfying showdown between the Democratic editor of the *World* and the Rough Rider-turned-Republican politician, one which lasts just long enough for Roosevelt to toss in a few pithy remarks about bullies, soft heads, and Pulitzer's grouchy demeanor ("He doesn't do 'happiness,' does he?" Roosevelt says with a smirk). It's also the place in which *Newsies the Musical* deviates most drastically from its historical text.

In an alternate universe, Roosevelt may very well have paid a visit to Printing House Square and demanded a reception with the owner of the bronze-topped *World* building. That kind of confrontation only plays well if Roosevelt is pitching into a much younger—and healthier—Pulitzer, though. The newspaper editor was well past his prime in 1899, beset with near-blindness and a debilitating sensitivity to sound that made him a poor sparring partner. Not only was he practically infirm by his mid-50s, but he didn't step foot in Park Row even once during the strike, sending all probability of a meeting between the two right out the metaphorical window.

Not only was Roosevelt's snark-laced confrontation with Pulitzer conveniently fabricated for *Newsies the Musical*, but any depiction of the governor's involvement in the strike would have been historically inaccurate as well. In 1899, Roosevelt was a plucky 40-year-old whose wartime exploits had recently earned him a lucrative seat in local government, but he was still several years away from developing some much-needed child labor reform policies.

It wasn't until the early 1900s that Roosevelt began speaking out in earnest about the perils of unregulated child labor. He made compelling arguments in favor of strict labor laws during his State of the Union addresses in 1902, 1904, 1906, 1907, and

1908, insisting on a thorough investigation into working conditions across the country and recommending that women and children be exempted from night work and excessive overtime.

> "The horrors incident to the employment of young children in factories or at work anywhere are a blot on our civilization," he said in 1906. "It is true that each state must ultimately settle the question in its own way; but a thorough official investigation of the matter, with the results published broadcast, would greatly help toward arousing the public conscience and securing unity of State action in the matter."[35]

Good intentions notwithstanding, Roosevelt didn't always back up his principles with concrete action. In 1903, 73-year-old "Mother" Mary Harris Jones caught wind of a massive strike among the Kensington silk mill workers in Pennsylvania. Six hundred mills had all but shut down after their workforce—totaling around 100,000 men, women, and children—refused to show up for work. They had formed a delegation and petitioned the mill owners for a workweek that was to be shortened by a mere five hours. In exchange, said the strikers, they would sacrifice part of their much-needed wages.

It was a no-go. The mill owners turned a blind eye to the exploitation of their young, impoverished workers. Long shifts and harsh working conditions were considered part and parcel of factory life, and it never crossed their minds that an extra five hours could be applied to the children's education—or, at the very least, for the sake of their physical health and emotional well-being. The mill owners had deluded themselves into believing that they had already extended more generosity than the children (or their families) deserved.*******

Mother Jones was horrified, first, by the injustice of the situation, then by the condition of the strikers themselves.

******* The mill owners weren't stupid. They recognized what a valuable commodity they had in the children: hundreds, if not thousands of nimble, dispensable, and vulnerable employees who weren't protected by the kind of labor laws that regulated pay and work hours. In 1896, Mother Jones saw the corruption of the mills firsthand. During a trip to Alabama, she requested a position in one of the local cotton mills and was flat-out denied—until she said she had six children. As if by a sudden and miraculous change of heart, the manager hired her on the spot.[36]

Underfed, underdressed, and underpaid seemed to be the norm among the working families of the silk mills, and it wasn't rare to find the child who had lost limbs and lives to the very machines they were tasked with maintaining.

The sight of starving women and gaunt, hunchbacked children would have moved anyone to tears; it merely moved Jones to action. Her crusade to illuminate the perils of child labor inspired her to march from Pennsylvania to New York with 300 strikers in tow. On a local level, it worked. Kensington newspapers wouldn't touch the movement, bound as they were to the mill owners' interests, but those from surrounding metropolises quickly picked up the heart-rending story.

Jones had bigger fish to fry. Two weeks after the start of her march, she made her way up to Oyster Bay, New York, where she knew then-President Theodore Roosevelt would be vacationing with his family for the summer. Who better to appeal to than a self-proclaimed child labor reform advocate?

There was just one hitch in her plan: Roosevelt didn't want to take a meeting with Jones or her children. By the time Jones showed up at the gates of the president's summer home, some 125 miles from her starting point in Kensington, Roosevelt had already departed for Sagamore Hill with his sons and nephews. Jones and her little delegation, including a handful of frayed, ragged strikers, were received instead by Roosevelt's private secretary, B.F. Barnes. Unfortunately for the crusader and her posse, they would get no closer to the president.

Barnes dissuaded Jones from interrupting the president's vacation and suggested she write another letter stating the purpose of her business. It was little more a thinly-veiled attempt to get rid of the woman and her push for federal child labor laws; as the *Buffalo Morning Express* later alleged, the president was wary of Jones' motives after reports that the woman had been put up to the publicity stunt by a Philadelphia newspaper that was trying to make amends with disgruntled boycotters.

"The President, under these circumstances, will, it is said, not consider granting an interview to Mrs. Jones," the paper read.[37]

Mother Jones headed back to Kensington, where many workers had already conceded defeat and resumed their shifts at the silk mills. The children returned to their 60-hour work-weeks, doomed by abject poverty and their innate helplessness against beleaguered parents and opportunistic mill owners. While the Children's Crusade succeeded in capturing the attention and hearts of sympathetic souls across the country, it had failed to make an impression on the one man powerful enough to enact lasting change.[†††††††]

It would be another six years before substantial reform measures were adopted in Pennsylvania and 35 years before Roosevelt's fifth cousin, President Franklin Delano Roosevelt, endorsed the groundbreaking Fair Labor Standards Act. Under the Act of 1938, federal restrictions were placed on the ages of child workers in mines and manufacturing plants. By 1949, no child under the age of 16 years old was permitted to work during school hours or to accept a position in industries of commerce and the production of goods.[‡‡‡‡‡‡‡] At long last, the child laborers of the United States were going to be seen for who they really were: children.

Despite Teddy Roosevelt's pro-labor reform stance, his inability and disinclination to get personally involved in such matters makes it difficult to imagine him swooping in on Pulitzer in order to rescue the newsies. If his heart was not stirred to action after Mother Jones and her army of child workers marched 125 miles across the country to plead for merciful labor regulations, if he was unmoved by the sob stories of young kids whose fingers had been sliced off and scalps pulled clean by the machines of textile mills and whose lungs were coated by rich black soot from the mines, then it seems doubtful that he would have spent the years leading up

---

[†††††††] Roosevelt's objection to Jones' crusade may have stemmed from a fundamental disagreement about the scope of her plans to rescue the children, too. Jones enjoined the president to establish federal labor laws that would sweep the whole of the United States' mills, mines, and factories, but she was swiftly reminded that all labor reform measures were created on the state, not federal, level.

[‡‡‡‡‡‡‡] The 1949 amendment was primarily designed to give American children the opportunity and time to better themselves through education, but it also helped equip them for more rigorous and demanding careers—in other words, it made them more efficient and knowledgeable laborers.

to his presidency running elaborate rescue operations in the House of Refuge or putting pressure on the yellow journals to raise the wages of their adolescent employees.§§§§§§§

In *Newsies* (1992), viewers are introduced to a man cut from an entirely different cloth. Roosevelt first catches wind of the newsies' plight when *New York Sun* reporter Bryan Denton swings by his office for a chat, a copy of the *Newsies Banner* in tow. The front-page article lays bare the horrors of the House of Refuge and exposes the collusion between Warden Snyder and Judge E.A. "Move-along" Monahan, the latter of whom funnels children into the juvenile detention center for a cut of Snyder's profits. More importantly, at least in this fictitious circumstance, it draws Roosevelt's attention to the layers of corruption that fester within the system:

"So steeped in corruption and hypocrisy is this institution, it has successfully managed to disguise its true nature from some of our more progressive politicians," the article reads. "The great hero of the Spanish-American War, Colonel Theodore Roosevelt himself, on a pre-election visit to this place of shame, was hoodwinked into believing the charade of humane conditions put forth by the Warden, L.A. Snyder."

"Disgraceful, Denty!" Roosevelt exclaims, slamming his fist on the table for emphasis. "Those poor boys. And I did nothing—until now."[41]

Without another word of explanation, the two shake on it. The next time we see the governor, he's sitting pretty outside the *World* building, doffing his hat and congratulating the

---

§§§§§§§ This isn't to say that Roosevelt was unfeeling toward the newsboys and newsgirls of the city. On the contrary, he was revered among the children. Newsgirl Winnie Horn sent funds to Roosevelt's campaign for state governor in the autumn of 1898; as her letter in the *Buffalo Enquirer* explained, "To the multitude that passes by me at the elevated station every afternoon and evening as I sell my papers I have constantly talked for you. [...] may you live long to enjoy your heroism."[38] The following June, a delegation of Rochester newsboys presented the governor with a medal, which prompted an effusive thank-you note in which Roosevelt lauded the children's profession as one that "teaches [...] the doctrine of self-help and the doctrine of help to others."[39] Even as Vice President, Roosevelt did not forget the children of New York City, but paid a visit to the West Side Boys' Home during their annual spring dinner and regaled the newsies with tales of his hunting exploits and travels with the Rough Riders.[40]

strikers swarming his carriage. He doesn't so much as say "Boo!" to Pulitzer; in fact, he doesn't even show up for the party until the newsboys have secured their victory. Instead, it's Jack and Davey alone who are left to wrap up their business (the particulars of which are laid out offscreen¶¶¶¶¶¶¶ with Pulitzer and Seitz). Later, the newly-freed Crutchy rhapsodizes about Roosevelt's heroics in the Refuge:

"Aw, Jack, you oughta seen it!" the boy squeals. "He comes stormin' into the Refuge, wavin' his walkin' stick like a sword, and he's leadin' this army of lawyers and cops—"

"Who comes walkin' in?" says Jack.

"Aw, you know, your friend. Him! Teddy Roosevelt!"[42]

As Jack rides off with Roosevelt to have a chat about his future, *Newsies* shifts from historical fiction to full-fledged Hollywood drama. On screen, it may make sense for Roosevelt to make a grand entrance at the last minute, free the pitiful creatures of the Refuge, and deliver a final blow to the sadistic Warden Snyder (whether or not Judge Monahan receives any penalty for his corrupt behavior is left to the viewer's imagination). It's a far cry from the way things worked out in New York's real House of Refuge, which persisted until 1935 and, when it was finally razed to the ground, saw its young inmates transferred out to alternative facilities rather than released.

In the *Newsies the Musical*, meanwhile, Roosevelt's role in settling the strike is far more pronounced. Jack, Davey, and Spot barge into Pulitzer's office to return the bribe money and personally deliver a copy of the newsies' banner. As Pulitzer glowers and Jack gloats, Katherine and Medda usher Roosevelt into the office to deliver the final blow: the threat of a state Senate investigation into the *World's* unethical employment practices. It's an ultimatum Pulitzer cannot dismiss without

---

¶¶¶¶¶¶¶ Following Jack and Davey's confrontation with Pulitzer, it isn't made explicitly clear that the original price of the newspapers has been reinstated. Jack simply shouts, "We beat 'em!" into an assembly of thousands of newsies, factory workers, and other child laborers. Some time later, we see Davey slap 50 cents on Mr. Wiesel's counter as he picks up his first hundred newspapers. No mention of Pulitzer buying back unsold copies of the *World* is mentioned either, though it becomes a key part of Jack's bargain with the villainous publisher in *Newsies the Musical*.

severe repercussions, and the only one that finally nudges him toward a compromise with Jack and his boys.^{********}

With the strike settled, Pulitzer gets in one last jab at the governor—the suggestion that Jack join the *World*'s staff as a political cartoonist. It's a position that would allow the talented young artist unfettered access to the "dealings in our own government's back rooms" and give Pulitzer yet another weapon against the Republican Party, an opportunity the real Pulitzer might have relished had it ever taken place in real life. In the musical, true to form, Jack reassures Roosevelt that he has better things to do than go poking and prodding into political affairs, and (after a brief bit of bellyaching over Santa Fe) gladly returns to his post as a newsboy.

The important thing to note here isn't the farfetched idea that Roosevelt was so invested in child labor reform that he personally made house calls to the Refuge, nor is it the manner in which he bullies Pulitzer into submission.[††††††††] No, it's the way that his involvement in the resolution of the newsies' strike overshadows the children's accomplishments. What should be a moment of triumph for Jack and his ilk—the way his drawings are used to expose the House of Refuge's seedy underbelly, the way the *Newsies Banner* calls attention to the inhumane conditions of working children across the city, etc.—is instead reduced to an entertaining bit of verbal sparring between Pulitzer and Roosevelt. Jack is ultimately granted a private audience with the publisher, during which they hammer out the details of their agreement, but some of the drama of the moment has already subsided due to the interruption.

******** Here, Pulitzer agrees to cut the wholesale price down to 55 cents per hundred papers and purchase all unsold stock from the children for full refunds. Though this puts the newsboys' story closer to actual events, it's still not quite right: The real newsies of 1899 were stuck at 60-cents-per hundred prices after the strike ended, and their unsold papers could only be returned for credit, not cash.

†††††††† Roosevelt even goes so far as to tell Pulitzer that his support of the newsies is at least partially driven by his desire for revenge, given the series of anti-Republican editorials Pulitzer printed during the Rough Rider's gubernatorial campaign in 1898.

The striking newsboys and newsgirls of 1899 didn't petition adults to bail them out of their dispute with Pulitzer and Hearst. While they might have jumped at the chance had it been presented to them (and especially if someone as influential as Roosevelt had put their weight behind the boycott) what made their movement so remarkable was the fact that they did everything themselves. It's true that local politicians, former newsies, reporters, and big-hearted benefactors sponsored the newsies' rally, helped the children unionize, and printed flattering, if condescending, coverage of the strike, but when it came to confronting the bigwigs of the yellow press, the boys and girls of New York City were wholly on their own.

A marriage of history and entertainment: What it means to preserve the legacy of *Newsies*

Between the soft buzz of Annie Wilkes' lawnmower and the monotonous pull of writer's block on a summer day, Paul Sheldon tries to forget about the string of increasingly gruesome events that led him to this exact kitchen table, this woman, and this broken typewriter. Trauma, most recently stemming from the charred flesh of his hobbled right foot, is all he can fixate on, and he eventually concludes that while trauma begets stories, it's the painful remembering and re-remembering that allows writers like himself to transform those stories into art.

Art consists of the persistence of memory, Paul decides.[43] It wasn't enough to have lived through something only once. His trauma had to be experienced again and again, with such clear and vivid recall that he cannot help but commit it to the page.

In the narrow and cruelty-laced world of Stephen King's *Misery*, memory is inextricably linked with both physical and psychological pain...but what about other forms of art that depend on active remembering? What about history, specifically the moments that so quickly recede from our social consciousness with no one to remind us over and over that so-and-so lived, or that such-and-such happened? How can we ever ensure that something will be remembered forever?

The simple answer: We can't. What is meaningful to one generation, at one point in time, has no guarantee of living on to see the next.

At the outset of *Newsies* (1992), Racetrack's expository monologue comes with a preface: "This story is based on actual events." It's a promise and a warning. Both *Newsies* and *Newsies the Musical* try, in their own ways, to capture a fraction of the lost history of the newsboys and newsgirls who once decorated the sidewalks of New York City, but both productions exist firmly in the realm of fiction. They cannot encompass all perspectives and events exactly as they unfolded some 93 years ago, nor should they.

Art may consist of the persistence of memory, but it also consists of the persistence of *imperfect* memory, of memories that are necessarily and inevitably altered by every person who comes into contact with them. The way we remember the newsies' strike today isn't the way the newsies remembered it in 1900, or the way Frank Luther Mott remembered it in 1941, or the way Bob Tzudiker and Noni White remembered it in 1985, or the way Harvey Fierstein remembered it in 2009, or the way, we hope, others will remember it in the decades that follow this one.

The responsibility we bear to history, both in art and in life, is not to tell it perfectly, but to do it justice. It doesn't take the keen eye of a critic to spot the flaws in *Newsies*, from Joseph Pulitzer's farcical attempts to blackmail and imprison his young workers to the unlikely (and, perhaps, unethical) romance that blooms between the newsies' underage strike leader and the *New York Sun*'s rookie reporter, but to harp only on its shortcomings would be to miss the point entirely. For all of its campy showtunes and contrived happy endings, *Newsies* did what even the most conscientious historian could not: Without agenda or malice, it amplified the newsies' voices in a world where they had long been silenced.

Assisted by Disney's thoughtful storytelling and direction, the narrative of the 1899 strike no longer belongs to those who profited most from its demise. The *World* and *Journal*'s condescending editorials would no longer paper over the real story of the newsies' protest, nor would the movement be reduced to a few pithy stories in the annals of the city's smaller papers or cast off as an inconsequential footnote to the larger labor reform movement that swept through the country nearly half a century later. *Newsies* makes a point of returning the story to its rightful owners: the thousands of poverty-stricken news-boys and homeless newsgirls who crawled out from coal boxes and fire escapes every morning to stand on street corners and fog-chilled ferry landings; who hawked their wares even when the summers ran hot and the rain doused their afternoon sheets and the winter air bit into their cheeks; who sacrificed their health and childhood to keep their parents and siblings clothed and sheltered; who, in a burst of righteous anger, demanded justice and respect from the two publishers least inclined to give it to them.

"You learn from the part of the story you focus on."[44] Those words were first delivered by Australian comedy writer Hannah Gadsby in 2017, but they ring true for the newsies even so. The lessons to be gleaned from the strike are mani-fold: the importance of news and art as purveyors of truth; the value of integrity in the face of adversity and corruption; the necessity of giving a platform to the rising generation.‡‡‡‡‡‡‡‡

Whether or not the newsies of 1899 will be remembered in the years to come remains to be seen. They mounted their strike without crowd-rousing anthems, prominent political allies, or synchronized pirouettes, but the spirit of their move-ment lives on in Newsies—and will continue to do so as long as there are people who believe in giving a platform, a voice, and a square deal to the young and vulnerable of the world.

As Jack Kelly might say, lip curled and palm outstretched for another of his famous spit-coated handshakes, "It's a com-promise we can all live with."

---

‡‡‡‡‡‡‡‡   "Each generation must, at the height of its power, step aside and invite the young to share the day," Theodore Roosevelt proclaims to an awed and hushed throng of newsboys. His message, while hardly faithful to any moment in history, is still an affecting one.[45]

Timeline of the 1899 Strike

July 18, 1899: Fed up with Joseph Pulitzer and William Randolph Hearst's refusal to reduce the wholesale price of their newspapers from 60 cents to 50 cents per hundred, the newsies began spreading the word of an impending boycott to be carried out over the next several days.

July 20, 1899: Three hundred newsies demonstrate along Park Row. The strike catches fire, spreading from Manhattan to Brooklyn, Long Island City, Newark, the Bowery, and other districts and boroughs of the greater New York City area.

July 22, 1899: *New York World* business manager Don Carlos Seitz reports losses of 60,000+ in a memo to Joseph Pulitzer. Seitz teams up with *New York Journal* business manager Solomon Carvalho to hire adult scab workers to fend off the strikers.

July 24, 1899: Over 5,000 newsies attend a rally at Irving Hall. Kid Blink, Racetrack Higgins, Annie Kelly, Bob Indian, and Dave Simons give rousing speeches, inspiring the children to continue the strike.

July 25, 1899: The *World* and *Journal* offer to sell papers to the newsies at 55 cents per hundred. The newsies refuse the offer and insist on holding out for another five-cent reduction.

July 26, 1899: The strike continues to spread. By this date, its reach has expanded to include Trenton, Yonkers, Troy, Mount Vernon, Plainfield, and Elizabeth, among other neighboring cities.

July 27, 1899: Strike leaders Kid Blink and Dave Simons are caught peddling papers for the *World* and *Journal*. Kid

Blink is taken to court and banned from the newsies' union, while Simons accepts a demotion after pleading his case to the strikers.

July 31, 1899: Three newsboys are arrested on charges of extortion after allegedly demanding a $600 fee to halt the strike. Though there are conflicting reports of the incident, the magistrate holds the boys for trial and sets bail at $1,000 per person.

August 2, 1899: The strike is brought to a sudden end when the *World* and *Journal* decide to buy back unsold papers at full price. No formal decision is made by the Newsboys' Union, but most newsies begin hawking the yellow papers again.

August 3, 1899: Joseph Pulitzer breaks his silence on the strike, publishing "A Plain Statement of Facts for Public Consideration" that seeks to discredit the legitimacy of the newsies' reasons for striking.

The Newsies
of the 1899 Strike

The following is an alphabetical list of some of the New York-based newsboys and newsgirls who participated in the 1899 strike, as well as those who defected or chose to continue selling the boycotted papers for personal reasons. All names and descriptions have been compiled from the various newspaper accounts that were drawn up in July and August 1899. In many cases, the *World* and *Journal*'s rivals offered conflicting reports of the roles the children played in the movement.* Additionally, nicknames were often used to identify the strikers and their allies, and some names were given multiple spellings in the press. This list reflects just a fraction of the thousands of newsies believed to have been involved in the 1899 strike and should be regarded as both incomplete and inconclusive.

JOHN J. ALLEPPO/GALLUPO, STRIKE LEADER (AGE 13-15)

One of the first strike leaders identified in the press, Alleppo marched into City Hall Park alongside a band of 24 newsies and was charged by a police officer, who scooped up half a dozen boys and tried to drag them away to the Center Street Court. All escaped except for Alleppo and fellow strike leader Moses Burns. The pair were promptly arrested and placed under the care of the Gerry Society.[1]

---

* This could have been for any number of reasons: 19th-century journalists were not pressured to stick to the facts, nor would most of the newsies have necessarily volunteered sensitive information concerning their real names, addresses, family situations, etc. for fear of incurring severe consequences.

"CRAZY" ARBORN/ABORN/ARBOR/ARBURN, STRIKE SYMPATHIZER AND MEMBER OF THE STRIKE COMMITTEE OF THE NEWSBOYS' UNION

While not a newsboy himself, Arborn put his disposable income to use and assisted the strikers by donating 1,500 pretzels to their cause.[†] In exchange, the newsies elected him to their union and strike committee as an honorary member.[2]

JOHN ARMSTRONG, NEWSBOY (AGE 14)

Among the many arrests made of a striking newsboy, Armstrong's case was one of the most dramatic. He was fined $5 for forcing newsboy James Tobin to swallow large pieces of the yellow journals he was attempting to sell.[3]

ORLANDO BALDECHAR, NEWSBOY

Baldechar assaulted a delivery wagon driver and was among a select few to get arrested for it, despite the supposed presence and involvement of at least a hundred other newsies during the incident.[4]

LOUIS "KID BLINK" BALLATT/BALETTI/"RED BLINK"/"MUG MAGEE," GRAND MASTER WORKMAN

The most well-known strike leader of 1899, Kid Blink organized thousands of newsboys and newsgirls in the movement to renegotiate their pay with the *World* and *Journal*. Described as a red-haired fellow with one glass eye, he was thought to be no older than 14 or 16 years old when the strike began.[‡] Kid Blink was a popular speaker at the newsies' various rallies and

---

[†] There are conflicting reports as to the nature of Aborn's business. The *Times* named him as a newsboy, but comments from strike committee spokesman Barney Peters suggested that he was only a sympathizer to the movement.

[‡] According to a comment made during the newsies' rally at Irving Hall, this wasn't Kid Blink's first strike—and it likely wasn't the first of its kind for many of his compatriots, either. He briefly mentioned the success of a similar strike against the Evening News, a newspaper which had previously raised its wholesale prices from 50 to 60 cents a hundred for its young vendors in 1893. Blink would have been around 10-12 years old at the time. Perhaps his memory was faulty; not only did the strike fail to attract much public support, but it quickly fizzled out after the *News* refused to lower their prices.

gatherings, and often encouraged the children to join forces and stand strong against the employees of the boycotted papers.

> "Fr'end's, Brudders and Feller Citerzens: We is unitered in a patriotic cause," he addressed his fellow strikers. "The time has cum when we mus' eder make a stan' or be downtrodden by the decypils of acrice and greed'ness. Dey wants it all, and when we cums to 'em dey sez we must take the papes at der own price or leave 'em. Dis ain't no time to temporize. Is ye all still wid us in de cause? Well, den, we'll go ahead wid de warfare, same as we done yistiday. Let no guilty man escape. Lay fer 'em and give it to 'em hot."

He later made a celebrated appearance during the strikers' gathering at New Irving Hall and insisted that the strikers cease violent actions against strikebreakers and scabs. The newsies respected his opinion, even as it was an unpopular one during the boycott. Kid Blink, too, had been the victim of assault after a character called "Mike the Greaser" attempted to shove a loaded revolver down the boy's throat.[5]

As the strike wound down, however, there were plenty of rumors that Kid Blink had struck a deal with the yellow journals, which seemed to be a proven fact after he showed up in a nice suit (rather than the tattered uniform of the average newsie) with a bundle of boycotted papers under his arm. The boy was arrested soon after the incident. A group of striking newsies spotted their so-called leader and chased him through the city, where he ran into a police officer who erroneously assumed that he was mobilizing another group of disgruntled children against the city. Kid Blink's mother posted the bail for his release, and he appeared to reconcile with his former companions after making an impassioned speech during the newsies' makeshift court hearing some time later.

"DINKY" BATEMAN, TROY NEWSBOY AND STRIKE COMMITTEE MEMBER

Along with newsboys "Foxey" Osborne and "Mugsey" McGrath, Bateman helped form a strike committee that was tasked with soliciting support from the city's merchants.

ALMO BAVITHARO, NEWSBOY (AGE 14)

Bavitharo was counted among a group of fifty newsboys who launched a targeted attack on delivery wagon drivers Perry Walton and Edward Openshaw. Both Walton and Openshaw had been spotted selling the *Journal* during the strike. Following the altercation, Bavitharo and newsboys Charles Bervino and Sebastian De Leo were sentenced to the care of the Gerry Society.[6]

CHARLES BERVINO, NEWSBOY (AGE 14)

Next to 14-year-old Almo Bavitharo and 16-year-old Sebastian De Leo (among several others), Bervino was apprehended following a brutal assault on *Journal* deliverymen Perry Walton and Edward Openshaw, the boy was committed to a room in the Gerry Society as a consequence for his participation in the attack.[7]

CORNELIUS "GRIN" BOYLE, STRIKE LEADER (AGE 13–14)

With the help of three of his friends—newsboys and strike leaders Abraham Greenhause, Isaac Miller, and Albert Smith—Boyle directed a parade of striking newsies down Park Row. The raucous bunch had just reached Frankfort Street when they were met by the law enforcement at Oak Street Station, who ordered the children to disperse after parading without a permit. The newsies gladly did so, only to reconvene on the street as soon as the cops turned their backs. Each of the leaders was apprehended for his role in the parade and turned over to the Gerry Society until he could pay his $5 fine.[8]

GEORGE BURLINGAME, POUGHKEEPSIE NEWSBOY AND STRIKE LEADER

Burlingame was presumed to be one of two strike leaders in Poughkeepsie, where an estimated one hundred newsies took to the streets, parading and incinerating as many newspapers as they could steal from distributors around the city.[9]

MOSES BURNS/BURRIS, STRIKE LEADER (AGE 11)

Burns was among the first newsboys the press identified during the strike. He led a demonstration through City Hall Park, but tried to flee the scene after a police officer confronted the strikers. Per the *Brooklyn Daily Eagle*'s report: "Policeman Furlong, who arrested them, said that little Burns was a perfect demon and had tried to brain another boy who wanted to sell papers." In the end, Burns and newsboy John J. Alleppo were given over to the care of the Gerry Society.[10]

HENRY "PUTTS"/"BUTTS" BUTLER, NEWSBOY

Butler found himself entangled in one of the most contentious events of the strike. According to the *World*'s formal complaint, he was among a group of boys accused of attempting extortion in exchange for a swift resolution of the strike. The boys, including Edward Fitzgerald, Jack Harney, and Jack Seeley, countered with a different version of events, one in which Kid Blink enticed them to take a meeting with circulation manager Patrick F. Duff and *Journal* employee Edward H. Harris at the *World*'s circulation office.

The men offered to satisfy the striker's terms for a sum of $300, but the boys refused the deal. When they were tricked into palming a $10 bill—the basis for the *World*'s claims of extortion—Detective Distler burst in on the scene to make his arrests. The boys scattered, with both Seeley and Butler diving out the nearest window to evade capture. Seeley was first onto the roof and down the water pipe, but the pipe broke under his weight and left Butler stranded and within easy reach of the detective's grasp. Later on, at the Center Street Court, Magistrate Mott sentenced them to the Tombs Prison after they failed to post a $1,000 bail.[11] Butler later claimed that he'd been made an offer of $500 to give up the newsies' cause.

DONATO "MUSTY PIP" CAROLUCI/CAROLUCCI, NEWSBOY AND JERSEY CITY DELEGATE (AGE 17)

Within the first few days of the strike, Carolucci jumped into the fray during a fight on Park Row. His fun was short-lived: he was detained after getting caught with his compatriots Joseph Mulligan and Frank Dresso.[12] The lot of them were fined $5 each and collectively charged with trying to organize a parade despite lack of an official permit.

STEPHEN CARROLL, NEWSBOY (AGE 12)

Carroll was among a horde of newsboys who descended on the home of Arthur and Solomon Loevine, two *World* employees who previously insisted on carrying the yellow journal. The boys intended to search the house and burn every remaining copy of the *World*, (an unsettling precursor to 1953 dystopia *Fahrenheit 451*), but the Loevines wielded baseball bats in self-defense until the police came to their rescue. In the mayhem that followed, 12-year-old Carroll sustained a head wound from the nightstick of one of the cops and was taken into custody.[13]

MRS. "AUNTY" COCHRAN/CORCORAN§, NEWSWOMAN AND STRIKE DEFECTOR

The newswomen walked a fine line between the strikers and publishers, knowing full well that they carried a certain immunity with both groups. The former refused to compel them to join the strike by force, which gave the women less incentive to stop selling the yellow journals, while the publishers didn't seem to regard them as a threat. At the outset of the strike, two prominent dealers, Mrs. Cochran and Mrs. Shea, agreed to support the children's cause by foregoing their usual stock of *World*s and *Journal*s. Not three days later, word came that the two women had reneged on their deal. Mrs. Cochran avoided any physical confrontation with the newsies, but instead sent threats to newswoman Annie Kelly after losing a few of her best customers to her rival.

Kelly, for her part, seemed unfazed by Mrs. Cochran's tantrums and told the *Sun* that she could "tie seven Mrs. Corcorans in a knot," then invited the woman "to come up to her stand and take a licking." The moment never came to pass. Eventually, helped by a few "hickory dissuaders," the newsies set out to persuade the women to reconsider and appeared to be successful in re-recruiting them to their side.[14]

---

§ While the girl was never mentioned in conjunction with the strike, Mrs. Corcoran had a daughter named Rosie who later proved to be a popular newsgirl at the Brooklyn Bridge.

JOHN CHARGE, NEWSBOY (AGE 16)

Charge was arrested during a skirmish between fifty Mount Vernon newsboys and *World* wholesale sellers, Arthur and Solomon Loevine. The boys swarmed the Loevine brothers with fists and kicks, destroyed the delivery wagon, and chased off the brothers' horse. Charge was the only boy taken into custody following the debacle (along with non-newsboy Thomas Madden), and a crowd of 1,000 bystanders and newsies followed him to the station.[15]

MORRIS COHEN, STRIKE LEADER AND PRESIDENT OF THE NEWSBOYS' UNION

Though active in the strike well before its leaders turned rogue, Cohen stepped into the spotlight as the new president of the Newsboys' Union when Kid Blink and Dave Simons were caught in the act of dealing banned copies of the *Journal*. He was responsible for helping arrange the newsies' parade, the very same that was swiftly nixed by Police Chief Devery.

MYER COHEN, NEWSBOY AND TREASURER OF THE NEWSBOYS' UNION

Although his name bears a striking resemblance to that of strike leader Morris Cohen, the *Tribune* listed the boys separately when they tallied up the members of the Newsboys' Union following Kid Blink and Dave Simons' simultaneous fall from grace. As Morris ran the lot in Blink's place, Myer was established as the lowly treasurer of the gang. His other exploits during the strike do not appear to have been recorded.[16]

SPOT CONLON, DISTRICT MASTER WORKBOY OF BROOKLYN UNION (AGE 14)

On the evening of July 20, strikers along Park Row caught sight of a 14-year-old newsboy clad in pink suspenders and cutting an "imposing figure," though by stature or demeanor it was not clear which. Conlon, self-titled District Master Workboy of the newsies' Brooklyn Union, emerged from his turf on the opposite end of the Brooklyn Bridge and requested an audience with General Master Workboy "Blind" Diamond. Newsies crowded close around the new boy for his address:

"We bring youse greetings an' promises of support," said Conlon. "We have tied up da scab sheets so tight dat y' can't buy one fer a dollar in de street. Hold out, me gallant, kids, an' tom-morrer I meself, at de head of t'ree t'ousand noble hearts from Brooklyn, will be over here t' help youse win yer noble scrap for freedom an' fair play."[17]

Promises of help, though fervently made, were hastily abandoned. Conlon may have meant well, but by the next morning, no Brooklyn contingent had arrived to help the strikers. They were too busy fending off scabs and strikebreakers in their own neighborhoods.

JACOB/ABE CUTLER/CUTTER, NEWSBOY AND SECRETARY OF THE NEWSIES' UNION

As the strike began to wind down, Pulitzer and Hearst seemed no closer to a peaceful resolution than they had been at the start. The newsies formed multiple unions, one of which enlisted Cutler as their secretary.[18] He was arrested toward the end of the strike after interfering—likely through violent methods—with another newspaper vendor.

SEBASTIAN DE LEO/DELO, NEWSBOY (AGE 16)

De Leo got a few last punches in before the strike officially ended in early August. Together with newsboys Orlando Baldechar and Tony Lessaro, among others, De Leo targeted two delivery wagon drivers who attempted to ply the newsies with copies of the *World* and *Journal*. The three boys were arrested, though their fate remains unknown.[19]

"BLIND"/"BLACK" DIAMOND, GENERAL MASTER WORKBOY AND EXECUTIVE COMMITTEE MEMBER

Thanks to the efforts of strike leader "Blind" Diamond, among hundreds of others, the trolley strike was soon relegated to yesterday's news. Diamond confessed to the *Sun* that he didn't expect the adults and their unions to come to the aid of the children—if for no other reason than the children's strike had interfered with the success of the trolley workers' boycott—but insisted that they would prevail against the *World* and *Journal* even so.

"Dem scab papes is crawlin' already," he said. "Dey'll give in, sure. Arbitrate? Ah, hell! W'at do we want t' arbitrate fer? Nah. De papes has got ter come down ter two fer a cent an' dey gotter put de agreement out on der bulletin boards. See? Den dey can't welch on it."[20]

THOMAS "NINEY" DONNIGAN/
"NINE-EYED" DONEGAN/
"NINE-FINGERED TOM," NEWSBOY (AGE 12–14)

Like Kid Blink, "Niney" was working with just one good eye (the other was stomped out during a street fight[21]) and nine fingers (one of which was chopped off in a similarly gory incident). Not much else was printed about him during the strike, except that he was a close friend of Kid Blink and was one of several to be selected as replacement strike leaders following Blink's betrayal of the newsies. Several days after the conclusion of the boycott, "Niney" ran into far more serious trouble when he was arrested for attempting to strangle a passerby. It was his seventh arrest to date.[22] Years later, he ran a branch of the infamous Cherry Hill Gang and was arrested for thievery and murder—the latter of which, he claimed, stemmed from a poker dispute in which he had been stiffed 10 cents by another gang member.

"DOPE"/"DOPEY," NEWSBOY

"Dope" delivered a brief but rousing speech during the strike, climbing atop the pedestal of the Horace Greeley statue to exhort his young colleagues:

> "Ladies and gentleman, us guys are on a strike! Are we goin' to win out? Well, I guess yes. As I was sayin', us guys are going to win. But to do it we must have some dough. Now we're going to take up a collection."[23]

"JUICY FRANK" DRESSO/GLASSO, NEWSBOY (AGE 17)

Several days into the strike, Dresso was arrested alongside Joseph Mulligan and Donato Caroluci, on charges of fighting.[24] The nature and outcome of the brawl was not reported, though the boys were later fined $5 after it was discovered they had tried to arrange a parade without filing the requisite paperwork to do so. Among those in attendance in court were a group of sociology students who were focused on studying criminal behavior. "Git on ter bloakies wid der swell rags wot tinks we'se a circus," Dresso told Caroluci.

"DUFSKY," STRIKE LEADER AND DEFECTOR

Dufsky was spotted hawking illicit copies of the *Journal* along fellow strike leader Dave Simons. Though Simons' betrayal stirred up more of a ruckus—not only was he in a prominent position among the striking newsies, but he had received more press coverage than most other boys and girls at the time— Dufsky's betrayal was noted in the papers as well.[25] It's unclear whether he suffered the same social ostracization, however.

SAMUEL EISENBERG, NEWSBOY (AGE 14)

While many of his fellow strikers incurred the wrath of local police officers for starting up a parade without the proper license, Eisenberg found himself arraigned in court on charges of disorderly conduct—namely, ganging up on newspaper distributor Daniel Moore, pilfering the man's stock of *World*s and *Journal*s, and threatening him with a horseshoe to his head. Moore identified the boy as the leader of the group and had him arrested and slapped with a $3 fine for his involvement in the assault. Like most adolescent detainees, Eisenberg could not furnish the money, but informed the magistrate that he was happy to be jailed for his efforts and vowed revenge by way of his fellow strikers.[26]

JOHN FALK, NEWSBOY

Falk, an African-American newsboy, took a club to two adult newspaper sellers. He was arrested alongside newsboy Mikki Fischler and slapped with a $3 fine.[27]

"BUCK" FARLEY/FARLY, NEWSBOY

About a week after the strike kicked off, Farley helped arrange a newsie rally in Brooklyn and claimed "to be ready to lick any newsboy found guilty of selling the two [boycotted papers]."[28]

MRS. FENTON, NEWSWOMAN

Mrs. Fenton was only photographed in the *Tribune*, appearing to be a middle-aged woman of medium height and build, with a fat sheath of newspapers tucked under one arm and a hat and shawl draped around her for protection. She sold papers at the Fulton Ferry, though her personal feeling about the strike went unrecorded.[29]

MIKKI FISCHLER, NEWSBOY (AGE 12)

Fischler was caught "casually clubbing" non-union newsboys who were hawking copies of the *World* and *Journal*. He was arrested with African-American newsboy John Falk and taken to court, where Magistrate Crane issued a $1 fine and made the boy cry.[30]

"KID" FISH, NEWSBOY

Fish was one of many newsboys to exhort the crowd assembled at New Irving Hall. The nature of his speech and the reception it garnered among the rest of the strikers is still unknown.

"YOUNG" FISHER, NEWSBOY AND COMMITTEE MEMBER

As with "Young Hawkeye," little was printed about Fisher's role in the strike. Following the newsies' rally at New Irving Hall, he was said to travel in Kid Blink's entourage as part of the central strike committee.[31]

EDWARD FITZGERALD, NEWSBOY

Fitzgerald was implicated in a claim of extortion, whereupon he and a few other boys were accused of trying to get $600 from the *World* in exchange for ceasing all strike activities. He was arrested and, after failing to procure the $1,000 bail, sent to the Tombs Prison by order of Magistrate Mott.[32]

"MICKY" FORD, CO-VICE PRESIDENT OF BROOKLYN UNION

Ford served as co-vice president of the Brooklyn union alongside newsboy "Johnnie" Gallagher. Together with their leader, "Half Dollar" Williams, the boys circulated some 5,000 strike pamphlets and plotted a course of action against the yellow journals.[33]

"FRIEDMAN FROCKETS," NEWSBOY

Despite possessing one of the more distinctive names among his fellow strikers, nothing else distinguished Frockets from the lineup of newsie speakers at New Irving Hall.

JIM GADY/GAITY/GAIETY, NEWSBOY AND COMMITTEE OF ARRANGEMENTS MEMBER

On an invitation from Hearst himself, Gady accompanied Kid Blink, Dave Simons, and Jim Seabook during a brief visit to the Journal's office. Blink gave a report of the meeting after its disappointing conclusion:

> "He wanted to know what the *World* was going to do. I told him that we was dealing with the *Journal* now, and that if he cut the *World* would cut quick enough. He says he had to talk it over with some other guys before he'd give an answer, and I then asked him if he wouldn't arbitrate, like his paper says. He laughed and said he'd give us an answer Monday right here, and that if he decided to arbitrate he'd meet us at the Broadway Central Hotel."[34]

A second meeting between the two sides was scrapped, and aside from a brief appearance at the newsies' rally later that week, news of Gady's strike-related activities did not appear in the press again.

"JOHNNIE" GALLAGHER, CO-VICE PRESIDENT OF BROOKLYN UNION

Both Gallagher and newsboy "Micky" Ford worked under Brooklyn union president "Half Dollar" Williams. It's not certain how many newsboys and newsgirls supported the union, but they likely undertook some of the same activities as other groups around the area: organizing rallies, passing out pro-strike pamphlets, and appealing to would-be supporters.[35]

MILO GREEN, STRIKE DEFECTOR (AGE 15)

For every newsboy and newsgirl who declined to protest the *World* and *Journal*, there were fifty more newsies prepared to give them grief for it. Green was one of many to discover that lesson firsthand. Shortly after he started hawking the yellow journals at Broadway and Thirty-Sixth Street, he was besieged by newsboy Emil Kahune and a swarm of fifty-odd protestors. They scared off Green's customers, ripped up his papers, and bestowed a sound thrashing on the boy. Green finally caught a break with the arrival of lawyer Hugh Coleman, who took Kahune over his knee for another beating and fended off the rest with his cane until the police arrived.[36]

ABRAHAM GREENHAUSE/GREENHOUSE, STRIKE LEADER (AGE 14)

Greenhause was one of four strike leaders apprehended for orchestrating a parade of newsies. flanked by fellow strikers Cornelius Boyle, Isaac Miller, and Albert Smith, the newsboy caused an unsightly commotion in front of the printers' offices that attracted the attention of local cops. When the boys continued to defy orders to disband, the leaders were arrested and fined $5 apiece. As no boy could pay the fee, they were taken into custody by the Gerry Society until they could scrape together the funds needed to pay their debts.[37]

"CHEEK" GRUBER, NEWSBOY

Gruber was listed among the speakers at the New Irving Hall assembly. The nature and content of his speech was not recorded.

WALTER GULLIVER, NEWSBOY (AGE 14)

Gulliver was among the boys involved in an intense assault on two *World* distributors. The mob descended on the delivery wagon, tied the wheels together, then upended it and nearly decimated the vehicle as the newspapers were shredded and tossed to the street below. The horse was chased off and pelted with stones, and the distributors themselves—brothers by the name of Arthur and Solomon Loevine—received still harsher punishment. The strikers dragged the men out to the sidewalk and rained down all matter of wounds and bruises until they were all but beaten unconscious.[38] Gulliver was arrested for his part in the attack, though just hours before he had been compelled by force to join the strikers himself.

"TOW-HEAD" HALLIGAN, NEWSBOY AND CHIEF EXECUTIVE OF NEWSIES

Halligan was appointed the chief executive of the striking newsies of Troy, New York. He led a meeting of the newsies on July 25, backed by a committee of "Foxey" Osborne, "Dinky" Bateman, and "Mugsey" McGrath.

JACK "BLY" HARNEY, NEWSBOY

Like Edward Fitzgerald and Henry Butler, Harney was arrested and sentenced to the Tombs Prison after the *World* accused the boy of trying to extort the paper for $600. The sum would have effectively ended the strike for good, though the boys insisted that they were tricked into visiting the *World*'s circulation office and had no intention of signing any agreement to end the strike for a lump sum (according to less biased sources, the *World* had reportedly offered them $300 for their cooperation).[39]

LOUIS/LEWIS HASS, NEWSBOY

Hass stepped in and took control of the striking newsboys following Kid Blink's arrest in late July.[40] By this point, most boys didn't feel the need for management, believing that as soon as one of their own was appointed to a position of power, he would be more prone to abuse it or, worse, become suscepti-ble to the sabotaging efforts of the *World* and *Journal*.

"YOUNG" HAWKEYE, NEWSBOY AND COMMITTEE MEMBER

Little is known about Hawkeye, save that he was appointed to a committee and made to accompany Kid Blink to the *Evening Telegram* office when Blink retrieved the floral horseshoe he won at the rally.[41]

JAMES HEFFERNAN, SCOUT FOR THE NEWSIES

Among the first acts of violence committed during the strike came at the hands—or, rather, the fists—of the newsies' scout. He was sent to Long Island City to make a report of the strike there, where he subsequently found Long Island News Company employee Lawrence Weggenman dealing banned papers. Heffernan gave Weggenman the opportunity to arbitrate; whether the newsdealer knew he was in for a fistfight or simply walked into an ambush, the result was the same. Weggenman received a bloody nose for his troubles, while Heffernan ran free...and straight into the arms of a police offer. The scout was just as quickly released from jail, however, and word traveled back to the newsies of New York City that Pulitzer and Hearst had conceded the 50-cent-per-hundred price.[42]¶

EDWARD HERBERT, NEWSBOY (AGE 21)

An accomplice to the strike, Herbert diligently trailed the customers who insisted on purchasing the *World* and *Journal*, plucking the papers from their palms and hopping aboard public cars to snatch them from the laps of unsuspecting readers. He was caught and arraigned at the Jefferson Market Police Court, where he received a $5 penalty for "[allowing] his enthusiasm and zealous desire to better the condition of the newspaper venders to lead him to acts of lawlessness."[43] Herbert was previously denoted as a strike leader during the newsies' parade on Herald Square.

RACETRACK HIGGINS, NEWSBOY AND STRIKE LEADER

Higgins was often mentioned as one of the more well-known leaders of the strike, and led a delegation of Brooklyn newsies through the streets of the city upon the evening of the mass gathering at New Irving Hall. Described in *Brooklyn Life* some days later, he was said to be a child with dark, handsome eyes that revealed qualities of defiance, tenderness, and sadness by turn. He took special care of a young boy of four or five years old who was the newsies' "mascot" and may have also been his younger brother.

Along with qualities of leadership, Higgins acquired a reputation as a captivating storyteller. This skill came in handy during the rally, when the newsboy amused the crowd with anecdotes of his run-ins with Police Chief Devery and the *Journal*'s staff:

¶ This, of course, was untrue. Neither Pulitzer nor Hearst ever made such a concession, and the strike itself didn't resolve until early August.

"I goes to him to-day and I says, just as perlite as I knows how: 'Mr. Devery, I wants to get a permit, please, to have a brass band lead me Brooklyn men to de meetin', to-night.' 'Go way, you slob!' he says—dats what de Chief says to me. And I told him I wasn't no slob, and some day I might be where he is.'"[44]

As there was a flowered horseshoe at stake for the newsie who made the best speech, Higgins tried another gag on the crowd. He claimed he had observed an exchange between a *Journal* employee and an unidentified scab worker, the latter of whom had refused the *Journal*'s offer of a $2 daily salary because "the *Journal* refused to contract to pay hospital expenses."

Higgins was ultimately awarded the horseshoe[**], but he promptly sold it to Kid Blink for seventy-five cents...a decision he came to regret, as Blink was photographed alongside the wreath and praised in the press as a "Young Strike Leader." "It makes a man cry to talk about it," Higgins said.[45]

When the strike drew near its conclusion, Higgins withstood a few accusations that he sold out for the sum of $300. He boldly refuted the claims.

"Do I look it?" he told the strikers and reporters along Park Row. "Why, here's me trousers, fringed like lambrequins, and weighting four pounds less than a straw hat. Look at me shoes—full of holes as a sand sieve. Do you t'ink I'd give up me floral horseshoe for seventy-five cents if I was getting three hundred cold plunks for me inflooence?"

By all accounts, the visage of the scraggly young newsboy backed up his statement more emphatically than his indignant exclamations ever could.

EMMA HORN, NEWSGIRL

One of the younger Horn girls, Emma studied under Winnie and Sadie as she learned the tricks of the newsgirl trade. During her first day on the job, she set down her papers and began dancing to attract a crowd; a ploy that worked as quickly

---

[**]   As with many aspects of the strike, there are conflicting reports on the outcome of this mini-competition. Some hold that Higgins won the horseshoe before selling it to Kid Blink, while other reports name Blink the initial victor.

as it was shut down by law enforcement. Though it's safe to assume Emma, Eva, Jennie, Sadie, and Winnie all remained active newsdealers in the summer of 1899, none of them were ever connected to the prominent events of the strike.

EVA HORN, NEWSGIRL

Eva was one of the five Horn sisters who sold papers in Manhattan, though the press often chose to focus more closely on her sisters, Winnie and Sadie. She married a Mr. Salsona and reportedly gave up a career in newspaper hawking, though it's not apparent whether that happened before or after the events of the newsies' strike.

JENNIE/JINNIE HORN, NEWSGIRL (AGE 11)

Little was printed about Jennie during her life, overshadowed as she was by her four newsgirl sisters. It's unlikely that she was involved in the strike; if so, her name has yet to be found in conjunction with reports of the protest. She later gave up the business after marrying a chauffeur, and at the young age of 22, committed suicide in 1910 shortly after the death of her mother, Elizabeth.

SADIE HORN, NEWSGIRL

"The pretty one" of the Horn sisters (at least according to Winnie Horn), Sadie helped her sister run the family newspaper business next to the Sixth Avenue train station. Though not as effervescent or well-known as her sister, Sadie more than held her own on the streets of New York City. She was fiercely loyal to Winnie and, in years to come, assisted her in petitioning for a newsstand of their own. Like the other Horn sisters, she was still running the family business during the summer of 1899, but was not mentioned in reports of the strike.

"WINSOME" WINNIE HORN, NEWSGIRL

An immensely popular newsgirl of her time, Winnie manned the Sixth Avenue train station entrance for nearly 20 years. She was an outspoken presence in a family of ten, including her three brothers and four sisters. A Russian-English girl with thick brown curls and one blind eye, Winnie often worked with Sadie in 12-hour shifts from 3 p.m. until 3 a.m., making $1-2.50 a day. Winnie was witty and easily humored, and found no shortage of ways to keep her customers entertained. She fended off interested gentleman suitors and was often spotted in the company of several newsboys, all of whom took it upon themselves to stand watch as various businessmen and commuters counted out their change for the sheets. Most found her delightful, especially once they discovered her wax likeness in the nearby Eden Musée or her parody in certain local theatre venues. There are no known reports of Winnie aiding or opposing the strikers' efforts in 1899, though she was undoubtedly still hawking her wares at the time.

JENNIE, NEWSGIRL

Red-haired and wild, Jennie[††] rushed to the defense of two young newsboys who had been bullied by bigger, brawnier non-strikers. As the older boys confidently hawked their wares on the corners of New York City streets, a shrill battle cry interrupted their sales pitches.

"It was Jennie the newsgirl," said the *Tribune*. "She wore no coat of mail, but armed in the justice of the cause, her red hair glinting in the sunlight, she came rushing onward. The small boys flocked about her. On they came. The traitors gave one more glance, dropped their papers, and fled."[46]

"JIMMY THE GOAT," STRIKE LEADER

Well over three hundred newsboys and newsgirls congregated at the intersection of Third Avenue and 125th Street on July 24. They overwhelmed five scab workers and confiscated bundles of the boycotted papers, which were sliced open and given to the breeze. Those who dared defy the strikers and pick up a copy were routinely discouraged from doing so. The newsies finally abandoned their post, with no light prodding from police officers, and made their way to the offices of the *World* and *Journal*.

There, a strike leader known only as "Jimmy the Goat" silenced the crowd to make his speech:

[††]   It's possible, though unlikely, that this Jennie belonged to the Horn family.

"Fellers, dem yallers sez dey symptize wid de car strikers, ain't it so?" the boy began. "Dey sez dem trolley men ain't gettin' a square deal an' can't make a livin'. Wot's de matter wid us? Is de *Wold* an' *Choinal* givin' us boys a square deal? Wot's sauce fer de gander is sauce fer de goose, and we'll boycott em 'ntil dey gives in. Dat's right, ain't it?"[47]

The strikers affirmed that it was, and Jimmy and his pals continued on to Eighth Avenue, where they changed the minds of six other scabs as well.

SAM KEELER, STRIKE SUPPORTER AND SON OF ANNIE KELLY

While it's likely that Keeler played a bigger role in the strike than the press let on, he was only mentioned toward the end of it. Following Kid Blink's unceremonious arrest, Keeler led 200 downtown strikers uptown to join the promised parade.[48]

ANNIE "SLOBBIE" KELLY/KEELER, NEWSWOMAN

Throughout the newsies' strike, most newswomen continued to sell the boycotted papers, confident that the boys wouldn't attack anyone of the female persuasion (some newsboys antagonized the newswomen who insisted on sabotaging the strike, though this doesn't appear to have been widely accepted behavior). Kelly was not among them; rather, she was considered the "patron saint" of the newsies and not only lent her support to the children, but spoke out against the traitors who sold scab papers. This didn't seem to hurt her bottom line much; she averaged an extra 66 cents in profits each day and told the *Tribune*, "Don't I make as much as I did? Oh, yes. I make more, for all my customers stan' by me an' a lot of new ones are helpin' me out."[49] Kelly was later invited to the newsies' rally, where she spoke briefly to much cheering and applause: "Well, boys, you know I'm with yer through thick and thin. Stick together and we'll win."

TIMMY KELLY, NEWSBOY

Kelly gave a speech alongside several other Brooklyn newsboys, during which the group explained that they had only raised $6.25 and were not yet ready to pay for the newsies' parade.[50]

LOUIS KERLOW/KIRLOW, STRIKE LEADER (AGE 13-16)

Kerlow was apprehended fairly early in the strike after he broke into the *Journal*'s distribution center and accosted the newsies who were waiting to receive the day's papers. Such violent methods did not go unpunished—Kerlow was arrested and brought before Magistrate Cornell, who found him to be a long-time offender and sentenced him to a six-month stay in the Juvenile Asylum.[51]

"HUNGRY JOE" KERNAN/KIERNAN, NEWSBOYS' MASCOT

Kernan, described in part as a "picturesque little fellow," entertained the crowd at the New Irving Hall assembly with a song about a one-legged newsboy. The lyrics, unfortunately, have been lost to time and circumstance, though the song so moved one of the two female reporters in attendance that she exclaimed, "Music hath charms."[52]

HANNAH "FIGHT" KLEFF, NEWSWOMAN

Kleff was briefly mentioned in a profile of some of New York City's more well-known newsboys, described by them as a "union [man] for fair" alongside the famous Annie Kelly. Exactly how she aided the striking newsies was not explained.[53]

A.J. KLOCK, STRIKE DEFECTOR (AGE 23)

Klock was among several newspaper hawkers who clearly opposed the strike. The boy was arrested after tangling with a band of strikers who had discovered him distributing the boycotted papers to newswoman Bertha Saffe at the Brooklyn Bridge. He was later discharged from the court by the order of Magistrate Cornell.[54]

H.H. KUEHN/EMIL KAHUNE, NEWSBOY (AGE 15)

Kuehn was apprehended several days into the strike after a cop caught him confiscating and shredding another newsie's papers. The boy refused to tell the officer his address and was promptly hauled off to the police station, his fellow newsies cheering him the whole way there. They plied him with copious amounts of fruit and candy as he awaited his sentencing: an involuntary commitment to the care of the Gerry Society.[55]

JAMES LAHEY/LEAHY, NEWSBOY (AGE 20)

One of the older newsies, Lahey was counted among the strike leaders. The morning of July 24, he led a contingent of strikers against one of the delivery wagons, surrounding and clubbing the driver until he was chased down the street by police officer Charles Zeeck. Zeeck arrested the boy and brought him to the nearest station. According to the *Evening Telegram*, "every striking newsboy within a radius of fifteen blocks followed Zeeck and his prisoner," but their pleas to release Leahy were refused. For his part, he told the officer he was happy to be jailed for the cause.[56]

TONY LESSARO/MISSARO, NEWSBOY (AGE 18)

Lessaro was accused of harassing and physically assaulting a pair of delivery drivers who were distributing the *World* and *Journal* shortly before the end of the strike. Three police officers on duty arrested three of the newsies, including Lessaro and newsboys Orlando Baldechar and Sebastian De Leo.[57]

CHARLES/"YELLOW" SIMON/SOLOMON "SOL" LEVY, NEWSBOY AND SECRETARY/SERGEANT AT ARMS OF THE NEWSIES' UNION

In the wake of Kid Blink's defection from the band of Manhattan strikers, Levy was appointed secretary of the newsies' union under then-president Morris Cohen. Several days later, Levy attempted to organize another rally for the newsies—this time, with the intent to form a union and select new leadership.[‡‡] He earned the position of sergeant at arms; together with the rest of the boys, they elected 50-year-old James G. Neill as president of the union.[58]

"LITTLE MIKE/KIKIE," NEWSBOY

One of many newsboy orators at the New Irving Hall rally, Mike also delivered a speech to the raucous crowd. It can safely be assumed that his was of a similar nature to those of

---

‡‡ Many newsies described themselves as strike leaders, possibly to elicit greater sympathy or admiration from the public. It's not clear what hierarchy was established in the newsies' ranks, nor the ratio of leaders to other striking newsboys and newsgirls.

Kid Blink, Bob "Indian" Stone, and others, though his words and sentiment have since been lost to time.

"HUNCH" MADDOX, NEWSBOY

Maddox was one of two known lieutenants in "Muggsy" McGee's posse of striking newsboys. Local news coverage failed to mention his specific responsibilities and attitude toward the strike.

"YOUNG" MALONEY, NEWSBOY[§§]

In the day following the newsies' rally, Maloney was sent to track a dozen *World* and *Journal* scabs to Hoboken. He reported that the twelve men only made 22 cents on their bundle of 500 yellow journals and were forced to solicit the publishers for return fare on the ferry.[59]

JOHN MASIN, NEWSBOY AND HEAD CAPTAIN OF NEWSIES' UNION

Little has been written about Masin, save that he was elected the head captain shortly after the newsies formed their union. He was then made responsible for choosing his own district captains.[60]

"BOOTS" MCALEENAN/MCALEEN, STRIKE LEADER AND SPOKESMAN OF THE ARBITRATION COMMITTEE (AGE 11)

Along with the likes of Jack Sullivan and "Young Monix," "Boots" was credited as one of the original leaders of the newsies' strike. He gave his version of the origins of the strike to the *Tribune*: "We went to de bloke wot sells de papers and we tells him dat its got to be two fer a cent or nuthin'. "He says, 'Wot are yer goin' to do about it if yer don't get 'em?'" "Strike,' sez I, and Monix, he puts in his oar and backs me up. The bloke sez 'Go ahead and strike,' and here we is—dat's all."[61]

---

§§   It is presumed that Maloney is a newsboy who joined the ranks of the strikers, though this is not explicitly mentioned by the press. Maloney was a common surname for the newsboys of the city, and without further information, it is impossible to identify him as any of the "Tommy," "Charles," or "James" Maloneys who were mentioned in the newspapers during the late 1800s and early 1900s.

He later specified that the newsies had decided to strike during the summer of 1899 precisely because the cops were too wrapped up with the trolley strike to bother with the children. "We're doin' it now because de cops is all busy, an' we can do any scab newsboy dat shows his face widout police interference," the boy revealed. "We're here fer our rights, an' we will die defendin' em."[62]

"MUGGSY" MCGEE, DISTRICT MASTER WORKMAN

McGee held court with the striking newsies in "Frankfurter John's" lunch wagon, where he sussed out the particulars of the boycott with self-proclaimed lieutenants "Hunch" Maddox and the "Speculator." In an interview with the *Evening Telegram*, he declared the newsies would soon force the *World* and *Journal* to return their wholesale papers to pre-war prices.[63]

"MUGSEY" MCGRATH, TROY NEWSBOY AND STRIKE COMMITTEE MEMBER

Along with Troy newsboys "Foxey" Osborne and "Dinky" Bateman, McGrath helped form a strike committee that was tasked with soliciting support from the city's merchants.¶¶

MCLINN, NEWSBOY

McLinn had his ups and downs within the newsies' organization. He was lauded for giving a non-union newsboy a bloody nose after he caught him dealing the yellow journals. A day later, he was hauled off to the children's court after pilfering a peach from a fruit stand. "Boots" McAleen handed down the sentencing: ten whacks with a stick.[64]

LOUIS MENDICK, NEWSBOY (AGE 14)

Mendick was briefly mentioned in the papers for daring to do what most newsboys would not: steal newspapers from the newsgirls and newswomen who hawked their wares at the Brooklyn Bridge. Like most offenders, he was charged a $5 fine by Magistrate Mott of the Centre Street Court.[65]

¶¶   He appears to be a different "Mugsey" than the newsboy who reigned over Park Row at the start of the strike, but their names are similar enough that it may be the same person.

ISAAC/IKE MILLER, STRIKE LEADER (AGE 13)

Miller helped lead a parade of one hundred newsboys down Park Row, where they jeered, waved homemade banners, and rattled the windows of the *World* and *Journal* offices so vociferously that their number seemed to have quadrupled by the volume of their shouting and chanting alone. The children managed to get as far as Frankfort Street before the police officers on duty demanded a cessation of all organized activity, but the newsies resumed their parade just as soon as the cops left the scene. Miller and his friends were arrested for their part in conspiring to parade without a permit, and each boy was committed to the Gerry Society after failing to pay the $5 fine issued by Magistrate Mott. [66]

"YOUNG MONIX"/"MANIX"/"YELLER," NEWSBOY, CHIEF ORGANIZER, AND MEMBER OF THE ARBITRATION COMMITTEE AND EXECUTIVE COMMITTEE OF THE NEWSBOYS' UNION

Monix helped form the center of the Executive Committee of the Newsboys' Union with Jim Gaiety, "Barney Peanuts," "Crutch" Morris, "Crazy" Arborn, David Simons, "Scabutch," and "Blind" Diamond. He was briefly mentioned as one of the newsies who confronted the newspaper distributors at the start of the strike, and later assumed Dave Simons' position as president of the newsboys' union and leader of the Park Row contingent of protesters.***

"CRUTCH"/"CRUTCHY"/ "CRUTCHIN'"/"ONE-LEGGED" MORRIS, NEWSBOY, RECORDING SECRETARY, AND MEMBER OF THE EXECUTIVE COMMITTEE OF THE NEWSBOYS' UNION

As his nickname implied, Morris was a one-legged newsboy who was counted among the leaders of the newsboys' union. He was given a variety of titles by his compatriots, but didn't appear to be heavily involved in some of the more violent protests and events of the strike.

*** It is entirely possible, albeit unconfirmed, that "Young Monix" is the same person as Morris Cohen, as both were listed in the press as the new strike leaders following Kid Blink and Dave Simons' defection from the movement.

"CROOKED MOUTH" MAX, NEWSBOY
AND COMMITTEE MEMBER

Like Fisher and Hawkeye, Max was assigned to a committee and helped chaperone Kid Blink's visit to the *Evening Telegram*'s office after the rally.[67]

JOSEPH "THIMBLEFINGER"
MULLIGAN, NEWSBOY (AGE 17)

Mulligan earned a brief mention in the *Times* after getting arrested for fighting. Two others, Frank Dresso and Donato Caroluci, were apprehended for similar reasons, though it's not apparent whether the boys were fighting each other or a common foe.[68] While awaiting their sentencing the next day, they were examined by Magistrate Mott, Charity Organization Society Assistant Secretary Philip W. Ayres, and a group of four sociology students.

Ayers felt the boys' heads for lumps, exclaiming, "Types of degeneracy, every one. Most interesting! Combativeness remarkably developed." Mulligan wasn't so keen on the analysis. "Wot's dat?" he asked the man. "Be you'se goin' ter write a book about de strike? I'm Timblefinger Joe, de delegate from de Borough of Kings. Kin I git one uv youse ter take a note ter Bun-Faced Ben an' me udder pals? We wants ter git out in time fer de p'rade termorrow night.[69] No such messenger was freely provided the newsies.

EDDIE/EDDY MURPHY, STRIKE LEADER

One of the smaller newsies, Murphy didn't let his short stature prevent him from getting into the thick of the mess between the newsboys and scab workers. He led an attack on *Journal* employee Michael Romeo, taking a club to the newsboy's wrist and leaving the boy bruised and beaten.[70] Five days later, he was spotted at a rally in Brooklyn, where he exhorted his fellow strikers to stand strong against the yellow journals:

> "Felly hustlers in de field of newspapes, youse all knows wot youse is here fur. W'en a bloke swipes de last dime youse has in her cloze, you don't have to kinsult a city directory or a cop t' know dat youse is a loser. Some folks is thick 'nuff ter say, 'Oh, it's only a matter of 10

cents a hundred papers, an' it'll blow over in a few days.'
Well, who's got a right to dat 10 cents—de blokes wot
ride in coupys or de boys wot git a hustle on and wolk
fur der butter cakes? Dat's wot I'd like ter know. Now,
we is goin' ter win dis strike. Don't get discouraged. De
peepuls is wid us."[71]

WALTER MURPHY, NEWSBOY

Murphy was one of the principal speakers during a newsie
rally in Brooklyn. The precise details of his speech were not
recorded by the press, though he was said to have "choked
a good deal."[72]

MRS. "BEAUTY" MYERS/MEYERS,
NEWSWOMAN AND STRIKE DEFECTOR

Unlike strike supporters Annie Kelly and, eventually, "The
Squealer," Mrs. Myers had no qualms about offering the *World*
and *Journal* to her customers. She kept them hidden under
her shawl, but was eventually discovered by the strikers and
chased away from her preferred selling spot at the Brooklyn
Bridge and into the less-desirable mouth of Nassau Street.

NICK/MICKEY MEYER/MYERS, NEWSBOY AND
VICE-PRESIDENT OF THE NEWSBOYS' UNION

Myers made a brief speech during the newsies' rally at New
Irving Hall. Neither his speech nor his pre- and post-rally
efforts were published for public consumption.[†††]

"YELL" MEYERS, NEWSIE

"Yell" might have been an alias for either Nick or "Mush"
Myers, or, equally likely, all three nicknames might have been
used interchangeably to describe the same newsboy. "Yell"
helped comprise a three-person advisory council to new strike
leader Morris Cohen.

[†††]   It's possible that Nick Myers also went by the moniker "Young Mush";
since there seems to be no definitive proof linking the two, they are listed
separately here.

YOUNG "MUSH" MYERS, NEWSBOY

The newsies often had to get creative in order to separate the scabs from the police protection they were afforded on the streets. In one such incident, "Mush" snatched a few copies of the *Journal* from a scab worker, then dashed down the block as the police officer chased him...giving the rest of the newsies plenty of time to wail on the scab. Per the *Sun*, "Mush" got his nickname "on account of his fondness for taking his girl to Corlears Hook Park [on] Sunday evenings."[73]

JAMES G. NEILL, UNION PRESIDENT

Neill was presumably the first adult to be placed in charge of the striking newsies. His appointment was suggested by another adult supporter of the strike, newsstand owner Abraham Lippman, a few days before the movement came to its natural end. The 50-year-old Neill had a few ideas for the newsboys and newsgirls' organization: first, that the union members wear identifying badges; second, that they take on affiliations with other labor organizations; third, that they divide New York City into districts and form a central union, to whom delegates from other areas of the city could report. All three suggestions were accepted, though it isn't known how fully they were implemented in the days that followed. Neill also told the children that the price hike imposed by the *World* and *Journal* amounted to a tax on newspaper sellers (both those who ran newsstands and those who sold on street corners), and it was a price hike that could not be transferred to the public.[74]

ABIE/"BIG ABE" NEWMAN, NEWSBOY

An employee and outdoor distributor of the *Evening Telegram*, Newman came under fire from a former coworker named William Fitzgibbons, who attempted to obtain a warrant for the boy's arrest on charges of attempted manslaughter. Fitzgibbons was allegedly telling the newsies that they had been conned into boycotting the yellow journals, which aggravated Newman so much that he pulled a pistol and tried to shoot him.[75]

"NINK" NUGENT, POUGHKEEPSIE
NEWSBOY AND STRIKE LEADER

In Poughkeepsie, unlike New York City, the price hike was 20 cents above the going rate rather than 10 cents. Nugent and fellow newsboy George Burlingame were named as two strike leaders in the city, where newsies knocked down newsdealers, filched the contraband papers, and burned the journals in an enormous bonfire to celebrate their victory.[76]

"FOXEY" OSBORNE, TROY NEWSBOY AND
STRIKE COMMITTEE MEMBER

Along with Troy newsboys "Mugsey" McGrath and "Dinky" Bateman, Osborne helped form a strike committee that was tasked with soliciting support from the city's merchants.

"BARNEY PEANUTS" PETERS/COHEN, NEWSBOY,
WALKING DELEGATE, AND SPOKESMAN OF THE
STRIKE COMMITTEE OF THE NEWSBOYS' UNION‡‡‡

Peters presided over a gathering of the Strike Committee of the Newsboys' Union on July 23, where he announced the newsies' intention to stage a meeting at New Irving Hall the following evening. He solicited help from the non-struck papers and asked them to advertise the event, then targeted the politicians and adult strike sympathizers who held the most sway in the city: senator Timothy "Dry Dollar" Sullivan, aspiring politician (and future Congressman and Tammany Hall boss) Christopher Sullivan, former Alderman Patrick Farley, Chinatown saloon owner James "Scotty" Lavelle, and others.

"All of these guys are going to do more than write notes," Peters told the crowd of newsies. "We also have ordered 10,000 circulars that will tell how we are being done by the 'ristrocrats that talk of the workingman and arbitration in their papers and then do us."[77]

---

‡‡‡ "Barney Peanuts" was listed alongside two surnames in the newspapers, but is likely the same fellow due to the uniqueness of his nickname. As with every lnewsie catalogued by the press, his real name has not and cannot be verified.

"CROSS-EYED" JOE PETERS, NEWSBOY REPRESENTATIVE

Peters, whose nickname was an apt description of his physical appearance, represented the uptown contingent of newsboys. "We're all out [protesting]," he told Kid Blink at the start of the strike. "We'll send a kid to de horspital in de rattler fer ever scab pape dat's sold above Fourteenth Street."[78] Later, when the boys were busy resisting bribes and defending their position against the *World* and *Journal*, he spoke to the *Herald* in favor of the newsies::

> "What do you expect? How do they t'ink a man can live? Suppose he don't bring home any house money. Why, he gets beaten and jumped on when he gets home. I've got to take home $6 a week house money. Ain't that ten cents on a hundred just as good to me as it is to anybody else?"[79]

"PIE-FACED JIM," STRIKE LEADER

As the boycott spread from its epicenter on Park Row, Jim collected the newsies of Harlem and assembled them at Third Avenue and 125th Street. Together, they drew up large placards and hung them around town:

> "We demand fair profits,
> fair methods. Won't you
> help us?"
> "Strike, newsboys!
> Do not buy the *Evening*
> *World* or *Journal*"
> "Strike, newsboys!
> We believe in fair play
> and arbitration."[80]

WILLIAM "COON" REESE/REISS, NEWSBOY
AND LEMONADE SELLER§§§

An African-American newsboy who doubled his profits by selling lemonade in Printing House Square, Reese was arrested after an agent of the *New York World* accused him of distributing pro-strike pamphlets. The *World* employee told a police officer that he was under orders to have any strike sympathizers arrested. Reese was charged with violating a corporation ordinance, but soon released after making his case to Magistrate Zeller.[81] Around the same time, the newsboy earned some positive press for supplying the strikers with an elaborate floral horseshoe, to be awarded to the best newsie orator during the rally at New Irving Hall.¶¶¶

MICHAEL ROMEO, STRIKE DEFECTOR

Romeo made a nearly-fatal error in the first days of the strike. He insisted on crossing the bridge with copies of the *Journal* in tow, but was soon met with an angry band of strikers. They brandished large sticks, which they would have used on him had he not procured a knife of his own. As Romeo made a stabbing motion toward newsie Eddy Murphy, Murphy struck the boy's wrist with the full weight of his club and knocked the knife into the gutter. By the time the brawl reached its bloody end, Romeo had been bruised, kicked, knocked about the head, and stripped of his papers.[82]

JOSEPH ROSENTHAL, ROSENTHAL STRIKE LEADER

While the strikers' efforts began to wind down in New York City, the outlying cities of New York continued to feel the

---

§§§   There seems to be some conflicting descriptions of the lemonade seller in the press. On several accounts, he was identified as a newsboy who split his time between hawking papers and selling lemonade in Printing House Square. Alternative reports describe him as an adult strike sympathizer who spent the entirety of the New Irving Hall assembly keeping the newsies in line with a "far-reaching switch." It is possible these were two different persons, though not enough information has been given to independently verify their identities.

¶¶¶   There does not seem to be a clear consensus about the origin of the horseshoe. According to various sources, it may have been presented by Reese or fellow newsies Racetrack Higgins and Nick Myers.

ripple effects of the boycott. Rosenthal directed the Rochester newsies to protest the sale of the *World* and *Journal*, saying, "The boys are only asking for what is right, and we ought to have it. In New York City newsboys get papers for 60 cents per 100, and they want to charge us $1.25 per 100 here."[83]

EDWARD ROWLAND, NEWSBOY (AGE 16)

Rowland was apprehended during the protests on July 24, though his exact crime was not described in the papers. He was locked up in the 125th Street station house.[84]

DAVID RUBEN, NEWSBOY AND TREASURER OF NEWSIES' UNION

Ruben hailed from Bleeker Street and the Bowery. He helped form a newsies' union several days before the end of the strike and served as treasurer.[85]

BERTHA SAFFE, STRIKE DEFECTOR (AGE 23)

Saffe sold the banned newspapers alongside 23-year-old newsboy A.J. Klock. She set up shop at the entrance to the Brooklyn Bridge, but attracted unwanted attention from a group of strikers and was arrested during the scuffle that followed. Like Klock, she was granted a reprieve by Magistrate Cornell, but it's not clear whether she returned to selling the banned journals or joined the newsies' ranks.[86]

JIMMIE SCABOOCH/SCABUTCH WOLFF, NEWSBOY AND FINANCIAL SECRETARY OF THE NEWSBOYS' UNION[****]

Wolff was listed among Kid Blink's posse as one of the few who confronted William Randolph Hearst face-to-face. During their brief meeting—arranged not at the *Journal* offices, but on a chance public encounter—Hearst told the young newsboy that he'd rather go out of business and close up shop than give into the children's demands. "I guess dat's wot he'll have to do," Blink concluded.[87]

[****] It's possible that Jimmie Scabooch and Jim Seabook are one and the same. As a strong link was not made between the two in the press, they are listed separately here.

JIM SEABOOK, NEWSBOY

Seabook earned little mention in the papers, save for a fruitless meeting between William Randolph Hearst and a four-person committee of striking newsboys. Hearst refused to arbitrate with the strikers on the spot, and wanted to know how the *World* planned to deal with the children before he made up his own mind.[88]

JACK SEELEY, NEWSBOY

Seeley's name didn't crop up in the newspapers until the newsies' biggest scandal hit the rumor mill: a claim that the strikers had tried to extort the *World* for $600 in order to end the boycott. Unlike newsboys Edward Fitzgerald, Henry Butler, and Jack Harney, Seeley dodged arrest by climbing onto the roof of the *World*'s circulation office and shimmying down the water pipe to make his escape. His fellow newsies were less fortunate, as they were captured by Detective Distler and committed to Tombs Prison soon afterward.[89]

MRS. SHEA, NEWSWOMAN AND STRIKE DEFECTOR

Mrs. Shea ran a competing enterprise against fellow news-woman Mrs. Cochran, but both women temporarily put aside their rivalry during the children's strike. It's not apparent whether the women considered themselves part of the strike or simply acted as a support system for the children who initiated it, though they were listed as members of the union at one point. Regardless of their personal motivations, Shea and her rival vacillated between lending their support to the newsies and selling the boycotted papers to gain an advantage in the market. They were most often opposed by newswoman and strike sympathizer Annie Kelly, who made a point of antagonizing strike dissenters whenever possible and later ratted them out to the *Tribune*: "There's them two old women. They sell the scab papers—an' Mis' Shea and Mis' Corcoran, both with big bank accounts to their names, they've gone back on the boys a' sell them on the sly."[90]

SHORTY, NEWSBOY (AGE 11)

Among the younger newsboys to participate in the strike, Shorty questioned the strike leaders' unanimous decision to stop "soaking" the scabs. "Who's been a-talkin' to yer like that, Dave [Simons]?" he piped up during the newsies' meeting. Simons refused to offer further explanation, but encouraged the newsboys and newsgirls to find more peaceful methods of persuasion.[91]

DAVE "DAVEE" SIMONS/SIMMONS/SIMONDS/ SIMMONDS/SYMONDS, NEWSBOY, TREASURER, EXECUTIVE COMMITTEE MEMBER, AND PRESIDENT OF THE NEWSBOYS' UNION (AGE 21)

The press never could decide on a definitive spelling for the newsboy's name, but there was no mistaking Simons' importance in the hierarchy of strike leaders. He was well-versed in the ways of the street trade; by his own account, he had started hawking newspapers at the ripe old age of eight years old and established himself as a regular in City Hall Park. Simons also received an education at the Norfolk St. School, though he never made it clear whether he took a break from selling papers in order to do so. By the time he reached his early twenties, he had several boys working under him,†††† and frittered away his free time in boxing matches at the local athletic clubs.

When the strike rolled around, Simons was elected one of the prominent newsie leaders and often made grand speeches to his fellow compatriots. He spoke during the newsies' rally at Irving Hall, both to instruct the newsboys and newsgirls not to "soak" the scab workers and to beseech the newsdealers and advertisers to aid the children:

---

†††† According to his own comments in the *Tribune*, Simons was generally of the attitude that any boy who could best him in a fight could take possession of his corner of the park. "If de man kin lick me, he kin have de place, and dat's de case all over," Simons said. "De newsboy has got to look out for himself, and if he's no good he'd better quit soon." He also gave the paper a rough overview of the group's demographics, describing four-fifths as Jewish, Irish, and Italian newsboys and the remaining one-fifth as an amalgamation of newswomen, African-American children, and disabled and impoverished newspaper sellers.[92]

"Please don't buy the *World* or *Journal,* because we refuse to sell these papers until some satisfactory terms can be reached. The *World* and the *Journal* demand arbitration for the striking railroad me, but why don't they arbitrate with the newsboys? If you have any sympathy with us help us to boycott these papers by not reading them. Take out your advertisements: as no one sells these papers no one will be able to see them. You will find all the news in the *The Evening Sun, Telegram* and *Daily News.* They give us a chance to make a living. Buy them and help us, and we will thank you very kindly. We remain yours humbly, The Newsboys' Union."[93]

It was also Simons who followed in Kid Blink's footsteps and was persuaded to turn traitor against the children's movement. He was spotted hawking the forbidden papers and consequently dethroned within the union, though his passionate entreaties to the strikers allowed him to keep a humbler position as the strike moved forward.

SKAGGS, NEWSBOY

Skaggs was fairly well known among the crowd of strikers helmed by Kid Blink. The boy's father owned a restaurant on the East Side and offered to treat the newsies to anything they needed. That was of little help against the newspapers in question—during a visit to one of the boycotted papers[‡‡‡‡], neither Kid Blink nor Skaggs made it past the lobby.

"Me an' me corp an' anoder of me men, wot his name is Skaggs, went to call on de guy what owns de paper last night," said Blink. "Wen we get sto de office a kid askes us our buzness. 'Say,' sez I, 'just take me card and put it onto a silver tray and take it inter de boss. I ain't in de habit of transachin' my bizness wid no office boys.' He started to talk, and I tole him to be mighty quick erbout it or I'd make him look like a stranger in his own family."**[94]**

---

‡‡‡‡   While pontificating in front of a large gathering of strikers, Kid Blink failed to specify which publisher they had visited.

"FISHBONE" SKINNEYS, NEWSBOY

Skinneys delivered a speech during the mass meeting of newsies on July 24, but his exact words were not recorded alongside those made by Kid Blink, Racetrack Higgins, and others.

ALBERT SMITH, STRIKE LEADER (AGE 15)

One of the young strike leaders, Smith collaborated with Cornelius Boyle, Abraham Greenhause, and Isaac Miller to organize and run a parade past the big newspaper buildings. The four boys were successful in their efforts, lining up a hundred newsies and marching through Printing House Square and on to Frankfort Street. It was there their happy parade came to its untimely end: after ignoring repeated warnings to disband, they were arrested by Detective Allen and Policemen Distler and Snydecker for carrying out a parade without permission from the city. Along with his fellow strike leaders, Smith was penalized $5 and placed under the custody of the Gerry Society until he was able to pay it.[95]

"SOCKS," NEWSBOY§§§§

"Socks" was one of the lucky souls who managed to cram into New Irving Hall during the newsies' assembly, leaving some 3,000 children pacing the streets outside. He might have gone unnoticed altogether had he not stirred up a ruckus when Annie Kelly took the stage, prompting a warning from one of the sergeant-at-arms: "Hey there, Socks, shut up, will yer?"[96]

"THE SPECULATOR," NEWSBOY

Like "Hunch" Maddox, "The Speculator" played second fiddle to strike leader "Muggsy" McGee. McGee and his compatriots reportedly set up shop in a local lunch wagon.

---

§§§§ Whether "Socks" was a newsboy might be contested, as he was never fully identified in the press as anything but an "unruly spirit."

"THE SQUEALER"/MRS. "CRY BABY," NEWSWOMAN AND STRIKE DEFECTOR

Known for her distinctive cry—one the *Sun* likened to that of an "enraged elephant"—the German newswoman known as "The Squealer" spent most afternoons and evenings peddling the evening editions and fending off the newsies who would divest her of a prime selling spot. She boldly refused to stop selling the *World* and *Journal* at the beginning of the strike and fell upon one of the strikers with an ear-piercing shriek after she was warned to detach herself from the yellow journals. The newsies weren't kept down for long: thirty of them rushed the woman, stripping her of her skirt and "[hoisting] the captured garments upon sticks, [parading] them as banners of victory."[97] "The Squealer" (aptly called by another nickname, Mrs. "Cry Baby") retreated to an alley until the newsies had finished their impromptu parade, then negotiated a trade— her clothing for her compliance in strike matters—and quietly returned to her stand by the day's end.

"STEAMBOAT MIKE," MOUNT VERNON NEWSBOY

Mike took charge of the Mount Vernon newsboys, though as he was a fair distance from the center of the movement, the papers didn't follow his efforts all that closely. Following a rally of 200 newsies in a vacant lot of the city, he proclaimed: "I tell youse this strike ain't no bluff. It's goin' to spread till it reaches de Klondike and puts de *World* and *Journal* on de bum."[98]

BOB "INDIAN" STONE, NEWSBOY AND MEMBER OF THE NEWSBOYS' UNION

Stone was among the first of the unioned newsboys to take the stand at New Irving Hall. His nickname was derived from the shriek he unleashed as he advertised his wares, often compared to that of a stereotypical Native American war cry. In front of the newsies, Stone gave a report on his trip to the offices of the *Journal* and informed the crowd that Hearst had not been receptive to the children's pleas.

> "Say, boys, I ain't much on de talk. Bu I'm wid yer to de end," said the newsboy. "We'se got a strike on 'De Evenin' Woild' and 'De Evenin' Joinal.' Dey knows it, you bet,

and I reckon about now dey'd like to quit. Well, if we stick togedder we'll win dis fight. And say, will we stick? I tinks we will-radder.

"Just tink wot dey makes on der ads. And dey wants our 10 cents profert, too. I went to see Mister Hearst, and he just as good as trun me outen his offiz. Let's not do nuthin' wrong. Let's tend to business, and not trow no sticks and stones, and not hit nobody over de head. Just let's sell dose papers wot treats us right."[99]

Like the other speakers that evening, Stone encouraged the strikers to abstain from violent methods of drumming up support. Whether the newsboys and girls intended to stick by that noble-hearted resolution was another story altogether.

MIKE "JACK"/"GAS HOUSE" SULLIVAN, STRIKE LEADER[¶¶¶¶]

Sullivan was counted among the early strike leaders of the newsies' movement. After receiving an unsavory report from the children's arbitration committee, he resolved to launch the boycott against the *World* and *Journal*.[*****]

"They tink we're cravens," he told the newsies, "but we'll show 'em dat we ain't. De time is overripe fer action. De cops won't have not time fer us. What is de sense of de meetin'? Is it strike? Well, den, de strike is ordered. Der must be no half measures, my men. If you sees any one sellin' de 'Woild' or 'Joinal,' swat 'em. [...] tear 'em up, trow 'em in de river, any ole ting."[100]

GEORGE "MICKY" THOMPSON, NEWSBOY

In yet another of the newsies' mass meetings, this one held on July 29, Thompson was deemed the best speaker after pleading for new funds for the strikers' next outing and promising to form another Newsboys' Association. He also maligned the

---

[¶¶¶¶] The year prior to the 1899 strike, both Sullivan and Bob "Indian" Stone went head-to-head in a newsboy boxing championship. After ten fierce rounds, played to a crowd of 4,000, the match ended in a draw.

[*****] His decision is not considered to be the true genesis of the strike, but one of many moments during which the boys and girls of the city found ample reason to protest their employers.

World and *Journal*—as the *Eagle* pointed out, he did so while avoiding any coarse or vulgar language. (They may also have been partial to the lad, seeing as how he was a familiar figure who hawked papers in front of their offices.)

> "[Scab workers] are mostly Italians and the sons of for-eigners," Thompson told the crowd. "They are willing to work for nothing. You see these night hawks. They are fly by nights, here to-day and at Coney Island to-mor-row. Most of us boys have regular corners and regular trade. These are the poor fellows who have no homes. They are not to be blamed if they do anything to make a few cents. Some of the boys who have homes say their mothers complain because they don't bring in as much money as before. Mine don't, but then she looks into these things different. Now, don't any of you boys sell the *World*. Sell the *Eagle* and other papers that treat us right, and people, don't you buy the yaller sheet."[101]

"TINY TIM," NEWSBOY

Tim, likely named for his diminutive frame, was regularly found with his bundle at the corner of 23rd Street and Sixth Avenue. When asked to predict the longevity of the strike, he displayed the same brash confidence put forth by many of the newsie leaders before him. "[The strike will last] forever," the boy was quoted, "and longer, if nesercery. I ain't got no famerly to support, an' I reckin der fellers wot has is makin' just as much as dey did before."[102]

He was right on two counts: a) the newsboys and news-girls who were orphaned or whose families did not depend on their income had less to lose in the strike, and b) what-ever losses the newsies had taken by refusing to peddle the popular *World* and *Journal*, they were partially compensating for by upping their intake of *Evening Telegrams* and other strike-supporting publications.

JAMES TOBIN, STRIKE DEFECTOR

Tobin elected not to join the newsboys' strike; or, if he had joined it, he walked back that decision just two days after it began. He was assaulted by two strikers when they ripped the yellow journals away from him and tried to literally shove them down his throat.[103]

"CHEEKY" WILITZ, NEWSBOY[†††††]

Wilitz reported to the *Tribune*, explaining the ploy of the young boys who were often spotted sleeping on curbstones with newspapers crumpled in their fists:

> "Dem kids is a disgrace. Dey stand in wid fellers dat give 'em de papers, and den dey do de cry act, de lost penny act and de sick story, and makes money for de big blokes. You can see 'em sneakin' into de open air places, beer gardens, and all over where dere's people, and some of 'em works do poor dodge so slick dat five papers 'll last 'em all night."[104]

"HALF DOLLAR" WILLIAMS, PRESIDENT OF BROOKLYN UNION

Together with co-vice presidents "Micky" Ford and "Johnnie" Gallagher, Williams formed a union of Brooklyn newsies.[‡‡‡‡‡] With union president Williams at the head of the group, they tended to the usual strike business—venting their grievances against their yellow-papered employers and distributing strike pamphlets, which read as follows:

> "Protect the newsboys, who work all day and sometimes all night. The Evening World and Evening Journal refuse us an opportunity to make even a fair profit."

According to the *Herald*, an estimated 5,000 flyers were distributed by the boys.

JOHN WILSON, NEWSBOY

Wilson was not listed among those who participated in the newsies' rallies and protests, though he may well have been involved in either. Instead, he outlined the purpose of the

---

††††† Wilitz was not identified as a New York newsboy, but the nature and proximity of his quote to those given by other newsboys seems to indicate that he was counted among their clan.

‡‡‡‡‡ It is not known how many unions existed within the numbers of the striking newsies or whether they coordinated their efforts from borough to borough and city to city.

strike in a letter that was then delivered to the *Tribune*:

> "For over a year the *World* and *Journal* have growned
> down the newsboys by making us pay 60 cts a hundred
> when 50 cts was a fair price and all we paid before. We
> have now boycotted their papers, don't let us sell them
> again until they agree to make the price 40 cts for
> a year,§§§§§ which will just even up what we lost. If they
> are not satisfied then let us arbitrate the matter, they
> want the car men to arbitrate now what is the harm of
> them doing some arbitrating [with the newsies]. Let us
> leave the matter if it shall be 40 or 50 cts to arbitration,
> that is the advice they give others and they should not
> object to their own medicine."[105]

Upon publication of the letter, Wilson was unfairly lambasted by the paper's editor, who went out of their way to
criticize the newsboy's poor orthography, grammar, and
vocabulary.¶¶¶¶¶ Rare was the newsboy or newsgirl who had
the luxury of a complete and prestigious education, as many
children spent morning, noon, and night working the streets
and had little time to improve their mastery of subjects like
English and composition.

SAMUEL WOLKINSKY, NEWSBOY (AGE 13)

Two days into the strike, Wolkinsky resorted to extreme measures. He was captured and fined $5 alongside fellow striker
John Armstrong after the pair began shoving pieces of newspaper down the throat of a non-compliant newsboy.[107]

---

§§§§§   In most reports of the strike, the newsies' demanded a 10-cent discount, not a 20-cent reduction.

¶¶¶¶¶   "The following communication was sent to *The Tribune* office yesterday," they wrote. "[...] if John Wilson expects to emulate the example of some
great men who have risen from the ranks he will have to take a few innings
with English grammar and a dictionary." The *Tribune* also made it apparent
that they did not want to take a side in the strike, though that could hardly
be said of other papers around town. The *Sun*, for instance, advertised on
the newsies' behalf, posting meeting times and announcements like, "Help
us in our struggle to get a fair play by not buying the *Journal* or the *World*.
Help us. Do not ask for the *World* or *Journal*. –Newsboys' Union."[106]

"BLACK WONDER," NEWSBOY

For two long hours, on nothing more ornate than a platform of dry goods boxes drawn up by the post office, the newsboy known as "Black Wonder" stood side-by-side with fellow Brooklyn strike leaders Timmy Kelly, Eddy Murphy, and Walter Murphy. The four delivered speeches and took up a collection in front of a crowd of 200-some newsies. Much of the content of their speeches was not recorded, except for this bit of information: according to Walter Murphy, the *World* and *Journal* made an offer to sell their papers wholesale for 55 cents a hundred, terms the newsboys and newsgirls of Brooklyn still found unsatisfactory.[108]

"YAK EGG," NEWSBOY

As Kid Blink and Dave Simons sank lower and lower in the estimation of their peers, the rest of the Manhattan-based strikers banded together and elected a new set of leaders. "Yak Egg" was among the boys they selected to spearhead the next phase of the strike, though the boy's instructions, qualities, and actions do not appear to have made it into the papers.[109]

Timeline of *Newsies*

April 28, 1985: Bob Tzudiker reads a *New York Times* review of David Nasaw's *Children of the City: At Work and at Play* and first learns about the 1899 strike.

1989: Tzudiker and White pitch *Newsies* to Walt Disney Productions executive Donald DeLine. The day after their presentation, Disney issues a verbal agreement to develop the film.

April 15, 1991: Production begins on the film. First-time director Kenny Ortega delays principal photography to give the young cast a 10-week crash course in singing, dancing, and stunt work.

April 10, 1992: *Newsies* is released in theaters across the country. It flops at the box office, drawing just $2.8 million against a budget of $15 million. Several theater owners ask to back out of their initial agreement with Disney and pull the film from theaters after a limited run.

October 14, 1992: Walt Disney Home Video releases *Newsies* on VHS and Betamax home video. For the first time, film begins to attract a wider following.

March 28, 1993: *Newsies* is nominated for Worst Picture, Worst Director (Kenny Ortega), Worst Supporting Actor (Robert Duvall), Worst Supporting Actress (Ann-Margret), and Worst Original Song ("High Times, Hard Times") at the 13th Golden Raspberry Awards. It eventually takes home a Razzie for Worst Song.

March 28, 1993: The same day that *Newsies* receives its first Razzie Award, it also premieres as part of the Disney Channel's "Free Spring Preview." The combination of home video sales and frequent cable airings gives rise to a dedicated and vocal fan base, one whose fever for the film, its characters, and message proves contagious in the best way possible.

2006: Following the success of TV movie-musical *High School Musical* and Disney Theatrical's push for more licensable theatre shows, Disney puts a stage version of *Newsies* into production. After two years and a couple of unsuccessful table reads, it becomes clear that the company lacks a unified vision for the project. In October 2008, *Newsies the Musical* is shelved indefinitely.

2009: Harvey Fierstein rediscovers *Newsies* during a collaborative session with composer Alan Menken. He mentions the idea to head of Disney Theatrical Group, Thomas Schumacher, and officially signs on as the musical's new book writer. With the help of Menken and writers Tzudiker and White, Fierstein starts to develop a new draft of the stage production.

May 14, 2010: Disney hosts a 29-hour reading presentation of *Newsies! The Stage Musical* at Ballet Hispanico. While the musical is designed to be revived and reconstructed for stock and amateur productions, the idea of a professional stage show starts to gain some traction as well...

September 25, 2011: Featuring a new book by Fierstein and several new songs from Menken and lyricist Jack Feldman, *Newsies the Musical* makes its auspicious debut at the Paper Mill Playhouse in Millburn, New Jersey.

March 29, 2012: Thanks to rave reviews and tremendous fan support, *Newsies the Musical* is authorized for a transfer to Broadway and stages its first official performance at the Nederlander Theatre.

May 16, 2012: *Newsies the Musical* is officially extended for an open-ended engagement on Broadway.

June 10, 2012: *Newsies the Musical* receives eight nominations during the 66th Annual Tony Awards: Best Musical, Best Book of a Musical (Harvey Fierstein), Best Performance by a Leading Actor in a Musical (Jeremy Jordan), Best Direction of a Musical (Jeff Calhoun), Best Choreography (Christopher Gattelli),

Best Original Score (Alan Menken and Jack Feldman), Best Orchestrations (Danny Troob), and Best Scenic Design of a Musical (Tobin Ost and Sven Ortel). It secures two wins for Best Choreography and Best Original Score.

December 20, 2012: *Newsies the Musical* recoups its initial $5 million investment, becoming the fastest Broadway production to turn a profit in Disney history.

August 24, 2014: After 1,005 performances at the Nederlander, *Newsies the Musical* officially ends its Broadway run.

October 11, 2014: A North American tour of *Newsies the Musical* begins, with performances scheduled to hit 25 cities in just 43 weeks.

September 11, 2016: A performance at the Hollywood Pantages Theatre is filmed for theatrical release. Select members of the original Broadway run—including Jeremy Jordan (Jack Kelly), Kara Lindsay (Katherine Plumber), Andrew Keenan-Bolger (Crutchie), and Ben Fankhauser (Davey)—reprise their roles for the taping.

October 2, 2016: The North American tour of *Newsies the Musical* is capped in Austin, Texas after 784 performances in 65 cities across the United States and Canada.

February 16-18, 2017: A filmed performance of *Newsies the Musical* receives a limited theatrical release in North America and grosses $3.47 million in sales. Due to overwhelming demand, encore showings are scheduled for March and August 2017 and, later, July 2018. The film is digitally released on May 23, 2017, a little over 25 years since *Newsies* (1992) first premiered in theaters.

Newsies (1992)

Newsies made its inauspicious debut in U.S. theaters on April 10, 1992. It was distributed by Buena Vista Pictures and received a PG rating from the Motion Picture Association of America. The film grossed $1,232,508 in 1,223 theaters during its opening weekend from April 10–12, and finished its run with a total domestic gross of $2,819,485. *Newsies* was released on VHS by Walt Disney Home Video in 1992 and re-released on a collector's edition DVD for the film's 10-year anniversary in 2002. On June 19, 2012, Walt Disney Studios Home Entertainment released a Blu-ray edition of the film for its 20th anniversary.

Cast and Crew

Directed by...Kenny Ortega
Produced by...Michael Finnell
Screenplay by...Bob Tzudiker and Noni White
Music by...Alan Menken
Lyrics by...Jack Feldman
Director of Photography...Andrew Laszlo
Production Designer...William Sandell
Film Editor...William Reynolds
Original underscore by...J.A.C. Redford
Songs orchestrated and conducted by...Danny Troob
Vocal arrangements by...Danny Troob
Choreography by...Kenny Ortega and Peggy Holmes
Costume design by...May Routh
Casting by...Elisabeth Leustig
Christian Bale...Jack Kelly

David Moscow...David Jacobs
Luke Edwards...Les Jacobs
Max Casella...Racetrack
Marty Belafsky...Crutchy
Arvie Lowe, Jr. ...Boots
Aaron Lohr...Mush
Trey Parker...Kid Blink
Gabriel Damon...Spot Conlon
Dee Caspary...Snitch
Joseph Conrad...Jake
Dominic Maldonado...Itey
Matthew Fields...Snipeshooter
Mark David...Specs
Ivan Dudynsky...Dutchy
Robert Feeney...Snoddy
Michael A. Goorjian...Skittery
Dominic Lucero...Bumlets
David Sidoni...Pie Eater
Kevin Stea...Swifty
Bill Pullman...Bryan Denton
Ann-Margret...Medda Larkson
Ele Keats...Sarah Jacobs
Jeffrey DeMunn...Mayer Jacobs
Deborra-Lee Furness...Esther Jacobs
Marc Lawrence...Kloppman
Kevin Michaels...Ten-Pin
Sylvia Short...Nun
Melody Santangelo...Nun
Lois Young...Nun
JoAnn Harris...Patrick's Mother
Gregg Kent-Smith...Toby the Candy Butcher
David James Alexander...Teddy Roosevelt
Robert Duvall...Weasel
Michael Lerner...Snyder
Kevin Tighe...Seitz
Charles Cioffi...Oscar Delancey

David Sheinkopf...Morris Delancey
Mark Lowenthal...Jonathan
William Boyett...Judge Move-along Monahan
Ryan MacDonald...Mayor Van Wyck
Frank Girardeau...Chief of Police Devery
Shay Duffin...Captain McSwain
Terry Kohl...Bailiff
Tom Finnegan...Bunsen
I.M. Hobson...Gammon
Frank Novak...Policeman
Ogie Banks III...Newsie dancer
Daxon Calloway...Newsie dancer
Scott Caudill...Newsie dancer
D.J. Dellos...Newsie dancer
Chris Dupré...Newsie dancer
Dak Eubanks...Newsie dancer
Brian Friedman...Newsie dancer
Todd Jenkins...Newsie dancer
Terry Lindholm...Newsie dancer
Alan Luzietti...Newsie dancer
Kevin McCasland...Newsie dancer
Dean McFliker...Newsie dancer
James Earl Miller...Newsie dancer
David Evans...Newsie dancer
Craig Raclawski...Newsie dancer
Michael Rohrbacher...Newsie dancer
Gregg Russell...Newsie dancer
Joshua Wiener...Newsie dancer
Jesus Fuentes...Newsie dancer
Tony Gonzales...Newsie dancer
Robert Jaquez...Newsie dancer
Larry Jones...Newsie dancer
Kevin Kruger...Newsie dancer
David Larson...Newsie dancer
Patrick Lars Olsen...Newsie dancer
Travis Payne...Newsie dancer

Jim Raposa...Newsie dancer
Damon Butler...Newsie dancer
Christopher Bonomo...Newsie dancer
Bret Dieball...Newsie dancer
Rob Grayson...Newsie dancer
Michael Irvin...Newsie dancer
Eric Pesqueira...Newsie dancer
Scott Thysell...Newsie dancer
Jeff Thysell...Newsie dancer
Wes Veldink...Newsie dancer
Michael Warwick...Newsie dancer
Jason Yribar...Newsie dancer

Synopsis

Manhattan, summer of 1899: The newsboys of New York City are roused from their sleep in the Newsboys' Lodging House and prepare for another day of work hawking newspapers ("Carrying the Banner"). At the *New York World* distribution center, they meet David and Les Jacobs. The brothers have been forced into the newspaper trade to help their father, who broke his arm and is unable to support the family. The newsboys arrange an introduction between David and Jack Kelly, the leader of the newsies and the best newspaper hawker in their company. Jack strikes a deal with the brothers: If he can sell alongside 10-year-old Les, who's guaranteed to attract more sympathy due to his young age, he'll train them how to hawk papers effectively and split their combined profits 60/40—in his favor. David and Les agree.

In the *World* building, newspaper magnate Joseph Pulitzer complains about the lack of news and his waning circulation. He hasn't been able to maintain a hefty profit margin thanks to his exorbitant spending habits and ongoing rivalry with fellow tycoon and *New York Journal* owner, William Randolph Hearst. His accountant, Bunsen, suggests pay cuts—if not to Pulitzer and his editors, then the newsboys themselves. By increasing the wholesale price of the newspapers from 50 to 60 cents per hundred, the newsies will be forced to sell more papers to maintain their daily wages and Pulitzer will be able to pocket the difference. Pulitzer decides to roll out the new price immediately.

Jack, David, and Les begin selling papers at a local boxing match. David is appalled when he finds Jack making up headlines and lying to customers, but Jack reassures him that a little white lie shouldn't stand in the way of starvation. The boys' workday is cut short when they are spotted by Warden Snyder, head of the orphanage and juvenile delinquency center termed "The Refuge." He chases them along the streets and rooftops of the city and eventually loses their trail when they duck into a theatre. Inside, Jack confesses that he escaped from the Refuge after he was caught stealing food, a claim that David finds hard to believe. Jack introduces the brothers to Medda Larkson, the vaudeville performer known as the "Swedish Meadowlark," and the three of them stay to watch her next show ("My Lovey-Dovey Baby").

On the way home from the theatre, the boys stumble across a demonstration by the trolley strikers, who have built a bonfire in the middle of the street and are beating up strikebreakers. Jack is stirred by the scene, but David convinces him to avoid trouble and take refuge in his house. He introduces Jack to his parents, Mayer and Esther, and his sister, Sarah. They discuss the newspaper trade and Mayer reassures his elder son that he plans to continue his children's education once he's able to return to work. Jack heads home for the night, shaken by the picture of the Jacobs' loving, stable family. He dreams about escaping West to Santa Fe, New Mexico, where he can be free of the drudgery and poverty of New York City ("Santa Fe").

The next morning, the newsboys are horrified to find that the *World* has increased the price of newspapers. News is slow and the demand for newspapers is minimal, meaning that any increase will cut into their profits. They vent to Jack, who refuses to purchase the papers and suggests that the boys form a union and stage a strike to stick it to Pulitzer—and anyone else who stands in their way ("The World Will Know"). David agrees to help if Jack will take the newsies' demands to Pulitzer; Jack reluctantly agrees, but is denied a meeting and swiftly tossed out of the *World* building.

New York Sun reporter Bryan Denton begins to take an interest in the newsboys' movement. The boys organize delegations to spread word of the strike to newsies of other boroughs and neighborhoods, hoping to put more weight behind their cause. Jack, David, and Boots cross the Brooklyn Bridge to discuss the strike with Brooklyn leader Spot Conlon, but Spot tells the boys that he won't give them reinforcements until he sees that the Manhattan newsies can withstand the pressure and violence that often accompanies a protest.

The newsboys get the chance to prove themselves soon enough. Disheartened by the lack of support from the rest of the city's child laborers, they decide to take on the delivery wagons and newspaper distributors themselves ("Seize the Day"). As soon as they reach the *World* circulation gates, however, they are ambushed by a mob of strikebreakers and goons. The newsboys scatter before the police arrive, but one—a lame newsboy named Crutchy—is caught and dragged away to the Refuge.

Jack and David attempt to break Crutchy out of the Refuge, but he has been too severely beaten to walk on his own and rejects their help. The next day, the newsboys spot replacement workers, or "scabs," coming out of the *World* center. Furious over Crutchy's beating, Jack incites the strikers to beat up the scabs. The police lock the strikers and strikebreakers inside of the distribution center, but the newsies are bailed out at the last minute by Spot and his cronies. Together, they combine their forces to overwhelm and defeat the *World* employees, if only for the day. Denton takes a photograph of the newsies and prints a front-page story about the strike in the *Sun*; thrilled, the kids begin to imagine how they'll cash in their newly-earned fame ("King of New York").

The newsboys aren't the only ones who are excited by the attention they're getting. Back at the Refuge, Crutchy inadvertently reveals Jack's identity to Snyder. The warden pays a visit to Pulitzer and the city mayor, who collectively decide to arrest the strike leaders during the newsboys' rally at Irving Hall the next night. Pulitzer promises to throw his support behind the mayor's next election as an incentive, while Snyder looks forward to recommitting Jack to the Refuge.

Riding the high of their latest victory, newsies gather from every street corner and alleyway of New York City. Jack and Spot pledge to work together to end Pulitzer's price hike and Medda stages another performance to cheer the boys' efforts ("High Times, Hard Times"). Denton spots Snyder lurking in the back of the theatre, but his warning to Jack comes too late—police officers ambush the strikers, grabbing and beating whatever newsboy they can get their hands on. Spot and several Manhattan newsies are hauled off to court, where Judge Monahan fines them $5 each for disrupting the peace. In the meantime, Jack is exposed as "Francis Sullivan," an escaped juvenile delinquent and troublemaker. The judge commits him to the Refuge until he reaches adulthood.

Dejected and leaderless, the newsboys turn to Denton for support, hoping that the injustice they suffered has been well-documented by the city's papers. Instead, they discover that Pulitzer has prohibited every rival publisher in New York from printing additional news about the strike. Afraid of losing his job, Denton abandons the boys and takes his old post as a war correspondent.

Pulitzer summons Jack to his office and issues a threat: He'll prevent David and the rest of the newsboys from ending up in the Refuge if Jack voluntarily ends the strike. The deal comes with a monetary bribe as well (more money, Pulitzer claims, than Jack could make in three lifetimes). Jack rebuffs the offer and makes a brief escape attempt, but realizes that he'd rather sell out his friends than see them sentenced to years of suffering in the orphanage. He returns to the Refuge and laments his imprisonment ("Santa Fe—Reprise").

The sun rises on another morning, and the price of papers remains unchanged. The newsboys are livid when they find Jack walking out with the scabs, clad in a new suit and shouldering a stack of boycotted newspapers. Jack doesn't reveal his true reasons for joining the scab workers, instead reassuring an infuriated David that he only intends to work for Pulitzer until he can collect enough money to travel out West. Later that afternoon, Sarah and Les are assaulted by *World* goons Oscar and Morris Delancey. David attempts to rescue his siblings, but finds himself overmatched by the two brothers until

Jack rushes to his defense. Jack admits that he can't hold up his end of the bargain he struck with Pulitzer and returns to help the newsboys.

Jack, David, Les and Sarah appeal to Denton. Using his unpublished article about the rally and an abandoned printing press in the basement of the *World* building, they print their own newspapers and distribute them to the working boys and girls of the city—and, thanks to Denton, Governor Theodore Roosevelt himself ("Once and For All"). Thousands of children descend on Newsie Square the next day. At last, Jack and his newsies have the support they need to force Pulitzer's hand. After a tense confrontation, during which Jack and David reveal that they used their banners to orchestrate the city-wide shutdown, Pulitzer is strong-armed into reversing the price hike.

Exhausted and jubilant, the newsies return to the *World* distribution center to purchase the day's supply of newspapers. Jack weighs the cost of pursuing his dreams in Santa Fe— namely, losing the family he's found with the newsboys—and decides to stay in New York City for good. He shares a kiss with Sarah as the newsies take to the streets once again ("Carrying the Banner—Finale").

Newsies the Musical

Newsies the Musical premiered at the Paper Mill Playhouse in Millburn, New Jersey on September 25, 2011. On March 29, 2012, it officially transferred to Broadway's Nederlander Theatre and became the fastest Broadway production to recoup its initial investment in Disney Theatrical Productions history, running for an incredible 1,005 performances before its closing date on August 24, 2014.[*] The North American tour of *Newsies the Musical* kicked off on October 11, 2014 in Schenectady, New York and played 784 performances in 65 U.S. and Canadian cities, shuttering two years later on October 2, 2016 in Austin, Texas. A filmed production of the show, *Newsies: The Broadway Musical*, was released in theaters on February 18, 2017 and drew a domestic total gross of $2,545,060 during its initial run. It was made available for digital release on May 23, 2017.

Cast and Crew

Directed by...Jeff Calhoun
Produced by...Disney Theatrical Productions
Book by...Harvey Fierstein
Music by...Alan Menken
Lyrics by...Jack Feldman
Choreography by...Christopher Gattelli

---

[*]   The cast list below names the cast members who comprised the show's Opening Night lineup on Broadway in 2012 and does not reflect the numerous cast changes made during the musical's run at the Paper Mill Playhouse, the Nederlander Theatre, the North American tour, or the subsequent filming of the production at the Pantages Theatre in 2016.

Music Supervision/Incidental Music and Vocal Arrangements by...Michael Kosarin
Orchestrations by...Danny Troob
Scenic design by...Tobin Ost
Costume design by...Jess Goldstein
Lighting design by...Jeff Croiter
Sound design by...Ken Travis
Projection and video design by...Sven Ortel
Hair and wig design by...Charles G. LaPointe
Fight direction by...J. Allen Suddeth
Casting by...Telsey & Company
Associate Producer...Annie Quart
Technical Supervision by...Neil Mazzella and Geoff Quart
Production Manager...Eduardo Castro
Production Stage Manager...Thomas J. Gates
Music Director/Dance music arrangements by...Mark Hummel
Music Coordinator...John Miller
Associate Director...Richard J. Hinds
Associate Choreographer...Lou Castro
Jeremy Jordan...Jack Kelly
John Dossett...Joseph Pulitzer
Kara Lindsay...Katherine Plumber/Pulitzer
Capathia Jenkins...Nun/Medda Larkin
Ben Fankhauser...Davey Jacobs
Andrew Keenan-Bolger...Crutchie
Lewis Grosso...Les
Matthew Schechter...Les
Aaron J. Albano...Finch
Mark Aldrich...Don Seitz
Tommy Bracco...Spot Conlon/Scab/Tommy Boy
John E. Brady...Wiesel/Mr. Jacobi/Mayor
Ryan Breslin...Race
Kevin Carolan...Nunzio/Teddy Roosevelt
Caitlyn Caughell...Swing
Kyle Coffman...Henry
Mike Faist...Mike/Morris Delancey

Michael Fatica...Swing
Julie Foldesi...Nun
Garett Hawe...Albert/Bill
Thayne Jasperson...JoJo/Darcy
Evan Kasprzak...Elmer
Jess LeProtto...Buttons/Scab
Stuart Marland...Snyder
Andy Richardson...Romeo
Jack Scott...Swing
Ryan Steele...Specs
Brendon Stimson...Ike/Oscar Delancey
Nick Sullivan...Bunsen/Stage Manager
Ephraim Sykes...Mush
Laurie Veldheer...Nun/Hannah/Smalls
Alex Wong...Sniper/Scab
Stuart Zagnit...Swing

Synopsis

ACT ONE

On a rooftop in New York City in 1899, newsboys Jack Kelly and Crutchie dream about life in Santa Fe, New Mexico ("Santa Fe—Prologue"). Jack fears he'll end up like his father, overworked and mistreated, and longs for a simple, quiet life away from the city. The two are joined by the rest of the newsboys as they head off to work for the day ("Carrying the Banner").

At the distribution center, the boys are disappointed to see the *New York World*'s lackluster headline—"Trolley Strike Drags on for 3rd Week"—as it means they'll have a harder time hawking newspapers. They order their papers from the circulation manager, Mr. Wiesel, and tangle with his two cronies, Oscar and Morris Delancey. Jack offers a partnership to two new newsboys, Davey and Les Jacobs: They'll split their combined profits 60/40 in Jack's favor if he can sell alongside 10-year-old Les, who will get more attention from prospective customers due to his young age.

In the *World* building, newspaper mogul Joseph Pulitzer mulls over his sales figures. His circulation and profits have been on the decline during his cutthroat battle with *New York Journal* publisher William Randolph Hearst, and he wants to know how he can get back on top. His bookkeeper, Bunsen, suggests that he charge the newsboys more for their papers. By raising the wholesale price of the newspaper, instead of the customer price, the newsboys will need to sell 10 more papers to turn the same profit every day[†] and Pulitzer will pocket the increase without losing any customers to the *Journal* ("The Bottom Line").

Jack, Davey, and Les finish selling papers for the day. Before they part ways, Les spots an ominous figure watching from the shadows, whom Jack later identifies as Warden Snyder. Snyder chases the boys through the city streets, but eventually loses them when they duck into the nearby Burlesque House. The owner, vaudeville star Medda Larkin, invites them to stay for her next performance ("That's Rich"). Jack climbs into a private box to meet Katherine Plumber, the young reporter assigned to cover the show for the *New York Sun*. Despite her continual protestations, he insists on staying by her side and expresses his attraction to her ("I Never Planned on You/Don't Come A-Knocking").

The next morning, the newsboys are appalled to hear the *World* has jacked up their price from 50 to 60 cents per hundred papers. Jack claims it's a prank, but Wiesel confirms the price increase and the boys quickly discover that the rest of the publishers in New York City have also increased their wholesale fees. Incensed by the news, Jack hastily forms the Newsboys' Union and declares a strike ("The World Will Know").

The newsboys gather at Jacobi's Deli to discuss their next plan of attack. Katherine interrupts the meeting and volunteers to write about their protest for the *Sun*, but the boys are quick to dismiss her lack of experience and insist on holding out for a "real reporter." In a vulnerable moment, Katherine admits that she's still struggling to be taken seriously as a journalist and vows to make the protest front-page news if

---

† While this is indeed the line Bunsen gives Pulitzer, his math is slightly inaccurate. Each newsboy would need to purchase an additional 14 papers to turn the same profit, not 10 papers.

they'll allow her to write about it. The newsboys agree to the deal. Later that night, Katherine starts to write the newsboys' story and finds herself getting emotionally invested in their cause ("Watch What Happens").

When the newsboys gather at the circulation gates the next day, Davey, Albert, Specs, and Race deliver some bad news: no one is coming to help them. The Brooklyn newsies have decided to wait and see how the strike progresses before lending their support, and the rest of the city's newsboys have followed their example. If the newsboys of Manhattan want to take on Pulitzer, they'll have to do so alone. Jack and Davey lift the newsies' spirits; even if their brothers refuse to join the protest, they have a responsibility to fight on their behalf ("Seize the Day"). They charge the distribution center, ripping up papers, staring down strikebreakers, and tussling with Wiesel and the Delancey brothers. Suddenly, reinforcements arrive—but not for the newsboys. Snyder, accompanied by a posse of policemen, charges into the crowd and attacks the boys. Everyone escapes except for Crutchie, who is beaten with his own crutch and dragged away to the Refuge. Back on the rooftop, Jack laments the capture of his friend and blames himself for the outcome of the strike, still yearning for the day when he can escape from New York and make a new life in Santa Fe ("Santa Fe").

ACT TWO

Bruised and beaten, the newsboys return to the deli after the protest, this time without Jack and Crutchie. Katherine attempts to cheer them up by waving a copy of the *Sun* that features the newsboys' strike—above the fold. The boys are thrilled, and take turns reveling in their newfound fame and success ("King of New York"). Over at the Refuge, Crutchie writes a letter to Jack. He exhorts him to press on with the strike and reminds him of their plan to travel out West together ("Letter from the Refuge").

Davey, Les, and Katherine find Jack squirreled away in Medda's Burlesque House. Davey shows off the article about the strike, but Jack no longer sees the point in endangering the newsboys' lives in order to fight Pulitzer. After a tense argument, Davey helps him realize that Pulitzer would never have sent the goons and cops to break up the protest if he didn't fear the boys' power ("Watch What Happens—Reprise").

Katherine is summoned to the *World* office, where she is privy to a meeting among Pulitzer, the city mayor, and Warden Snyder. Snyder reveals Jack's tragic backstory: As a young newsboy, he was apprehended for loitering and vagrancy and committed to the Refuge for six months. Pulitzer demands that the mayor arrest Jack during the newsboys' rally at the Burlesque House, claiming that his status as a criminal supersedes the law that forbids arrests on private property. Jack arrives and asks for an audience with Pulitzer, who quickly blackmails him into shutting down the strike lest the rest of his friends get imprisoned in the Refuge as well ("The Bottom Line—Reprise"). Katherine is revealed to be Pulitzer's daughter.

News of the protest spreads. Every newsboy from New York shows up to the rally, led by Spot Conlon and his posse of Brooklyn newsies ("Brooklyn's Here"). Jack shows up late to the rally and advises the newsboys to take Pulitzer's deal. If they go back to hawking newspapers again, he tells them, the publishers won't raise their wholesale prices for two years. The newsies erupt in anger, and Bunsen exacerbates the situation by handing Jack a wad of cash in full view of the crowd. Angry and alone, he retreats to the rooftop, followed by Katherine. They fight about their perceived betrayals—Jack selling out the strikers, Katherine lying about her identity—and end up sharing their first kiss. Katherine develops a plan to save the newsboys and the two pledge their love to each other ("Something to Believe In").

Jack and Katherine lead the newsies to the basement of the *World* building, where they use an old printing press to print strike pamphlets that will expose the injustices of the Refuge ("Once and for All"). The papers go out to every newsboy and child laborer in New York City, as well as Joseph Pulitzer himself. Accompanied by Davey and Spot Conlon, Jack returns to the *World* office to confront Pulitzer and return his bribe ("Seize the Day—Reprise").

They are soon joined by Governor Theodore Roosevelt, who has also received a copy of the newsies' banner and Jack's incriminating drawings of the inhumane living conditions at the Refuge. Roosevelt threatens Pulitzer with a state Senate investigation unless he rolls back the price increase. The publisher strikes a deal with Jack: If the strike is put to an immediate stop, he'll reduce the wholesale price to 55 cents per hundred papers and agree to buy back all unsold newspapers at full price. The two shake on it.

With the strike over, Jack reconsiders his move to Santa Fe. While the idea of escape still appeals to him, he chooses to stay in New York City with his family—which now includes Davey, Les, and Katherine ("Santa Fe—Reprise"). Crutchie is freed from the Refuge and uses his newfound freedom to help apprehend Warden Snyder, who is arrested for the abuse he has perpetuated at the juvenile delinquency center. The newsboys celebrate their victory and return to selling newspapers once again ("Finale").

Newsies Trivia

Newsies (1992)

Newsies marked Kenny Ortega's feature film directorial debut. Ortega was already well-known for his choreography work on previous hits and cult films like *Xanadu* (1980), *Ferris Bueller's Day Off* (1986), *Pretty in Pink* (1986), and *Dirty Dancing* (1987) and was uniquely suited to oversee Disney's first live-action musical.

Alan Menken might never have composed music for *Newsies* if not for the prompting of Howard Ashman. The legendary lyricist was too ill to work with Menken in 1991, but encouraged his collaborator to find another writing partner for the project. Menken eventually reached out to a longtime colleague, Jack Feldman, who would go on to script the lyrics for each *Newsies* song—on screen *and* stage.[1]

The cast was largely comprised of 11 "featured newsies" and 40 newsie dancers. Twenty newsies are listed by name in the official credits: Jack Kelly/Francis Sullivan, David "Davey" Jacobs, Les Jacobs, Racetrack, Crutchy, Boots, Mush, Kid Blink, Spot Conlon, Snitch, Jake, Itey, Snipeshooter, Specs, Dutchy, Snoddy, Skittery, Bumlets, Pie Eater, and Swifty.

When casting Sarah Jacobs, Christian Bale ("Jack Kelly") was allegedly given permission to "[dismiss] any actress he felt was too modern-looking since *Newsies* was set in 1899."[2] Burgeoning actress Milla Jovovich was said to have been eliminated from the audition process after rehearsing scenes with Bale that, to him, felt "abrasive." The part eventually went to 19-year-old Ele Keats.

For all of his hemming and hawing about the movie's musical numbers, Christian Bale handled his new role as a showman and dramatist with professionalism. "I never recorded before but I got used to it real quick," he said. "I was nervous only one day. I went into the recording studio and there was a whole orchestra waiting for me to record it. And, you know, the only time I've sung before is just in the car singing [by] myself, which is not great practice for something like this."[3]

David Moscow ("David 'Davey' Jacobs") was also nervous about accepting a starring role in a movie-musical. In the four months of rehearsal leading up to the filming, he worked with an experienced vocal coach whose clientele included the Queen of Pop herself: Madonna.[4]

Singin' in the Rain (1952) star and mentor to Kenny Ortega, Gene Kelly, visited the rehearsal space for *Newsies* one afternoon. He likened the dance moves of David Sidoni ("Pie Eater") to those of Donald O'Connor during the infamous "Make 'Em Laugh" sequence.[5]

Ortega, co-choreographer Peggy Holmes, and assistant choreographer William Holden Jr. tailored each newsboy's dance moves to his abilities and personal style. Christian Bale was taught martial arts-infused dance movements that incorporated kicks, jumps, and punches—moves that are clearly played up in his solo number, "Santa Fe." Max Casella ("Racetrack"), meanwhile, helped develop the tap dance-heavy "King of New York."[6]

For the 40 professional dancers who fleshed out the rest of the newsboys' troupe, the issue wasn't developing personal style or technique, but making their polished moves feel more spontaneous and rough around the edges. "We had to take away some of their training so that the musical pieces were believable; so you don't feel that all of a sudden it turned into a dance number and the characters were lost," Holmes said.[7]

The day before set construction was scheduled to begin, the New York City backlot at Universal Studios was torched by an arsonist.[8] Disney was later able to rebuild the set to their exact specifications, with one hitch: Universal wanted to keep the buildings once production wrapped. A minor tiff arose between *Newsies* production designer William Sandell and Hollywood director and producer Francis Ford Coppola, the latter of whom wanted to use some of the backdrops for *Bram Stoker's Dracula* (1992). While Sandell insisted that the sets were Disney property, and therefore unavailable for Coppola's use, the buildings became permanent fixtures on the backlot once Disney was informed that they would be charged for every piece they removed from the property.[9]

A special schedule had to be devised for the filming of *Newsies* so that the modern-day sounds of the studio tram tours wouldn't interfere with the background noise during takes.[10]

Newsies was filmed in 16 different locations: three studio backlots, seven sets on various soundstages, and six Los Angeles-area locales.[11]

"The World Will Know" involved the choreographed talents of 99 different actors, including 19 principal and featured newsies, 20 dancers, and 60 extras. The crew was forced to film the scene over six separate days in order to keep the lighting consistent from beginning to end.[12] Between takes, the young actors would occasionally run over to the adjacent *Back to the Future* courtyard set on the Universal Studios backlot and stage water balloon and Super Soaker fights to beat the miserable, 110-degree heat.*

Costumes for the principal and ensemble cast were sourced from flea markets, clothing collectors, costume shops, and antique stores. Some were authentic 19th century garments made of extremely delicate material, like the dress Ele Keats wore during the rally at Irving Hall. Costumers were on high alert during the film's more intense musical numbers, as they

---

* In an interview with BroadwayWorld.com in 2017, David Moscow revealed that Ortega had put the kibosh on another favorite pastime: paintballing. "When you get hit by a paintball, you get a red welt," Moscow admitted. "We all had welts all over. I got one in the cheek and that was the end of that."[13]

frequently needed to repair rips and tears in the costumes between takes.[14]

Special footwear had to be ordered for the young actors, as the authentic cobblestone streets they danced on created unusual wear and tear on the soles of their shoes. The newsies were also required to cover their faces and arms with sunscreen and their hair with a special conditioner that prevented it from lightening in the sun.[15]

Christian Bale's sister, Louise, makes a brief cameo in the film. She's seen pulling Ann-Margret ("Medda Larkson") off the stage during the newsies' rally. Bale's girlfriend, Natalie, also appears on screen: she's the young woman who walks by the newsies as they exit the World's distribution center.

After securing roles for his sister and girlfriend, Bale wanted to cast his dog, Mojo, in the film. The idea was quickly nixed as Mojo was neither trained nor comfortable in large crowds of people.[16]

Ele Keats was tone-deaf and could not sing at all, despite working with a vocal coach throughout the rehearsal process. Ortega ultimately decided to cut her character's solo from the film rather than dub over her singing voice.[17]

The toe-tapping dance number, "King of New York," was initially cut from the shooting schedule. It was an inadvertent blow to Ortega's vision of the film; he saw the scene as an opportunity to unite Denton and the newsboys before they pressed on with their strike. Together with co-choreographer Peggy Holmes, composer Alan Menken, and lyricist J.A.C. Redford, Ortega petitioned Disney to keep the song in the film. "It just felt right, organic to the movie, to the storytelling and where the characters were," he added, "and finally the studio said, 'OK. Look, if you can rehearse it in a weekend and shoot it in a day, we can do it.' So we did and shot it in one afternoon on the stage. And I'm so thrilled we did."[18]

When Jack, Davey, Sarah, Les, and Denton spend the night in the basement of the *New York World* building, they were originally supposed to sing a number called "Point of No Return." The lyrics read in part:

> Don't you bummers get what I'm sayin'
> This ain't hide and seek that we're playin'
> One false step and they'll be in here
> One stray hair, they'll know we been here
> Questions—it's too late for 'em
> Answers—we can't wait for 'em
> We're at the point of no return

The child actors enjoyed pranking Ortega, dousing him with the spray from their water guns and filling his trailer to the brim with newspapers. "For some reason, I don't know why, these guys felt like they had to torture me at the end of every week," Ortega jested. "They liked to let me know that they were in charge, that's what it was. David Moscow always wanted me to know that he had the upper hand."[19]

Between rehearsals, filming, and practical jokes, a few members of the *Newsies* cast and crew produced a short horror spoof called *Blood Drips Heavily on Newsie Square* (1991). Directed by Michael Goorjian ("Skittery"), the film features washed-up actor Don Knotts, who exacts gruesome revenge on the cast of *Newsies* after he gets rejected for a bit part.[†]

Only two years after the theatrical release of *Newsies*, tragedy struck one of the young actors. Dominic Lucero ("Bumlets") died on July 1, 1994 following a protracted battle with lymphatic cancer. He was 26 years old.

---

† The full synopsis of *Blood Drips Heavily on Newsie Square* can be located in the next section of this book.

Newsies the Musical

While reworking the lyrics for many of the musical's beloved songs, lyricist Jack Feldman made the unpopular decision to cut a verse from "Carrying the Banner" in which a young mother searches for her missing son, Patrick. After weathering considerable backlash from devoted fans, Feldman issued an apology: "Guys, please forgive me and take comfort in knowing that it will always be there on the soundtrack, haunting me until the day I die."[20]

Patrick's mother would never be reinserted as an official character in the formal stage production of *Newsies*, but that didn't stop Andrew Keenan-Bolger ("Crutchie") and his castmates from having some fun with it. Before the closing of the show in 2014, the cast recreated the iconic scene with the help of ensemble member Julie Foldesi in the role of Patrick's mother.[21]

During one of the first table reads for the stage musical, Feldman revealed the lyrics for the show's new opening number, a slow-tempo song called "Fallen Angels." They read in part:

> Show every urchin
> There's a church in his heart where he may pray.[22]

The song was eventually scrapped and a reworked version of "Santa Fe" was used in its place.

Three more songs were tossed in the dustbin between the musical's 2011 run at the Paper Mill Playhouse and its Broadway debut at the Nederlander Theatre in 2012: Pulitzer's expository solo, "The News Is Getting Better"; Medda's innuendo-laced showstopper, "Don't Come A-Knocking"; and Jack and Katherine's Act 2 duet, "Then I See You Again." They were respectively replaced with "The Bottom Line," "That's Rich," and "Something to Believe In" during the same scenes in the show.‡ "Don't Come A-Knocking" wasn't fully removed from

---

‡ A version of the script dated November 2, 2011 suggests that another song called "Legyen Egyszer!" was in the works for Pulitzer's first scene during Act 1. (The phrase, a Hungarian quip often used by Pulitzer's mother, roughly

the production, but instead given to the Bowery Beauties to perform as Jack belts his first romantic solo, "I Never Planned on You," to an oblivious and uninterested Katherine.

Although newsgirls were conspicuously absent from the Paper Mill Playhouse staging of *Newsies*, as well as many Broadway and national tour performances, Disney Theatrical Productions attempted to rectify the matter when they licensed the show out to amateur high school and community theatre groups. In an attempt to present more inclusive options,§ multiple roles were marked as 'gender-flexible': Crutchie, Spot Conlon, Seitz, Bunsen, Snyder, Mr. Jacobi, Darcy, Buttons, Specs, Finch, Splasher, Jo Jo, Stage Manager, Photographer, and an unlimited number of ensemble newsies and scabs. Of those roles, however, only Crutchie, Spot Conlon, Snyder, Mr. Jacobi, and Darcy received script modifications,¶ as most others are non-speaking parts or speaking parts that do not use any gendered language.[23]

From the original script to the 1992 film and, later, the Broadway adaptation, the character of Jack Kelly went through a variety of potential romantic partners. Screenwriters Bob Tzudiker and Noni White initially envisioned young Jack pairing up with a newsgirl named Charlie, but eventually

---

translated to "Keep it simple.") Whether a full rendition was ever drafted by Alan Menken and Jack Feldman is uncertain, though that spot in the show was later co-opted by "The News Is Getting Better" and, ultimately, "The Bottom Line."

§   Disney should be credited for increasing the representation of non-male characters in their show; still, they ran no real risks by choosing to do so *after* the Broadway and touring productions of *Newsies* had already reached their natural end. Furthermore, adapting canonically male roles for women and non-binary actors and actresses may be a small step toward true inclusion, but it's worth remembering that no historical newsgirl figures were written into the musical—either before or after the licensed version was made accessible for schools and community theatres.

¶   These approved changes do not currently extend to any casting choices and libretto modifications that may be made in a professional production of *Newsies*. Per the official production handbook: "Any additional requested changes must be submitted in writing and be approved by your licensing representative at Music Theatre International. Professional productions should consult with MTI before making any alterations to the libretto as written."

incorporated Davey's sister, Sarah, into the story. When Disney rewrote *Newsies* for the stage, Sarah was cut from the script and *New York Sun* reporter Katherine Plumber/Pulitzer became Jack's primary love interest.

Katherine Plumber/Pulitzer's character was inspired by 23-year-old *New York World* journalist Elizabeth Cochran, who wrote under the pseudonym "Nellie Bly."[24] Bly made a name for herself by going where others feared to tread: passing herself off as an insane patient at a local mental asylum, posing as a lobbyist to catch professional political bribers, and embarking on a race around the world to beat the 80-day record set by Jules Verne's famous fictional protagonist Phileas Fogg, among other stunts and escapades. Her audacious journalistic endeavors were both highly respected and imitated among her peers and, more often than not, led to positive social change.

Before Menken and Feldman developed Katherine's showstopping number, "Watch What Happens," they drafted another solo for her called "The Story of My Life."[25]

When the newsies congregate in the basement of Joseph Pulitzer's *New York World* building, Katherine writes an exposé titled "The Children's Crusade."[23] This is a nod to the Children's Crusade of 1903, when "Mother" Mary Harris Jones brought adolescent mill workers to President Theodore Roosevelt's summer home in Oyster Bay, New York. Roosevelt's secretary refused to allow the meeting and dismissed Jones by asking her to formalize her request with another letter to the president. The meeting was never officially arranged, but the relentless passion and concern of "Mother" Jones helped illuminate the perils of child labor in the years leading up to the widespread labor reform movement of the early 1900s.

Several characters' names were inexplicably altered or shortened from the 1992 film. Medda Larkson became "Medda Larkin," Crutchy was rewritten as "Crutchie," and David/Davey and his brother Les both dropped the surname "Jacobs."

Ben Fankhauser's ("Davey") familiarity with *Newsies* dates back to his childhood, when he was cast in a summer camp adaptation of the 1992 film. "I remember we all wanted to play Racetrack," Fankhauser confessed. He was later cast as "Crutchy."[26]

As Jack, Davey, and Les seek refuge in Medda's theatre, during Act I of the show, the faint refrain of "My Lovey-Dovey Baby" can be heard in the background, a callback to Medda's first solo performance in *Newsies* (1992).

While Medda Larkin was patterned after the larger-than-life personas of former Bowery comedienne Aida Overton Walker and 1930s cinema star Mae West, understudy-turned-replacement Julie Reiber took the character in a different direction during the show's final months on Broadway. "I've gotten to be the first-ever 'Cockney Medda,'" she told Broadway.com.[28]

The *Newsies Banner* that Jack and Katherine print during "Once and For All" is an obvious reference to the same paper that is distributed at the end of *Newsies* (1992). In order to accurately recreate the banner as an homage to the film, projection designer Sven Ortel partnered with Woodside Press, a traditional letterpress printing studio in Brooklyn, New York. "We picked type and set it, cut historical newspaper paper to size, applied ink to an old letterpress, and then went on to print about 50 *Newsies Banner*s by hand after the printing plate was fixed down," Ortel said.[29]

Set designer Tobin Ost constructed 24-foot-tall metal towers to represent the complex backdrop of New York City. Per director Jeff Calhoun, the towers composed a "vertical landscape meant to dwarf and intimidate, and [...] represent the city's obstacles that the boys must scale and traverse to escape trouble."[30]

The movable towers also complicated the major fight scene among the newsies, scabs, and police officers in Act 2. Fight director J. Allen Suddeth created a meticulous color-coded Excel spreadsheet just to keep track of the blocking, partner changes, entrances, and exits for each of the 20 actors.[31]

The iconic newsboy leap that decorated the show's playbills and banners is called "The Kyle," named for ensemble dancer and newsboy Kyle Coffman ("Henry"). The raised arm indicates an act of resistance, the crossed leg suggests the act of running, and the clenched fist is a clear sign of determination and protest.[32]

Choreographer Christopher Gattelli wanted the newsies' dancing to evolve as their revolution progressed. Audiences with a perceptive eye might notice that the dance numbers at the beginning of the show appear rougher and more juvenile (fittingly, Gattelli labeled them with names like "Kick the Curb" and "Hopscotch"). Toward the end of the show, Gattelli refines and polishes the newsies' moves in hopes that the subtle arc in their movements will convey a newly-developed maturity.[33]

Reams of 1899 newspapers were stored backstage for the "newspaper dance" that the newsies stage during "Seize the Day." The dance itself was partially conceived by Evan Kasprzak, who improvised the handspring that allowed the dancers to gracefully retrieve the newspapers from the stage without breaking the fluidity of their movements.[34]

Although it was never performed for a live audience, swing performer Stuart Zagnit composed a song for the character of Don Carlos Seitz called "That Old Printing Press in the Cellar." Seitz ruminates on his usefulness to Joseph Pulitzer, singing:

> So don't ever count out an oldsie,
> Don't laugh 'cause they're creaky and gray,
> You need not be young to have value,
> Don't let them just toss you away.[352]

The melody for Katherine's tongue-twisting solo, "Watch What Happens," was originally conceived as a ditty for Les, to be sung in the second scene of Act 2. Eventually, Jack Feldman admitted, they realized that no child singer would be able to pull it off.[36]

After two weeks of previews, *Newsies the Musical* made its inaugural Broadway performance on March 29, 2012. It was the first original production in Paper Mill Playhouse's 78-year history to premiere at the Millburn theatre and successfully transfer to Broadway.

In addition to two Tony Awards for Best Choreography and Best Original Score, *Newsies* won two Drama Desk Awards (Outstanding Choreography and Outstanding Music) and two Outer Critics Circle distinctions (Outstanding Choreography and Outstanding New Score). In total, the show received 30 nominations and six awards from the Astaire Awards, Drama Desk Awards, Drama League, Outer Critics Circle, Tony Awards, and Grammy Awards.

Newsies wrapped its first year on the Great White Way with the Broadway debuts of 25 performers: Tommy Bracco ("Spot Conlon"), Ryan Breslin ("Race"), Caitlyn Caughell (swing), Joshua Colley ("Les"), Corey Cott ("Jack Kelly"), Julian DeGuzman (Swing), Michael Fatica (swing), John Michael Fiumara ("Specs"), Hogan Fulton ("Darcy"), David Guzman ("Mush"), Jacob Guzman ("Sniper"), Thayne Jasperson ("Darcy"), Adam Kaplan ("Morris Delancey"), Evan Kasprzak ("Elmer"), Nicholas Lampiasi ("Les"), Kara Lindsay ("Katherine Plumber"), Jake Lucas ("Les"), Tommy Martinez ("Romeo"), Jack Scott (swing), Clay Thomson ("Spot Conlon"), Madeline Trumble ("Katherine Plumber"), Laurie Veldheer ("Hannah"), Alex Wong ("Sniper"), and Iain Young ("Henry"). By the time it shuttered in August 2014, that total had risen to 32 first-timers.

After the matinee wrapped on June 19, 2013, the cast of *Newsies* held an informal high school graduation ceremony for four of their members: Hogan Fulton ("Darcy"), David Guzman ("Mush"), Jacob Guzman ("Sniper"), and Andy Richardson ("Crutchie"**). While the orchestra played the grandiose notes of "Pomp and Circumstance," the graduates strode across the stage in bright red caps and gowns to receive their diplomas

---

** Andrew Keenan-Bolger originated the role of Crutchie when *Newsies the Musical* first premiered at Paper Mill Playhouse in 2011 and stayed with the company when it transferred to Broadway in 2012. In 2013, he accepted the leading role of "Jesse Tuck" in *Tuck Everlasting* and was replaced by Andy Richardson—formerly "Romeo"—as Crutchie.

from John Dossett ("Joseph Pulitzer") and Tom Alan Robbins ("Theodore Roosevelt"), the latter two decked out in their finest 19th-century garb.

All told, *Newsies* played 16 previews and 1,005 performances to Broadway audiences. Only *Beauty and the Beast*, *Mary Poppins*, and *Aida* logged more performances before they closed their respective runs on Broadway.[††]

Following *Newsies'* successful run on Broadway, Disney Theatrical president Thomas Schumacher asked Alan Menken and Jack Feldman to invent a new song for the production as part of American Theatre Wing's "Working in the Theatre" series. Out of this brainstorming session, Menken and Feldman first developed the concept and lyrics for Crutchie's forlorn solo, "Letter from the Refuge." The song would later be incorporated into *Newsies'* first touring run in 2014 and *Disney's Newsies the Broadway Musical* in 2016.[37]

Disney Theatrical premiered the "NEWSIES: Get Up and Go" campaign at PS 254 in Queens, New York in the autumn of 2014. The program was designed in conjunction with *Disney Magic of Healthy Living*, an extension of Michelle Obama's 2010 *Let's Move!* initiative that sought to diminish childhood obesity by encouraging children to embrace balanced nutrition and exercise. During sessions facilitated by Christopher Gattelli and several members of the *Newsies* cast, students from New York City-based schools were invited to learn the simplified choreography to "Seize the Day."

Prior to the professional taping of *Newsies the Musical* in 2016, select numbers from the show were professionally telecast on several occasions, including the tap dance-heavy "King of New York" during the 2011 Macy's Thanksgiving Day Parade; abridged performances of "Seize the Day" and "Santa Fe" on both *The View* and (six months later) *Good Morning America*;

[††]   This list does not account for the performance data of still-running shows like *The Lion King*, *Frozen*, *Aladdin*, etc.

a medley of "Once and For All" and "Seize the Day" in the middle of the 66ᵗʰ Annual Tony Awards; a rousing rendition of "Seize the Day" on ABC's *Dancing with the Stars: All-Stars*; a brief cameo during the opening montage of the 67th Annual Tony Awards; and a "Seize the Day" dance tutorial on *Good Morning America* in July 2014.

During the annual Newsboys' Variety Show at Feinstein's/54 Below in November 2016, a different version of "Watch What Happens (Reprise)" was performed by six of the young actors who had appeared as Les during the Broadway and touring productions of *Newsies*: Turner Birthisel, Vincent Crocilla, Jonathan Fenton, John Michael Pitera, Anthony Rosenthal, and Ethan Steiner. The lyrics to the reprise helped flesh out Les's Act 2 reveal—his impending date at Medda's Burlesque House with an 11-year-old girl named Sally—and read in part:

> Wait! She ain't done, she says, "Ooh,
> what's a rally?
> 'Course I'm too scared to go,
> but I'd go if my chaperone
> had big, bulging muscles like—
> ooh, by the way,
> I don't suppose you know Jack Kelly?"
> "Know him?" I says,
> "We sell papers together
> every day, him and me—
> well, and also my brother.
> We're a team! Thick as thieves! Jack's my pal."
> Then, she smiles at me
> and says her name is Sally.
> Then, outta nowhere, I still can't believe it,
> she leans over and plants me
> this kiss on the cheek!
> So I don't care, Jack,
> if I have to drag you myself,
> we're gonna have that stupid rally![38]

Blood Drips Heavily on Newsie Square (1991)

The amateur short horror film *Blood Drips Heavily on Newsie Square* (1991) does not appear to have been released by the Walt Disney Studios in any official format. The synopsis below has been sourced from the video footage that surfaced online in 2004 and makes no claim to represent the entirety of the film or the opinions and intentions of Walt Disney Studios or the cast and crew of *Newsies* (1992).

Cast and Crew

Producer...Max Casella
Director...Michael A. Goorjian
Cinematographer...Ivan Dudynsky
Creative consultant...Trey Parker
Prop master...Russell Bobbit
Equipment supplier...Kevin Stea
Christian Bale...Himself
Marty Belafsky...Himself
Lucy Boryer...Newswoman
Max Casella...Himself
Dee Caspary...Himself
Mark David...Don Knotts
Brett Dieball...Fire Marshall [sic]
Ivan Dudynsky...Himself
Luke Edwards...Himself
Michael A. Goorjian...Himself
Shon Greenblatt...Sunnyside Mental Institution Guard

Gregg Smith...Himself
Michael Lerner...Himself
Aaron Lohr...Himself
Dominic Lucero...Himself
Dominic Maldonado...Himself
David Moscow...Himself
Kenny Ortega...Himself
Trey Parker...Himself
Bill Pullman...News reporter
David Sidoni...Himself
Mary...Gate lady

Synopsis

In 1991, down-on-his-luck Hollywood actor Don Knotts (Mark David) stands on the precipice of a building overlooking the Universal Studios backlot, where a production of *Newsies* is underway. *Newsies* director Kenny Ortega cusses Knotts out and dismisses him after realizing the 67-year-old's last big movie part involved "playing a fish in a cartoon." Knotts is tossed off the set. He unsuccessfully pleads his case to a stoic security guard, then vows revenge on the entire production, shouting, "If I can't be in this movie, nobody will!"

Disgruntled and disgraced, Knotts soon sneaks back onto the lot and eavesdrops on a group of cast members swapping dirty jokes. After lurking behind the set pieces, he stalks one of the actors (Ivan Dudynsky) back to his trailer. Dudynsky is preoccupied with his own troubles—namely, his inability to locate a stash of porn magazines. He curses to himself and begins rifling through the cabinets, only to catch sight of Knotts standing behind him in the mirror, holding a knife. Knotts repeatedly stabs the young actor and leaves him to die a slow death.

At midday, the cast breaks for lunch. Knotts impersonates a food service staff member and empties an entire packet of Ex-Lax into actor Trey Parker's cup. Parker consumes the drug when he returns to his trailer.

Another child actor, Max Casella, finds himself the third target of Knott's evil machinations. Knotts lures Casella to the roof of the faux *New York World* building and pushes him off the edge of the roof. Casella strives to hang onto the ledge by his fingertips, but after taunting Knotts ("Aren't you that bad actor, Don Knotts?"), he is given a fatal push onto the movie set below.

The cast and crew become frantic over the recent murders. Crew member Gregg Smith assembles what's left of the cast and likens the Universal Studios lot to a "veritable slaughter-house," with the cast and crew of *Newsies* playing the role of the "piggies." He instructs the actors to return to their dressing rooms and await the summons of an A.D. (assistant director).

Frightened by the outbreak of violence, "newsboys" Marty Belafsky, David Sidoni, Dee Caspary, and David Moscow entreat fellow cast member Michael Goorjian to accompany them on the long walk back to their trailers. Goorjian advises them to stay out of the nearby set buildings, watch out for falling objects, tell someone if they spot the killer, and use the buddy system, but eventually turns around to find that all four of his companions have been murdered in precisely those ways.

Terrified and alone, Goorjian flees to his trailer, where he is soon found by Knotts. Knotts pretends to be an A.D. and orders Goorjian to exit his trailer and report to the Old Road for filming. The actor arrives to find the long gravel road some 200-miles from Los Angeles, deserted save for a lone white car parked several yards away from him. Now behind the wheel, Knotts attempts to run over Goorjian twice, succeeding in hitting him both times but failing to deliver a fatal blow. Even his most brutal tactics fail to inflict lasting damage on the actor: choking Goorjian with a bathrobe sash, dragging him behind the car, hanging him, shooting him in the chest, setting him on fire.

Back at Universal Studios, an exhausted Knotts devises a plan to rid the world of the rest of the *Newsies* cast and crew in one fell swoop. Aided by "Fire Marshall [sic] Brett" (Brett Dieball), the pair strap crude explosives to a movie clapper. The detonation causes a nuclear explosion that wipes out everyone on set and levels buildings for miles around. Only the indestructible Goorjian—his face blackened and burned beyond repair—and Knotts survive. Knotts is accused of homicide and committed to the Sunnyside Mental Institution, where he is locked in a padded cell and finally forced to confront the voices in his head.

The Rebirth of *Newsies* at the Disney Parks

The problem with Disney's California Adventure was that it looked like an airport gift shop that had been inexplicably converted into a theme park. Even the entrance resembled a 50-cent postcard: pastel mountains converging on a bright red replica of the Golden Gate Bridge and 11-foot-tall letters that spelled "C-A-L-I-F-O-R-N-I-A" in front of the turnstiles. If you stood far back enough in the Esplanade, you might be able to capture the tableau as it was intended to be seen, but more often than not, the structures functioned solely as a make-shift jungle gym for kids who were bored in line.

Inside the park, only the most banal elements of California were on display: palm trees, sunglasses, tractors, the baggage claim at LAX, a half-peeled orange, the sun. Marquee attractions like California Screamin' and the Sun Wheel played on the idea of California boardwalks during the summertime, which felt downright charming compared to the neon kitsch of Mulholland Madness and Superstar Limo. At Bountiful Valley Farm, Imagineers had dispensed with the idea of rides altogether. Instead, guests were invited to watch crops of Valencia oranges blossom, get their feet wet at an "Irrigation Station," admire sculptures of real California cows, and climb into the cab of a stationary Caterpillar Challenger 95E tractor. It was thrilling stuff.

The experience felt like seeing a billboard for your hometown, well, *in* your hometown. Local passholders were well-versed in the pros and cons of living in California, and out-of-towners had already agreed to fork over a sizable wad of cash to visit Anaheim. They didn't need to be sold on the concept twice.

By 2007, even Disney had soured on its six-year-old park. Disney's California Adventure didn't just need a fresh coat of paint, it needed a fresh coat of everything. With rapidly dwindling profits and attendance numbers, the company committed to a five-year, $1.1 billion overhaul and expansion that transformed the park from a tacky tourist trap into an elegant, beautifully-themed tourist trap.

Imagineers focused on bringing the park back to its Disney roots; or, to paraphrase CEO Bob Iger, correcting "brand withdrawal."[1] As the ceramic mural overlooking the turnstiles was carefully deconstructed and the jumbo letters shipped off to adorn the entrance to Sacramento's Cal Expo, Disney put special emphasis on redesigning the vibrant promenade leading up to the now-defunct Sunshine Plaza. They wanted to make guests feel the same way they did when they emerged from Disneyland's entrance tunnels onto Main Street, U.S.A.—as if they had traveled back in time to a simpler, more refined era.

There was still something missing. Disneyland's Main Street was decorated with pinstriped barbershop quartets, piano players, and brass bands, while the newly-christened Disney California Adventure clearly lacked the same kind of pep. And it just so happened Disney *did* have a wildly successful adaptation of *Newsies* playing on Broadway. So what if the newsies of 1899 were born on the sidewalks of New York City instead of the streets of Los Angeles? Who cared if their strike preceded Walt Disney's arrival in Burbank by 24 years? Not Disney, that's who.*

Buena Vista Street officially opened to the public on June 15, 2012. Its warm earth tones and seamless blend of Spanish Revival and Art Deco architecture evoked the atmosphere of 1920s Los Angeles, where Pacific Electric Railway trolleys transported riders to the heart of Hollywood and the lights of Carthay Circle Theatre sizzled with the latest motion picture

---

* Of course, we're dabbling in a little hyperbole here. The Red Car Trolley News Boys Show isn't based strictly (or loosely) on *Newsies*, nor does it treat the events of the 1899 strike in any shape or form. Rather, the inclusion of the musical number "Seize the Day" suggests that *Newsies* served as partial inspiration for the show. Certainly, Walt Disney's arrival in California—as characterized by Mickey Mouse's arrival in the second half of the show—was a more significant inspiration for the production.

titles. In this careful reconstruction of Hollywood's Golden Age, guests were invited to mingle with classic Disney characters and the special, era-specific "Citizens of Main Street": Molly the Messenger, Milly the Messenger, Donna the Dog Lady, Phi Phi Francis the Photographer, and Officer Calvin Blue.

Over at Carthay Circle Plaza, visitors were treated to the inaugural performance of the Red Car Trolley News Boys Show. These newsboys differed in size and demeanor from the ones found in 19th century Manhattan. Clad in multi-colored caps and trousers and grins that stretched from ear to ear, they sold the crowd on good times and high spirits. Instead of unions and strikes, they discussed baseball and the Charleston; instead of Joseph Pulitzer's wily schemes, they dissected Charles Lindbergh's solo flight across the Atlantic; instead of scabs and "girl reporters," they heralded the arrival of Walt Disney and his newest star-to-be, Mickey Mouse.

In other words, they were the "Disneyfied" newsies: a little cleaner, cheerier, and well-off than the real newsboys and newsgirls who once cried the news in metropolitan America. But had Disney gone too far? Did the newsies of Buena Vista Street pay homage to the children who inspired Disney's franchise—or had they become more fiction than fact?

A brief synopsis of the Red Car Trolley News Boys Show

Location: Disney California Adventure, Buena Vista Street
Duration: 15-20 minutes

Watch out: The Pacific Electric Red Car trolley is rolling down Sunset Boulevard. The newsies are hanging out of every open window—there's Sal, the tomboy who filched her brother's clothes; Kip, the mischievous teenager with a flair for the dramatic; Feets Charming, dancer extraordinaire; Brass Tacks, the funny one; Shorty McGuire, the short one; and Johnny, Kip's older brother and the starry-eyed leader of the pack. Outfitted in smart caps and colorful garb, the newsboys flutter their papers and sing about California as the trolley curves around the plaza and comes to a final stop in front of Carthay Circle ("California, Here I Come").

Johnny runs roll call and the newsies spill out of the trolley to make their enthusiastic introduction to the crowd:

"Hey there, we're the News Boys,

And we got to pay our dues:

Sellin' late editions

And singin' 'bout the news!"

Johnny gives everyone a crash course in newspaper hawking. His first tip: Sell your customers on good times. "Extra! Extra!" he crows. "'Can-Do Spirit Sweeping California!' Looks like the bad days are behind us, eh?"

The crew launches into their next musical number ("Happy Days Are Here Again") and Feets and Tacks lift Sal onto their shoulders. She has a headline, too: Charles Lindbergh has crossed the Atlantic Ocean in the *Spirit of St. Louis*.

"All I can say about 'Lucky Lindy' is, 'Attaboy, Charlie!'" Sal shouts. The newsboys swarm around her, holding their arms out like airplane wings as they cheer on Charlie ("Clap Hands! Here Comes Charley!").

It's Shorty's turn next. He grabs a baseball bat and shouts the headline: Babe Ruth has broken another baseball record! Maybe California will get a team of their very own someday. Maybe not, says Kip. Johnny joins his kid brother in a rendition of an old ballpark classic ("Take Me Out to the Ball Game") before Brass Tacks brings the focus back to the paper itself.

"Barney Google always makes me bust out laughin'!" Tacks chortles, pointing at the funnies in the paper and swinging to and fro on the trolley bars. He reenacts a few *Singin' in the Rain* gags with Shorty until the rest of the newsies are inspired to join in, pulling faces and tossing Sal in the air ("Make 'Em Laugh").

Tacks' crash course in physical comedy soon gives way to Feets Charming's dancing demonstration. "Hey guys, look: 'Dance Craze Sweeps Country!'" he says. "It's a good thing I've been brushing up on my dance steps." There's no time to sing here: the whole company is focused on getting the Charleston just right ("The Charleston").

Before long, Kip breaks up the festivities with a newsworthy item from the business sector: "Market Grows by Leaps and Bounds." The newsies brainstorm ways to use their newfound wealth ("The Gold-Diggers' Song") and finish off the number with a sales pitch: "Latest edition: two cents."

As the group disband to sell their papers, Kip refocuses their attention as he notices that a lot of their front-page stories feature 'nobodies' like them who ended up making it big. Johnny agrees. In fact, he says, there's even one such a fellow in the paper now: Walt Disney.

"Just goes to show," Johnny tells the newsies, "everybody who's anybody started off as a nobody before they became a somebody."

The gang is soon distracted when Mickey Mouse crash-lands in the middle of their next song to deliver his big solo ("Suitcase and a Dream"). They all have advice for the enterprising young mouse, none more fitting than the line Johnny delivers: "No matter how tough things get, you just gotta believe in yourself, push forward, and seize the day!"

Mickey and the newsies find common ground as they sing about seizing the opportunity to make their dreams come true, no matter the obstacles in front of them ("Seize the Day"). Another interruption brings the last little glimmer of inspiration: a telegram from Molly the Messenger, who tells Mickey it's time to prepare for his upcoming audition in Hollywood Land.

Feeling energized despite of their remarkable lack of sales, the newsies hop on the trolley with Mickey and wave a fond farewell to the crowd as they trundle back down Sunset, straight into the heart of Hollywood itself ("Side by Side").

Who are the Red Car Trolley News Boys?

Compared to the wealth of available information about the newsboys and newsgirls of New York City, relatively little has been documented about the child newspaper hawkers of California. Perhaps newsies were in fewer numbers on the West Coast, or perhaps there were simply fewer big-name publishers and fewer papers interested in the exploits and struggles of their young workers. Perhaps it had less to do with an underlying bias against child workers and more to do with the changing tide of the industry itself.

By the early 20th century, children had started to disappear from the streets of metropolitan cities as concerned activists enacted child labor laws and stringent age restrictions were placed on street traders. Adult salesmen and saleswomen began opening their own newsstands, eliminating the need for young boys and girls to wander the sidewalks in search of a dwindling customer base.† Your average American newsboy was no longer the pitiful waif scavenging for scraps among the trash heaps and alleyways, but the teenage entrepreneur who could afford to take up his business in the afternoons and evenings, trading in a 9-to-5 workday for something akin to leisure.

This gives us a general framework for the Red Car Trolley News Boys Show, which features Californian newsboys (and one newsgirl-in-disguise) at the zenith of the Roaring Twenties. Just how closely does the show hew to history? Let's break it down.

"CALIFORNIA, HERE I COME." At the beginning of the show, the newsboys arrive to the staging area in one of two Red Car Trolleys. Red Car #623, distinguished by its deep cherry finish and dark green trim, has been modeled after the 600-series St. Louis Car Co. Hollywood cars that debuted in 1922 and 1923. While the number "623" suggests that this specific Red Car trolley model dates back to 1922, it was chosen to pay homage to a 21-year-old Walt Disney, who made his trek out west in August 1923 to find a job in a real Hollywood studio.[2]

Red Car #717 is similarly inspired by the 700-series J.G. Brill Hollywood cars of the 1920s. Its bright red exterior is bisected by orange butterfly wing stripes, with orange doors and red trim around the windows. "717" is the number of a retired Red Car trolley at the Orange Empire Railway Museum, but it's connected in a more significant way to Disney lore as it harkens back to the opening of Disneyland on July 17, 1955.[3]

The newsboys travel down Sunset Boulevard in style, belting the modified refrain of Buddy DeSylva and Joseph Meyer's smash hit, "California, Here I Come." The tune also establishes

---

† This phenomenon was exacerbated during the Great Depression, when unemployment skyrocketed and adults began reclaiming factory and street jobs—the primary domain of 19th-century child laborers.

the newsboys' show in the early 1920s, as it was recorded and released in 1924 for the Broadway musical *Bombo*. For a time, "California, Here I Come" was marketed as the state song for California, but it was ultimately replaced by Francis Beatty Silverwood's more popular "I Love You, California" in 1951. The newsies would only have recognized it as a showtune; here, they use it to hint at Walt's impending arrival in Hollywood.

"HAPPY DAYS ARE HERE AGAIN." Unlike the newsboys of decades past, Red Car Trolley News Boys' leader Johnny eschews bloodthirsty, sellable headlines for feel-good topics like the "can-do" spirit of California. (This is a family theme park, after all.) As he flaps his copy of the *Buena Vista Bugle* at the crowd, eagle-eyed audience members might catch a few historical inconsistencies. The paper is dated February 10, 1923, a full year before "California, Here I Come" was recorded and six months before Walt began his migration to the Golden State. "Happy Days Are Here Again," on the other hand, wasn't dreamed up by Milton Ager and Jack Yellen until 1929, and wouldn't become popularized until the premiere of the romantic musical *Chasing Rainbows* in 1930.

At this point in the show, it's clear that the plot isn't going to adhere to a concrete timeline. The glaring continuity problems only continue to snowball, from the way the newsies' conversation encompasses years of current events and pop culture references to the way each character hawks a different headline for the same edition of the same newspaper. Based on the various stories they advertise, we can roughly place the show's timeline around 1922-1930. The rest is better left to the happy suspension of disbelief.

"CLAP HANDS! HERE COMES CHARLEY!" Sal introduces us to the first "current event" of the show: The completion of Charles Lindbergh's first solo transatlantic flight. While it didn't have a spot of blood or gore to recommend it, this was undoubtedly a hot news item when it broke. Lindbergh landed in Le Bourget Aerodrome on May 21, 1927, only to be instantly encircled by a hundred thousand spectators and well-wishers. One Californian paper, the *Oakland Tribune*, distilled the essence of Lindbergh's mission thusly:

"The man who pioneers in the air, accepts adventure for the sake of achievement rather than the material reward, may never have bothered to analyze his reasons. It is fortunate for the world that men have dared the unknown for it is on what they have found and learned that much of our progress is indebted."[4]

The newsies of Buena Vista Street celebrate the event with a rousing rendition of "Clap Hands! Here Comes Charley!" The ditty, composed by Billy Rose, Ballard McDonald, and Joseph Meyer in 1925, predates Lindbergh's milestone flight by two years.

"TAKE ME OUT TO THE BALL GAME." Shorty follows the celebration with news about New York Yankees darling Babe Ruth, who he claims has broken another record in baseball. Though that might have been impossible in *February* 1923, owing to the April—October schedule the Yankees kept that year, Ruth did reach a few major-league milestones by season's end. The "Bambino" enjoyed the lush grounds of the newly-constructed Yankee Stadium, one where the right field porch was perfectly angled to welcome his home runs. He tied Philadelphia Phillies rival Cy Williams with a league-leading 41 home runs, set a new all-time record after reaching base 399 times, and helped catapult the Yankees to their first franchise World Series championship.

Shorty leads the gang in a hearty round of "Take Me Out to the Ball Game" as the newsies toss popcorn kernels in the air and pantomime striking out swinging. Baseball's beloved anthem was first invented by non-baseball fans Jack Norworth and Albert Von Tilzer in 1908, though it wouldn't be performed in a proper ballpark until the mid-1930s.

"Just think, maybe California will have a team of their own one day!" Shorty exclaims, perhaps unfamiliar with the plethora of baseball teams that had already been established in California by the 1920s and 30s, including the Hollywood Stars, San Francisco Seals, Los Angeles Angels, Oakland Oaks, Mission Bells/Reds, Vernon Tigers, and Sacramento Senators of the Pacific Coast League.[‡]

---

‡   Shorty was right about one thing: California wouldn't see its first major-league club until the spring of 1958, when the Los Angeles Dodgers and

"MAKE 'EM LAUGH." The show then pivots to its resident funny man, Brass Tacks, who introduces the audience to famed cartoonist Billy DeBeck and his most famous character, shrimp-sized, down-on-his-luck sportsman "Barney Google" of *Barney Google and Snuffy Smith*.§

Barney Google's humorous exploits inspired at least two songs during 1923: "Come On, Spark Plug!" and "Barney Google (with the Goo-Goo-Googly Eyes)." Neither song is used here. Instead, Tacks launches into a poor man's version of Donald O'Connor's infamous "Make 'Em Laugh" sequence from the 1952 film *Singin' in the Rain*.¶

"THE CHARLESTON." The newsboys take a much-needed vocal rest as Feets Charming demonstrates the Charleston. The heart-stopping ragtime jazz dance was culled from Black communities in the United States as early as 1903, and achieved widespread popularity in 1923 when James P. Johnson composed a song called "The Charleston" for an all-Black production of *Runnin' Wild* at the New Colonial Theatre in New York City. Dawn Lille of Dance Heritage Coalition describes the infectious nature of its introduction to white mainstream society:

> "When it was performed by a group of chorus boys called 'the dancing redcaps,' the only accompaniment was hand clapping, body slapping, and foot stomping—the way it had been performed in the south. The audience reaction to this previously unseen combination of jazz rhythms and body movements was explosive."[5]

As the Charleston moved from stage to ballroom to screen, it spawned endless new variations. A number of distinct styles remain today, each one characterized by the decade in

---

San Francisco Giants migrated from New York City to stake new territory on the West Coast.

§ Don't squint too closely at Tacks' newspaper prop: not only does the front page advertise a full spread of comic strips, instead of a conventional headline and news story, but the cartoons are all of Mickey Mouse, who didn't occupy the funny pages until 1930.

¶ This is the most blatant incongruity in the show, given that "Make 'Em Laugh" was originally written around the early 1950s and doesn't fit the time period of the show.

which it was most popular: solo 20s Charleston, partner 20s Charleston, solo 30s Charleston, partner 30s Charleston, solo 40s Charleston, etc. The newsboys, twisting and cavorting about the staging area, perform a looser, more stylized version of the dance in both solo and partner variations.

"THE GOLD-DIGGERS' SONG (WE'RE IN THE MONEY)." Kip piggybacks on the boys' chatter about fame and glory with a pipe dream of his own. "Market Grows by Leaps and Bounds!" he cries. "New Era of Optimism Upon Us!" He isn't wrong: The United States enjoyed an enormous financial bubble during the early- to mid-1920s before the Wall Street Crash of 1929 ushered in the decade-long Great Depression. Whether newsboys regularly stumbled into untold riches prior to Black Tuesday is less certain—and less likely.

Fueled by the promise of unfettered wealth and prosperity, the boys begin to belt "The Gold-Diggers' Song (We're in the Money)," Al Dubin and Henry Warren's opening musical number for the 1933 film *Gold Diggers of 1933*. In the musical, Ginger Rogers fantasizes about paying rent on time and putting food on the table when "Ol' Man Depression" finally takes his leave, though the real nationwide crisis wouldn't resolve itself for another six years.

"SUITCASE AND A DREAM." Johnny and Kip marvel over the next headline: "Walt Disney Arrives in Hollywood: Mickey Mouse to Star in First Feature!" The arrival of a shabbily-dressed, little-known animator in 1923 Burbank wasn't exactly front-page news; more importantly, Mickey Mouse wouldn't be invented until 1928 and wouldn't star in his first feature film until 1940's *Fantasia*.

Nevertheless, this is still a Disney Parks show, one that might feel incomplete without some overt nod to the company's most iconic character. Mickey emerges from the trolley in suspenders and a newsboy cap, clutching his cardboard suitcase and waxing poetic about his dreams, and it's here that his place in the story becomes obvious: He's not Mickey Mouse at all, but a convincing stand-in for Walt himself.

Cue the show's first original song: "Suitcase and a Dream." This earworm was specifically scripted for the Red Car Trolley

News Boys Show, and its saccharine lyrics deliver the show's over-reaching moral:

"It don't matter if you're rich or broke,

It don't matter if you've given up hope—

All you need is a little drive

To make your dreams begin to come alive!"

It's an appealing rebranding of the old Horatio Alger myth: Work hard, nurture your ambition, and you'll be able to rise above your circumstances. That may have worked well for Walt and Mickey, but the same couldn't be said for the scores of real newsboys and newsgirls who lived and died on the streets of American cities. Those who managed to break free of the poverty cycle were few and far between.

"SEIZE THE DAY." The newsboys follow one feel-good anthem with another, this time drawing from a combination of Disney's 1992 film *Newsies* and its Broadway stage adaptation, *Newsies the Musical*. Noticeably, no mention of opening the gates, righting the wrongs, beholding brave battalions, answering the call, joining the fray, drawing near, letting them hear it loud and clear, or starting the strike "right damn now" is made. Instead, the modified lyrics exhort Mickey and his crew to stare down the odds and "win it"—which in this case likely refers to the audition Mickey just booked in Hollywood and *not* a wearying battle against Joseph Pulitzer.

"SIDE BY SIDE." The show concludes as Mickey and the newsboys finally take their leave of Carthay Circle Plaza, rumbling back down the road to the tune of Harry McGregor Woods' "Side by Side."** The audience knows where Mickey is headed; he's going to become a big star for Walt Disney. The newsboys' future, on the other hand, is less certain. They aren't given a happy ending. In fact, they're not given any clear ending at all.

Maybe they'll continue hawking newspapers in the entryways to Hollywood movie palaces, collecting spare pennies for tickets to the shows inside. Maybe they'll begin their own fight against injustice, like the newsies of 1881 and 1884 and 1886

** Woods, himself a Tin Pan Alley pianist, composed the standard in 1927.

and 1887 and 1894 and 1898 and 1899 and 1914 and 1920 did. Maybe they'll find a way to make their own American Dreams come true: chartering solo missions to foreign countries, swatting home runs in the big leagues, dancing the Charleston in front of sold-out crowds on Broadway. Who knows what their future holds?

It's a question that haunted generations of forgotten child newspaper hawkers before them, and one that is never given a satisfying resolution.

Reconciling the newsies of Buena Vista Street with *Newsies*

The Red Car Trolley News Boys Show represents a small but imperfect triumph for *Newsies* and the real newsboys and newsgirls who served as their inspiration. Four times a day, every day of the week, the red trolley slithers up and down Buena Vista Street and deposits its newsboys in front of Carthay Circle to hawk faux newspapers and sing an upbeat refrain from "Seize the Day." It's as close to immortality as *Newsies* will ever get.

But has Disney done enough? The problem with the newsies' musical revue isn't that it sheds light on the children's hopes and dreams, however unrealistic those may be. After all, it's not so ludicrous to imagine that the young newspaper hawkers of 19th and 20th century America yearned for better lives or kinder circumstances. As newspaper stands began sprouting on street corners and the role of the child newspaper hawker became less vital to publishers and more of a novelty, children had more time for daydreaming and play. Perhaps a few even fantasized about escaping West to Santa Fe.

The concern here is that Disney fails to strike a balance between the newsboys' dreams and the harsh realities of child labor. Sal and the boys carefully steer clear of describing any hardship that might be perceived as unpleasant (or un-*Disney*): poverty, homelessness, freak accidents, turf wars, profane headlines, child labor exploitation, union disputes, and the like.†† While the newsboys and newsgirls of the early 1900s enjoyed a more relaxed schedule and stable home environment than those of the previous century, they still wrestled with these issues—and more.

That said, it's worth mentioning that the Red Car Trolley News Boys Show was written for a theme park environment. The newsboys aren't hidden in a theatre or sequestered in a remote location. They're smack dab in the middle of Disney California Adventure Park. It's only understandable that Disney would want to refrain from endorsing overt pro-union messages or complex discussions about the afflictions of young, exploited child workers.

By failing to address some of the realities of the newsies' lives, Disney loses some much-needed nuance and perspective. They rob themselves of the opportunity to showcase fascinating aspects of the newsboys' lives: their ingenious selling methods and fierce brotherhood, their tenacious hold on every saloon entrance, trolley seat, and street corner of Los Angeles and New York City, the way they tricked generous tips out of stingy customers and defended their rights against the publishers and police officers who sought to strip them of all agency. On Buena Vista Street, the audience is trained to think of the newsboys not as historical figures, but as mere caricatures of the boys and girls who once ran the megalopolises of America. Here, the newsboys are once again relegated to the background as Mickey Mouse takes center stage, deprived of the opportunity to tell their own stories.

---

†† Early in the show, the newsboys seem to imply that any adversity they experience is part and parcel of "paying their dues."

Acknowledgments

No book is made in a vacuum. This one was written in a living room full of cats; the darkened pews of AMC Bay Street 16, Rialto Cinemas Elmwood, and Lark Theater; the Kaiser Permanente Richmond Medical Center cafeteria; Southwest Airlines flights 5485, 1961, and 5809; Philz Coffee Shop; Peet's Coffee Shop; Fiddler, Fifer & Practical Cafe; Carnation Café; the cliffs of Sea Ranch, California; the hollowed-out canoes of Splash Mountain; the solarium of PeaceHealth St. Joseph Hospital; and the re-imagined streets of turn-of-the-century New York City, as wonderfully and graciously painted by Bob Tzudiker, Noni White, and Harvey Fierstein, among so many talented others.

I will forever be appreciative for a brief sentence on page 598 of Frank Luther Mott's 1941 survey of American journalism:

"The newsboy strike of the next year to force the *World* and *Journal* to allow the half-cent per copy paid by other penny papers was eventually successful."[1]

Had that observation not helped inspire David Nasaw's 1985 exposé *Children of the City: At Work and at Play*, had his chapters on 19th and 20th century newsboys not piqued the interest of *New York Times* columnist Avery Corman, had Tzudiker never stumbled across Corman's subsequent book review, had both Tzudiker and White not been so captivated by the newsboys' plight that they developed the first draft of what would later become one of Disney's biggest commercial failures of the 1990s, had that failure not been embraced by an entire generation of passionate fans, had that passion not breathed new life into an award-winning Broadway adaptation, the newsies' remarkable story might have been lost forever.

My gratitude extends to the rest of Disney's team: legendary composer Alan Menken and lyricist Jack Feldman, for capturing the spirit of the strike and finally giving the newsies an anthem (or three) to rally around; director and choreographer Kenny Ortega, for the most precious cowboy dance solo in cinematic history; legendary book writer Harvey Fierstein, for seeing treasure where everyone else saw trash; Christian Bale and Jeremy Jordan, for imbuing Jack Kelly's character with fervor, wit, and some truly terrible New Yawk accents; and every supporting and ensemble member of the film and stage adaptation of *Newsies*, for reviving the valiant hearts and souls of the mostly-forgotten children of New York City.

I am also indebted to the many digital newspaper archives and carefully-sourced *Newsies* fan sites that made some of the research for this book so effortless and enjoyable, including Newspapers.com, Chronicling America, NewspaperArchive. com, the New York Public Library, Columbia University's Rare Book & Manuscript Library, City Hall Park 1899, A Spoonful of Research, and NewsiesAndHistory.

This book would never have been possible without the generosity of Bob McLain and his team at Theme Park Press. The time, effort, and trust you invested in me has made this whole project an absolute joy, and I cannot thank you enough for the opportunity and the platform to share a story that is so dear to my heart.

To my amazing partner, Danny, thank you for fanning the flames of my *Newsies* obsession, indulging endless bits of 19th century trivia and nerdiness, and remembering to feed our cats (and me) on the days that I couldn't or wouldn't leave my office. You enable me to pursue my dreams every day, and I love you for that and so much more.

To my family—Mom, Dad, Alyssa, AJ, Bill, Sue, Razi, and Leah—your encouragement and enthusiasm helped me believe I could do something as crazy as write a book. Now that I've written this one, you'll definitely watch *Newsies* with me... right? (I'm not kidding. Also, I love you.)

Last, but never least, my thanks go out to the scores of newsboys and newsgirls who dared to fight for their right to livable wages, fair treatment, and the respect of the most powerful publishers in New York City.

Your sacrifice did not go unnoticed; your efforts were not in vain.

Notes

INTRODUCTION

1. Corman, Avery. "Street Scenes." *The New York Times*, 28 Apr. 1985. Web. <http://www.nytimes.com/1985/04/28/books/street-scenes.html>

2. "Great Meet of Newsboys." *The New York Sun*, 25 Jul. 1899, p. 2.

3. Milzoff, Rebecca. "How Does Newsies Hold Up?" *Vulture*, 29 Feb. 2012. Web. <vulture.com/2012/02/how-does-newsies-hold-up.html>

4. Maher, Kathleen. "Newsies." Review of *Newsies*, directed by Kenny Ortega, *The Austin Chronicle*, 10 Apr. 1992. Web. <austinchronicle.com/calendar/film/1992-04-10/newsies/>

5. Ebert, Roger. "Newsies." Review of *Newsies*, directed by Kenny Ortega, *RogerEbert.com*, 10 Apr. 1992. Web. <rogerebert.com/reviews/newsies-1992>

6. "Newsies." Review of *Newsies*, directed by Kenny Ortega, *TVGuide.com*, 9 Mar. 2009. Web. <tvguide.com/movies/newsies/review/129134>

7. Howe, Desson. "'Newsies' (PG)." Review of *Newsies*, directed by Kenny Ortega, *The Washington Post*, 10 Apr. 1992. Web. <washingtonpost.com/wp-srv/style/longterm/movies/videos/newsiespghowe_a0aebb.htm>

8. Hunter, Stephen. "Disney's new musical 'Newsies' won't grab the headlines." *The Baltimore Sun*, 10 Apr. 1992. Web. <articles.baltimoresun.com/1992-04-10/entertainment/1992101067_1_kenny-ortega-christian-bale-newsies>

9. Gelber, Cari. "Movie Generation Gap." Letter. *The New York Times*, 29 Apr. 1992. Web. <nytimes.com/1992/04/29/opinion/l-movie-generation-gap-304292.html>

10. Cerniglia, Ken. *Newsies: Stories of the Unlikely Broadway Hit*. Disney Editions, 2013, p. 42. Print.

11. Cerniglia, *Newsies*, p. 43.

12. Ibid.

13. Healy, Patrick. "Limited Broadway Run for Disney's 'Newsies'." *The New York Times*, 15 Nov. 2011. Web. <nytimes.com/2011/11/16/theater/Disney-starts-small-for-newsies-the-musical.html>

14. Healy, "Limited Broadway Run for Disney's Newsies."

15. Healy, Patrick. "'Newsies' Recoups Initial Investment." *The New York Times*, 20 Dec. 2012. Web. <artsbeat.blogs.nytimes.com/2012/12/20/newsies-recoups-initial-investment/>

16. La Gorce, Tammy. "Get Me Rewrite: It's a Fresh 'Newsies'." *The New York Times*, 9 Sep. 2011. Web. < www.nytimes.com/2011/09/11/nyregion/newsies-reimagined-by-harvey-fierstein-at-the-paper-mill-playhouse.html>

A NOTE ON SOURCES

1. Nasaw, David. *Children of the City: At Work and at Play*. Anchor Press/Doubleday, 1985, pp. 72-75. Print.

2. "The Only Tie-Up in Town." *The New York Sun*, 21 Jul. 1899, p. 2.

3. "Plain Statement of Facts for Public Consideration." *The New York World*, 3 Aug. 1899, p. 12.

CHAPTER ONE:
CARRYING THE BANNER

1. *The New-York Tribune*, 4 Feb. 1846, p. 2.

2. Goodman, Matthew. *The Sun and the Moon: The Remarkable True Account of Hoaxers, Showman, Dueling Journalists, and Lunar Man-Bats in Nineteenth-Century New York*. Basic Books, 2008, p. 33. Print.

3. Thompson, Susan. *The Penny Press: The Origins of the Modern News Media, 1833-1861*. Vision Press, 2004, p. 220. Print.

4. Goodman, *The Sun and the Moon*, p. 20.

5. Goodman, *The Sun and the Moon*, p. 28.

6. Goodman, *The Sun and the Moon*, p. 33.

7. Nasaw, David. *Children of the City: At Work and at Play*. Anchor Press/Doubleday, 1985, pp. 74-76. Print.

8. McCabe, James D. *Lights and Shadows of New York Life; Or, the Sights and Sensations of a Great City*. National Publishing Company, 1872. Print.

9. *The Brooklyn Daily Eagle*, 29 Aug. 1868, p. 1.

10. "Newsboys and Newsgirls." *The New York Sun*, 25 Jul. 1886, p. 6.

11. "News-girls of New York." *The New York Sun*, 06 Dec. 1896, p. 16.

12. "Newsgirls about Town." *The New York Sun*, 26 Apr. 1896, p. 29.

13. *The New York Sun*, "News-girls of New York," p. 16.

14. *The New York Sun*, "Newsgirls about Town," p. 29.

15. *The New York Sun*, "News-girls of New York," p. 16.

16. "The Newsgirl." *The Buffalo Enquirer*, 09 Sep. 1892, p. 4.

17. *Elmira Daily Gazette*, 11 May 1895, p. 4. Web.

18. *The New York Sun*, "News-girls of New York," p. 16.

19. Ibid.

20. Ibid.

21. Paulding, James K. "Enforcing Newsboy Law in New York and Newark." *Charities* XIV, 10 Jun. 1905, pp. 836-837.

22. Goodman, *The Sun and the Moon*, p. 2.

23. Foster, George G. *New York in Slices by an Experienced Carver.* 1849, p. 104. Print.

24. Brown, Thomas Allston. *A History of the New York Stage from the First Performance in 1732 to 1901*, 1902, p. 271. Print.

25. Foster, *New York in Slices by an Experienced Carver*, p. 105.

26. Brace, Charles Loring. *Short Sermons to News Boys: with a History of the Formation of the News Boys' Lodging-House.* Scribner, 1866, pp. 16-22. Print.

27. Brace, *Short Sermons to News Boys*, p. 45.

28. Brace, *Short Sermons to News Boys*, p. 38.

29. Brace, *Short Sermons to News Boys*, p. 27.

30. Brace, *Short Sermons to News Boys*, p. 44.

31. Brace, *Short Sermons to News Boys*, p. 35.

32. Brace, *Short Sermons to News Boys*, p. 47.

33. "Country Estate of the 'Newsies.'" *The New-York Tribune*, 21 Jun. 1914, p. 28.

34. "Our Working Women." *The New York Herald*, 27 Nov. 1869, p. 2.

35. O'Connor, Stephen. *Orphan Trains: The Story of Charles Loring Brace and the Children He Saved and Failed.* The University of Chicago Press, 2001, p. 222. Print.

36. "The Newsboy Has Something." *The New-York Tribune*, 12 May 1915, p. 9.

37. "Children's Lodging-Houses." *The New York Times*, 20 Dec. 1868, p. 3.

38. Justice Harvey Baker to C. Watson. NYCLC, box 31, folder 15, 13 Mar. 1911.

39. Lankford, Susan. "Punishing Children: Houses of Refuge & Juvenile Justice." *U.S. Prison Culture*, 03 Feb. 2011. Web. <http://www.usprisonculture.com/blog/2011/02/03/punishing-children-houses-of-refuge-juvenile-justice/>

40. "The House of Refuge Horror." *The New York Daily Herald*, 13 Jun. 1872, p. 10.

41. "The Killing of Calvert." *The New York Daily Herald*, 12 Jun. 1872, p. 4.

CHAPTER TWO:
KING OF NEW YORK

1. "Amusements This Evening." *St. Louis Post-Dispatch*, 14 Oct. 1880, p. 4.

2. Morris, James McGrath. *Pulitzer: A Life in Politics, Print, and Power.* HarperCollins, 2010, p. 18. Print.

3. Seitz, Don Carlos. *Joseph Pulitzer: His Life and Letters.* Simon and Schuster, 1924, p. 43.

4. "A Newspaper Romance." *The Washington Post*, 28 Sep. 1890, p. 2.

5. Seitz, *Joseph Pulitzer*, p. 58.

6. Seitz, *Joseph Pulitzer*, p. 60.

7. Morris, *Pulitzer*, p. 62.

8. Seitz, *Joseph Pulitzer*, p. 72.

9. Chernow, Ron. *Grant.* Penguin Press, 2017, p. 740. Print.

10. Chernow, *Grant*, p. 745.

11. Chernow, *Grant*, p. 741.

12. Seitz, *Joseph Pulitzer*, p. 79.

13. Seitz, *Joseph Pulitzer*, p. 80.

14. Brian, Denis. *Pulitzer: A Life.* John Wiley & Sons, 2001, p. 29.

15. Morris, *Pulitzer*, p. 155.

16. Seitz, *Joseph Pulitzer*, p. 100.

17. Seitz, *Joseph Pulitzer*, p. 101.

18. "A Broadhead Broadside." *St. Louis Post-Dispatch*, 26 Sep. 1882, p. 2.

19. Swanberg, W.A. *Pulitzer.* Scribner, 1967, pp. 80-81. Print.

20. Juergens, George. *Joseph Pulitzer and the* New York World. Princeton University Press, 1966, p. 12.

21. *The New York World*, 16 Mar. 1885, p. 1.

22. Morris, *Pulitzer*, p. 239.

23. Brian, *Pulitzer*, pp. 176-177.

24. Brian, *Pulitzer*, p. 185.

CHAPTER THREE:
THE CHIEF

1. "In Ashes." *The Los Angeles Times*, 3 Apr. 1887, p. 4.

2. Nasaw, David. *The Chief: The Life of William Randolph Hearst*. Houghton Mifflin, 2000, p. 75.

3. Hearst, William Randolph Jr. *The Hearsts: Father and Son*. Roberts Rinehart, 1991, p. 9.

4. Coblentz, Edmond D. *William Randolph Hearst: A Portrait in His Own Words*. Simon and Schuster, 1952, pp. 10-19.

5. Swanberg, W.A. *Citizen Hearst: A Biography of William Randolph Hearst*. Scribner, 1961, p. 15.

6. Nasaw, *The Chief*, p. 25.

7. Procter, Ben. *William Randolph Hearst: The Early Years, 1863-1910*. Oxford University Press, 1998, p. 32.

8. Swanberg, *Citizen Hearst*, p. 29.

9. Whyte, Kenneth. *The Uncrowned King: The Sensational Rise of William Randolph Hearst*. Knopf Canada, 2009, p. 21.

10. Whyte, *The Uncrowned King*, p. 23.

11. Proctor, *William Randolph Hearst*, p. 35.

12. Proctor, *William Randolph Hearst*, p. 43.

13. Creelman, James. "The Real Mr. Hearst." *Pearson's Magazine*, Sep. 1906, pp. 256-257.

14. Swanberg, *Citizen Hearst*, p. 40.

15. Coblentz, *William Randolph Hearst*, pp. 28-29.

16. Nasaw, *The Chief*, p. 62.

17. Nasaw, *The Chief*, p. 54.

18. Swanberg, *Citizen Hearst*, p. 44.

19. Steffens, Lincoln. "Hearst, the Man of Mystery." *The American*, Nov. 1906, pp. 10-11.

20. Lewis, Oscar. *Bay Window Bohemia: An Account of the Brilliant Artistic World of Gaslit San Francisco*. Doubleday & Company, 1956, p. 133.

21. Creelman, "The Real Mr. Hearst," p. 257.

22. *The New York World*. 28 Dec. 1890, p. 1.

23. "A City's Disgrace." *The San Francisco Examiner*, 19 Jan. 1890, p. 11.

24. *The New York World*. 28 Dec. 1890, p. 1.

CHAPTER FOUR:
A CROOKED GAME

1. Creelman, James. *On the Great Highway: The Wanderings and Adventures of a Special Correspondent.* Lothrop Publishing, 1901, pp. 177-178.

2. Campbell, W. Joseph. *Yellow Journalism: Puncturing the Myths, Defining the Legacies.* Praeger Publishers, 2001, p. 77.

3. Creelman, *On the Great Highway*, p. 177.

4. "A Type of Old Journalism." *The New York Journal*, 12 Oct. 1897, p. 6.

5. "The Yellow War." *The New York Tribune*, 19 Feb. 1897, p. 6.

6. "For God's Sake Kill Me!" *The New York World*, 22 Apr. 1885, p. 8.

7. Hachten, William A. *The Troubles of Journalism: A Critical Look at What's Right and Wrong with the Press.* Lawrence Erlbaum Associates, 1998, p. 52.

8. "Local Streak of Yellow." *The Buffalo Enquirer*, 02 Jul. 1897, p. 4.

9. "Views of New Journalism." *The New York Times*, 4 Mar. 1897, p. 3.

10. Campbell, *Yellow Journalism*, p. 34.

11. "Vile Newspapers Put Out." *The New York Sun*, 10 Mar. 1897, p. 1.

12. *The New York Times*, "Views of New Journalism," p. 3.

13. "The Garbage of Literature." *The New York Sun*, 20 December 1897, p. 4.

14. Swanberg, W.A. *Citizen Hearst: A Biography of William Randolph Hearst.* Scribner, 1961, p. 96.

15. Pfaff, Daniel W. *Joseph Pulitzer II and the* Post-Dispatch: *A Newspaperman's Life.* Pennsylvania State University Press, 1991, p. 36.

16. Pfaff, *Joseph Pulitzer II and the* Post-Dispatch, p. 26.

17. Ibid.

18. "Climax to Recent Victories." *The New York World*, 13 Feb. 1896, p. 1.

19. *The New York World*, "Climax to Recent Victories," p. 3.

20. Nasaw, David. *The Chief: The Life of William Randolph Hearst.* Houghton Mifflin, 2000, p. 111.

21. "The First Electrocide." *The New York World*, 07 Aug. 1890, p. 1.

22. "Led Like Lambs to the Slaughter." *The New York World*, 07 Jul. 1892, p. 2.

23. Carlson, Oliver. *Brisbane: A Candid Biography.* Stackpole Sons, 1937, pp. 43-45. Print.

24. Morris, James McGrath. *Pulitzer: A Life in Politics, Print, and Power.* HarperCollins, 2010, p. 365. Print.

25. "The Attempt to Disgrace Mr. Low." *The New York Sun*, 12 Aug. 1897, p. 6.

26. *The Fourth Estate*, 25 Mar. 1897.

27. Henken, Ted A. *Cuba.* ABC-CLIO, 2013, p. 45. Print.

28. "Has a Red Record." *The News-Courant*, 23 Jan. 1896, p. 1.

29. Creelman, *On the Great Highway*, p. 177.

30. "Miss Evangelina Cisneros Rescued by the *Journal*." *The New York Journal*, 10 Oct. 1897, p. 1.

31. "Maine Explosion Caused by Bomb or Torpedo?" *The New York World*. 17 Feb. 1898, p. 1.

32. *The New York Journal*. 20 Feb. 1898, p. 1.

33. *The New York Evening Post*. 17 Mar. 1898.

34. "On the Newspaper Habit." *The Fourth Estate*. 19 Oct. 1899.

35. Godkin, Edwin Lawrence. "The Influence of the Press," p. 411.

36. Whyte, Kenneth. *The Uncrowned King: The Sensational Rise of William Randolph Hearst*. Knopf Canada, 2009, p. 443.

37. "Boycott by Newsboys." *The Brooklyn Daily Eagle*, 09 May 1898, p. 16.

38. "The Central Labor Union." *The New York Times*, 16 May 1898, p. 3.

CHAPTER FIVE
STRIKE!

1. "Memo for Mr. Pulitzer on the Newsboys' Strike." 27 Jul. 1899. The World *(New York) Records, 1882-1940*. Box 12.

2. "Memo for Mr. Pulitzer on the Newsboys' Strike." 20 Jul. 1899. The World *(New York) Records, 1882-1940*. Box 12.

3. "Newsboys Go on Strike." *The New-York Tribune*, 21 Jul. 1899, p. 10.

4. "Brooklyn Trolley Roads Only Half Crippled by the Strike." *The New York World*, 17 Jul. 1899, p. 1.

5. "Not a Line Tied Up." *The New York Sun*, 17 Jul. 1899, p. 1.

6. "The Brooklyn Strike." *The New York Times*, 17 Jul. 1899, p. 6.

7. "Preferred Fire to Mob." *The New York World*, 18 Jul. 1899, p. 1.

8. "Night Riot in South Brooklyn." *The New York World*, 19 Jul. 1899, p. 1.

9. "Strike Spreads to Manhattan and There is Fierce Rioting." *The New York World*, 20 Jul. 1899, p. 1.

10. "'No Strike,' Says the Metropolitan. 'Fight to a Finish,' Says Parsons." *The New York World*, 20 Jul. 1899, p. 1.

11. "Newsboys 'Go Out.'" *The New York Sun*, 20 Jul. 1899, p. 3.

12. Ibid.

13. "The Only Tie-Up in Town." *The New York Sun*, 21 Jul. 1899, p. 2.

14. Ibid.

15. Note to Mr. Pulitzer from Don Carlos Seitz. Jul. 1899. The World *(New York) Records, 1882-1940*. Box 12.

16. *The New York Sun*, "The Only Tie-Up in Town," p. 2.

17. *The New-York Tribune*, "Newsboys Go on Strike," p. 10.

18. Seitz, Don Carlos. "Memo for Mr. Pulitzer on the Newsboys' Strike." *Columbia University Libraries Online Exhibitions*. Web. <https://exhibitions.library.columbia.edu/exhibits/show/pulitzer/item/2948>

19. "The Strike of the Newsboys." *The New York Times*, 22 Jul. 1899, p. 4.

20. "Strike That Is a Strike." *The New York Sun*, 22 Jul. 1899, p. 3.

21. Ibid.

22. Ibid.

23. Ibid.

24. "Newsboys' Strike Swells." *The New York Sun*, 23 Jul. 1899, p. 2.

25. "Plan to Down Newsboys." *The New York Sun*, 24 Jul. 1899, p. 3.

26. *The New York Sun*, "Strike That Is a Strike," p. 3.

27. *The New York Sun*, "Newsboys' Strike Swells," p. 2.

28. Ibid.

29. Ibid.

CHAPTER SIX
ONCE AND FOR ALL

1. "Plan to Down Newsboys." *The New York Sun*, 24 Jul. 1899, p. 3.

2. Ibid.

3. "Great Meet of Newsboys." *The New York Sun*, 25 Jul. 1899, p. 2.

4. "Newsboys Act and Talk." *The New York Times*, 25 Jul. 1899, p. 3.

5. Ibid.

6. *The New York Sun*, "Great Meet of Newsboys," p. 2.

7. "Boys Foresee a Victory." *The New-York Tribune*, 25 Jul. 1899, p. 1.

8. *The New York Sun*, "Great Meet of Newsboys," p. 2.

9. Ibid.

10. "Parade To-night, Sure." *The New York Sun*, 27 Jul. 1899, p. 3.

11. Seitz, Don Carlos. "Telegram on Newsboys' Strike." *Columbia University Libraries Online Exhibitions*. Web. <https://exhibitions.library.columbia.edu/exhibits/show/pulitzer/item/2951>

12. "Newsboys' New Leader." *The New York Sun*, 29 Jul. 1899, p. 2.

13. "'World' Jails Newsboys." *The New York Sun*, 01 Aug. 1899, p. 3.

14. "You Can't Fool All the People All the Time." *The New York Journal*, 30 Jul. 1899, p. 40.

15. "The Evening Journal and the Newsboys." *The New York Journal*, 28 Jul. 1899, p. 3.

16. "Tried for High Treason." *The New-York Tribune*, 27 Jul. 1899.

17. Nasaw, David. *Children of the City: At Work and at Play*. Anchor Press/Doubleday, 1985, p. 192. Print.

18. "Newsboys' Boycott Over." *The New-York Tribune*, 02 Aug. 1899, p. 3.

19. "Plain Statement of Facts for Public Consideration." *The New York World*, 03 Aug. 1899, p. 12.

20. T.H.L. "A Kindergarten for Strikers." Letter. *The New York Sun*, 29 Jul. 1899, p. 6.

21. Seitz, Don Carlos. "Memo for Mr. Pulitzer on the Newsboys' Strike." *Columbia University Libraries Online Exhibitions*. Web. <https://exhibitions.library.columbia.edu/exhibits/show/pulitzer/item/2952>

22. "Fable Repeated in Fact." *The New-York Tribune*, 30 Jul. 1899, p. 5.

23. Nasaw, *Children of the City*, pp. 200-203.

CHAPTER SEVEN
THE STORY BEHIND THE STORY

1. Corman, Avery. "Street Scenes." *The New York Times*, 28 Apr. 1985. Web. <http://www.nytimes.com/1985/04/28/books/street-scenes.html>

2. Cerniglia, Ken. *Newsies: Stories of the Unlikely Broadway Hit*. Disney Editions, 2013, p. 14. Print.

3. Ibid.

4. Cerniglia, *Newsies*, p. 27.

5. Cerniglia, *Newsies*, p. 28.

6. Cerniglia, *Newsies*, pp. 30-31.

7. The Walt Disney Company. *Disney's Newsies the Musical Media Kit*. 1992, p. 10. Print.

8. Atkinson, Michael. "The Mystery of Christian Bale." *Movieline*, 01 Mar. 1997. Web. <http://movieline.com/1997/03/01/the-mystery-of-christian-bale/>

9. The Walt Disney Company, *Disney's Newsies the Musical Media Kit*, p. 17.

10. The Walt Disney Company, *Disney's Newsies the Musical Media Kit*, p. 11.

11. Cerniglia, *Newsies*, p. 32.

12. Fox. David J. "It Looks Like Bad 'Newsies' for Disney." *The Los Angeles Times*, 15 Apr. 1992. Web.

13. Ebert, Roger. "Newsies." Review of *Newsies*, directed by Kenny Ortega, *RogerEbert.com*, 10 Apr. 1992. Web. <rogerebert.com/reviews/newsies-1992>

14. Howe, Desson. "'Newsies' (PG)." Review of *Newsies*, directed by Kenny Ortega, *The Washington Post*, 10 Apr. 1992. Web. <washingtonpost.com/wp-srv/style/longterm/movies/videos/newsiespghowe_a0aebb.htm>

15. Hunter, Stephen. "Disney's 'Newsies' is no special edition." Review of *Newsies*, directed by Kenny Ortega, *The Baltimore Sun*, 10 Apr. 1992. Web. <http://articles.baltimoresun.com/1992-04-10/features/1992101221_1_kenny-ortega-christian-bale-newsies>

16. Howe, "'Newsies.'"

17. Siskel, Gene. "Lively 'Newsies' Best When It's in Tune." Review of *Newsies*, directed by Kenny Ortega, *The Chicago Tribune*, 10 Apr. 1992. Web. <http://articles.chicagotribune.com/1992-04-10/entertainment/9202020132_1_newsies-water-tower-star>

18. Kehr, Dave. "Cold Type: 'Newsies' as Fresh as Yesterday's Headlines." Review of *Newsies*, directed by Kenny Ortega, *The Chicago Tribune*, 10 Apr. 1992. Web. <http://articles.chicagotribune.com/1992-04-10/entertainment/9202020140_1_newsies-kenny-ortega-ele-keats>

19. Ibid.

20. Gleiberman, Owen. "Newsies." Review of *Newsies*, directed by Kenny Ortega, *Entertainment Weekly*, 17 Apr. 1992. Web. <http://ew.com/article/1992/04/17/newsies-2/>

21. Ebert, "Newsies."

22. Cerniglia, *Newsies*, p. 32.

23. Ibid.

24. Ebert, Roger. "Swing Kids." Review of *Swing Kids*, directed by Thomas Carter, *RogerEbert.com*, 05 Mar. 1993. Web. <https://www.rogerebert.com/reviews/swing-kids-1993>

25. Collis, Clark. "Spotlight on Christian Bale." *Entertainment Weekly*, Aug. 31 2007. Web. <http://ew.com/article/2007/08/31/spotlight-christian-bale/>

26. Gelber, Cari. "Movie Generation Gap." Letter. *The New York Times*, 29 Apr. 1992. Web. <nytimes.com/1992/04/29/opinion/l-movie-generation-gap-304292.html>

27. Marshall, Sarah. "The Afterlife of *Newsies*." *The Baffler*, 5 Jan. 2018. Web. <https://thebaffler.com/latest/newsies-marshall>

28. Ibid.

29. Cerniglia, *Newsies*, p. 98.

30. Cerniglia, *Newsies*, p. 45.

31. Cerniglia, *Newsies*, p. 37.

CHAPTER EIGHT
NEWSIES FOREVER

1. Wilson, John. *The Official Razzie Movie Guide: Enjoying the Best of Hollywood's Worst*. Hachette Book Group, 2005. Print.

2. Ibid.

3. Itzkoff, Dave. "Alan Menken Goes for the EGOT (and the REGOT)." *The New York Times*, 5 Aug. 2013. Web. <https://artsbeat.blogs.nytimes.com/2013/08/05/alan-menken-goes-for-the-egot-and-the-regot/>

4.   Keveney, Bill. "Can 'High School Musical' do it again?" *USA Today*, 9 Aug. 2007. Web. < https://usatoday30.usatoday.com/life/television/news/2007-08-09-high-school-musical2_N.htm>

5.   Cerniglia, Ken. *Newsies: Stories of the Unlikely Broadway Hit*. Disney Editions, 2013, p. 8. Print.

6.   Cerniglia, *Newsies*, p. 43.

7.   Itzkoff, Dave. "Extra, Extra! 'Newsies' Musical to Open Paper Mill Playhouse Season." *The New York Times*, 14 Feb. 2011. Web. <https://artsbeat.blogs.nytimes.com/2011/02/14/extra-extra-newsies-musical-to-open-paper-mill-playhouse-season/>

8.   Cerniglia, *Newsies*, p. 44.

9.   Healy, Patrick. "Limited Broadway Run for Disney's 'Newsies.'" *The New York Times*, 15 Nov. 2011. Web. <http://www.nytimes.com/2011/11/16/disney-starts-small-for-newsies-the-musical.html>

10. Barry, Dan. "Read All About It! Kids Vex Titans!" *The New York Times*, 2 Mar. 2012. Web. <https://www.nytimes.com/2012/03/04/theater/disneys-newsies-the-musical-comes-to-broadway.html>

11. Fierstein, Harvey. "Reimagining the Story of *Newsies*." *The Huffington Post*, 29 Mar. 2012. Web. <http://huffingtonpost.com/harvey-fierstein/newsies-broadway_b_1385817.html>

12. La Gorce, Tammy. "Get Me Rewrite: It's a Fresh 'Newsies'." *The New York Times*, 9 Sep. 2011. Web. < www.nytimes.com/2011/09/11/nyregion/newsies-reimagined-by-harvey-fierstein-at-the-paper-mill-playhouse.html>

13. Cerniglia, *Newsies*, p. 44.

14. *Disney's Newsies the Broadway Musical*. Dir. Brett Sullivan. Perf. Jeremy Jordan, Kara Lindsay, Ben Fankhauser. Disney Theatrical Group and Fathom Events, 2017. *Netflix*. Web.

15. Ibid.

16. Cerniglia, *Newsies*, p. 47.

17. Ibid.

18. Futterman, Erica. "The Real-Life 'Smash' Story of *Newsies*' Star Jeremy Jordan." *Rolling Stone*, 7 Jun. 2012. Web. <https://www.rollingstone.com/music/news/the-real-life-smash-story-of-newsies-star-jeremy-jordan-20120607>

19. Cerniglia, *Newsies*, p. 46.

20. "Staged Reading Guidelines ('29-Hour Reading')." *Actors' Equity*, May 2016. Web. <http://actorsequity.org/docs/codes/Stage_Reading_Guidelines.pdf>

21. Cerniglia, *Newsies*, p. 46.

22. Cerniglia, *Newsies*, p. 47.

23. Hetrick, Adam. "Extra! Extra! Disney's *Newsies* Will Debut at Paper Mill Playhouse." *Playbill*, 14 Feb. 2011. Web. <http://www.playbill.com/article/extra-extra-disneys-newsies-will-debut-at-paper-mill-playhouse-com-176155>

24. Jordan, Jeremy; Keenan-Bolger, Andrew. "Santa Fe (Prologue)." *Newsies (Original Broadway Cast Recording)*, Ghostlight Records, 2012.

25. Cerniglia, *Newsies*, p. 52.

26. Cerniglia, *Newsies*, p. 59.

27. Cerniglia, *Newsies*, p. 71.

28. That unity, perhaps, is solidified most clearly in the syncopated beats of their tap dance moves during the Act 2 opener, "King of New York," when Gattelli again advances the story as the newsboys adopt Katherine as one of their own.

29. Cerniglia, *Newsies*, p. 72.

30. Thomas, Aaron C. "Dancing toward Masculinity: Newsies, Gender and Desire." *The Disney Musical on Stage and Screen: Critical Approaches from 'Snow White' to 'Frozen.'* Bloomsbury, 2017, p. 162.

31. Rothenberg, Adam. "Interview With Choreographer And Tony Nominee Christopher Gattelli." *CBS Boston*, 01 Jun. 2012. Web. <https://boston.cbslocal.com/2012/06/01/interview-with-choreographer-and-tony-nominee-christopher-gattelli/>

32. Cerniglia, *Newsies*, p. 81.

33. Cerniglia, *Newsies*, p. 87.

34. Rooney, David. "Newsboy Strike? Sing All About It." *The New York Times*, 27 Sep. 2011. Web. <https://www.nytimes.com/2011/09/28/theater/reviews/newsies-the-musical-review.html>

35. Brown, Scott. "Theater Review: *Newsies'* Time Is Now." *Vulture*, 04 Oct. 2011. Web. <http://www.vulture.com/2011/10/stage_dive_newsies.html>

36. Geier, Thom. "Newsies: The Musical." *Entertainment Weekly*, 27 Sep. 2011. Web. <http://ew.com/article/2011/09/27/newsies-musical/>

37. Healy, Patrick. "An Opening for Some Song and Dance." *The New York Times*, 02 Nov. 2011. Web. <https://www.nytimes.com/2011/11/03/theater/a-rush-to-get-musicals-to-broadway.html>

38. Ibid.

39. Healy, Patrick. "Limited Broadway Run for Disney's 'Newsies.'" *The New York Times*, 15 Nov. 2011. Web. <https://www.nytimes.com/2011/11/16/theater/disney-starts-small-for-newsies-the-musical.html>

40. Dizney CTC DePaoli, Jeff and Dougall, Patrick. "*Newsies* Director Jeff Calhoun Interview." Audio blog post. Dizney Coast to Coast. 15 Feb. 2017. Web.

41. Cerniglia, *Newsies*, p. 118.

42. Cerniglia, *Newsies*, p. 119.

43. Healy, Patrick. "Even Before Broadway Openings, 'Newsies' and 'Evita' Show Box Office Strength." *The New York Times*, 19 Mar. 2012. Web. ‹https://artsbeat.blogs.nytimes.com/2012/03/19/even-before-broadway-openings-newsies-and-evita-show-box-office-strength/›

44. Geier, Thom. "*Newsies*." *Entertainment Weekly*, 29 Mar. 2012. Web. ‹http://ew.com/article/2012/03/29/newsies/›

45. Rooney, David. "*Newsies*: Theater Review." *The Hollywood Reporter*, 29 Mar. 2012. Web. ‹https://www.hollywoodreporter.com/review/newsies-review-theater-305971›

46. Suskin, Steven. "*Newsies*: The Musical." *Variety*, 29 Mar. 2012. Web. ‹https://variety.com/review/VE1117947318›

47. "2012 Tony Awards: The Winners' Remarks—All the Speeches1" *Broadway World*, 10 Jun. 2012. Web. ‹https://www.broadwayworld.com/article/2012-Tony-Awards-The-Winners-Remarks-Updating-LIVE-20120610›

48. Healy, Patrick. "'Newsies' Recoups Initial Investment." *The New York Times*, 20 Dec. 2012. Web. ‹https://artsbeat.blogs.nytimes.com/2012/12/20/newsies-recoups-initial-investment/›

49. Healy, Patrick. "'Smash' Schedule Prompts Jeremy Jordan To Depart 'Newsies' on Sept. 4." *The New York Times*, 14 Aug. 2012. Web. ‹https://artsbeat.blogs.nytimes.com/2012/08/14/smash-schedule-prompts-jeremy-jordan-to-depart-newsies-on-sept-4/›

50. Hetrick, Adam. "Why Disney Decided *Newsies* Was Ready for the Big Screen." 06 Feb. 2017. Web. ‹http://www.playbill.com/article/why-disney-decided-newsies-was-ready-for-the-big-screen›

51. "'Disney's *Newsies*: The Broadway Musical!" Becomes Top-Grossing Broadway Event in Fathom Events History." *Celluloid Junkie*, 23 Feb. 2017. Web. ‹https://celluloidjunkie.com/wire/disneys-newsies-broadway-musical-becomes-top-grossing-broadway-event-fathom-events-history/›

CHAPTER NINE
THE STORY THEY NEEDED TO WRITE

1. Korkis, Jim. "Some Thoughts on Pocahontas." *Mouse Planet*, 25 Apr. 2018. Web. ‹http://mouseplanet.com/12084/Some_Thoughts_on_Pocahontas›

2. Cochran, Jason. "Pocahontas needed an ethnic look." *Entertainment Weekly*, 16 Jun. 1995. Web. ‹http://ew.com/article/1995/06/16/pocahontas-needed-ethnic-look/›

3.   Townsend, Camilla. *Pocahontas and the Powhatan Dilemma: The American Portraits Series*. Hill and Wang, 2007, p. 74. Print.

4.   Mansky, Jackie. "The True Story of Pocahontas." *Smithsonian.com*, 23 Mar. 2017. Web. <https://www.smithsonianmag.com/history/true-story-pocahontas-180962649/>

5.   Townsend, *Pocahontas and the Powhatan Dilemma*, pp. 52-54.

6.   Culhane, John. *Disney's* Aladdin: *The Making of an Animated Film*. Hyperion, 1992, pp. 41 and 63. Print.

7.   Koenig, David. *Mouse Under Glass: Secrets of Disney Animation & Theme Parks*. Bonaventure Press, 1997, p. 240.

8.   Cochran, "Pocahontas needed an ethnic look."

9.   Ibid.

10. Jordan, Jeremy; Fankhauser, Ben; Lindsay, Kara; Grosso, Lewis. "Watch What Happens (Reprise)." *Newsies (Original Broadway Cast Recording)*, Ghostlight Records, 2012.

11. Itzkoff, Dave. "Extra, Extra! 'Newsies' Musical to Open Paper Mill Playhouse Season." *The New York Times*, 13 Feb. 2011. Web. <https://artsbeat.blogs.nytimes.com/2011/02/14/extra-extra-newsies-musical-to-open-paper-mill-playhouse-season/>

12. "Meet the Newsies: Liana Hunt." 13 Jun. 2014. YouTube. <https://www.youtube.com/watch?v=3Gx4YbiPxyo>

13. "'Newsboy' Josephine Beck?" *The New York Sun*, 01 May 1904, p. 2.

14. Maloney, Wendi. "Inquiring Minds: Director Casts Girls as 'Newsies,' Citing Library's Historical Photos." *Library of Congress Blog*, 17 Jan. 2018. Web. <https://blogs.loc.gov/loc/2018/01/inquiring-minds-director-casts-girls-as-newsies-citing-librarys-historical-photos/>

15. "And Now the Newsboys Strike." *The Brooklyn Daily Eagle*, 30 Mar. 1886, p. 6.

16. "The Newsboys' Strike Ended." *The Brooklyn Daily Eagle*, 02 Apr. 1886, p. 6.

17. "Newsboys on Strike." *The New York Times*, 13 Aug. 1889, p. 8.

18. "Cause of a Strike," *The Buffalo Evening News*, 15 Jan. 1890, p. 1.

19. "A Newsboys' Union." *The Buffalo Morning Express*, 13 Aug. 1892, p. 5.

20. "Strike That Is a Strike." *The New York Sun*, 22 Jul. 1899.

21. "Newsboys' Strike Swells." *The New York Sun*, 23 Jul. 1899.

22. "Can't Break Boys' Tie-Up." *The Evening Telegram*, 24 Jul. 1899.

23. *Disney's Newsies the Broadway Musical*. Dir. Brett Sullivan. Perf. Jeremy Jordan, Kara Lindsay, Ben Fankhauser. Disney Theatrical Group and Fathom Events, 2017. *Netflix*. Web.

24. *The New York Sun*, "Newsboys' Strike Swells," 23. Jul. 1899.

25. "'Newsies' Standing Fast." *The New-York Tribune*, 26 Jul. 1899.

26. "Newsboys Ready to Show Strength." *The Evening Telegram*, 26 Jul. 1899.

27. Morris, James McGrath. *Pulitzer: A Life in Politics, Print, and Power.* HarperCollins, 2010, p. 356. Print.

28. Cerniglia, Ken. *Newsies: Stories of the Unlikely Broadway Hit.* Disney Editions, 2013, p. 14. Print.

29. *Disney's Newsies the Broadway Musical*, 2017.

30. *Newsies.* Dir. Kenny Ortega. Perf. Christian Bale, Bill Pullman, Ann-Margret, and Robert Duvall. Buena Vista Pictures, 1992. DVD.

31. Ibid.

32. Ibid.

33. Churchill, Allen. *Park Row*. Rinehart, 1958, p. 43.

34. *Newsies*, 1992.

35. "State of the Union Message." *Theodore-Roosevelt.com*, 03 Dec. 1906. Web. <http://www.theodore-roosevelt.com/images/research/speeches/sotu6.pdf>

36. Bartoletti, Susan Campbell. *Kids on Strike!* Houghton Mifflin Company, 1999, p. 117.

37. "Slept on the Ground." *The Buffalo Morning Express*, 30 Jul. 1903, p. 2.

38. "Newsboy-Soldier in the Fighting 13th." *The Buffalo Enquirer*, 16 Nov. 1898, p. 9.

39. "From the Governor." Democrat and Chronicle, 15 Jun. 1899, p. 11.

40. "Roosevelt a Waiter." *The Buffalo Enquirer*, 19 Apr. 1901, p. 6.

41. *Newsies*, 1992.

42. *Newsies*, 1992.

43. King, Stephen. *Misery*. New English Library, 1988. Print.

44. *Hannah Gadsby: Nanette*. Dir. Jon Olb, Madeleine Parry. Perf. Hannah Gadsby. Guesswork Television, 2018. *Netflix*. Web.

45. *Disney's Newsies the Broadway Musical*, 2017.

THE NEWSIES OF THE 1899 STRIKE

1. "Newsboys Start a Strike." *The Brooklyn Daily Eagle*, 20 Jul. 1899, p. 2.

2. "Plan to Down Newsboys." *The New York Sun*, 24 Jul. 1899, p. 3.

3. "Strike That Is a Strike." *The New York Sun*, 22 Jul. 1899.

4. "Three Newsboys Arrested for Assault." *The New York Sun*, 02 Aug. 1899, p. 2.

5. "Newsboys' Strike Goes On." *The New-York Tribune*, 22 Jul. 1899.

6. "Newsboys' Boycott Over." *The New-York Tribune*, 02 Aug. 1899.

7. *The New-York Tribune*, "Newsboys' Boycott Over."

8.   "A Newsboys' Meeting." *The New-York Tribune*, 24 Jul. 1899.

9.   "Newsboys Strike Up the State." *The New York Sun*, 02 Aug. 1899.

10. *The Brooklyn Daily Eagle*, "Newsboys Start a Strike," p. 2.

11. "*World* Jails Newsboys." *The New York Sun*, 01 Aug. 1899.

12. *The New York Times*, "Striking Newsboys are Firm," p. 3.

13. "Newsboys Riot in Mount Vernon." *The New-York Tribune*, 25 Jul. 1899.

14. *The New York Sun*, "Strike That Is a Strike."

15. "Great Meet of Newsboys." *The New York Sun*, 25 Jul. 1899.

16. "New-York Newsboys." *The New-York Tribune*, 30 Jul. 1899.

17. *The New-York Tribune*, "Newsboys Go on Strike," p. 10.

18. "Newsboys Form a New Union." *The New York Times*, 31 Jul. 1899.

19. *The New York Sun*, "Three Newsboys Arrested for Assault," p. 2.

20. *The New York Sun*, "Strike That Is a Strike."

21. "The Wickedest Boy on the East Side. *The Evening World*, 7 Mar. 1905, p. 8.

22. "Here Are Newsboy Highwaymen." *The New York Sun*, 04 Aug. 1899.

23. "Newsboys Parade To-Night." *The New York Sun*, 26 Jul. 1899.

24. *The New York Times*, "Striking Newsboys are Firm," p. 3.

25. *The New York Sun*, "Newsboys Get New Leaders," p. 2.

26. *The New York Sun*, "Plans to Down Newsboys."

27. *The New York Sun*, "Great Meet of Newsboys."

28. "Boys Eloquent in Brooklyn." *The New-York Tribune*, 27 Jul. 1899, p. 2.

29. *The New-York Tribune*, "New-York Newsboys."

30. *The New York Sun*, "Great Meet of Newsboys."

31. "Newsboy Strike Gains Ground." *The Evening Telegram*, 25 Jul. 1899.

32. *The New York Sun*, "*World* Jails Newsboys."

33. "Spread of Strike Fever Among Lads." *The New York Herald*, 22 Jul. 1899.

34. "Newsboys' Strike Swells." *The New York Sun*, 23 Jul. 1899, p. 2.

35. *The New York Herald*, "Spread of Strike Fever Among Lads."

36. "The Only Tie-Up in Town." *The New York Sun*, 21 Jul. 1899, p. 2.

37. *The New-York Tribune*, "A Newsboys' Meeting."

38. *The New-York Tribune*, "Newsboys Riot in Mount Vernon."

39. *The New York Sun*, "*World* Jails Newsboys."

40. "Newsboys See Victory Ahead." *The Evening Telegram*, 28 Jul. 1899, p. 8.

41. *The New York Evening Telegram*, "Newsboy Strike Gains Ground."

42. *The Evening Telegram*, "Newsboys 'Go Out.'"

43. "Boy Strikers Sweep the City." *The Evening Telegram*, 22 Jul. 1899.

44. "Boys Foresee a Victory." *The New-York Tribune*, 25 Jul. 1899.

45. "Some Incidents That Made Memorable the New York Newsboys' Most Halcyon and Vociferous Week." *The New York Herald*, 30 Jul. 1899.

46. "Newsboys Go on Strike." *The New-York Tribune*, 21 Jul. 1899, p. 10.

47. "Violent Scenes During Day." *The New York Times*, 25 Jul. 1899.

48. "Newsboys' New Leader." *The New York Sun*, 29 Jul. 1899, p. 2.

49. "Park Row Capulets and Montagues." *The New-York Tribune*, 25 Jul. 1899.

50. *The New-York Tribune*, "Boys Eloquent in Brooklyn," p. 2.

51. *The Brooklyn Daily Eagle*, "Newsboys Start a Strike," p. 2.

52. *The New York Times*, "Newsboys Act and Talk," p. 3.

53. *The New-York Tribune*, "New-York Newsboys."

54. "Newsboys Strike for Better Terms." *The New York Herald*, 21 Jul. 1899.

55. *The New York Times*, "Newsboys Go on Strike," p. 2.

56. "Can't Break Boys' Tie-Up." *The Evening Telegram*, 24 Jul. 1899.

57. *The New York Sun*, "Three Newsboys Arrested for Assault," p. 2.

58. *The New York Times*, "Newsboys Form a New Union."

59. *The New York Evening Telegram*, "Newsboy Strike Gains Ground."

60. *The New York Times*, "Newsboys Form a New Union."

61. *The New-York Tribune*, "Newsboys Go on Strike," p. 10.

62. "Newsboys 'Go Out.'" *The Evening Telegram*, 20 Jul. 1899.

63. "Newsboys Strike Against Two Papers." *The Evening Telegram*, 20 Jul. 1899.

64. *The New York Sun*, "Strike That Is a Strike."

65. "Stole Newspapers from Girls and Women." *The New York Sun*, 28 Jul. 1899.

66. *The New-York Tribune*, "A Newsboys' Meeting."

67. *The New York Sun*, "Great Meet of Newsboys."

68. *The New York Times*, "Striking Newsboys are Firm," p. 3.

69. "Sociological Students in Court." *The New York Sun*, 24 Jul. 1899, p. 2.

70. *The New York Sun*, "Strike That Is a Strike."

71. *The New-York Tribune*, "Boys Eloquent in Brooklyn," p. 2.

72. Ibid.

73. *The New York Sun*, "Newsboys' Strike Swells," p. 2.

74. *The New York Times*, "Newsboys Form a New Union."

75. "*Herald* Employees Sued for $10,000." *The New York World*, 30 Jul. 1899.

76. *The New York Sun*, "Newsboys Strike Up the State."

77. *The New York Sun*, "Plan to Down Newsboys," p. 3.

78. *The New York Sun*, "Strike That Is a Strike."

79. "Striking Newsboys Stand Firm." *The New York Herald*, 30 Jul. 1899.

80. "Newsboys' Strike Spreads to Harlem." *The Evening Telegram*, 21 Jul. 1899.

81. *The New York Sun*, "Great Meet of Newsboys."

82. *The New York Sun*, "Strike That Is a Strike."

83. "'Strike' Still On." *Democrat and Chronicle*, 03 Aug. 1899.

84. *The New York Times*, "Violent Scenes During Day."

85. *The New York Times*, "Newsboys Form a New Union."

86. *The New York Herald*, "Newsboys Strike for Better Terms."

87. "'Newsies' Standing Fast." *The New-York Tribune*, 26 Jul. 1899.

88. *The New York Sun*, "Newsboys' Strike Swells," p. 2.

89. *The New York Sun*, "*World* Jails Newsboys."

90. *The New-York Tribune*, "Park Row Capulets and Montagues."

91. *The New York Sun*, "Great Meet of Newsboys."

92. *The New-York Tribune*, "New-York Newsboys."

93. *The New York Sun*, "Great Meet of Newsboys."

94. "Newsboys' Word Stands." *The New-York Tribune*, 23 Jul. 1899.

95. *The New-York Tribune*, "A Newsboys' Meeting."

96. *The New York Times*, "Newsboys Act and Talk," p. 3.

97. *The New York Sun*, "The Only Tie-Up in Town," p. 2.

98. *The New York Sun*, "Strike That Is a Strike."

99. "Boys Foresee a Victory." *The New-York Tribune*, 25 Jul. 1899.

100. *The New-York Tribune*, "Newsboys Go on Strike," p. 10.

101. "The Newsboys' Strike." *The Brooklyn Daily Eagle*, 20 Jul. 1899, p. 36.

102. *The New-York Tribune*, "Newsboys' Word Stands."

103. *The New York Sun*, "Strike That Is a Strike."

104. *The New York Herald*, "Spread of Strike Fever Among Lads."

105. *The New-York Tribune*, "Newsboys' Word Stands."

106. *The New York Sun*, "Newsboys' Strike Swells," p. 2.

107. *The New York Sun*, "Strike That Is a Strike."

108. "Parade To-night, Sure." *The New York Sun*, 27 Jul. 1899, p. 3.

109. "Newsboys Get New Leaders." *The New York Sun*, 28 Jul. 1899, p. 2.

NEWSIES TRIVIA

1. Watts Jr., James D. "'Newsies' goes from Razzies to riches." *Tulsa World*, 11 Sep. 2016. Web. <http://www.tulsaworld.com/scene/artsandentertainment/newsies-goes-from-razzies-to-riches/article_ce66df7b-4bd0-5547-8a99-3be16773ba20.html

2. Cheung, Harrison, & Pittam, Nicola. *Christian Bale: The Inside Story of the Darkest Batman*. BenBella Books, Inc., 2012, p. 56. Print.

3. 3. The Walt Disney Company. *Disney's Newsies the Musical Media Kit*. 1992, pp. 12-13. Print.

4. 4. Wong, Wayman. "BWW Exclusive: David Moscow Shares His Secrets From NEWSIES on Its 25th Anniversary! Read All About It!" *Broadway World*, 31 Jul. 2017. Web. <https://www.broadwayworld.com/article/BWW-Exclusive-David-Moscow-Shares-His-Secrets-From-NEWSIES-on-Its-25th-Anniversary-20170731>

5. 5. The Walt Disney Company, *Disney's Newsies the Musical Media Kit*, pp. 13-14.

6. The Walt Disney Company, *Disney's Newsies the Musical Media Kit*, pp. 11-12.

7. The Walt Disney Company, *Disney's Newsies the Musical Media Kit*, p. 12.

8. Fox, David J. "Out of the Ashes: Universal Rebuilds N.Y. Set After Devastating Fire." *Los Angeles Times*, 13 Mar. 1991. Web. <http://articles.latimes.com/1991-03-13/entertainment/ca-277_1_universal-studios>

9. Bjornas, Michelle. "*Newsies* (1992)." American Film Institute. Web. <http://catalog.afi.com/Catalog/MovieDetails/67295>

10. The Walt Disney Company, *Disney's Newsies the Musical Media Kit*, p. 14.

11. Ibid.

12. The Walt Disney Company, *Disney's Newsies the Musical Media Kit*, p. 16.

13. Wong, *Broadway World*.

14. The Walt Disney Company, *Disney's Newsies the Musical Media Kit*, p. 15.

15. The Walt Disney Company, *Disney's Newsies the Musical Media Kit*, pp. 15-16.

16. *Christian Bale*, Cheung and Pittam, p. 57.

17. Ibid.

18. Etkin, Jaimie. "The Man Behind Your Favorite Onscreen Dance Numbers, From 'Dirty Dancing' to 'HSM.'" *Buzzfeed*, 31 Jul. 2015. Web. <https://www.buzzfeed.com/jaimieetkin/the-best-of-kenny-or-tega-from-dirty-dancing-hsm?utm_term=.mvm4dpxWb#.lcAqg7lkZ>

19. "*Newsies*: The Inside Story." *Newsies*. Dir. Kenny Ortega. Perf. Christian Bale, Bill Pullman, Ann-Margret, and Robert Duvall.

Buena Vista Pictures, 1992. DVD.

20. Cerniglia, Ken. *Newsies: Stories of the Unlikely Broadway Hit*. Disney Editions, 2013, p. 45. Print.

21. "'Patrick's Mother'—A NEWSIES Thank You!" 17 Oct. 2011. YouTube. <https://www.youtube.com/watch?v=B-FVyxbD3jQ>

22. 22. Cerniglia, Newsies, p. 43.

23. 23. Haverkate, Julie (ed.). <i>Newsies: The Broadway Musical: Production Handbook</i>, pp. 26-27.

24. 24. Cerniglia, Newsies, p. 18.

25. Cerniglia, *Newsies*, pp. 46-47.

26. Cerniglia, *Newsies*, p. 19.

27. Cerniglia, *Newsies*, p. 37.

28. "King of New York: Backstage at 'Newsies' with Corey Cott, Bonus Episode: Bye, Fansies!" 21 Aug. 2014. YouTube. <https://www.youtube.com/watch?v=bwpPSZT8sks>

29. Cerniglia, *Newsies*, p. 61.

30. Cerniglia, *Newsies*, p. 53.

31. Cerniglia, *Newsies*, p. 83.

32. Catton, Pia. "The Jump That Saved a Season." *The Wall Street Journal*, 29 Apr. 2012. Web. <https://www.wsj.com/articles/SB1000 1424052702304050304577374243401040090>

33. Cerniglia, *Newsies*, p. 80.

34. Cerniglia, *Newsies*, p. 82.

35. Cerniglia, *Newsies*, p. 136.

36. "The Anatomy of a Song (Working In The Theatre #417)." 04 Mar. 2013. YouTube. <https://www.youtube.com/watch?v=70OkaohKrjw>

37. Ibid.

38. "A Multitude of Leses—'Watch What Happens (Reprise)' (Alan Menken & Jack Feldman)." 13 Nov. 2016. YouTube. <https://www.youtube.com/watch?v=IbS1Sgss7As>

THE REBIRTH OF *NEWSIES* AT THE DISNEY PARKS

1. Smith, Ethan. "Disney CEO Turns Slump Into a Springboard." *The Wall Street Journal*, 8 Nov. 2010. Web. <https://www.wsj.com/news/articles/SB10001424052748704580304575600134000523928>

2. Milzoff, Rebecca. "How Does Newsies Hold Up?" *Vulture*, 29 Feb. 2012. Web. <vulture.com/2012/02/how-does-newsies-hold-up.html>

3. Gabler, Neal. *Walt Disney: The Triumph of the American Imagination*. Vintage Books, 2006, p. 77. Print.

4.   "Red Car Trolley." *Duchess of Disneyland*, 13 Aug. 2015. Web. <http://duchessofdisneyland.com/california-adventure/red-car-trolley/>

5.   "Lindbergh Leaps Off." *The Oakland Tribune*, 21 May 1927, p. 12.

6.   Lille, Dawn. "The Charleston." *Dance Heritage Coalition*, 2012. Web. <http://www.danceheritage.org/treasures/charleston_essay_lille.pdf>

7.   "Miss Horace Greeley Perry." *The Springville Journal*, 04 Aug. 1898, p. 6.

ACKNOWLEDGEMENTS

1.   Mott, Frank Luther. *American Journalism: A History of Newspapers in the United States Through 250 Years, 1690 to 1940*. The Macmillan Company, 1941, p. 598.

Index

About the Author

Ashley Varela is a professional writer and author based in the San Francisco Bay Area. Through 2019, she has published over 2,000 articles online and in print with USA Today, NBC Sports, SB Nation, and Theme Park Tourist, among other outlets. Her writing was most recently featured in the 24th edition of the *Baseball Prospectus Annual*, a *New York Times'* bestselling guide to the baseball industry.

Guided by a profound passion for history, she has conducted original research and put forth multi-part analyses on many topics, including the development of Major and Minor League Baseball in the Pacific Northwest; the creation of the four main theme parks of the Walt Disney World Resort; and the contributions of prominent women designers and costumers at Walt Disney Imagineering.

Her full portfolio and personal writing is available online at www.AshleyVarela.com.

ABOUT THEME PARK PRESS

Theme Park Press publishes books primarily about the Disney company, its history, culture, films, animation, and theme parks, as well as theme parks in general.

Our authors include noted historians, animators, Imagineers, and experts in the theme park industry.

We also publish many books by first-time authors, with topics ranging from fiction to theme park guides.

And we're always looking for new talent. If you'd like to write for us, or if you're interested in the many other titles in our catalog, please visit:

www.ThemeParkPress.com

• •

Theme Park Press Newsletter

Subscribe to our free email newsletter and enjoy:

- ◆ Free book downloads and giveaways
- ◆ Access to excerpts from our many books
- ◆ Announcements of forthcoming releases
- ◆ Exclusive additional content and chapters
- ◆ And more good stuff available nowhere else

To subscribe, visit www.ThemeParkPress.com, or send email to newsletter@themeparkpress.com.

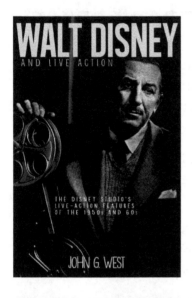
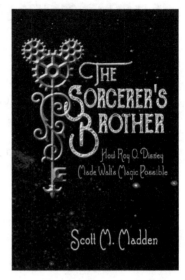
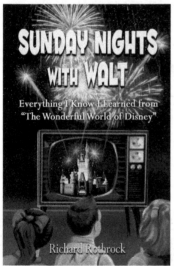